THE DISCOVERY
OF POETRY

Second Edition

THE DISCOVERY OF
POETRY

Second Edition

Frances Mayes

San Francisco State University

HARCOURT BRACE COLLEGE PUBLISHERS

Fort Worth Philadelphia San Diego New York Orlando Austin San Antonio

Toronto Montreal London Sydney Tokyo

Editor in Chief	Ted Buchholz
Acquisitions Editor	Stephen T. Jordan
Developmental Editor	Camille Adkins
Project Editor	Kelly Riche
Production Manager	Jane Tyndall Ponceti
Book Designers	Jeanette Barber & Sue Hart
Photo/Permissions Editor	Lili Weiner

Address for editorial correspondence
Harcourt Brace College Publishers
301 Commerce Street
Suite 3700
Fort Worth, Texas 76102

Address for orders
Harcourt Brace & Company
6277 Sea Harbor Drive
Orlando, Florida 32887
1-800-782-4479; in Florida 1-800-433-0001

Cover: Susan Rothenberg, Cabin Fever, *1976. Acrylic and tempera on canvas, 67 × 84 inches. Collection of the Modern Art Museum of Fort Worth, museum purchase, Sid W. Richardson Foundation Endowment Fund and an anonymous donor. 1991.10.P.P*

Illustrations: p. 5, Studio Laborie / p. 115, Reprinted by permission of Jeanette Ferrary / p. 353, Dr. William F. King, IBM Corporation / p. 400, Drawing by Booth; © 1976 The New Yorker Magazine, Inc. / p. 432, Kunsthistorisches Museum, Vienna / p. 445, Philadelphia Museum of Art, The Louise and Walter Arensburg Collection / p. 476, Hirshhorn Museum and Sculpture Garden, Smithsonian Institution; gift of Joseph H. Hirshhorn, 1966; photo by Lee Stalsworth.

Copyrights and acknowledgments continue on p. 591.

ISBN: 0-15-500162-0

Library of Congress Catalog Card Number: 92-75794

Printed in the United States of America

7 8 9 0 1 2   016   9 8 7 6 5

Preface

A Note on the Text

The Discovery of Poetry, second edition, introduces you to the art and craft of poetry. From an early tribal orison on the rising sun to a recent freeway lyric just out of the word processor, poems always reveal the writer's concerns, feelings, and values. All literature does this, of course. Essays, stories, and plays show the pleasures and problems of the writer and, usually, of the time when they were written. But poetry differs from other kinds of literature in several ways. Poems are structured in lines rather than in margin-to-margin sentences that build into paragraphs. Poets often arrange words in sound and rhythm patterns to accent and intensify meanings. And poetry deeply involves the imagination, both writer's and reader's; a poem can create a many-layered world. The present, a dream, a memory, a conversation—several aspects of experience may operate simultaneously. These special characteristics require more of us than casual reading. The *how*—the crafting of the poem—has everything to do with the subject. Craft and subject are identical. At the conclusion of one poem, William Butler Yeats asks:

> O body swayed to music, O brightening glance,
> How can we know the dancer from the dance?

We can't know. Why should we want to? In poetry, subject and craft are as inseparable as the dancer and the dance. A close reading of a poem for meaning involves a close analysis of the poet's craft.

Although you will understand many poems on the first reading, you will find others less accessible. Poems come from inspiration and sweat. The spark or seed that starts the poem and the (sometimes) thirty or more revisions needed to complete it are equal parts of the writer's process. As the reader, you too may perceive the poem's essence at once, but you may require many readings to satisfy all your questions. A good, practical approach is always to reread and to read out loud.

The Discovery of Poetry starts with words and images, the basic raw materials of the poet's art. Understanding word choice and image-making is vital to understanding later chapters on rhythm, voice, and structure. The first poems in the book are primarily modern poems because their language and subjects are familiar. As your knowledge of terminology and craft increases, more and more poems from earlier centuries are offered. In the course of the book, poems from the entire diverse tradition of poetry in English, plus a selection of translations, are included. The text progresses by adding new elements of poetry in a sequence that encourages you to use your new knowledge as you go along. You read *whole* poems, but as you study you will focus on one aspect or another—imagery here, repetition there. Keep in mind that a poem is more than a sum of these parts. Once you cover all the basics, the concluding chapters give you a chance to approach and interpret poems with an integrated knowledge of subject and craft.

Discussion is crucial. Saying what you think and asking others about parts of poems that puzzle you will bring out much more than silently reading on your own. The exercises in this book include questions for discussion, many of which ask you to look at another poem in relation to the one at hand. In every chapter you will also see frequent suggestions for writing. First-hand experience, such as trying out a suggested form or a rhyme scheme with your own pen, is the quickest way to grasp the real working significance of the topic under discussion. Don't think anyone expects Shakespearean results. That is not the point—although you *may* discover your own talent for writing in the process.

For those who wish to experiment further, a new last chapter, "A Poet's Handbook," has been added. It is a brief guide to the art: the writing process, getting started, finding your strongest material, limbering the imagination, revision. No one can teach you how to be a great poet. If your blood is on fire with the love of language and the desire to *make* something in words, you probably know that. You might have known since you were a child. You probably know too that no matter how awkward your writing is right now, something in you will make you a writer. The German poet Rilke pinpointed this phenomenon when he said, "The future enters us in order to transform us long before it happens." Working on your craft with good guidance can save you years. Many other people find an interest in writing late; their talent is just waiting to be uncovered and developed. They're the ones Ben Jonson had in mind when he said, "A good poet's made as well as born." As a writing teacher in a large university, I've been surprised to find that genuine talent is not at all unusual. What is unusual is the perseverance and will it takes to become a writer. Even without a blazing talent, almost everyone can learn to write some good poems, and that is a great pleasure.

Reasons for Reading Poetry

The study of poetry proves to be excellent training for the mind. Poetry is *the* language art. Learning to *see* precisely how words work teaches you how to come closer to what you want to write, whether it's a newspaper article, a law brief, a cost estimate, or a letter home. The ability to hear the literal level of what a poem is saying, to discern a tone of voice, to learn *why* one poem is interesting and another is not, to pick up suggested meanings, to see the logic of the imagination—all are valuable analytical tools. By studying poetry element by element, you learn to synthesize these components into a whole appreciation. Apprehending the range of a poem is a skill that transfers directly to any intellectual consideration or work in which analysis and interpretation are needed.

I hope this book offers you much more. Consider these more personal reasons for studying poetry.

We look to art for clues about our lives. When you take a walk at night, lighted windows are irresistible. You see a child setting the table, a vase of wildflowers, a stack of books on a chair; all these sights form a quick glimpse of how those mysterious others behind the glass live their lives. At a more complex level, we ask the poem, the painting, the piece of music for these glimpses. The most natural question we ask of a work of art is, "What does it say about life?"

All art, no matter how "serious," involves a sense of play. As children, we easily enter the spirit of make-believe and accept temporary worlds. We pretend we are pioneers or explorers; we follow our imaginations on marvelous journeys. Samuel Taylor Coleridge called this process the "willing suspension of disbelief." As adults, we abandon much of our sense of play. Yet we still enter temporary worlds when we yell at a soccer game or swim meet, cry or applaud at a movie, or get caught up in a friend's story. For a while we forget the immediacy of ourselves and go *with* the witnessed experience. Like child's play, poetry lets us enter other worlds. We are imaginatively placed in contexts different from the ones in which we live. The ability to "suspend disbelief" and enter the world of a poem is a primary pleasure. Active reading enables us to participate in more than we can possibly experience first-hand. After reading the poem, it is as if we have had the experience ourselves.

Poems can also change an experience by imaginatively naming or extending the feeling or thought. I went to college in Virginia, hundreds of miles north of my Georgia hometown. I was used to deep South seasons, a subtle blend of each one into the next. In Virginia, the first autumn startled me. The whole landscape along the James River transformed, especially the ginkgo trees, which turned gold and suddenly, all on the same day, rained their fan-shaped leaves in circles around their trunks. I observed this with no accurate words to describe my astonishment. The next spring, the enormous old weeping cherry outside my dorm bloomed as though it had invented the word. Have you ever stood under a blossoming cherry tree and looked up through almost transparent petals at the sky? I was taking a poetry class at the time. Leafing through the textbook I came across the following poem:

LOVELIEST OF TREES

Loveliest of trees, the cherry now
Is hung with bloom along the bough,
And stands about the woodland ride
Wearing white for Eastertide.

Now, of my threescore years and ten,
Twenty will not come again,
And take from seventy springs a score,
It only leaves me fifty more.

And since to look at things in bloom
Fifty springs are little room,
About the woodlands I will go
To see the cherry hung with snow.

A. E. Housman, 1859–1936

I read the poem out loud until I had memorized it. I was struck that I had lost nineteen years of seeing a cherry tree in bloom. I liked the softspoken sound of the poem's language. Its lightness seemed to suit the tree. "Loveliest of Trees" may not be one of the great poems of the western world, but for me it *connected* with an important experience, giving me perceptions in addition to my own. I copied the poem and tacked it to the tree. Every day I would see people stop to read the poem and look up.

For years after that (and perhaps still) someone tacked the poem to the tree each spring. I already liked poems, but this changed my relationship to them. I discovered that the poet's experience was like mine, yet it also stretched my perceptions. This book offers you similar connections.

Acknowledgments

A laurel crown to Daniel Orozco, who took over the chore of permissions with great grace. A grant from San Francisco State University also helped enormously. I would like to thank Nancy McDermid, Dean of the School of Humanities, for that support. My gratitude also to friends and colleagues: Steve Barkley, Susan MacDonald, Judy Breen, Kit Wallingford, and Steve Arkin. Letters and suggestions from teachers and students around the country have been a pleasure to receive. To Edward Kleinschmidt of Santa Clara University and to Ashley King, again, my boundless gratitude.

At Harcourt Brace, I am especially grateful to Camille Adkins, Stephen T. Jordan, Kelly Riche, Tammi Price, Lili Weiner, and Bill McLane. Continuing thanks to Gary Burke, who first suggested this book.

I thank the following people who reviewed this second edition of *The Discovery of Poetry* and gave me good advice: Robert S. Mikkelsen, Weber State University, Ogden, Utah; Sylvia G. Wheeler, University of South Dakota, Vermillion; and Margaret Garrett, Dickinson College, Carlisle, Pennsylvania.

Contents

2 *Words: Texture and Sound* 35

4 The Speaker: The Eye of the Poem

Poems for Discussion   446

11   *Writing about Poetry*   547

12   *A Poet's Handbook*   567

Sources and Approaches

*If I feel physically as if the top of my head were taken off,
I know that is poetry.*

Emily Dickinson

The Origin of a Poem

Diverse impulses motivate poets to write. When Emily Dickinson said about her art, "My business is circumference," she was talking about her desire to explore experience by drawing it into a circle of her own, a world. Similarly, Wallace Stevens wanted each poem to give "a sense of the world." D. H. Lawrence thought the essence of good poetry was "stark directness." Telling or uncovering truth is the prime motive of poets like Muriel Rukeyser, who once asked, "What would happen if one woman told the truth about her life? / The world would split open." William Wordsworth valued "the spontaneous overflow of powerful feelings." When William Carlos Williams called a poem "a machine made of words," he simply meant to say that the best-formed poems function smoothly, with oiled and well-fitted parts. This is not far from Samuel Taylor Coleridge's ideal, "The best words in the best order."

Many poets aspire to reach "the condition of music"—some aim for the heavenly music of the spheres, while others want the words to "boogie." William Butler Yeats thought, "We make out of the quarrel with others, rhetoric, but of the quarrel with ourselves, poetry." His writing emerged from the internal faultline between conflicting thoughts and emotions. Yeats's desire to understand his human condition echoes Walt Whitman, who wanted the reader to "stand by my side and look in the mirror with me." For Matthew Arnold the impulse was external, not internal. His poetry came from "actions, human actions; possessing an inherent interest in themselves, and which are to be communicated in an interesting manner by the art of the poet." Some pull of inner necessity draws the poet to the page, whether to explore a problem, pursue a rhythm, break apart logic, express an emotion, tell a story, or simply to sing. When asked the familiar question, "Why do you write?", writers often answer, "Because I have to," (though prose writer Flannery O'Connor replied, "Because I'm good at it."). The impetus of *having to*, for any or all of the reasons named above, gives poetry its fire and urgency.

Because of all these diverse sources, no one ever has come up with a satisfactory definition of poetry, just as no one can define music or art. Those who want to proclaim what is or isn't poetry have thankless work cut out for themselves. No umbrella is wide enough to cover the myriad versions, subjects, and forms. If a poem interests you, better to just go along with Walt Whitman's assertion, ". . . what I assume you shall assume, / For every atom belonging to me, as good belongs to you." Reasons for reading and for writing seem almost as numerous as atoms.

Sometimes poets write to recreate an experience, as in this poem about a childhood moment of exhilaration and terror:

CHILD ON TOP OF A GREENHOUSE

The wind billowing out the seat of my britches,
My feet crackling splinters of glass and dried putty,
The half-grown chrysanthemums staring up like accusers
Up through the streaked glass, flashing with sunlight,
A few white clouds all rushing eastward,
A line of elms plunging and tossing like horses,
And everyone, everyone pointing up and shouting!

Theodore Roethke, 1908–1963

In seven brief lines, Roethke isolates an unforgettable moment. He keeps the precarious child on the roof present to the reader by his use of *billowing, rushing, flashing*, and other *-ing* verbs. This participle form maintains an ongoing feeling of action and excitement. This immediacy of language stirs the reader's sense of motion. Roethke repeats "up" three times, accentuating the tension of the boy's position. The poet wants the reader to *feel* the process of the experience, not just *hear* the story of it.

"Child on Top of a Greenhouse" reports an experience in vivid language. "A Blessing" proceeds in the same manner until the last three lines:

A BLESSING

Just off the highway to Rochester, Minnesota,
Twilight bounds softly forth on the grass.
And the eyes of those two Indian ponies
Darken with kindness.
They have come gladly out of the willows   5
To welcome my friend and me.
We step over the barbed wire into the pasture
Where they have been grazing all day, alone.
They ripple tensely, they can hardly contain their happiness
That we have come.   10
They bow shyly as wet swans. They love each other.
There is no loneliness like theirs.
At home once more,
They begin munching the young tufts of spring in the darkness.
I would like to hold the slenderer one in my arms,   15
For she has walked over to me
And nuzzled my left hand.
She is black and white,
Her mane falls wild on her forehead,
And the light breeze moves me to caress her long ear   20
That is delicate as the skin over a girl's wrist.
Suddenly I realize
That if I stepped out of my body I would break
Into blossom.

James Wright, 1927–1980

What happens at the end? After a simple, sensuous description of stepping over barbed wire into the field with the Indian ponies, the poem abruptly changes. The speaker (the "I" in the poem) stops describing external action. He shifts to the *inner* experience of his happiness. The last two lines surprise us with their bold originality. Rapport with the natural world is a common experience, but the speaker here reacts intensely. He expresses an *imaginative* level of that experience, allowing us to recognize our own feelings in a new way. If he'd ended the poem at "wrist," we could not possibly have imagined the powerful idea of the spirit transforming into blossom.

A poet may write primarily out of a delight with the sounds of language:

COUNTING-OUT RHYME

Silver bark of beech, and sallow
Bark of yellow birch and yellow
   Twig of willow.

Stripe of green in moosewood maple,
Colour seen in leaf of apple,   5
   Bark of popple.

Wood of popple pale as moonbeam,
Wood of oak for yoke and barn-beam,
   Wood of hornbeam.

Silver bark of beech, and hollow   10
Stem of elder, tall and yellow
   Twig of willow.

Edna St. Vincent Millay, 1892–1950

Millay plays with words, rhymes, and repeating patterns of vowels and consonants. There is nothing to understand, only something to hear and imagine. Even though it has no message, the poem evokes reactions. It sounds like a chant. You probably remember the one-potato, two-potato counting-out rhymes from childhood, and how repetition can cast a spell. Perhaps Millay's words call up images of trees in different seasons or memories of playing in a forest. You might recall such childhood nonsense as:

Tinky toesy timbo nosey
Hooey booey booskie
Pin pin rickey
Pom pom mickey
No me oh non phooey hoo.

Who knows where such rhymes come from, except from the basic fun of making noises with words?

   The sources of poems, like their subjects, approaches, and meanings, are endless. Whatever the motivation might be, the making of all art is a fundamental and instinctive impulse. More than twenty thousand years ago, at Pech Merle in France, the earliest artists painted a group of spotted horses on the damp walls of caves. Around the realistic forms are several handprints. No one who has seen them could forget these strange reminders, like signatures, of the cave painters. These are startling images of the human desire to create. Did the drawings give magic control over hunting that animal? Was the horse a religious image? Were the paintings done for entertainment on long, cold nights in the cave? Were the horses so beautiful that the painter searched for just the right spot, placing the chest of the animal over a swelling in the cave wall to get the right sense of the animal's form? Perhaps none—or all—of these possible sources were in the artist's mind. As we look at the pictures, the artist mixing paints from blood and soot and ashes

The spotted horses of Pech Merle, France.

seems very close. We have to resist matching our hands to the black ones outlined on the wall. The natural desire to make art easily spans the epochs.

Art is the real "news" source of any culture. The cave paintings are the liveliest news items from prehistory. Today, as ever, movements in art reveal more about a moment of human consciousness than newspaper headlines can. Art reveals a culture's values, pressures, breakdowns, new directions. Contemporary poems are comments on our time; poems from other times and places give us glimpses into other lives.

The Art of Reading

When an interviewer asked William Stafford how old he was when he started writing poems, Stafford replied, "How old were you when you stopped?" Writing poetry, he meant, is a normal function. So is reading. This is especially important to realize because many of us are overtrained to read for factual information. Overly pragmatic, we look for a result, a conclusion. In addition, Americans are particularly time-conscious. Stories in the old *Saturday Evening Post* used to have notations to let you know how long it would take to read each one. Presumably, you could zip through the first few paragraphs and decide whether the story was worth the allotted twelve minutes, two seconds.

Although poems may include useful information, results, and conclusions, these aren't prime reasons for reading. Poems take concentration and time. Because many people assume they cannot understand poetry, they bring to it an overly serious mindset. They fear that complex meanings must be wrung from the poem like water out of a dishrag.

The writer starts and ends elsewhere:

from AN ATLAS OF THE DIFFICULT WORLD

XIII (Dedications)

I know you are reading this poem
late, before leaving your office
of the one intense yellow lamp-spot and the darkening window
in the lassitude of a building faded to quiet
long after rush-hour. I know you are reading this poem   5

standing up in a bookstore far from the ocean
on a grey day of early spring, faint flakes driven
across the plains' enormous spaces around you.
I know you are reading this poem
in a room where too much has happened for you to bear   10
where the bedclothes lie in stagnant coils on the bed
and the open valise speaks of flight
but you cannot leave yet. I know you are reading this poem
as the underground train loses momentum and before running up
    the stairs
toward a new kind of love   15
your life has never allowed.
I know you are reading this poem by the light
of the television screen where soundless images jerk and slide
while you wait for the newscast from the *intifada*.
I know you are reading this poem in a waiting-room   20
of eyes met and unmeeting, of identity with strangers.
I know you are reading this poem by fluorescent light
in the boredom and fatigue of the young who are counted out,
count themselves out, at too early an age. I know
you are reading this poem through your failing sight, the thick 25
lens enlarging these letters beyond all meaning yet you read on
because even the alphabet is precious.
I know you are reading this poem as you pace beside the stove
warming milk, a crying child on your shoulder, a book in your hand
because life is short and you too are thirsty.   30
I know you are reading this poem which is not in your language
guessing at some words while others keep you reading
and I want to know which words they are.
I know you are reading this poem listening for something, torn
    between bitterness and hope
turning back once again to the task you cannot refuse.   35
I know you are reading this poem because there is nothing else left
    to read
there where you have landed, stripped as you are.

1990–1991

Adrienne Rich, 1929–

Many poems, on first reading, are as direct as this one.

The most important aspect of appreciating any poem is extensive
reading—the more the better—of poems of all kinds. The best reader
is the one most open to the poem on the page; this reader is likely to
be an experienced one. Novelist Henry James said, "Be one on whom
nothing is lost." Here are eight guidelines toward that ideal:

1. Poems are written in lines. The length of the line and where it breaks help establish the poem's rhythm. We'll discuss this in detail later. For now, let the punctuation mark at the end of the line guide you. A comma indicates a distinct pause; a period indicates a full stop. If there is no punctuation mark where the line breaks, regard that break as a very slight pause, like a half-comma, that emphasizes the last word on the line. Lines are not necessarily units of sense. Often the sense flows on from line to line in a continuous sentence. If there's no period, keep reading; don't interrupt your reading of the sentence just because the line stops:

    > I met a traveler from an antique land
    > Who said: Two vast and trunkless legs of stone
    > Stand in the desert . . .
    >
    > *Percy Bysshe Shelley*

    New lines often start with capital letters, but this does not necessarily indicate that a new sentence is starting. Understand the lines above as: ''I met a traveler from an antique land who said, 'Two vast and trunkless legs of stone stand in the desert.''' Capitals along the left margin of a poem add a formality to the poem and give a slight emphasis to the opening words of the lines. Practice pausing for the line break but continuing the thought. Note, for example, the importance of the *realize*, *break*, and *blossom* at the line breaks in this excerpt from James Wright's ''A Blessing'':

    > Suddenly I realize
    > That if I stepped out of my body I would break
    > Into blossom.

    Emphasis on *realize* signals a change in the speaker's thinking. The emphasis on *break* is tricky: for a suspenseful instant, we don't know what will come next. *Blossom* is the most important word in the poem. Coming last in the shortest line, it gets strong emphasis both visually and orally.

2. Read the poem once silently, then once aloud, listening to the sounds. With long poems, read at least a few sections aloud. Notice the action of the verbs.

3. Characterize the poem. Old wisdom claims that all poems come from courting, praying, or fighting. The traditional classification of poetry is into lyric, narrative, and dramatic. A **lyric** is a song-like poem (originally played on the lyre), usually told in first person; a **narrative** is a story poem; and a **dramatic** poem demonstrates a conflict, often using the third-person voice. These categories tend to blur, however: a narrative may have lyric passages, a lyric may be dramatic, a dramatic poem may tell a story. More useful for sharp-focusing a poem will be to pinpoint two or more basic qualities of its subject: Is it a poem of personal experience? A description? A revelation of a single moment? A poem of political or social comment? A poem of word play? A retelling of a myth? A memory? A meditation on a spiritual or religious question? A song? A sermon? An argument?

4. Is the poem effective? You gradually will build a critical vocabulary for *why* and *how* rhythm, image, and word choice help you determine effectiveness. At the outset, notice your general responses to the poem. What is your first impression? Is the poem interesting? Does each line propel your attention down the page? What personal associations does the poem evoke? A poem usually has plural meanings; some of them are entirely personal to an individual reader.

5. Who is speaking? "I"? "We"? A character, historical or invented? To whom is the poem addressed? "You"? The reader? A character, named or unnamed? A nation or group? What is the overall tone of voice of the speaker? Sincere? Ironic? Intimate? Matter of fact? Mocking? Distant? Contemplative? Frenzied? Questioning? **Tone** of voice shows the speaker's emotion and sense of the situation. Reading aloud will help you hear the speaker's tone.

6. Note difficult sections. Sometimes typing or copying these parts will clarify them. Look up unfamiliar words. If you miss a word in line 1 that is referred to in lines 2 and 3, you'll lose the opening. Look up **allusions,** those references to people, objects, or events outside the poem. A poem might mention Norse gods, brand names, or English spies; it might refer to a biblical story, a battle, an ancient tool—or another work of literature. Not every allusion is important to understand, and many are self-explanatory in the

context of the poem. Arm yourself with a good dictionary (a paper-back desk dictionary won't do) and a book of myths. When you see a poem titled "Leda and the Swan," you'll need to track down exactly who Leda was.

7. Don't overinterpret. Meanings don't hide behind every bush. If you **paraphrase** (put what the poem says into your own words), that will be a useful prose replica of the poem, a flat rendition of what the poem says without the qualities of craft that make it a poem. Poems usually suggest much more than they actually say; some are complex, with layers of meanings that repay weeks of study. However, when one student wrote that the black and white ponies in "A Blessing" symbolized good and evil, he'd gone too far. Nothing in the poem suggests this interpretation. The ponies are themselves. They suggest also the beauty of the natural world and something of its mystery—but not good and evil.

8. Comment and ask questions in class. You're a student; if you already understand everything, then the teacher has no job to do. Sometimes everyone in class, even the teacher, must probe a line or a section of a poem. If all of you discuss your impressions and insights, the meanings often get pieced together. Writing papers and discussing them with others offer further chances to explore the poem. Some people fear that analysis takes away from enjoy-ment; "explain it, drain it," they say. Protracted discussions can wear everybody out, but good critical consideration is creative and rewarding. As you hear other opinions, some very different from your own, you sharpen and widen your perceptions.

Like a loaf of bread—which is somehow more than flour, yeast, salt, and water—a poem is more than words, rhythm, and lines. Samuel Taylor Coleridge once said that the pleasure of poetry comes from the "whole, consistent with a consciousness of pleasure from the compo-nent parts. . . ." In the following chapters, you'll focus attention on various topics, one at a time. As much as possible, the goal always is synthesis: putting the parts together to comprehend the whole.

By way of an introduction to close reading, consider the following poems, each quite different from the next. Use the eight guidelines to direct your attention.

If you have read Shakespeare's *Macbeth*, you probably remember the witches' chant (Act IV, scene i). Here is an excerpt:

Double, double toil and trouble;
Fire, burn; and, cauldron, bubble.
Fillet of a fenny[1] snake,
In the cauldron boil and bake;
Eye of newt, and toe of frog,
Wool of bat, and tongue of dog,
Adder's fork, and blind-worm's sting,
Lizard's leg, and owlet's wing,—
For a charm of powerful trouble,
Like a hell-broth boil and bubble.

[1] *fenny:* from boggy ground (a fen).

EXERCISES

1. Look at the words Shakespeare uses. Compare his words with Millay's in "Counting-Out Rhyme" (page 4). Compare the use of consonants and vowel sounds; what effect do these choices have on each poem?
2. What further uses of sound is Shakespeare making?
3. Do the ingredients of the "hell-broth" really seem horrifying? Why or why not?

● ● ●

THE SUNNE RISING

Busie old foole, unruly Sunne,
    Why dost thou thus,
Through windowes, and through curtaines call on us?
Must to thy motions lovers seasons run?
    Sawcy pedantique wretch, goe chide   5
    Late schoole boyes and sowre prentices,
  Goe tell Court-huntsmen, that the King will ride,
  Call countrey ants to harvest offices;
Love, all alike, no season knowes, nor clyme,
Nor houres, dayes, months, which are the rags of time.   10

Thy beames, so reverend, and strong
Why shouldst thou thinke?
I could eclipse and cloud them with a winke,
But that I would not lose her sight so long:
   If her eyes have not blinded thine,   15
   Looke, and to morrow late, tell mee,
Whether both the India's of spice and Myne
Be where thou leftst them, or lie here with mee.
Aske for those Kings whom thou saw'st yesterday,
And thou shalt heare, All here in one bed lay.   20

She is all States, and all Princes, I,
Nothing else is.
Princes doe but play us; compar'd to this,
All honor's mimique; All wealth alchimie.
   Thou sunne art halfe as happy as wee,   25
   In that the world's contracted thus;
Thine age askes ease, and since thy duties bee
To warme the world, that's done in warming us.
Shine here to us, and thou art every where;
This bed thy center is, these walls, thy spheare.   30

John Donne, 1572–1631

EXERCISES

1. Poems written on waking at dawn are called **aubades.** Usually a
    lover is leaving the bed, regretfully, after a night of passion. This
    speaker has no intention of getting out of bed. Whom is he address-
    ing? Read the first three lines aloud. What attitude or emotion is
    revealed by his tone of voice?

2. Sometimes archaic spellings are modernized. Here they are not.
    Often the words aren't as odd as they appear at first glance. If you
    read by sound, they should be clear. *Sowre prentices*, for example,
    is "sour apprentices"; *pedantique* and *clyme* are seventeenth-cen-
    tury spellings of "pedantic" and "clime" (climate). "Both the In-
    dia's of spice and Myne" (line 17) refers to the East and West
    Indies, where there are spices and gold mines. What other clues
    indicate when the poem was written? In what ways does it still
    seem contemporary?

3. How does Donne convince us that the lovers are a world unto
    themselves?

TO A CHILD TRAPPED IN A BARBER SHOP

You've gotten in through the transom
    and you can't get out
till Monday morning or, worse,
    till the cops come.

That six-year-old red face   5
    calling for mama
is yours; it won't help you
    because your case

is closed forever, hopeless.
    So don't drink   10
the Lucky Tiger, don't
    fill up on grease

because that makes it a lot worse,
    that makes it a crime
against property and the state   15
    and that costs time.

We've all been here before,
    we took our turn
under the electric storm
    of the vibrator   20

and stiffened our wills to meet
    the close clippers
and heard the true blade mowing
    back and forth

on a strip of dead skin,   25
    and we stopped crying.
You think your life is over?
    It's just begun.

Philip Levine, 1928–

EXERCISES

1. Paraphrase the poem; that is, tell in your own words what it says.
2. What do these phrases suggest: "the true blade mowing"; "strip of dead skin"; "your case / is closed forever"?
3. What does climbing through the transom suggest?
4. What does Levine imply about the boy's control over his life? Do you agree?
5. What is the speaker's attitude toward the trapped boy?
6. Compare your experience of this poem with that of "Child on Top of a Greenhouse" (page 2). How does each author's tone of voice affect your response?

• • •

THE ROAD NOT TAKEN

Two roads diverged in a yellow wood,
And sorry I could not travel both
And be one traveler, long I stood
And looked down one as far as I could
To where it bent in the undergrowth;   5

Then took the other, as just as fair,
And having perhaps the better claim,
Because it was grassy and wanted wear;
Though as for that the passing there
Had worn them really about the same,   10

And both that morning equally lay
In leaves no step had trodden black.
Oh, I kept the first for another day!
Yet knowing how way leads on to way,
I doubted if I should ever come back.   15

I shall be telling this with a sigh
Somewhere ages and ages hence:
Two roads diverged in a wood, and I—
I took the one less traveled by,
And that has made all the difference.   20

Robert Frost, 1874–1963

EXERCISES

1. What is the poem's literal subject? How far do you read before you begin to pick up suggestions of other meanings?

2. How does the speaker regard the unchosen way? Both paths were "worn" about the same; the one he took was slightly "less traveled by." Why did that make "all the difference"?

3. Why did Frost write about choosing between two roads rather than two jobs, two mates, or other specific alternatives?

4. If you've ever read poetry, you're probably familiar with this poem. Is it just a worn "old chestnut"? Are its pleasures enduring?

● ● ●

STEPPING WESTWARD

What is green in me
darkens, muscadine.

If woman is inconstant,
good, I am faithful to

ebb and flow, I fall   5
in season and now

is a time of ripening.
If her part

is to be true,
a north star,   10

good, I hold steady
in the black sky

and vanish by day,
yet burn there

in blue or above   15
quilts of cloud.

There is no savor
more sweet, more salt

than to be glad to be
what, woman,   20

and who, myself,
I am, a shadow

that grows longer as the sun
moves, drawn out

on a thread of wonder.   25
If I bear burdens

they begin to be remembered
as gifts, goods, a basket

of bread that hurts
my shoulders but closes me   30

in fragrance. I can
eat as I go.

                    Denise Levertov, 1923–

1. Is this poem mostly lyric, narrative, or dramatic?

2. What is the significance of the title?

3. Muscadine (rhymes with *green*) is a grapevine with dark purple fruit used for dense wines. What change does this rhyme indicate the speaker is experiencing?

4. Most of the poem is in the first person. Who is the "her" in line eight?

5. What is the effect of the poem's simple, mostly one-syllable, nature words *(north star, black sky, clouds, salt, shadow, sun)*? How do these words reflect the speaker's relationship to the natural world?

• • •

DOG UNDER FALSE PRETENCES

Not very affectionate; she likes to kiss,
but not to stay still long and be petted.
Yet if she is shut outside, she barks angrily.
If I move from one room to another, she moves too.
Is it a confusion in her history?   5

Now, after these months, I have her papers
from her first owner. Why was she given up?
The pet groomer who had her, and the birds, and Norman
the Great Dane, od'd on speed, disappeared,
was found later in a mental hospital.   10

It has worked out in different ways.
Norman is in the High Sierra, killing his own deer.
The birds have been killed by a raccoon, who slit
their nylon cage, ate most of them. Imogene,
like a mafia *capo*,[1] is taking over.   15

---

[1] *capo:* chief.

Nothing is as it was guaranteed to be.
She is not a Lhasa Apso, she is a Shih Tzu.
She has grandfathers and great-grandfathers, she has
her own number with the American Kennel Club.
She is in fact known, an aristocrat.   20

For the first three days I thought she was
timorous, elderly, a quiet dog
who would sit by the fireplace of evenings, who
could be taught to knit. After all these years
I should recognize, when I see it, shock.   25

I could and do recognize resilience.
Out of the wound of loss, of nobody,
it takes little to make her again feel
a person, to bark angrily, to say
"I am a person again. Let me in."   30

What were those weeks like, in the almost
unattended pet shop, where there was food
but nothing else? Svidrigailov says of eternity
"What if it were only a small bath-house
full of spiders?"   35

It is something, at least, to be in time
rather than in eternity. We may howl,
child, dog, at being bathed, tied up
while we dry. Yet it is a touch.
Why bark if you know there is no one listening?   40

So the aristocrats must have
crossed the Russian border to Shanghai,
knowing that they were nothing they had been before,
must have got jobs as *maîtres-d'hôtel*,
as cafe waitresses.   45

Must have come out of shock, into
a knowledge, tentative at first, that
it was possible to be human, must have said
to the world that was not their world "I have revised
my conceptions of being human. Let me in."   50

For many, there will have been those weeks
in the abandoned pet shop, when one was neither
owned nor believed in. There will have been
a break in the continuity of life.
"I was myself, or nothing. Nothing, then."   55

And as the Jews walked in their ritual order
to the chambers that would displace them, a space
opened in the middle of life, empty. Then
to one woman boarding the train, a neighbor
finally offered a sandwich.   60

A raccoon has eaten the birds, we do not
all survive, there is final and less than final.
Imogene will survive, she is fortunate.
I have given her a name other than her own name.
It is a device to change her luck.   65

And perhaps there is no place in her memory
to remember when she was nothing. If so, good.
She has now a plastic beetle that squeaks to play with.
She plays with it enthusiastically, wants other people
to play with her. It may be enough.   70

William Dickey, 1928–

EXERCISES

1. Starting from the particular example of a domestic pet, what general subjects does the poet move on to consider? Is this enlargement of the subject effective? How do you think the poem would work if he'd focused only on the dog?

2. What are the allusions? Is it necessary to your understanding to look them up?

3. Is there any humor in the poem?

4. What expectations does the title give you toward the poem?

5. Would you argue with the conclusion?

Poems for Discussion

I WANDERED LONELY AS A CLOUD

I wandered lonely as a cloud
That floats on high o'er vales and hills,
When all at once I saw a crowd,
A host, of golden daffodils,
Beside the lake, beneath the trees,   5
Fluttering and dancing in the breeze.

Continuous as the stars that shine
And twinkle on the milky way,
They stretched in never-ending line
Along the margin of a bay;   10
Ten thousand saw I at a glance,
Tossing their heads in sprightly dance.

The waves beside them danced, but they
Outdid the sparkling waves in glee;
A poet could not but be gay,   15
In such a jocund company;
I gazed—and gazed—but little thought
What wealth the show to me had brought:

For oft, when on my couch I lie
In vacant or in pensive mood,   20
They flash upon that inward eye
Which is the bliss of solitude;
And then my heart with pleasure fills,
And dances with the daffodils.

William Wordsworth, 1770–1850

SPRING AND ALL

By the road to the contagious hospital
under the surge of the blue
mottled clouds driven from the
northeast—a cold wind. Beyond, the
waste of broad, muddy fields   5
brown with dried weeds, standing and fallen

patches of standing water
the scattering of tall trees

All along the road the reddish
purplish, forked, upstanding, twiggy   10
stuff of bushes and small trees
with dead, brown leaves under them
leafless vines—

Lifeless in appearance, sluggish
dazed spring approaches—   15

They enter the new world naked,
cold, uncertain of all
save that they enter. All about them
the cold, familiar wind—

Now the grass, tomorrow   20
the stiff curl of wildcarrot leaf
One by one objects are defined—
It quickens: clarity, outline of leaf

But now the stark dignity of
entrance—Still, the profound change   25
has come upon them: rooted, they
grip down and begin to awaken

William Carlos Williams, 1883–1963

CHANSON INNOCENTE[1]

in Just-
spring   when the world is mud-
luscious the little
lame balloonman

whistles   far   and wee   5

and eddieandbill come
running from marbles and
piracies and it's
spring

when the world is puddle-wonderful   10

[1] *Chanson Innocente:* Innocent Song.

the queer
old balloonman whistles
far   and   wee
and bettyandisbel come dancing

from hop-scotch and jump-rope and   15

it's
spring
and
    the

    goat-footed   20

balloonMan   whistles
far
and
wee

                        e. e. cummings, 1894–1962

MENDING WALL

Something there is that doesn't love a wall,
That sends the frozen-ground-swell under it,
And spills the upper boulders in the sun;
And makes gaps even two can pass abreast.
The work of hunters is another thing: 5
I have come after them and made repair
Where they have left not one stone on a stone,
But they would have the rabbit out of hiding,
To please the yelping dogs. The gaps I mean,
No one has seen them made or heard them made,   10
But at spring mending-time we find them there.
I let my neighbor know beyond the hill;
And on a day we meet to walk the line
And set the wall between us once again.
We keep the wall between us as we go.   15
To each the boulders that have fallen to each.
And some are loaves and some so nearly balls
We have to use a spell to make them balance:
'Stay where you are until our backs are turned!'
We wear our fingers rough with handling them.   20
Oh, just another kind of outdoor game,

One on a side. It comes to little more:
There where it is we do not need the wall:
He is all pine and I am apple orchard.
My apple trees will never get across   25
And eat the cones under his pines, I tell him.
He only says, 'Good fences make good neighbors.'
Spring is the mischief in me, and I wonder
If I could put a notion in his head:
'*Why* do they make good neighbors? Isn't it   30
Where there are cows? But here there are no cows.
Before I built a wall I'd ask to know
What I was walling in or walling out,
And to whom I was like to give offense.
Something there is that doesn't love a wall,   35
That wants it down.' I could say 'Elves' to him,
But it's not elves exactly, and I'd rather
He said it for himself. I see him there
Bringing a stone grasped firmly by the top
In each hand, like an old-stone savage armed.   40
He moves in darkness as it seems to me,
Not of woods only and the shade of trees.
He will not go behind his father's saying,
And he likes having thought of it so well
He says again, 'Good fences make good neighbors.'   45

Robert Frost, 1874–1963

NAMING OF PARTS

Today we have naming of parts. Yesterday,
We had daily cleaning. And to-morrow morning,
We shall have what to do after firing. But to-day,
To-day we have naming of parts. Japonica
Glistens like coral in all of the neighboring gardens,   5
        And to-day we have naming of parts.

This is the lower sling swivel. And this
Is the upper sling swivel, whose use you will see,
When you are given your slings. And this is the piling swivel,
Which in your case you have not got. The branches   10
Hold in the gardens their silent, eloquent gestures,
        Which in our case we have not got.

This is the safety-catch, which is always released
With an easy flick of the thumb. And please do not let me
See anyone using his finger. You can do it quite easy   15
If you have any strength in your thumb. The blossoms
Are fragile and motionless, never letting anyone see
      Any of them using their finger.

And this you can see is the bolt. The purpose of this
Is to open the breech, as you see. We can slide it   20
Rapidly backwards and forwards: we call this
Easing the spring. And rapidly backwards and forwards
The early bees are assaulting and fumbling the flowers:
      They call it easing the Spring.

They call it easing the Spring: it is perfectly easy   25
If you have any strength in your thumb; like the bolt,
And the breech, and the cocking-piece, and the point of balance,
Which in our case we have not got; and the almond-blossom
Silent in all of the gardens and the bees going backwards and forwards,
      For to-day we have naming of parts.   30

Henry Reed, 1914–

THOSE WINTER SUNDAYS

Sundays too my father got up early
and put his clothes on in the blueblack cold,
then with cracked hands that ached
from labor in the weekday weather made
banked fires blaze. No one ever thanked him.   5

I'd wake and hear the cold splintering, breaking.
When the rooms were warm, he'd call,
and slowly I would rise and dress,
fearing the chronic angers of that house,

Speaking indifferently to him,   10
who had driven out the cold
and polished my good shoes as well.
What did I know, what did I know
of love's austere and lonely offices?

Robert Hayden, 1913–1980

A FATHER AT HIS SON'S BAPTISM

Cutlet carved from our larger carcasses:
thus were you made—from spit and a hug.
The scratchy stuff you're lying on is wool.
You recognize the pressure of your mother's hand.
That white moon with a bluish cast is a priest's face,   5
frowning over a water bowl. Whatever befalls you now,
you've been blessed, in a most picturesque
and ineffective ceremony dating from the Middle Ages.
Outdoors, the church lawn radiates a lethal green.
A gas truck thunders down the street.   10
Why, at emotional moments, do the placid trees
and landscape look overexposed, almost ready
to bleach away, and reveal the workings
of "the Real" machine underneath?
All bundled up on such a hot day: 15
whose whelp, pray tell, or mutton chop are you?
—tail-less, your cloudy gaze a vague accusation,
not of the sins of my history, but ignorance
to come, future cruelty. You're getting red
in the face, blotchy, ready to wail. Good.   20
From now on protest and remember everything.
Your cries assail even the indigent dead,
buried in charity plots right outside,
slowly releasing their heat, while you,
born out of the blue into a wheezing spring,   25
watch a chaotic mosaic assemble itself.
You tune up. My love for you is half adrenaline,
half gibberish. More Latin and the priest
splatters you. He's got one good eye,
and a black patch, like a pirate.   30
Now, smiling as if he knows something I don't,
he hands you to me. If I drop you, loudmouth,
will you bounce or fly? You were chalky
and bloody at first, in the doctor's grip,
looking skinned and inside-out.   35
Boyhood, a dangling carrot. I stare at you
and experience the embarrassment of riches. I
need to loosen my tie or I'll faint.
Outside a rake scrapes, sprinklers hiss.
It might be best to set you down   40
in one of these squares of light on the floor,
striped by venetian blinds, and leave you safe
in that bright cage. I could go have coffee,
and come back when we can carry on

a conversation. Men and women are afraid   45
of each other. It's true. Whisper
and drool of my flesh, I'm terrified of you.

Amy Gerstler, 1956–

GO, LOVELY ROSE

Go, lovely rose,
Tell her that wastes her time and me,
    That now she knows,
When I resemble her to thee,
How sweet and fair she seems to be.   5

Tell her that's young
And shuns to have her graces spied,
    That hadst thou sprung
In deserts where no men abide,
thou must have uncommended died.   10

Small is the worth
Of beauty from the light retired;
    Bid her come forth,
Suffer herself to be desired,
And not blush so to be admired.   15

Then die, that she
The common fate of all things rare
    May read in thee;
How small a part of time they share
That are so wondrous sweet and fair.   20

Edmund Waller, 1607–1687

THE CONCERT

In memory of Dimitri Mitropoulos

The harpist believes there is music
in the skeletons of fish

The French horn player believes
in enormous golden snails

The piano believes in nothing   5
and grins from ear to ear

Strings are scratching their bellies
openly, enjoying it

Flutes and oboes complain
in dialects of the same tongue   10

Drumsticks rattle a calfskin
from the sleep of another life

because the supernatural crow
on the podium flaps his wings

and death is no excuse   15

Lisel Mueller, 1924–

THE LEAP

The only thing I have of Jane MacNaughton
Is one instant of a dancing-class dance.
She was the fastest runner in the seventh grade,
My scrapbook says, even when boys were beginning
To be as big as the girls,   5
But I do not have her running in my mind,
Though Frances Lane is there, Agnes Fraser,
Fat Betty Lou Black in the boys-against-girls
Relays we ran at recess: she must have run

Like the other girls, with her skirts tucked up   10
So they would be like bloomers,
But I cannot tell; that part of her is gone.
What I do have is when she came,
With the hem of her skirt where it should be
For a young lady, into the annual dance   15
Of the dancing class we all hated, and with a light
Grave leap, jumped up and touched the end
Of one of the paper-ring decorations

To see if she could reach it. She could,
And reached me now as well, hanging in my mind   20
From a brown chain of brittle paper, thin
And muscular, wide-mouthed, eager to prove
Whatever it proves when you leap
In a new dress, a new womanhood, among the boys
Whom you easily left in the dust   25
Of the passionless playground. If I said I saw
In the paper where Jane MacNaughton Hill,

Mother of four, leapt to her death from a window
Of a downtown hotel, and that her body crushed-in
The top of a parked taxi, and that I held   30
Without trembling a picture of her lying cradled
In that papery steel as though lying in the grass,
One shoe idly off, arms folded across her breast,
I would not believe myself. I would say
The convenient thing, that it was a bad dream   35
Of maturity, to see that eternal process

Most obsessively wrong with the world
Come out of her light, earth-spurning feet
Grown heavy: would say that in the dusty heels
Of the playground some boy who did not depend   40
On speed of foot, caught and betrayed her.
Jane, stay where you are in my first mind:
It was odd in that school, at that dance.
I and the other slow-footed yokels sat in corners
Cutting rings out of drawing paper   45

Before you leapt in your new dress
And touched the end of something I began,
Above the couples struggling on the floor,
New men and women clutching at each other
And prancing foolishly as bears: hold on   50
To that ring I made for you, Jane—
My feet are nailed to the ground
By dust I swallowed thirty years ago—
While I examine my hands.

James Dickey, 1923–

THE UNKNOWN CITIZEN

(To JS/07/M/378
This Marble Monument
Is Erected by the State)

He was found by the Bureau of Statistics to be
One against whom there was no official complaint,
And all the reports on his conduct agree
That, in the modern sense of an old-fashioned word, he was a saint,
For in everything he did he served the Greater Community.   5
Except for the War till the day he retired
He worked in a factory and never got fired,
But satisfied his employers, Fudge Motors Inc.
Yet he wasn't a scab or odd in his views,
For his Union reports that he paid his dues,   10
(Our report on his Union shows it was sound)
And our Social Psychology workers found
That he was popular with his mates and liked a drink.
The Press are convinced that he bought a paper every day
And that his reactions to advertisements were normal in every
    way.   15
Policies taken out in his name prove that he was fully insured,
And his Health-card shows he was once in hospital but left it cured.
Both Producers Research and High-Grade Living declare
He was fully sensible to the advantages of the Installment Plan
And had everything necessary to the Modern Man,   20
A phonograph, a radio, a car and a frigidaire.
Our researchers into Public Opinion are content
That he held the proper opinions for the time of year;
When there was peace, he was for peace; when there was war, he
    went.
He was married and added five children to the population,   25
Which our Eugenist says was the right number for a parent of his
    generation,
And our teachers report that he never interfered with their education.
Was he free? Was he happy? The question is absurd:
Had anything been wrong, we should certainly have heard.

W. H. Auden, 1907–1973

WE REAL COOL

The Pool Players.
Seven at the Golden Shovel.

We real cool. We
Left school. We

Lurk late. We
Strike straight. We

Sing sin. We
Thin gin. We

Jazz June. We
Die soon.

Gwendolyn Brooks, 1917–

DEATH BE NOT PROUD

Death be not proud, though some have callèd thee
Mighty and dreadful, for thou art not so;
For those whom thou think'st thou dost overthrow
Die not, poor Death, nor yet canst thou kill me.
From rest and sleep, which but thy pictures be,   5
Much pleasure; then from thee much more must flow,
And soonest our best men with thee do go,
Rest of their bones, and soul's delivery.
Thou are slave to Fate, Chance, kings, and desperate men,
And dost with Poison, War, and Sickness dwell;   10
And poppy or charms can make us sleep as well,
And better than thy stroke; why swell'st thou then?
One short sleep past, we wake eternally
And death shall be no more; Death, thou shalt die.

John Donne, 1572–1631

IF THIS BE LOVE

To live in hell, and heaven to behold;
To welcome life, and die a living death;
To sweat with heat, and yet be freezing cold;
To grasp at stars, and lie the earth beneath;
To tread a maze that never shall have end;   5
To burn in sighs, and starve in daily tears;
To climb a hill, and never to descend;
Giants to kill, and quake at childish fears;
To pine for food, and watch the Hesperian[1] tree;
To thirst for drink, and nectar still to draw;   10
To live accurst, whom men hold blest to be;
And weep those wrongs which never creature saw;
If this be love, if love in these be founded
My heart is love, for these in it are grounded.

Henry Constable, 1562–1613

[1] *Hesperian:* In Greek mythology, the daughters of Hesperus watched over a garden where golden apples grew.

986[1]

A narrow Fellow in the Grass
Occasionally rides—
You may have met Him—did you not
His notice sudden is—

The Grass divides as with a Comb—   5
A spotted shaft is seen—
And then it closes at your feet
And opens further on—

He likes a Boggy Acre
A Floor too cool for Corn—   10
Yet when a Boy, and Barefoot—
I more than once at Noon
Have passed, I thought, a Whip lash
Unbraiding in the Sun
When stooping to secure it   15
It wrinkled, and was gone—

[1] *986:* Dickinson did not title her works; after her death, editors numbered her poems in approximate chronological order.

Several of Nature's People
I know, and they know me—
I feel for them a transport
Of cordiality—   20

But never met this Fellow
Attended, or alone
Without a tighter breathing
And Zero at the Bone—

Emily Dickinson, 1830–1886

SALT

I

They drag the dead pony out of the field,
wet snowflakes over the surface of her eyes.
Those slumped axhandle bones and her hair still shimmering
needles, or the wet slick in the arch of a shoe.

They drag her in her husk.   5
If only the hacker could lift her
before opening that slat-backed truck
spilling out its yellow dog straw.

She still smells like a sweater where kittens are born.

II

I sweep the tack room where touches of cold   10
dust stick to spider webs.
I cover the saddle with a carrot sack
and fold her bridle in a box
with my helmet, now too small.
In her trough, the thick cake of rusty salt   15
is smoothed where she polished her tongue.
It is the common objects, the shoes,
that become our pictures of grief.

Stumbling back to the house, my hands
are in my pockets   20
and my elbows pull me from
side to side.

I move through chores as if
this were any day.
Then, stretching the laundry   25
across the line;
a sudden wet mouth of sheet
wraps around my arms.

III

I watch the window where a great snail of dusk
leaves a silvery trail   30
across the ledge.
Inside the hot house, a ripe tomato smell.
Through the dark boards I slip
slowly into fretful sleep.

If I get out of bed I am alone   35
with the salt on the floor.
I sweep it into a pile
and throw blue lumps of it
out the open window.
The floor is iron gray and tilted   40
as if we are sailing.

Frances Phillips, 1951–

INTRO TO POETRY

You thought it was math that taught
the relation of time and speed
but it's farther than you knew
from that sun-lit white-walled classroom
to this darkened lounge with its couch   5
and overstuffed chairs. How many miles,
would you say, since you talked
as if poetry were no distorting mirror,
one-way street? But listen, sometimes
it's like this, a stranger's Ford pulls up,   10
and you, with no plans for the afternoon,
get in. He doesn't talk, stares at the road
and it's miles before you understand
you didn't want to travel. His lips say *no*
as you reach for the radio's knob.   15

In this silence you fall deeper
into yourself, and even the car
disappears, the stranger's face blurs
into faded upholstery, and all things
being equal, you're alone as though   20
you've wandered into a forest with night
coming on, no stars, the memory of sun
and a voice asking *Is this my life?*

Steven Bauer, 1948–

2

Words: Texture and Sound

One deep feeling called by its right name names others.

Eudora Welty

A poem on a stately theme often will use measured, exalted language. A poem on marlin fishing in rough seas will be lively, "salty." If the subject is jazz, the words will play a riff of their own in your ear; if they don't, the poem probably will seem "off." Whatever the subject, the writer works with words to fit the best sounds and sound patterns to the subject.

A computer calculated that James Joyce used 29,899 different words in his novel *Ulysses*. Obviously, writers in English have rich choices to make. And each word has layers of meaning; few, if any, are confined to a single interpretation. We bring our personal associations to a word along with our knowledge of its dictionary meanings. The dictionary defines *chocolate* or *dog*, but we have hundreds of further links to the words. Every word has **denotation** (explicit meaning) and **connotation** (suggested meaning).

Texture of Language

Equally crucial to what the poet has to say is how it is said. Words have meaning and also texture. There's more than difference in meaning between *summer smoke, cellar door* and *rot gut, mug shot*. English branched from complex Teutonic (Germanic) roots but also absorbed much of the more mellifluous Latin (Romance) languages. The texture of a one-syllable word with two or three consonants sounds harder to the ear than a word such as *mellifluous*, which seems to drift along. As you listen, you respond to texture. It is as if you could run your hand over the poem's surface. Are the words soft and flowing, or chopped and harsh? Are they worn down, heavy and flat, or light and smooth? Sound alone tells us a lot about the poem.

Words are the basic building blocks of poetry. The poem is made word by word. No other choices the poet makes—subject, structure, speaker—are more important than the quality of individual words.

Sometimes a poem can mean little or nothing, yet the stimulus of words alone wins our attention. We begin to invent for ourselves. Our ears prick up for the pleasure of listening to interesting sounds. The invented and odd words in this poem from *Through the Looking-Glass* hook the ear. Our eyes also are attracted by words' textures. Poetry is partly a visual experience; the shape of the poem on the page and the look of the words claim our interest. Humpty Dumpty had no trouble explaining every word of this to Alice. He maintained he could explain all poems, even "a good many" not yet written.

JABBERWOCKY

'Twas brillig, and the slithy toves
   Did gyre and gimble in the wabe;
All mimsy were the borogoves,
   And the mome raths outgrabe.

"Beware the Jabberwock, my son!   5
   The jaws that bite, the claws that catch!
Beware the Jubjub bird, and shun
   The frumious Bandersnatch!"

He took his vorpal sword in hand:
   Long time the manxome foe he sought—   10
So rested he by the Tumtum tree,
   And stood awhile in thought.

And as in uffish thought he stood,
   The Jabberwock, with eyes of flame,
Came whiffling through the tulgey wood,   15
   And burbled as it came!

One, two! One, two! And through and through
   The vorpal blade went snicker-snack!
He left it dead, and with its head
   He went galumphing back.   20

"And hast thou slain the Jabberwock?
   Come to my arms, my beamish boy!
O frabjous day! Callooh! Callay!"
   He chortled in his joy.

'Twas brillig, and the slithy toves   25
  Did gyre and gimble in the wabe;
All mimsy were the borogoves,
  And the mome raths outgrabe.

Lewis Carroll, 1832–1898

The sentences sound real; the invented words could be real. Often, people like to hear poets read in languages they cannot understand. A woman leaving a reading by the Polish poet Czeslaw Milosz said she was glad he'd read some of his work in Polish because the language sounded exciting, like horse hooves over cobblestones. Her friend said one poem sounded like books dropped down a stairwell. Unable to hear nuances in the foreign language, they still responded to the overall texture of sound. Story writer Isak Dinesen's workers in Africa asked her to read to them because her voice sounded like rain falling. The *noise* a poem makes is part of its meaning. Just the sound of the words and the patterns of the sounds make direct connections to the senses and extend to the imagination.

Many poets begin writing out of love for the sounds of language. Dylan Thomas, who wrote poems characterized by exuberant language, remembers:

> The first poems I knew were nursery rhymes, and before I could read them for myself I had come to love just the words of them, the words alone. What the words stood for, symbolized, or meant, was of very secondary importance; what mattered was the *sound* of them as I heard them for the first time on the lips of the remote and incomprehensible grownups who seemed, for some reason, to be living in my world. And these words were, to me, as the notes of bells, the sounds of musical instruments, the noise of wind, sea, and rain, the rattle of milk carts, the clopping of hooves on cobbles, the fingering of branches on a windowpane, might be to someone, deaf from birth, who has miraculously found his hearing. I did not care what the words said, overmuch, nor what happened to Jack & Jill & the Mother Goose rest of them; I cared for the shapes of sound that their names, and the words describing their actions, made in my ears; I cared for the colors the words cast on my eyes. . . . I tumbled for words at once. And when I began to read the nursery rhymes for myself, and, later, to read other verses and ballads, I knew that I had discovered the most important things, to me, that could be ever.

from *Poetic Manifesto*

Thomas probably would appreciate this poem about "the naming of things into their thing," which explores the elemental pleasure of words:

SAYING THINGS

Three things quickly—pineapple, sparrowgrass, whale—
and then on to asbestos. What I want to say tonight is
words, the naming of things into their thing,
yucca, brown sugar, solo, the roll of a snare drum,
say something, say anything, you'll see what I mean.   5
Say windmill, you feel the word fly out from under and away.
Say eye, say shearwater, alewife, apache, harpoon,
do you see what I'm saying, say celery, say Seattle,
say a whole city, say San Jose. You can feel the word
rising like a taste on the palate, say   10
tuning fork, angel, temperature, meadow, silver nitrate,
try carbon cycle, point lace, helium, Micronesia, quail.
Any word—say it—belladonna, screw auger, spitball,
any word goes like a gull up and on its way,
even lead lifts like a swallow from the nest   15
of your tongue. Say incandescence, bonnet, universal joint,
lint—oh I invite you to try it. Say cold cream,
corydalis, corset, cotillion, cosmic dust,
you are all of you a generous and patient audience,
pilaster, cashmere, mattress, Washington pie,   20
say vise, inclinometer, enjambment, you feel your own voice
taking off like a swift, when you say a word you feel like
a gong that's been struck, to speak is to step out of your skin,
stunned. And you're a pulsar, finally you understand light
is both particle and wave, you can see it, as in   25
parlour—when do you get a chance to say parlour—
and now mackinaw, toad and ham wing their way
to the heaven of their thing. Say bellows, say sledge,
say threshold, cottonmouth, Russia leather,
say ash, picot, fallow deer, saxophone, say kitchen sink.   30
This is a birthday party for the mouth—it's better than ice cream,
say waterlily, refrigerator, hartebeeste, Prussian blue
and the word will take you, if you let it,
the word will take you along across the air of your head
so that you're there as it settles into the thing it was made for,   35

adding to it a shimmer and the bird song of its sound,
sound that comes from you, the hand letting go
its dove, yours the mouth speaking the thing into existence,
this is what I'm talking about, this is called saying things.

Marilyn Krysl, 1942–

Words *are* names, and naming is a rite. It's bad luck to rename a boat. Babies' name, once the birth certificate is filled in, are seldom changed. Once called by an unfortunate nickname like "Lard" or "Pug," a person can be stuck for life. Your own name has a sound like no other; it seems to belong to you as intrinsically as "chair" does to chair or "book" does to book.

Naming is one of the great involvements of the writer, the bonding of words as close to the subject as possible. In *Let Us Now Praise Famous Men*, James Agee wrote about Southern sharecroppers during the Great Depression. In his frustration over finding words powerful enough to make tangible the farmers' poverty, Agee said he would like to glue one of their shoes to a page of each book. He wanted the word to have the power of the actual object. Words are chosen for poems with the same passion for precision.

Choosing Words

This morning I deleted the hyphen from "hell-hound" and made it one word; this afternoon I redivided it and restored the hyphen.

Edward Arlington Robinson

Given that poets can't glue shoes on the page, how do they find the best words? Good poems use language with freshness. What is a fresh word? Some always seem new: star, biscuit, carnation, mint, foot, hair, rock, knot, cat, seed, goat, worm, ruby, salt, thorn, rooster, sock, milk. . . . The endless list of totally ordinary nouns never seems old because these **concrete words** name specific things. (**Abstract words** describe generalizations or concepts such as work, generosity, jealousy, pain.)

Shakespeare must have been thinking of concrete naming when he wrote:

> Fie, fie upon her!
> There's language in her eye, her cheek, her lip,
> Nay, her foot speaks; her wanton spirits look out
> At every joint and motive of her body.

The language *in* her eye is the point here. The words to describe her are all over her body; every part of her speaks. If Shakespeare decided to describe those eyes, chances are he would not be content to say they were dark brown. He would want the *exact* quality of the brown—say, sun on sherry in a glass; in a different mood, he'd describe her with round, bulging eyes like an old horse.

Onomatopoeia always sounds fresh. *Hiss, slap, rip, buzz, sizzle, pop*: an onomatopoeiac word is one whose sound imitates meaning. *Bang, burp, gargle, screech, gabble, croak*: onomatopoeiac words are noise words. Many words in our language have hidden onomatopoeiac connections. *Barbarian*, for instance, comes from the ancient Greek's mimicking of foreign invaders' speech. The Greeks thought the invaders sounded as though they were saying, "bar, bar, bar, bar." Noise words are direct. They're used for their impact and immediacy. Writers invent onomatopoeiac words: she *shugs* through in her slippers, he *hoicks* the chair closer, a boat *thucks* across the water. Some of these inventions become part of everyday speech. This is one of the ways languages grow.

When words lose their voltage through overuse, they become **clichés**. We're familiar with clichés in ordinary speech: working like a mule, busy as a beaver, warm as toast, the fact of the matter, first and foremost, sigh of relief, short but sweet, fatal flaw. These once-strong expressions now pass—to use a cliché—in one ear and out the other.

Poetry has its own stock of phrases and words that have been used up. In certain poems perhaps a cliché can be revived, but most of these old warhorses deserve a long rest:

mirror of my mind	grim reaper
thou art true	eternal sleep
soaring spirit	veil is parted
crystal clear	shining hosts
spectral ships	on golden wings
purple twilight	dwelt
truth and beauty	O, time
drenched by light	heavenly sphere
soul-enhancing	night is falling

sweetness and grace	alas
afar	memory weaves
voice of the wind	voice of woe
dreams go with you always	threads of memory
brief years	shadow of death
radiant glow	dying embers
press your lips to mine	crimson tide
golden mist	time immemorial
enchanted realms	dewdrops
days to come	undimmed
alien lands	infinity
muted strings	dispel the clouds
your essence	endless horizon
bitter end	shaft of light
tracery	crystalline

Some of the phrases on the list were brilliant when they were first used: "crimson tide," though now a hand-me-down, was new in Shakespeare's *Richard III*. Others, however, were lazy language all along. It's hard to imagine that "grim reaper" was ever fresh.

Besides the ground-down quality of poetic clichés, they usually sound archaic. We don't say *oft, o'er,* or *yon* anymore, so the sudden appearance of such a word in a contemporary poem displaces the tone into another time. In a poem from an earlier century we accommodate our ears to the language of the era. We may still have some difficulty learning to read early poems with vocabularies very different from our own. Those poems require us to work a little harder in order to participate as readers. Sometimes we need to learn obsolete words and figure out references to customs and past events.

Even the subject of a poem can be a cliché. Only through a sharp ear for language can a well-worn subject such as the moon be refreshed. The face and being of the beloved is certainly such a subject too. We can find rosebuds in many cheeks in English literature. We expect lavish praise and superlatives—but look at this early fifteenth-century poet's unexpected assessment of his love.

OF MY LADY

Of my lady well me rejoise I may!
Hir golden forheed is full narw° and small;   *narrow*
Hir browes been lik to dim, reed coral;
And as the jeet° hir yën° glistren ay.   *jet, eyes*

5	Hir bowgy° cheekës been as softe as clay,	*bulging*
	With largë jowës° and substancial;	*jowls*
	Hir nose a pentice° is that it ne shal	*penthouse*
	Reine in hir mouth though she uprightës lay.	

	Hir mouth is nothing scant with lippës gray;	
10	Hir chin unnethë° may be seen at al;	*hardly*
	Hir comly° body shape as a footbal,	*comely*
	And she singeth full like a papëjay°.	*parrot*

Thomas Hoccleve, (ca 1369–1450)

EXERCISES

1. Leaf through several books or spend an hour with a dictionary. Make a list of your fifty favorite words. Pick what your eyes, ears, and imagination particularly respond to. This will sharpen your ear for the use of words in the poems that follow. After you've made the list, look at it as a whole. What do your words have in common? Are they vivid? Quiet? Concrete? Rowdy? Do you like active verbs? Nouns? Reread "Jabberwocky" and "Counting-Out Rhyme" (pages 36 and 4); then try writing a poem for the pleasure of sound from your list.

2. You know the denotative meanings of *soup, snow, midnight, siren, candlelight, moon, terror, mist, escape, privacy.* Select three of these words and list your connotations for each.

The Muscle of Language

When the poet strengthens certain aspects of language, it's for particular purposes. The use of many active verbs, for instance, gives force and movement. The use of many adjectives or adverbs gives an impression of abundance, whereas an absence of modifiers pares language down to the bones. A high density of one-syllable words gives a definite, emphatic impression. Any *one* effect used over and over has an impact. In "Pied Beauty," Gerard Manley Hopkins selected fresh and surprising words such as *brinded, tackle, adazzle, fallow, fickle, rosemole, stipple.* He uses several hyphens to get words as close together as possible. When you see an emphasized usage like this, pay special attention. The poet purposefully draws your attention to his word choice. Although the meaning of the poem is simple—praising God for creating dappled beauty—many of the packed-tight words need to be thought through or looked up in the dictionary.

PIED[1] BEAUTY

> Glory be to God for dappled things—
>   For skies of couple-colour as a brinded cow;
>   For rose-moles all in stipple upon trout that swim;
> Fresh-firecoal chestnut-falls; finches' wings;
>   Landscape plotted and pieced—fold, fallow, and plough;   5
>   And all trades, their gear and tackle and trim.
>
> All things counter, original, spare, strange;
>   Whatever is fickle, freckled (who knows how?)
>   With swift, slow; sweet, sour; adazzle, dim;
> He fathers-forth whose beauty is past change: 10
>   Praise him.

> *Gerard Manley Hopkins*, 1844–1889

[1] *Pied:* patchy in color.

In praising God for diversity, Hopkins, by his word choice, means also to praise God for the variety in language. The poem itself is "dappled," "stippled" with unusual words. Obviously, Hopkins delights in the sounds of such words as *firecoal, rose-moles*, and *couple-colour*. In each line, the word choice reflects his admiration for the dappled things of the world *and* his joy in matching them to language.

Sound Patterns

In "Pied Beauty," Hopkins arranges certain sounds. Look at each line and see how often he repeats the initial consonants of words, as in line 4:

> *F*resh-*f*irecoal chestnut-*f*alls; *f*inches' wings

Repeating an initial consonant sound is called **alliteration**. Like rhyme, alliteration ties sounds together, reinforcing, by repetition, a unity in the poem. By placing like sounds close together, the words are subtly linked, as in this passage from the Preface to Walt Whitman's *Leaves of Grass*:

> All beauty comes from beautiful blood and a beautiful brain.

Alliteration is one of the oldest formal devices of English poetry, older than rhyme. *Beowulf*, the Anglo-Saxon epic composed between 650–750 A.D., was written in short, strongly alliterative lines, a tradition still lively in English poetry.

According to this clattering poem of the fifteenth century, noise pollution is nothing new. Blacksmiths (smoked black smithys) working at night drove the anonymous poet to use the loudest words he could find for his complaint. He generally keeps to the traditional four alliterations per line.

THE BLACKSMITHS

	Swarte smeked° smithes smatered with smoke	*black smoked*
	Drive me to deth with din of here dintes.°	*their blows*
	Swich° nois on nightes ne herd men never:	*such*
	What knavene cry° and clatering of knockes!	*workmen shouting*
5	The cammede kongons° cryen after 'coal, coal'	*snub-nosed brutes*
	And blowen here bellowes, that al here brain brestes:°	*bursts*
	'Huf, puf!' said that one; 'haf, paf!' that other.	
	They spitten and sprawlen and spellen many spelles;°	*curses*
	They gnawen° and gnachen°, they grones togedere,	*grind, gnash*
10	And holden hem hote° with here hard hamers.	*keep themselves hot*
	Of a bulle-hide been here barm-felles;°	*leather aprons*
	Here shankes been shakled for the fire-flunderes;[1]	
	Hevy hameres they han°, that hard been handled°,	*have, wielded*
	Stark strokes they striken on a steled stokke:°	*steel anvil*
15	Lus, bus! las, das! rowten by rowe.°	*crash in turn*
	Swich dolful a dreme° the devil it to-drive!	*noise*
	The maister longeth a litel, and lasheth a lesse,	

---

[1] *shankes . . . flunderes:* shanks have been protected against fire sparks.

Twineth hem twain, and toucheth a treble:[2]
Tik, tak! hic, hac! tiket, taket! tik, tak!
20   Lus, bus! lus, das! swich lif they leden,
Alle clothemeres°: Crist hem give sorwe!   *horse-clothers*
May no man for bren-wateres[3] on night han his rest.

[2] *The maister . . . treble:* master smith lengthens a little piece and beats out a smaller
one, twists the two together, and strikes a treble note.
[3] *bren-wateres:* water-sizzlers; refers to hot iron cooling in water.

Gerard Manley Hopkins was drawn to these early uses of sound
patterning. He was interested also in forgotten language. He never
hesitated to use words that had rested quietly in dictionaries for years.
Observe the "new" words in the following poem. Note the addition of
accents to words he wanted to stress:

INVERSNAID

This darksome burn, horseback brown,
His rollrock highroad roaring down,
In coop and in comb the fleece of his foam
Flutes and low to the lake falls home.

A windpuff-bonnet of fáwn-fróth   5
Turns and twindles over the broth
Of a pool so pitchblack, féll-frówning,
It rounds and rounds Despair to drowning.

Degged with dew, dappled with dew
Are the groins of the braes that the brook treads through,   10
Wiry heathpacks, flitches of fern,
And the beadbonny ash that sits over the burn.

What would the world be, once bereft
Of wet and of wildness? Let them be left,
O let them be left, wildness and wet;   15
Long live the weeds and the wilderness yet.

Gerard Manley Hopkins, 1844–1889

"Degged with dew, dappled with dew" packs alliteration into the line. (Fortunately Hopkins did not go on to say, "Are the dips of the ditch that the drips drop through.") *Degged* means "sprinkled," "damped," "drizzled"—a perfectly good word rescued from oblivion. The key word is *burn*, the Scottish word for "brook." The words in the first three stanzas attempt to capture the fast-flowing motion of the burn. In stanza 4 the words slow down; the poem turns out to be a plea for the wilderness. A few minutes spent looking up unfamiliar words (such as *twindle, braes, flitches*) can make this poem come alive. *The Oxford English Dictionary* will be the best source for the more recondite words you will encounter.

Consonance and **assonance** are, respectively, repetitions of consonant and vowel sounds. Consonance differs from alliteration only in that alliteration repeats the first letter, while consonance repeats sounds within a word. The line

His rollrock highroad roaring down

uses alliteration of the *r* in *roll* and *roar* and consonance in the *r* sounds within *rollrock, highroad,* and *roaring.* The line has five *o* sounds: assonance. Assonance is more pronounced in: "In coop and in comb the fleece of his foam."

Passages which arrange and repeat vowels (and smooth consonants: l, m, n, y, w) have **euphony**—that is, flowing and pleasing sound without disruption. Read aloud this famous example of euphony:

The moan of doves in immemorial elms,
And murmuring of innumerable bees.

Alfred, Lord Tennyson

Cacophony is the opposite quality, a group of harsh sounds:

double-tongued mud brain, hypocrite
hiss, the heft of blood's blind demand

As in "Inversnaid," the muscles of the tongue work hard in this example. The effect on meaning is also tensile. Since language is taut and hard, that quality infuses the meaning.

EXERCISES

1. Identify these sound patterns:

> The surgy murmurs of the lonely sea.
>
> *John Keats*

> the tawny gutteral water
> spells itself: Moyola.
>
> *Seamus Heaney*

2. Read "He Remembers Forgotten Beauty" aloud. How does the euphony work *with* the subject? Compare the texture with "Inversnaid."

HE REMEMBERS FORGOTTEN BEAUTY

When my arms wrap you round I press
My heart upon the loveliness
That has long faded from the world;
The jewelled crowns that kings have hurled
In shadowy pools, when armies fled;   5
The love-tales wrought with silken thread
By dreaming ladies upon cloth
That has made fat the murderous moth;
The roses that of old time were
Woven by ladies in their hair,   10
The dew-cold lilies ladies bore
Through many a sacred corridor
Where such grey clouds of incense rose
That only God's eyes did not close:
For that pale breast and lingering hand   15
Come from a more dream-heavy land,
A more dream-heavy hour than this;
And when you sigh from kiss to kiss
I hear white Beauty sighing, too,
For hours when all must fade like dew,   20

But flame on flame, and deep on deep,
Throne over throne where in half sleep,
Their swords upon their iron knees,
Brood her high lonely mysteries.

William Butler Yeats, 1865–1939

3.   Nineteenth-century poets like Algernon Swinburne were especially
fond of alliteration, consonance, and assonance. Swinburne had a
weakness for **sibilance**, patterning *s* and hissing sounds. Underline
his use of sound patterns in these sections from a longer poem:

from IN THE BAY

xix

The shadow stayed not, but the splendor stays,
Our brother, till the last of English days.
No day nor night on English earth shall be
Forever, spring nor summer, Junes nor Mays,
But somewhat as a sound or gleam of thee   5
Shall come on us like morning from the sea.

xx

Like sunrise never wholly risen, nor yet
Quenched; or like sunset never wholly set,
A light to lighten as from living eyes
The cold, unlit, close lids of one that lies   10
Dead, or a ray returned from death's far skies
To fire us living lest our lives forget.

xxi

For in that heaven what light of lights may be,
What splendor of what stars, what spheres of flame
Sounding, that none may number nor may name,   15
We know not, even thy brethren; yea, not we
Whose eyes desire the light that lightened thee,
Whose ways and thine are one way and the same.

xxii

But if the riddles that in sleep we read,
And trust them not, be flattering truth indeed,   20
As he that rose our mightiest called them,—he,
Much higher than thou as thou much higher than we,—
There, might we say, all flower of all our seed,
All singing souls are as one sounding sea.

Algernon C. Swinburne, 1837–1909

The Surprise of Language

Often a poem includes one or two little-known words, or an unusual
use of a familiar word which ruffles the surface of the poem or shifts
your attention just when you thought you knew where you were going.
One poem by Theodore Roethke begins:

Once upon a tree
I came upon a time

A poem titled "Boustrophedon" sends you to the dictionary before
you begin reading. A volume titled *Bilingual Wholes* alerts you to the
possibilities of word play in the book. In one of his "non-lectures,"
e.e. cummings says, ". . . although [my mother's] health eventually
failed her, she kept her sense of humor to the beginning." The surprise
word pulls the rug out from under our expectations. In the following
poem, James Wright uses an ordinary word with a powerful effect.

AUTUMN BEGINS IN MARTINS FERRY, OHIO

In the Shreve High football stadium,
I think of Polacks nursing long beers in Tiltonsville,
And gray faces of Negroes in the blast furnace at Benwood,
And the ruptured night watchman of Wheeling Steel,
Dreaming of heroes.   5

All the proud fathers are ashamed to go home.
Their women cluck like starved pullets,
Dying for love.

Therefore,
Their sons grow suicidally beautiful   10
At the beginning of October,
And gallop terribly against each other's bodies.

James Wright, 1927–1980

Here the language is exact. The names of the stadium, the town, the
factory, the place where workers drink beer, all orient the reader
clearly. The men Wright thinks of are *nursing* beers. Their faces turn
gray in the furnace light; the watchman is *ruptured*. He compares the
women to starved chickens. The words are concrete; we can see these
people. Wright never generalizes or moralizes by resorting to abstractions about the tragic state of the steelworkers' lives; instead, with just
a few words, he makes us see several precise views of these lives.
Then, in the last stanza, the reflections take a turn. "Therefore," he
says. The single word on a line by itself turns the poem inside out.
Why? *Therefore* is not at all the kind of word he has used so far. If you
read aloud, you'll also change your tone of voice at that point. *Therefore* catapults us toward a conclusion which suddenly seems to be the
proof for an equation we did not realize was being set up. After *therefore*, he continues the change in language. The two words *suicidally
beautiful* shock each other powerfully. The words, it turns out, allow
us a new and more complex vision of an ordinary game of football. The
unusual, disturbing juxtaposition of *suicidally beautiful* is reinforced by
the additional pairing of other surprising words in the last line. *Gallop
terribly* pairs words that jolt our attention. Wright's conclusions about
the fall ritual at Shreve High provoke the reader to agree or argue with
his explanation of football.

The Kinship of Words

A poem's language usually has a coherence we may be unaware of
until it's interrupted. In Wright's poems, the word *Therefore* signals a
switching of gears; from then on, the vivid, descriptive words intensify.
Diction is a poem's entire word choice, the selection taken from the
poet's whole knowledge of language. Diction is somewhat analogous
to a recipe a chef devises from his whole familiarity with cuisines. A
fiery pepper on a clam has consequences, as does a hot word in a cold

poem. The chef wants his dish to balance and contrast tastes for the entire experience. The quality of every ingredient contributes to this.

"Words, words, words," Shakespeare wrote. Poems are mysteriously made of words just as a great dish is, as one cook explained, "only a combination of ingredients." Words for a poem are generated from a particular area of language. We talk about rowing with a special vocabulary, as we do with ballet, gambling, law, and computer programming. Glassblowers and rabbit raisers, short-order cooks and moving van drivers—all have characteristic phrases and terms appropriate to their activities. Groups of words are particular to places also. Many words you'd say in Oregon you would not use in Maine or Arizona. Poems often partake of special limitations of word choice. For a rabbit poem or a death poem, the writer dips into different dictions.

The **tone**, or mood, the poet wants the poem to have also influences word choice. In two poems about mountain climbing, the same poet may use similar technical terms and place names, but the diction will be guided differently by each poem's mood. Tension or exuberance lead the poet to make different word choices. In speech, you tell a lot about people's moods by their tones of voice. Even if you can't hear the words, you pick up quickly whether commotion in the street at night is someone getting mugged or someone going home from a party, whether the low voice on the telephone is a friend or an obscene caller, whether your father doesn't mind that you came in at four in the morning or is barely hiding his fury. In poems, too, emotions and attitudes show in the *tone*. Anger, sarcasm, boisterousness, teasing, boredom, exultation, sadness, querulousness—these emotions are currents we sense running through word selection.

"Cherrylog Road" tells about a meeting which could take place in any rural area. But, at the outset, "kudzu" and "corn whiskey" begin to focus sharply on the specific location of the poem. What other words are *of* that place? Unlike Wright's "Autumn Begins in Martins Ferry, Ohio," this poem contains no shift in diction. It stays right in the hot Southern junkyard. Both the boy and Doris Holbrook climb through a series of cars. Doris has "escaped" from her father's farm; the boy imagines the Pierce-Arrow's former owner being driven to an orphanage. Even the sun is active "eating the paint in blisters / From a hundred car tops and hoods." Dickey chooses words of constant motion and of location to lead to the wild parting at the end. A paraphrase of any section of the poem will reveal how Dickey's vibrant, exact word choice makes the story exhilarating.

CHERRYLOG ROAD

Off Highway 106
At Cherrylog Road I entered
The '34 Ford without wheels,
Smothered in kudzu,
With a seat pulled out to run   5
Corn whiskey down from the hills,

And then from the other side
Crept into an Essex
With a rumble seat of red leather
And then out again, aboard   10
A blue Chevrolet, releasing
The rust from its other color,

Reared up on three building blocks.
None had the same body heat;
I changed with them inward, toward   15
The weedy heart of the junkyard,
For I knew that Doris Holbrook
Would escape from her father at noon

And would come from the farm
To seek parts owned by the sun   20
Among the abandoned chassis,
Sitting in each in turn
As I did, leaning forward
As in a wild stock-car race

In the parking lot of the dead.   25
Time after time, I climbed in
And out the other side, like
An envoy or movie star
Met at the station by crickets.
A radiator cap raised its head,   30

Become a real toad or a kingsnake
As I neared the hub of the yard,
Passing through many states,
Many lives, to reach

Some grandmother's long Pierce-Arrow   35
Sending platters of blindness forth

From its nickel hubcaps
And spilling its tender upholstery
On sleepy roaches,
The glass panel in between   40
Lady and colored driver
Not all the way broken out,

The back-seat phone
Still on its hook.
I got in as though to exclaim,   45
"Let us go to the orphan asylum,
John; I have some old toys
For children who say their prayers."

I popped with sweat as I thought
I heard Doris Holbrook scrape   50
Like a mouse in the southern-state sun
That was eating the paint in blisters
From a hundred car tops and hoods.
She was tapping like code,

Loosening the screws,   55
Carrying off headlights,
Sparkplugs, bumpers,
Cracked mirrors and gear-knobs,
Getting ready, already,
To go back with something to show   60

Other than her lips' new trembling
I would hold to me soon, soon,
Where I sat in the ripped back seat
Talking over the interphone,
Praying for Doris Holbrook   65
To come from her father's farm

And to get back there
With no trace of me on her face
To be seen by her red-haired father
Who would change, in the squalling barn,   70
Her back's pale skin with a strop,
Then lay for me

In a bootlegger's roasting car
With a string-triggered 12-gauge shotgun
To blast the breath from the air.   75
Not cut by the jagged windshields,
Through the acres of wrecks she came
With a wrench in her hand,

Through dust where the blacksnake dies
Of boredom, and the beetle knows   80
The compost has no more life.
Someone outside would have seen
The oldest car's door inexplicably
Close from within:

I held her and held her and held her,   85
Convoyed at terrific speed
By the stalled, dreaming traffic around us,
So the blacksnake, stiff
With inaction, curved back
Into life, and hunted the mouse   90

With deadly overexcitement,
The beetles reclaimed their field
As we clung, glued together,
With the hooks of the seat springs
Working through to catch us red-handed   95
Amidst the gray breathless batting

That burst from the seat at our backs,
We left by separate doors
Into the changed, other bodies
Of cars, she down Cherrylog Road   100
And I to my motorcycle
Parked like the soul of the junkyard

Restored, a bicycle fleshed
With power, and tore off
Up Highway 106, continually   105
Drunk on the wind in my mouth,
Wringing the handlebar for speed,
Wild to be wreckage forever.

James Dickey, 1923–

Both "Oh, Lovely Rock" and "Crystals Like Blood" use language that focuses on geographical and geological terminology.

OH, LOVELY ROCK

We stayed the night in the pathless gorge of Ventana Creek, up
    the east fork.
The rock walls and the mountain ridges hung forest on forest
    above our heads, maple and redwood,
Laurel, oak, madrone, up to the high and slender Santa Lucian
    firs that stare up the cataracts
Of slide-rock to the star-color precipices.
    We lay on gravel and
Kept a little camp-fire for warmth   5
Past midnight only two or three coals glowed red in the cooling
    darkness; I laid a clutch of dead bay-leaves
On the ember ends and felted dry sticks across them and lay
    down again. The revived flame
Lighted my sleeping son's face and his companion's, and the
    vertical face of the great gorge-wall
Across the stream. Light leaves overhead danced in the fire's
    breath, tree-trunks were seen: it was the rock wall
That fascinated my eyes and mind. Nothing strange: light-gray
    diorite with two or three slanting seams in it,   10
Smooth-polished by the endless attrition of slides and floods; no
    fern nor lichen, pure naked rock . . . as if I were
Seeing rock for the first time. As if I were seeing through the
    flame-lit surface into the real and bodily
And living rock. Nothing strange . . . I cannot
Tell you how strange: the silent passion, the deep nobility and
    childlike loveliness: this fate going on
Outside our fates. It is here in the mountain like a grave smiling
    child. I shall die, and my boys   15
Will live and die, our world will go on through its rapid agonies
    of change and discovery; this age will die,
And wolves have howled in the snow around a new Bethlehem:
    this rock will be here, grave, earnest, not passive: the
    energies
That are its atoms will be bearing the whole mountain above:
    and I, many packed centuries ago,
Felt its intense reality with love and wonder, this lonely rock.

Robinson Jeffers, 1887–1962

CRYSTALS LIKE BLOOD

I remember how, long ago, I found
Crystals like blood in a broken stone.

I picked up a broken chunk of bed-rock
And turned it this way and that,
It was heavier than one would have expected   5
From its size. One face was caked
With brown limestone. But the rest
Was a hard greenish-gray quartz-like stone
Faintly dappled with darker shadows,
And in this quartz ran veins and beads   10
Of bright magenta.

And I remember how later on I saw
How mercury is extracted from cinnabar
—The double ring of iron piledrivers
Like the multiple legs of a fantastically symmetrical spider   15
Rising and falling with monotonous precision,
Marching round in an endless circle
And pounding up and down with a tireless, thunderous force,
While, beyond, another conveyor drew the crumbled ore
From the bottom and raised it to an opening high   20
In the side of a gigantic gray-white kiln.

So I remember how mercury is got
When I contrast my living memory of you
And your dear body rotting here in the clay
—And feel once again released in me   25
The bright torrents of felicity, naturalness, and faith
My treadmill memory draws from you yet.

Hugh MacDiarmid, 1892–1978

EXERCISES

1. Compare the tone of voice in "Cherrylog Road" to "Autumn Begins in Martins Ferry, Ohio." What is the attitude of each speaker toward his subject? What lets you know this?

2. How do the sounds in the last line of "Cherrylog Road" bring out the sensation of the boy speeding off on his motorcycle?

3. Compare the diction and sound in "Oh Lovely Rock" and "Crystals Like Blood."
4. Do the three preceding poems keep to a kinship of words, or are there significant shifts in diction?
5. Describe how the tone of each poem might have influenced word choice.
6. Discuss the title "Oh, Lovely Rock" in relation to the poem's last three words.
7. Does one poem have more immediacy than the others? If so, why?

• • •

DOLOR

I have known the inexorable sadness of pencils,
Neat in their boxes, dolor of pad and paper-weight,
All the misery of manila folders and mucilage,
Desolation in immaculate public places,
Lonely reception room, lavatory, switchboard,   5
The unalterable pathos of basin and pitcher,
Ritual of multigraph, paper-clip, comma,
Endless duplication of lives and objects.
And I have seen dust from the walls of institutions,
Finer than flour, alive, more dangerous than silica,   10
Sift, almost invisible, through long afternoons of tedium,
Dropping a fine film on nails and delicate eyebrows,
Glazing the pale hair, the duplicate grey standard faces.

Theodore Roethke, 1908–1963

EXERCISES

1. In "Dolor," is there a kinship of words? How does the mood of the title affect the word choice?
2. What words suggest the "inexorable sadness" of institutions? Is the list believable?
3. Try writing a ten-line poem titled "Celebration." Beginning with "I know the incomparable thrill of . . ." follow Roethke's pattern with words that fit your title.

FERN HILL

Now as I was young and easy under the apple boughs
About the lilting house and happy as the grass was green,
     The night above the dingle starry,
       Time let me hail and climb
     Golden in the heydays of his eyes,   5
And honoured among wagons I was prince of the apple towns
And once below a time I lordly had the trees and leaves
     Trail with daisies and barley
     Down the rivers of the windfall light.

And as I was green and carefree, famous among the barns   10
About the happy yard and singing as the farm was home,
     In the sun that is young once only,
       Time let me play and be
     Golden in the mercy of his means,
And green and golden I was huntsman and herdsman, the
     calves   15
Sang to my horn, the foxes on the hills barked clear and cold,
       And the sabbath rang slowly
     In the pebbles of the holy streams.

All the sun long it was running, it was lovely, the hay
Fields high as the house, the tunes from the chimneys, it was
     air   20
     And playing, lovely and watery
       And fire green as grass.
     And nightly under the simple stars
As I rode to sleep the owls were bearing the farm away,
All the moon long I heard, blessed among stables, the night-jars   25
     Flying with the ricks, and the horses
       Flashing into the dark.

And then to awake, and the farm, like a wanderer white
With the dew, come back, the cock on his shoulder: it was all
     Shining, it was Adam and maiden,   30
       The sky gathered again
     And the sun grew round that very day.
So it must have been after the birth of the simple light
In the first, spinning place, the spellbound horses walking warm
     Out of the whinnying green stable   35
       On to the fields of praise.

And honoured among foxes and pheasants by the gay house
Under the new made clouds and happy as the heart was long,
   In the sun born over and over,
      I ran my heedless ways,   40
   My wishes raced through the house high hay
And nothing I cared, at my sky blue trades, that time allows
In all his tuneful turning so few and such morning songs
   Before the children green and golden
      Follow him out of grace,   45

Nothing I cared, in the lamb white days, that time would take me
Up to the swallow thronged loft by the shadow of my hand,
   In the moon that is always rising,
      Nor that riding to sleep
I should hear him fly with the high fields   50
And wake to the farm forever fled from the childless land.
Oh as I was young and easy in the mercy of his means,
      Time held me green and dying
   Though I sang in my chains like the sea.

Dylan Thomas, 1914–1953

EXERCISES

1. Analyze the sound patterns and word choices in "Fern Hill."

2. How does the language compare to "Cherrylog Road"? To "Inversnaid"?

3. What are the emotions of the speaker? How do his adjectives, verbs, colors convey emotion?

4. What phrases surprised you? Do these surprises seem akin to the general diction of the poem or are they shifts in the tone and word choice?

Poems for Discussion

from THE CANTERBURY TALES

The General Prologue

Whan that Aprill with his shoures soote
The droghte of March hath perced to the roote
And bathed every veyne in swich licour
Of which vertu engendred is the flour,
Whan Zephirus eek with his sweete breeth   5
Inspired hath in every holt and heeth
The tendre croppes, and the yonge sonne
Hath in the Ram his half cours y-ronne,
And smale foweles maken melodye
That slepen al the nyght with open eye,   10
So priketh hem Nature in hir corages,
Than longen folk to goon on pilgrymages,
And palmeres for to seken straunge strondes,
To ferne halwes kouthe in sondry londes.
And specially, from every shires ende   15
Of Engelond, to Caunterbury they wende,
The holy, blisful martir for to seke
That hem hat holpen whan that they were seeke.

Geoffrey Chaucer, 1343–1400

Note: *The Canterbury Tales*, a group of stories told by pilgrims, opens with this prologue. Pilgrimages often started in April, the beginning of good weather. Thomas à Becket was martyred at Canterbury.

"When that April with its sweet showers/ The drought of March has pierced to the root,/ And bathed every vein in such liquor/ By virtue of which is engendered the flower;/ When Zephyrus, [west wind] also, with his sweet breath/ Inspired has in every wood and field/ The tender shoots, and the young sun/ Has in the Ram [Aries] half his course run,/ And small birds make melody,/ That sleep all night with open eye/ So Nature pricks them in their hearts,/ Then folks long to go on pilgrimages,/ And palmers [palm branch signified a trip to the Holy Land] to seek strange shores,/ To far shrines known in sundry lands;/ And especially from every shire's end/ Of England to Canterbury they wend,/ The holy, blissful martyr [Thomas à Becket] for to seek,/ Who had helped them when they were sick."

WHEN THAT I WAS AND A LITTLE TINY BOY[1]

When that I was and a little tiny boy,
  With hey, ho, the wind and the rain,
A foolish thing was but a toy,
  For the rain it raineth every day.

But when I came to man's estate,   5
  With hey, ho, the wind and the rain,
'Gainst knaves and thieves men shut their gate,
  For the rain it raineth every day.

But when I came, alas! to wive,
  With hey, ho, the wind and the rain,   10
By swaggering could I never thrive,
  For the rain it raineth every day.

But when I came unto my beds,
  With hey, ho, the wind and the rain,
With toss-pots still had drunken heads,   15
  For the rain it raineth every day.

A great while ago the world begun,
  With hey, ho, the wind and the rain,
But that's all one, our play is done,
  And we'll strive to please you every day.   20

William Shakespeare, 1564–1616

[1] *When That I Was and a Little Tiny Boy:* the clown's song at the close of *Twelfth Night.*

THE SNOWSTORM

Announced by all the trumpets of the sky,
Arrives the snow, and, driving o'er the fields,
Seems nowhere to alight: the whited air
Hides hills and woods, the river, and the heaven,
And veils the farmhouse at the garden's end.   5
The sled and traveler stopped, the courier's feet
Delayed, all friends shut out, the housemates sit
Around the radiant fireplace, enclosed
In a tumultuous privacy of storm.

Come see the north wind's masonry.   10
Out of an unseen quarry evermore
Furnished with tile, the fierce artificer
Curves his white bastions with projected roof
Round every windward stake, or tree, or door.
Speeding, the myriad-handed, his wild work   15
So fanciful, so savage, nought cares he
For number or proportion. Mockingly,
On coop or kennel he hangs Parian[1] wreaths;
A swan-like form invests the hidden thorn;
Fills up the farmer's lane from wall to wall,   20
Maugre[2] the farmer's sighs; and, at the gate,
A tapering turret overtops the work.
And when his hours are numbered, and the world
Is all his own, retiring, as he were not,
Leaves, when the sun appears, astonished Art   25
To mimic in slow structures, stone by stone,
Built in an age, the mad wind's night-work,
The frolic architecture of the snow.

Ralph Waldo Emerson, 1803–1882

---

[1] *Parian:* marble.
[2] *maugre:* in spite of.

THE NIGHT IS FREEZING FAST

The night is freezing fast,
    To-morrow comes December;
        And winterfalls of old
Are with me from the past;
    And chiefly I remember   5
        How Dick would hate the cold.

Fall, winter, fall; for he,
    Prompt hand and headpiece clever,
        Has woven a winter robe,
And made of earth and sea   10
    His overcoat for ever,
        And wears the turning globe.

A. E. Housman, 1859–1936

SONNET LXXIII

That time of year thou mayst in me behold
When yellow leaves, or none, or few, do hang
Upon those boughs which shake against the cold,
Bare ruined choirs, where late the sweet birds sang.
In me thou see'st the twilight of such day   5
As after sunset fadeth in the west;
Which by and by black night doth take away,
Death's second self, that seals up all in rest.
In me thou see'st the glowing of such fire,
That on the ashes of his youth doth lie,   10
As the deathbed whereon it must expire
Consumed with that which it was nourished by.
   This thou perceiv'st, which makes thy love more strong,
   To love that well which thou must leave ere long.

William Shakespeare, 1564–1616

THE SOOTE SEASON

The soote° season that bud and bloom forth brings   *sweet*
With green hath clad the hill and eke° the vale,   *also*
The nightingale with feathers new she sings,
The turtle° to her make° hath told her tale.   *turtledove, mate*
Summer is come, for every spray now springs,
The hart hath hung his old head on the pale,
The buck in brake his winter coat he flings,
The fishes float with new repairèd scale,
The adder all her slough away she slings,
The swift swallow pursueth the flyès smale,
The busy bee her honey now she mings,°—   *remembers*
Winter is worn, that was the flowers' bale:°   *woe*
   And thus I see, among these pleasant things
   Each care decays—and yet my sorrow springs.

Henry Howard, Earl of Surrey, 1517–1547

ON THE ICE ISLANDS SEEN FLOATING
IN THE GERMAN OCEAN

What portents, from what distant region, ride,
Unseen till now in ours, the astonished tide?
In ages past, old Proteus,[1] with his droves
Of sea-calves, sought the mountains and the groves:
But now, descending whence of late they stood,   5
Themselves the mountains seem to rove the flood.
Dire times were they, full-charged with human woes;
And these, scarce less calamitous than those.
What view we now? More wondrous still! Behold!
Like burnished brass they shine, or beaten gold;   10
And all around the pearl's pure splendour show,
And all around the ruby's fiery glow.
Come they from India? where the burning earth,
All-bounteous, gives her richest treasures birth;
And where the costly gems, that beam around   15
The brows of mightiest potentates, are found?
No. Never such a countless dazzling store
Had left unseen the Ganges' peopled shore.
Rapacious hands, and ever-watchful eyes,
Should sooner far have marked and seized the prize.   20
Whence sprang they then? Ejected have they come
From Vesuvius', or from Aetna's[2] burning womb?
Thus shine they self-illumed, or but display
The borrowed splendours of a cloudless day?
With borrowed beams they shine. The gales that breathe   25
Now land-ward, and the current's force beneath,
Have borne them nearer: and the nearer sight,
Advantaged more, contemplates them aright.
Their lofty summits, crested high, they show,
With mingled sleet and long-incumbent snow.   30
The rest is ice. Far hence, where, most severe,
Bleak winter well-nigh saddens all the year,
Their infant growth began. He bade arise
Their uncouth forms, portentous in our eyes.
Oft as, dissolved by transient suns, the snow   35
Left the tall cliff, to join the flood below,
He caught and curdled, with a freezing blast,
The current, ere it reached the boundless waste.
By slow degrees uprose the wondrous pile,

---

[1] *Proteus:* sea god.
[2] *Vesuvius, Aetna:* volcanoes in Italy.

And long-successive ages rolled and while;   40
Till, ceaseless in its growth, it claimed to stand
Tall as its rival mountains on the land.
Thus stood—and, unremovable by skill
Or force of man, had stood the structure still;
But that, tho' firmly fixt, supplanted yet   45
By pressure of its own enormous weight,
It left the shelving beach—and, with a sound
That shook the bellowing waves and rocks around,
Self-launched, and swiftly, to the briny wave,
As if instinct with strong desire to lave,[3]   50
Down went the ponderous mass. So bards of old,
How Delos swam the Ægean deep, have told.
But not of ice was Delos. Delos bore
Herb, fruit, and flower. She, crowned with laurel, wore,
E'en under wintry skies, a summer smile;   55
And Delos was Apollo's favorite isle.
But, horrid wanderers of the deep, to you
He deems Cimmerian[4] darkness only due.
Your hatred birth he deigned not to survey,
But, scornful, turned his glorious eyes away.   60
Hence! Seek your home; no longer rashly dare
The darts of Phoebus,[5] and a softer air;
Lest ye regret, too late, your native coast,
In no congenial gulf for ever lost!

William Cowper, 1731–1800

[3] *lave:* bathe.
[4] *Cimmerian:* refers to a mythical people who lived in perpetual darkness.
[5] *Phoebus:* Apollo, the sun god.

THE FISH, THE MAN, AND THE SPIRIT

To Fish

You strange, astonished-looking, angle-faced,
Dreary-mouthed, gaping wretches of the sea,
Gulping salt water everlastingly,
Cold-blooded, though with red your blood be graced,
And mute, though dwellers in the roaring waste;   5
And you, all shapes beside, that fishy be,—
Some round, some flat, some long, all devilry,
Legless, unloving, infamously chaste:—

O scaly, slippery, wet, swift, staring wights,
What is't ye do? what life lead? eh, dull goggles?   10
How do ye vary your vile days and nights?
How pass your Sundays? Are ye still but joggles
In ceaseless wash? Still nought but gapes and bites,
And drinks, and stares, diversified with boggles?

A Fish Answers

Amazing monster! that, for aught I know,   15
With the first sight of thee didst make our race
Forever stare! Oh flat and shocking face,
Grimly divided from the breast below!
Thou that on dry land horribly dost go
With a split body and most ridiculous pace,   20
Prong after prong, disgracer of all grace,
Long-useless-finned, haired, upright, unwet, slow!

O breather of unbreathable, sword-sharp air,
How canst exist? How bear thyself, thou dry
And dreary sloth? What particle canst share   25
Of the only blessed life, the watery?
I sometimes see of ye an actual pair
Go by! linked fin by fin! most odiously.

The Fish turns into a Man, and then into a Spirit, and again speaks

Indulge thy smiling scorn, if smiling still,
O man! and loathe, but with a sort of love: 30
For difference must its use by difference prove,
And, in sweet clang, the spheres with music fill.
One of the spirits am I, that at his will
Live in whate'er has life—fish, eagle, dove—
No hate, no pride, beneath nought, nor above,   35
A visitor of the rounds of God's sweet skill.

Man's life is warm, glad, sad, 'twixt loves and graves,
Boundless in hope, honored with pangs austere,
Heaven-gazing; and his angel-wings he craves:
The fish is swift, small-needing, vague yet clear,   40
A cold, sweet, silver life, wrapped in round waves,
Quickened with touches of transporting fear.

Leigh Hunt, 1784–1859

THE FISH

I caught a tremendous fish
and held him beside the boat
half out of water, with my hook
fast in a corner of his mouth.
He didn't fight.   5
He hadn't fought at all.
He hung a grunting weight,
battered and venerable
and homely. Here and there
his brown skin hung in strips   10
like ancient wallpaper,
and its pattern of darker brown
was like wallpaper:
shapes like full-blown roses
stained and lost through age.   15
He was speckled with barnacles,
fine rosettes of lime,
and infested
with tiny white sea-lice,
and underneath two or three   20
rags of green weed hung down.
While his gills were breathing in
the terrible oxygen
—the frightening gills,
fresh and crisp with blood,   25
that can cut so badly—
I thought of the coarse white flesh
packed in like feathers,
the big bones and the little bones,
the dramatic reds and blacks   30
of his shiny entrails,
and the pink swim-bladder
like a big peony.
I looked into his eyes
which were far larger than mine   35
but shallower, and yellowed,
the irises backed and packed
with tarnished tinfoil
seen through the lenses
of old scratched isinglass.   40
They shifted a little, but not
to return my stare.
—It was more like the tipping
of an object toward the light.

I admired his sullen face,   45
the mechanism of his jaw,
and then I saw
that from his lower lip
—if you could call it a lip—
grim, wet, and weaponlike,   50
hung five old pieces of fish-line,
or four and a wire leader
with the swivel still attached,
with all their five big hooks
grown firmly in his mouth.   55
A green line, frayed at the end
where he broke it, two heavier lines,
and a fine black thread
still crimped from the strain and snap
when it broke and he got away.   60
Like medals with their ribbons
frayed and wavering,
a five-haired beard of wisdom
trailing from his aching jaw.
I stared and stared   65
and victory filled up
the little rented boat,
from the pool of bilge
where oil had spread a rainbow
around the rusted engine   70
to the bailer rusted orange,
the sun-cracked thwarts,
the oarlocks on their strings,
the gunnells—until everything
was rainbow, rainbow, rainbow!   75
And I let the fish go.

Elizabeth Bishop, 1911–1979

BEAUTY

   Beauty, thou wild fantastic ape,
Who dost in ev'ry country change thy shape!
Here black, there brown, here tawny, and there white;
Thou flatt'rer which compli'st with every sight!
   Thou babel which confound'st the eye   5
With unintelligible variety!
   Who hast no certain what, nor where,
But vary'st still, and dost thy self declare
   Inconstant, as thy she-professors are.

Beauty, love's scene and masquerade,   10
So gay by well-plac'd lights, and distance made;
False coin, with which th' impostor cheats us still;
The stamp and colour good, but metal ill!
   Which light, or base we find, when we
Weigh by enjoyment, and examine thee!   15
   For though thy being be but show,
'Tis chiefly night which men to thee allow:
And choose t'enjoy thee, when thou least art thou.

Beauty, thou active, passive ill!
Which diest thy self as fast as thou dost kill!   20
Thou tulip, who thy stock in paint dost waste,
Neither for physic good, nor smell, nor taste.
   Beauty, whose flames but meteors are,   .
Short-liv'd and low, though thou wouldst seem a star,
   Who dar'st not thine own home descry,   25
Pretending to dwell richly in the eye,
When thou, alas, dost in the fancy lie.

Beauty, whose conquests still are made
O'er hearts by cowards kept, or else betray'd!
Weak victor! who thy self destroy'd must be   30
When sickness storms, or time besieges thee!
   Thou'unwholesome thaw to frozen age!
Thou strong wine, which youth's fever dost enrage,
   Thou tyrant which leav'st no man free!
Thou subtle thief, from whom nought safe can be!   35
Thou murth'rer which hast kill'd, and devil which wouldst damn me.

Abraham Cowley, 1618–1667

A HO! A HO!

   A ho! A ho!
   Love's horn doth blow,
   And he will out a-hawking go.
His shafts are light as beauty's sighs,
And bright as midnight's brightest eyes,   5
   And round his starry way
The swan-winged horses of the skies,
With summer's music in their manes,
Curve their fair necks to zephyr's reins,
   And urge their graceful play.   10

A ho! A ho!
Love's horn doth blow,
And he will out a-hawking go.
The sparrows flutter round his wrist.
The feathery thieves that Venus kissed   15
And taught their morning song,
The linnets seek the airy list,
And swallows too, small pets of Spring,
Beat back the gale with swifter wing,
And dart and wheel along.   20

A ho! A ho!
Love's horn doth blow,
And he will out a-hawking go.
Now woe to every gnat that skips
To filch the fruit of ladies' lips,   25
His felon blood is shed;
And woe to flies, whose airy ships
On beauty cast their anchoring bite,
And bandit wasp, that naughty wight,
Whose sting is slaughter-red.   30

Thomas Lovell Beddoes, 1803–1849

THE MARSHES OF GLYNN

Glooms of the live-oaks, beautiful-braided and woven
With intricate shades of the vines that myriad-cloven
    Clamber the forks of the multiform boughs,—
        Emerald twilights,—
        Virginal shy lights,   5
Wrought of the leaves to allure to the whisper of vows,
When lovers pace timidly down through the green colonnades
    Of the dim sweet woods, of the dear dark woods,
        Of the heavenly woods and glades,
That run to the radiant marginal sand-beach within   10
    The wide sea-marshes of Glynn;—

Beautiful glooms, soft dusks in the noon-day fire,—
Wildwood privacies, closets of lone desire,
Chamber from chamber parted with wavering arras of leaves,—
Cells for the passionate pleasure of prayer to the soul that
    grieves,   15
    Pure with a sense of the passing of saints through the wood,
    Cool for the dutiful weighing of ill with good;—

O braided dusks of the oak and woven shades of the vine,
While the riotous noon-day sun of the June-day long did shine,
Ye held me fast in your heart and I held you fast in mine;   20
   But now when the noon is no more, and riot is rest,
     And the sun is a-wait at the ponderous gate of the West,
       And the slant yellow beam down the wood-aisle doth seem
       Like a lane into heaven that leads from a dream,—
Ay, now, when my soul all day hath drunken the soul of the
    oak,   25
And my heart is at ease from men, and the wearisome sound of
    the stroke
Of the scythe of time and the trowel of trade is low,
And belief overmasters doubt, and I know that I know,
And my spirit is grown to a lordly great compass within,
That the length and the breadth and the sweep of the
    marshes of Glynn   30
Will work me no fear like the fear they have wrought me of
    yore
   When length was fatigue, and when breadth was but
    bitterness sore,
   And when terror and shrinking and dreary unnamable pain
   Drew over me out of the merciless miles of the plain,—
     Oh, now, unafraid, I am fain to face   35
       The vast sweet visage of space.
     To the edge of the wood I am drawn, I am drawn,
   Where the gray beach glimmering runs, as a belt of the
    dawn,
      For a mete and a mark
      To the forest-dark:—   40
       So:
     Affable live-oak, leaning low,—
   Thus—with your favor—soft, with a reverent hand,
   (Not lightly touching your person, Lord of the land!)
   Bending your beauty aside, with a step I stand   45
      On the firm-packed sand,
        Free
   By a world of marsh that borders a world of sea,
Sinuous southward and sinuous northward the shimmering
    band
Of the sand-beach fastens the fringe of the marsh to the folds
    of the land.   50
Inward and outward to northward and southward the beachlines
    linger and curl
As a silver-wrought garment that clings to and follows the firm
    sweet limbs of a girl.
   Vanishing, swerving, evermore curving again into sight,
   Softly the sand-beach wavers away to a dim gray looping of
    light.

And what if behind me to westward the wall of the woods
    stands high?   55
The world lies east: how ample, the marsh and the sea and
    the sky!
A league and a league of marsh-grass, waist-high, broad in
    the blade,
Green, and all of a height, and unflecked with a light or a
    shade,
    Stretch leisurely off, in a pleasant plain,
    To the terminal blue of the main.   60
    Oh, what is abroad in the marsh and the terminal Sea?
    Somehow my soul seems suddenly free
From the weighing of fate and the sad discussion of sin,
By the length and the breadth and the sweep of the marshes of
    Glynn.
Ye marshes, how candid and simple and nothing-withholding
    and free   65
Ye publish yourselves to the sky and offer yourselves to the
    sea!
Tolerant plains, that suffer the sea and the rains and the sun,
Ye spread and span like the catholic man who hath mightily
    won
God out of knowledge and good out of infinite pain
And sight out of blindness and purity out of a stain.   70

As the marsh-hen secretly builds on the watery sod,
Behold I will build me a nest on the greatness of God:
I will fly in the greatness of God as the marsh-hen flies
    In the freedom that fills all the space 'twixt the marsh and
    the skies:
    By so many roots as the marsh-grass sends in the sod   75
    I will heartily lay me a-hold on the greatness of God:
    Oh, like to the greatness of God is the greatness within
    The range of the marshes, the liberal marshes of Glynn.

And the sea lends large, as the marsh: lo, out of his plenty the
    sea
Pours fast: full soon the time of the flood-tide must be: 80
    Look how the grace of the sea doth go
About and about through the intricate channels that flow
    Here and there,
    Everywhere,
Till his waters have flooded the uttermost creeks and the low-
    lying lanes,   85
    And the marsh is meshed with a million veins,
    That like as with rosy and silvery essences flow

In the rose-and-silver evening glow.
    Farewell, my lord Sun!
The creeks overflow: a thousand rivulets run   90
'Twixt the roots of the sod; the blades of the marsh-grass
    stir;
Passeth a hurrying sound of wings that westward whirr;
Passeth, and all is still, and the currents cease to run;
    And the sea and the marsh are one.
    How still the plains of the waters be!   95
    The tide is in his ecstasy.
    The tide is at his highest height:
        And it is night.

And now from the Vast of the Lord will the waters of sleep
    Roll in on the souls of men,   100
    But who will reveal to our waking ken
    The forms that swim and the shapes that creep
        Under the waters of sleep?
And I would I could know what swimmeth below when the tide
comes in
On the length and the breadth of the marvellous marshes of
    Glynn.   105

Sidney Lanier, 1842–1881

A SMALL EXCURSION

Take a trip with me
through the towns in Missouri.
Feel naming in all its joy
as we go through Braggadocio, Barks, Kidder, Fair Play,
Bourbon, Bean Lake   5
and Loose Creek.
If we should get lost
we could spend the night at
Lutesville, Brinktown, Excello, Nodaway,
Humansville or Kinderpost.   10

If we liked Bachelor we could bypass
with only slight compunction
another interesting place,
Conception Junction.

I think you would feel instant intimacy   15
with all the little flaws
of an Elmer, Esther, Ethel, Oscar or Archie,
all the quirky ways
of a Eunice or a Bernice,
at home in a   20
Hattie or even an Amazonia.

I'd enjoy, wouldn't you, saying that I came from
Chloride, or Map or Boss or Turtle
Or Arab or Chamois or Huzzah or Drum.

Surely the whole world loves the lover of men   25
who calls a tiny gathering
in midwest America
Paris, Carthage or Alexandria,
Odessa, Cairo, Arcadia or Milan,
as well as the one who calls   30
his clump of folk
Postoak,
the literalist who aims low
and calls it Shortbend or Old Mines
or Windyville or Iron or Nobby or Gumbo.   35

Riding along together,
we could think of all we'd had
at both Blooming Rose and Evening Shade.
Heading into the setting sun,
the gravel roads might get long and rough,   40
but we could make the difficult choice between
Minimum and Enough,
between Protem and Longrun.
And if it got very late
we could stay at Stet.   45

Isn't there something infinitely appealing
in the candor
of calling a collection of human beings
Liberal, Clever, Bland, or
Moody, Useful, Handy, or   50
Rich, Fertile and Fairdealing?
People who named these towns
were nobody's fools.
Passing through Peculiar, we could follow
a real school bus labelled Peculiar Public Schools.   55

O to be physically and aesthetically
footloose,
travelling always,
going through
pure sound that stands for a space,   60
like Cabool, Canalou, Plad, Auxvasse,
Koshkonong, Weaubleau, Roubïdoux,
Hahn Dongola, Knob Noster and Foose!

Mona Van Duyn, 1921–

UPSTATE

A knife blade of cold air keeps prying
the bus window open. The spring country
won't be shut out. The door to the john
keeps banging. There're a few of us:
a stale drunk or stoned woman in torn jeans,   5
a Spanish-American salesman, and, ahead,
a black woman folded in an overcoat.
Emptiness makes a companionable aura
through the upstate village—repetitive,
but crucial in their little differences   10
of fields, wide yards with washing, old machinery—where people live
with the highway's patience and flat certainty.

Sometimes I feel sometimes
the Muse is leaving, the Muse is leaving America.
Her tired face is tired of iron fields,   15
its hollows sing the mines of Appalachia,
she is a chalk-thin miner's wife with knobbled elbows,
her neck tendons taut as banjo strings,
she who was once a freckled palomino with a girl's mane
galloping blue pastures plinkety-plunkety,   20
staring down at a tree-stunned summer lake,
when all the corny calendars were true.
The departure comes over me in smoke
from the far factories.

But were the willows lyres, the fanned-out pollard willows   25
with clear translation of water into song,
were the starlings as heartbroken as nightingales,
whose sorrow piles the looming thunderhead
over the Catskills, what would be their theme?

The spring hills are sun-freckled, the chaste white barns flash   30
through screening trees the vigour of her dream,
like a white plank bridge over a quarreling brook.
Clear images! Direct as your daughters
in the way their clear look returns your stare,
unarguable and fatal—   35
no, it is more sensual.
I am falling in love with America.

I must put the cold small pebbles from the spring
upon my tongue to learn her language,
to talk like birch or aspen confidently.   40
I will knock at the widowed door
of one of these villages
where she will admit me like a broad meadow,
like a blue space between mountains,
and holding her arms at the broken elbows   45
brush the dank hair from a forehead
as warm as bread or as a homecoming.

Derek Walcott, 1930–

PHOSPHOR READING BY HIS OWN LIGHT

It is difficult to read. The page is dark.
Yet he knows what it is that he expects.

The page is blank or a frame without a glass
Or a glass that is empty when he looks.

The greenness of night lies on the page and goes   5
Down deeply in the empty glass . . .

Look, realist, not knowing what you expect.
The green falls on you as you look,

Falls on and makes and gives, even a speech.
And you think that that is what you expect,   10

That elemental parent, the green night,
Teaching a fusky alphabet.

Wallace Stevens, 1879–1955

THAT SONG

I will use the cormorant on his rope at night diving
Into the sea, and the fire on the prow, and the fish
Like ribbons sliding toward the green light in the dark.

I will remember the baneberry and the bladderwort
And keep the white crone under the bosackle tree   5
And the translucent figs and the candelabra burning alone
In the middle of the plains, and the twig girdler,
And the lizard of Christ running over the waves.

I will take the egg bubble on the flute
Of the elm and the ministries of the predacious   10
Caul beetle, the spit of the iris, the red juice shot
From the eye of the horny toad, and I will use
The irreducible knot wound by the hazel scrub
And the bog myrtle still tangling, and the sea horse
With his delicate horn, the flywheel of his maneuvering.   15

I will remember exactly each tab folded down
In the sin book of Sister Alleece and each prayer
Hanging in its painted cylinder above the door
And the desert goat at noon facing
The sun to survive.   20

I will include the brindled bandicoot and the barnacle
Goose and the new birds hatching from mussels
Under the sea and the migrating wildebeests humming
Like organs, moaning like men.

The sand swimmers alive under the Gobi plateau,   25
The cactus wren in her nest of thorns and the herald
Of the tarantula wasp and each yellow needle
In the spring field rising, everything will be there,
And nothing will be wasted.

Pattiann Rogers, 1940–

WORDS

Axes
After whose stroke the wood rings,
And the echoes!
Echoes traveling
Off from the center like horses.   5

The sap
Wells like tears, like the
Water striving
To re-establish its mirror
Over the rock   10

That drops and turns,
A white skull,
Eaten by weedy greens.
Years later I
Encounter them on the road—   15

Words dry and riderless,
The indefatigable hoof-taps.
While
From the bottom of the pool, fixed stars
Govern a life.   20

Sylvia Plath, 1932–1963

TODAY

Oh! kangaroos, sequins, chocolate sodas!
You really are beautiful! Pearls,
harmonicas, jujubes, aspirins! all
the stuff they've always talked about

still makes a poem a surprise!
These things are with us every day
even on beachheads and biers. They
do have meaning. They're strong as rocks.

Frank O'Hara, 1926–1966

Images: The Perceptual Field

It is better to present one Image in a lifetime than to produce voluminous works.

Ezra Pound

When a runner describes the last quarter-mile of the marathon, he might say that his left calf felt tied in a granny knot and his lungs were on fire. He might say instead that he sailed along smoothly and finished like a boat slipping into the berth or that, when he saw the red ribbon ahead at the finish line, he felt a tidal wave of energy pulling him across.

These specific details give you an active sense of the runner's experience. The tight muscle, the pressure in his chest, the feeling of ease, the sight of the red ribbon—all these are images. We usually think of an image as a picture of something, like a photograph is an image of its subject, but an image is *any* physical sensation. In poetry, an **image** is a word "picture" of any sense impression, not necessarily the visual. We see the red ribbon; we can't see lungs on fire but we "picture" in our mind's eye the sensation of heat in the chest. The imaginative re-creation of a sensation (touch, smell, auditory, visual, taste, motion) through words is an image. If the runner says, "I ran the marathon and the last quarter-mile was really hard," he conveys information; he doesn't recreate the experience. He *tells*; he doesn't *show*. To use images is to show details that appeal directly to the senses as well as to the mind.

If you read, "He walks like a giraffe belly-deep in cold water," the words call up a humorous picture of a man moving along awkwardly, slowly, and laboriously. The image also recalls your own experience of the difficulty of moving in cold water. You recognize the sensation through your own body. This *showing* of the man is livelier than the writer's simply telling us, "The awkward man is walking with some difficulty." Physical detail makes the man's motion specific. The language is concrete, as opposed to abstract. **Concrete** derives from root words meaning "to grow together." **Abstract** comes from root words meaning "to remove" and "to pull away." Abstract words *(progress, jealousy, pleasure, experience)* seem distant, while concrete words *(sunlight, smile, fork, sandwich)* are solid and right next to direct experience. Abstract words and statements are sometimes important and necessary, but a string of them is tedious. Too much abstract language quickly begins to sound like white noise. Because readers respond more to the particular than to the general, imagery is a most important element in the craft of poetry. Compare the following examples, which point out the difference between "showing" and "telling."

To Tell	*To Show (with concrete details)*
She dresses sloppily.	She wears her clothes as if they were thrown on with a pitchfork.
	Jonathan Swift
The sea is rough.	A sea Harsher than granite.
	Ezra Pound
I saw the harvest moon come up.	And saw the ruddy moon lean over a hedge Like a red-faced farmer.
	T. E. Hulme
The old woman got ready for bed.	You stood at the dresser, put your teeth away, washed your face, smoothed on Oil of Olay.
	Mona Van Duyn

He'd do anything for her.	He'd cut off his thumbs for her.

C. D. Wright

She was absurdly pleased.	. . . pleased as a dog with two tails.

Ozark folk expression

He has an unpleasant hand.	A hand like a fat maggot.

Jean-Paul Sartre

The dog's eyes are unusually large.	The dog in the next room has eyes big as ferris wheels.

Forrest Gander

The sentences on the left suffer from what Henry James called "weak specification"; that is, the statements are too generalized. We understand "an unpleasant hand," but Sartre's "a hand like a fat maggot" stimulates the senses of touch and sight. "The sea is rough" is a clear enough sentence. But if the sea is "harsher than granite," then it has a *more* resistant quality: the waves appear to be as hard as rocks.

Three Image Poems

The next three poems make extensive use of sensory details. In "Gloire de Dijon," D. H. Lawrence almost paints a picture of a woman bathing by a window. He is not the first poet to compare a woman to a rose. Notice how unobtrusively the "I" participates, just enough to give the reader a grounded vantage point.

GLOIRE DE DIJON[1]

When she rises in the morning
I linger to watch her;
She spreads the bath-cloth underneath the window
Glistening white on the shoulders,
While down her sides the mellow   5
Golden shadow glows as
She stoops to the sponge, and her swung breasts
Sway like full-blown yellow
Gloire de Dijon roses.

She drips herself with water, and her shoulders   10
Glisten as silver, they crumple up
Like wet and falling roses, and I listen
For the sluicing of their rain-disheveled petals,
In the window full of sunlight
Concentrates her golden shadow   15
Fold on fold, until it glows as
Mellow as the glory roses.

D. H. Lawrence, 1885–1930

[1] *Gloire de Dijon* ("Glory of Dijon"): a kind of rose.

The sense most active here is the kinetic sense, the motions of spreading, swaying, swinging, stooping, dripping. These actions belong not only to the woman but to the roses the poet is comparing her with. Visually we see many colors and lights: white shoulders, gold shadow on her sides, the full-blown roses, her shoulder slivered when wet, a window full of sunlight, and her shadow glowing and golden. The watcher of the woman bathing re-creates his experience through the careful selection and fusion of sensory details common to both the woman and the roses.

"What the Dog Perhaps Hears" concentrates on auditory images:

WHAT THE DOG PERHAPS HEARS

If an inaudible whistle
blown between our lips
can send him home to us,

then silence is perhaps
the sound of spiders breathing   5
and roots mining the earth;
it may be asparagus heaving,
headfirst, into the light
and the long brown sound
of cracked cups, when it happens.   10
We would like to ask the dog
if there is a continuous whirr
because the child in the house
keeps growing, if the snake
really stretches full length   15
without a click and the sun
breaks through clouds without
a decibel of effort;
whether in autumn, when the trees
dry up their wells, there isn't a shudder   20
too high for us to hear.

What is it like up there
above the shut-off level
of our simple ears?
For us there was no birth-cry,   25
the newborn bird is suddenly here,
the egg broken, the nest alive,
and we heard nothing when the world changed.

Lisel Mueller, 1924–

We can't actually hear "the long brown sound / of cracked cups" or
the snake's clicking sound as it stretches out. The poem is playful. By
speculating on what the dog possibly hears, Mueller lets these sounds
resonate in the reader's imagination. By implication, too, she raises the
question of other events around us that we are unaware of. The poem
works with primarily auditory images, but Mueller ties them to images
involving other senses. The asparagus is "heaving, / headfirst, into the
light," the sun "breaks through clouds," roots are "mining" and trees
are drying up—all images of sight, motion, or touch.

Because it is grounded in the senses, Shakespeare's "Winter" still
seems immediate to contemporary readers.

WINTER

When icicles hang by the wall,
   And Dick the shepherd blows his nail,
And Tom bears logs into the hall,
   And milk comes frozen home in pail,
When blood is nipped, and ways be foul,   5
Then nightly sings the staring owl:
       "To-who!
Tu-whit, tu-who!" a merry note,
While greasy Joan doth keel¹ the pot.

When all aloud the wind doth blow,   10
   And coughing drowns the parson's saw,
And birds sit brooding in the snow,
   And Marian's nose looks red and raw,
When roasted crabs hiss in the bowl,
Then nightly sings the staring owl: 15
       "To-who!
Tu-whit, tu-who!" a merry note,
While greasy Joan doth keel the pot.

William Shakespeare, 1564–1616

¹ *keel:* to cool by stirring.

Shakespeare appeals to many of the senses in this brief poem. We see frozen milk and Marian's red nose. We hear the wind blowing, crab apples hissing as they roast, and coughs drowning out the parson. The sense of touch is affected by "nipped," "greasy," "blows his nail," and Joan's stirring the pot. The icicles hang, the logs are brought in, the winds blow, and the birds sit brooding—all arresting images of motion or the lack of it. Smell and taste, the only senses not directly evoked, are hinted at as Joan stirs and the crab apples hiss.

Images and Perception

It is too extreme to maintain, as Theodore Roethke did in "The Waking" (page 383), that "We think by feeling. What is there to know?", but it is true that a large proportion of what we know, think, and remember is held in mind by images. Thought involves textures, smells, colors. Your own memories of winter, if you were writing a list of them, might include smoke rising from a factory chimney, a leak in the ceiling of a closet, the steamy smell of wool mittens drying on the radiator, charred marshmallows toasted over leaf smoke, your aunt's curried tomato soup simmering on the back burner. Such sensory experience is the basic material of imagery.

Each sense can divide and combine with others. Sight, the strongest sensory perception, also includes qualities of focus, shape, color, perspective, shadow, speed of movement, brightness, clarity, and composition. The auditory sense involves sounds of all pitches, ranges, and rhythms—along with silences (as in "What the Dog Perhaps Hears"). The kinetic sense Lawrence works with in "Gloire de Dijon" includes tension, the pull of weight, muscular balance, and gravity. Temperature, texture, and density are three qualities of the tactile sense, which is active in "Winter." The whole complex of tastes and smells, and the combinations of these, is crucial to perception. In addition to the five external senses, we also have an inner organic sense of pulse, heartbeat, cycles, and digestion.

No one knows exactly how images work. True, people have basically the same primary senses. True, language related closely to the senses is processed by the brain almost immediately, with no pause for complex connections to take place. We recognize "the hot aroma of dark roasted coffee" quicker than "the complex acrid smell of a heating beverage." But why? Is one more pleasurable than the other? We respond immediately to language that seems to *be* experience, rather than language that seems to *describe* experience from a distance.

A whiff of a musty coat as you pass someone on the sidewalk can release a flood of memories of your grandfather's old age. Almost all of these will be images: his white mustache, his way of slurping his tea or jingling the change in his pocket, his habit of dabbing a white handkerchief at the corners of his eyes. Imagery is a constant sound-and-light show taking place in our heads. But the language of philosophical ideas and abstractions can be pleasurable, too. As you walk along the sidewalk with your grandfather's image in mind, you may begin to speculate and to draw conclusions about his life (he was a sweet man with a good sense of humor or he was a crochety old grump) that are far removed from the intense first impression you got from the dank, mildewed smell. These ideas can be just as important and powerful as the images that provoke them. How imagery works is at the root of how we perceive and remember. As a reader told the ancient Chinese poet TuFu, "It is like being alive twice." The sharp focus of imagery on the senses guarantees a reader's emotional, connotative, and physical involvement. Generalizations or abstractions have a wider angle. A *particular* experience, such as one foot in the cold ocean, can evoke an experience of a place much more powerfully than a *general* statement about the coastal terrain. The painter Degas said he had many ideas for poems but couldn't manage to say what he wanted. His friend, the poet Mallarmé, replied, "My dear Degas, one does not make poetry with ideas but with words."

EXERCISES

1. What are the exact senses evoked in the following images? Discuss how each image focuses the experience described.

    a. A tap at the pane, the quick sharp scratch
        And blue spurt of a lighted match.

        Robert Browning

    b. The old star eaten blanket of the sky.

        T. E. Hulme

    c. Her knee feels like the face
        Of a surprised lioness.

        James Wright

    d. Purple is black blooming.

        Christopher Smart

    e. With my whole body I taste these peaches.

        Wallace Stevens

    f. I should have been a pair of ragged claws
        Scuttling across the floors of silent seas.

        T. S. Eliot

g. The blindman placed
    a tulip on his tongue for purple's taste.

    May Swenson

h. A woman so skinny I could smell her bones.

    Miller Williams

i. . . . a collarpoint of light.

    Mei-Mei Berssenbrugge

j. When you are old and gray and full of sleep,
    And nodding by the fire, take down this book.

    W. B. Yeats

2. First memories are largely sensory. Write a list of your earliest
    memories, including all the colors, shapes, movements, tastes you
    can recall.

Literal Images

The two kinds of images, literal and figurative, are different. "Her wet
pink lips" is a literal image; "her ripe plum lips" is a figurative image.
A **literal image** aims to replicate in words the object or experience. The
poet tries to reproduce the subject realistically, without comparing it
to anything else. A **figurative image** likens an object or experience to
something else, usually something surprising, as in "his eye is like a
burnt hole in a blanket"; a literal image would be "his black eye is
almost swollen shut."

The Spanish writer Juan Ramón Jiménez said, "I want my word
to be the thing itself, created by my soul a second time." William Carlos
Williams's "Nantucket" is a clear word picture of the "thing itself."
Nothing in the room is likened to anything else.

NANTUCKET

Flowers through the window
lavender and yellow

changed by white curtains—
Smell of cleanliness—

Sunshine of late afternoon—   5
On the glass tray

a glass pitcher, the tumbler
turned down, by which

a key is lying—And the
immaculate white bed.   10

William Carlos Williams, 1883–1963

The room in Nantucket is easy to enter, although we are not sure if it is a hotel, a summer house, a hospital, or what. Williams presents the room: its view of flowers, its clean smell, and its feeling of austerity. Everything in the room is "just so." The poem is like the room, spare and simple. The literal imagery seems appropriate to this room one might walk in and see.

"A Description of the Morning" takes place on a Dublin street in the early eighteenth century. Like "Nantucket," it sticks to literal imagery. Note how Swift presents the commotion of the city scene.

A DESCRIPTION OF THE MORNING

Now hardly here and there an hackney-coach
Appearing, showed the ruddy morn's approach.
Now Betty from her master's bed had flown,
And softly stole to discompose her own.
The slipshod 'prentice from his master's door,   5
Had pared the dirt, and sprinkled round the floor.
Now Moll had whirled her mop with dext'rous airs,
Prepared to scrub the entry and the stairs.
The youth with broomy stumps began to trace

The kennel[1] edge, where wheels had worn the place.   10
The small-coal man was heard with cadence deep,
'Till drowned in shriller notes of chimney sweep,
Duns[2] at his lordship's gate began to meet,
And brickdust Moll had screamed through half a street.
The turnkey[3] now his flock returning sees,   15
Duly let out a-nights to steal for fees.
The watchful bailiffs take their silent stands;
And schoolboys lag with satchels in their hands.

Jonathan Swift, 1667–1745

[1] *kennel:* gutter.
[2] *duns:* bill collectors.
[3] *turnkey:* jailkeeper.

The active sequence of people doing what needs to be done vivifies the description. Betty musses her bed so it will appear that she slept there, the apprentice tidies his master's workshop, schoolboys dawdle on the way to class. Each line is dense with imagery—shrill voices, screaming, the whirling mop—and with active verbs: *flown, stole, pared, sprinkled, scrubbed.* A description of a street in Baltimore or Atlanta today, packed with freeways, busses, digital clocks, and fast-food breakfasts, would not be remote in effect from Swift's Dublin street waking up.

ELEGY FOR A WHITE COCK

White cock in my courtyard,
feathers white as white lard:
wild dogs were his daily fear;
malicious foxes never worried him.
Evenings, he'd roost in a nook in the eaves;   5
mornings, he'd peck by the foot of the stairs.
He crew before all the other birds,
even in wind and rain.
My granaries were running low
but I always gave him rice to eat.   10
Last night when the sky turned black,
a creature of darkness prowled and spied.
Stealthily it seized the cock—
I only heard the squawks of pain.
When I came to the rescue through the gate,   15
it was already past the eastern wall.

At the sound of my shouts, not daring to eat,
it dropped the cock and made its escape.
Throat covered with gushing blood,
the cock gasped for air on the brink of death.   20
Brilliant white breast stained deep vermilion,
frost pinions broken and torn.
Compassionate, I wished him to live,
but his head was crushed and could not be healed.
I'll accept his fate and bury him;   25
who could bear to use cinnamon and ginger on him now?
Still I see his scattered feathers
floating, dancing with the breath of the wind.
I remember when he first came to this place,
how many favors he received: 30
he never had to fear the block,
and never passed his days in hunger.
Why did he meet this vicious beast?
Who ever thought he'd be destroyed!
Though this may be a trifling matter,   35
a deeper meaning may be discerned:
Mr. Teng[1] could coin a mountain of cash,
but starved to death in the end.
Such too, then, is the way of man—
I bow my head, full of sorrow.   40

Mei Yao-ch'en, 641–680

[1] *Mr. Teng:* a government official who acquired a lot of money and lost it.

EXERCISE

"Elegy for a White Cock" is a seventh-century Chinese poem. Except for "white as lard," "breath of the wind," and "frost pinions," the author keeps to literal imagery. How does imagery enable a 1,300-year-old poem to communicate so directly to contemporary readers? Discuss the "deeper meaning" the poem refers to at the end.

TRAVELING THROUGH THE DARK

Traveling through the dark I found a deer
dead on the edge of the Wilson River road.
It is usually best to roll them into the canyon:
that road is narrow; to swerve might make more dead.

By glow of the tail-light I stumbled back of the car   5
and stood by the heap, a doe, a recent killing;
she had stiffened already, almost cold.
I dragged her off; she was large in the belly.

My fingers touching her side brought me the reason—
her side was warm; her fawn lay there waiting,   10
alive, still, never to be born.
Beside that mountain road I hesitated.

The car aimed ahead its lowered parking lights;
under the hood purred the steady engine.
I stood in the glare of the warm exhaust turning red;   15
around our group I could hear the wilderness listen.

I thought hard for us all—my only swerving—,
then pushed her over the edge into the river.

William Stafford, 1914–

EXERCISES

1. Which literal images suggest further meaning?
2. Compare "Traveling Through the Dark," a twentieth-century poem, with "Elegy for a White Cock." Is the use of imagery similar? The tone of the speaker's voice? How do the endings compare? What is the range of sensory impressions in each poem? Is any one sense predominant in either poem?
3. Reread Jonathan Swift's "Description of Morning." Try writing your own description of night where you live, using as many literal images as possible.
4. For further practice in recognizing literal images, write three specific images of each of the following: speed, orange, fear, boredom,

greed, yellow. (For example: *yellow*—petals of daffodils in a glass
beaker, the last tooth in an old man's mouth, the bill of a duck.)
Choose original images that *show* the subject.

Poems for Discussion

PRELUDES

1

The winter evening settles down
With smell of steaks in passageways.
Six o'clock.
The burnt-out ends of smoky days.
And now a gusty shower wraps   5
The grimy scraps
Of withered leaves about your feet
And newspapers from vacant lots;
The showers beat
On broken blinds and chimney-pots,   10
And at the corner of the street
A lonely cab-horse steams and stamps.
And then the lighting of the lamps.

2

The morning comes to consciousness
Of faint stale smells of beer   15
From the sawdust-trampled street
With all its muddy feet that press
To early coffee-stands.
With the other masquerades
That time resumes,   20
One thinks of all the hands
That are raising dingy shades
In a thousand furnished rooms.

3

You tossed a blanket from the bed,
You lay upon your back, and waited;   25
You dozed, and watched the night revealing
The thousand sordid images
Of which your soul was constituted;
They flickered against the ceiling.

And when all the world came back   30
And the light crept up between the shutters
And you heard the sparrows in the gutters,
You had such a vision of the street
As the street hardly understands,
Sitting along the bed's edge, where   35
You curled the papers from your hair,
Or clasped the yellow soles of feet
In the palms of both soiled hands.

4

His soul stretched tight across the skies
That fade behind a city block,   40
Or trampled by insistent feet
At four and five and six o'clock;
And short square fingers stuffing pipes,
And evening newspapers, and eyes
Assured of certain certainties,   45
The conscience of a blackened street
Impatient to assume the world.

I am moved by fancies that are curled
Around these images and cling:
The notion of some infinitely gentle   50
Infinitely suffering thing.

Wipe your hand across your mouth, and laugh;
The worlds revolve like ancient women
Gathering fuel in vacant lots.

T. S. Eliot, 1888–1965

STUDY OF TWO PEARS

I

Opusculum paedagogum.[1]
The pears are not viols,
Nudes or bottles.
They resemble nothing else.

---

[1] *opusculum paedagogum:* a little lesson that teaches.

II

They are yellow forms   5
Composed of curves
Bulging toward the base.
They are touched red.

III

They are not flat surfaces
Having curved outlines.   10
They are round
Tapering toward the top.

IV

In the way they are modelled
There are bits of blue.
A hard dry leaf hangs   15
From the stem.

V

The yellow glistens.
It glistens with various yellows,
Citrons, oranges and greens
Flowering over the skin.   20

VI

The shadows of the pears
Are blobs on the green cloth.
The pears are not seen
As the observer wills.

Wallace Stevens, 1879–1955

EPITAPH ON A HARE

Here lies, whom hound did ne'er pursue,
  Nor swifter greyhound follow,
Whose foot ne'er tainted morning dew,
  Nor ear heard huntsman's halloo;

Old Tiney, surliest of his kind,   5
   Who, nursed with tender care,
And to domestic bounds confined,
   Was still a wild jack hare.

Though duly from my hand he took
   His pittance every night;   10
He did it with a jealous look,
   And, when he could, would bite.

His diet was of wheaten bread
   And mild, and oats, and straw;
Thistles, or lettuces instead,   15
   With sand to scour his maw.

On twigs of hawthorn he regaled,
   On pippins' russet peel;
And, when his juicy salads failed,
   Sliced carrot pleased him well.   20

A Turkey carpet was his lawn,
   Whereon he loved to bound,
To skip and gambol like a fawn,
   And swing his rump around.

His frisking was at evening hours,   25
   For then he lost his fear;
But most before approaching showers,
   Or when a storm drew near.

Eight years and five round-rolling moons
   He thus saw steal away,   30
Dozing out all his idle noons,
   And every night at play.

I kept him for his humor's sake,
   For he would oft beguile
My heart of thoughts that made it ache,   35
   And force me to a smile.

But now beneath this walnut shade
   He finds his long last home,
And waits, in snug concealment laid,
   Till gentler Puss shall come.   40

He, still more aged, feels the shocks,
    From which no care can save,
And, partner once of Tiney's box,
    Must soon partake his grave.

William Cowper, 1731–1800

BADGER

When midnight comes a host of dogs and men
Go out and track the badger to his den,
And put a sack within the hole, and lie
Till the old grunting badger passes by.
He comes and hears—they let the strongest loose.   5
The old fox hears the noise and drops the goose.
The poacher shoots and hurries from the cry,
And the old hare half wounded buzzes by.
They get a forked stick to bear him down
And bait him all the day with many dogs,   10
And laugh and shout and fright the scampering hogs.
He runs along and bites at all he meets:
They shout and hollo down the noisy streets.

He turns about to face the loud uproar
And drives the rebels to their very door.   15
The frequent stone is hurled where'er they go;
When badgers fight, then everyone's a foe.
The dogs are clapped and urged to join the fray;
The badger turns and drives them all away.
Though scarcely half as big, demure and small,   20
He fights with dogs for hours and beats them all.
The heavy mastiff, savage in the fray,
Lies down and licks his feet and turns away.
The bulldog knows his match and waxes cold,
The badger grins and never leaves his hold.   25
He drives the crowd and follows at their heels
And bites them through—the drunkard swears and reels.

The frighted women take the boys away,
The blackguard laughs and hurries on the fray.
He tries to reach the woods, an awkward race,   30
But sticks and cudgels quickly stop the chase.
He turns again and drives the noisy crowd
And beats the many dogs in noises loud.
He drives away and beats them every one,

And then they loose them all and set them on.   35
He falls as dead and kicked by boys and men,
Then starts and grins and drives the crowd again;
Till kicked and torn and beaten out he lies
And leaves his hold and cackles, groans, and dies.

John Clare, 1793–1864

SOME VERSES UPON THE BURNING
OF OUR HOUSE JULY 10TH, 1666

In silent night when rest I took
For sorrow near I did not look
I wakened was with thund'ring noise
And piteous shrieks of dreadful voice.
That fearful sound of "Fire!" and "Fire!"   5
Let no man know is my desire.
I, starting up, the light did spy,
And to my God my heart did cry
To strengthen me in my distress
And not to leave me succorless.   10
Then, coming out, beheld a space
The flame consume my dwelling place.
And when I could no longer look,
I blest His name that gave and took,
That laid my goods now in the dust.   15
Yea, so it was, and so 'twas just.
It was His own, it was not mine,
Far be it that I should repine;
He might of all justly bereft
But yet sufficient for us left.   20
When by the ruins oft I past
My sorrowing eyes aside did cast,
And here and there the places spy
Where oft I sat and long did lie:
Here stood that trunk, and there that chest,   25
There lay that store I counted best.
My pleasant things in ashes lie,
And them behold no more shall I.
Under thy roof no guest shall sit.
Nor at thy table eat a bit.   30
No pleasant tale shall e'er be told,
Nor things recounted done of old.
No candle e'er shall shine in thee,
Nor bridegroom's voice e'er heard shall be.

In silence ever shall thou lie,   35
Adieu, Adieu, all's vanity.
Then straight I 'gin my heart to chide,
And did thy wealth on earth abide?
Didst fix thy hope on mold'ring dust?
The arm of flesh didst make thy trust?   40
Raise up thy thoughts above the sky
That dunghill mists away may fly.
Thou hast an house on high erect,
Framed by that mighty Architect,
With glory richly furnished,   45
Stands permanent though this be fled.
It's purchased and paid for too
By Him who hath enough to do.
A price so vast as is unknown
Yet by His gift is made thine own;   50
There's wealth enough, I need no more,
Farewell, my pelf[1], farewell my store.
The world no longer let me love,
My hope and treasure lies above.

Anne Bradstreet, 1612–1672

---

[1] *pelf:* money.

THE GERANIUMS

Even if the geraniums are artificial
Just the same,
In the rear of the Italian café
Under the nimbus of electric light
They are red; no less red   5
For how they were made. Above
The mirror and the napkins
In the little white pots . . .
. . . In the semi-clean café
Where they have good   10
Lasagne. . . . The red is a wonderful joy
Really, and so are the people
Who like and ignore it. In this place
They also have good bread.

Charles Reznikoff, 1894–1975

THE RUNNER

On a flat road runs the well-train'd runner,
He is lean and sinewy with muscular legs,
He is thinly clothed, he leans forward as he runs,
With lightly closed fists and arms partially rais'd.

Walt Whitman, 1819–1892

Figurative Images

Our use of language is naturally figurative. We say "slick as glass,"
"ugly as sin," "hard as rock," "soft as silk," "mad as a wet hen,"
"slow as molasses," "pale as a ghost," "dog-tired," "blood red,"
"weak as a kitten." We take for granted expressing one thing in terms
of another. Some of the expressions above have become clichés which
have lost their original surprise. Good figurative images seem new to
the reader, not just decorative.

Figurative imagery functions quite differently from literal imagery.
A literal image *remakes* something in words in order to describe a
reality as vividly as possible. A figurative image establishes connections
between things we normally would *not* associate. By using a figurative
image, the poet intends to do one or all of these:

1. *Expand sensory perception beyond the literal meaning.* "His death
   came slowly like a Mexican bus," adds other qualities to the fact
   of the slow death by connecting it to the characteristics of the old,
   over-laden Mexican buses that stop at every crossroad.

2. *Give pleasure or surprise to the imagination.* We have never connected a slow death and a Mexican bus before. We experience
   finding the connection, which gives a sense of discovery and participation. We reach imaginatively beyond our usual grasp, yet cre-
   dulity is not destroyed. Yes, his death *could* come slowly like a
   Mexican bus.

3. *Impart vigor by the inclusion of another active sensory detail.* The
   sudden appearance of the Mexican bus is a vivid image. It startles
   our normal expectations of where "His death came slowly . . ."
   was headed.

4. *Intensify the deeper intention in the poem by adding the new dimension of the figurative image.* Any of us making an image for a

slow death might have chosen a number of comparisons. *Only* this poet (Ann Gleeson) chose the Mexican bus, thereby putting *her* intuitive sense of death on the line. Like word choice, the choice of figurative images contributes to the overall mood, or tone, of the poem. "His death came slowly like an island emerging from the sea" would have to belong in a different poem than the more humorous bus image. Any image works within the whole poem as well as on its own.

In reading poems it is important to ask *why* the poet uses a figurative image. What does the image add to the whole poem? As you read, refer to the four intentions described above.

Figurative images fall into several distinct categories:

Similes

A *simile* is an explicit equation: *A* is like *B*. (The word *simile* comes from the Latin *similis*, meaning "similar" or "like.") *Like, as, as if,* and sometimes *seems* or *appears* are used in making the comparison.

> . . . the bulb hangs in the hot dark
> like a white blood drop.
>
> *Michael Dennis Browne*

> The Roman Road runs straight and bare
> As the pale parting-line in hair.
>
> *Thomas Hardy*

> Jane, Jane
> Tall as a Crane.
>
> *Edith Sitwell*

> I spied a very small brown duck
> Riding the swells of the sea
> Like a rocking-chair.
>
> *Galway Kinnell*

> The blood of the children ran in the street
> like the blood of children.
>
> *Pablo Neruda*

Saying Jane is as tall as a crane adds something to Jane's height: A crane seems to have little in common with a girl, but by linking the two, Sitwell gives Jane a particular angularity and a rather humorous posture. The lightbulb, as seen by Browne, hangs like a drop of blood. We know white blood doesn't exist, but a drop of blood, about to fall, is in the *shape* of a lightbulb. We see the bulb in a different way than we could if he had not made the comparison. The simile by Neruda affects us because of the surprise. We expect a dissimilar comparison after *like*. By employing the simile construction, the poet tells us that there *can be* no figurative image which *adds* to the impact of the first statement.

A simile is usually weak if it is abstract, vague, or stale. The reader experiences not a glimmer of interest in

> lazy as a day in June

> clean as soap

> the sun shone like hope

> the rain fell like tears

If the comparison on the other side of *like* is not different *enough*, the simile will not work for the poem. For instance, if the small brown duck rides the waves like a seagull, we have simply a comparison between like things. The reader will discover something new only if the writer finds an image with enough electricity to travel back through the word *like* and recharge the original image. Similes that don't work sometimes use vague words with inappropriate comparatives, as in ". . . a lilac bush bloomed, pulsating / here and there like a delicate blue vein in the violet light." "Here and there" are not helping the reader see anything, and clusters of lilac blossoms look nothing like pulsating veins. The writer could have made an interesting simile comparing the *color* of veins to lilacs. As it is, the simile in ineffective.

An **epic simile** makes an extended comparison. In Frost's poem below, "she" is compared to a tent in a field.

THE SILKEN TENT

She is as in a field a silken tent
At midday when a sunny summer breeze
Has dried the dew and all its ropes relent,
So that in guys it gently sways at ease,
And its supporting central cedar pole,   5
That is its pinnacle to heavenward
And signifies the sureness of the soul,
Seems to owe naught to any single cord,
But strictly held by none, is loosely bound
By countless silken ties of love and thought   10
To everything on earth the compass round,
And only by one's going slightly taut
In the capriciousness of summer air
Is of the slightest bondage made aware.

Robert Frost, 1874–1963

The simile spins out from "She is as . . . ," the poem's first three
words. The whole poem compares a woman to an exotic tent in a field
at noon. Most tents are synthetic fabrics or rough canvas. This one is
silk. The choice imparts a fine, luxurious quality to the woman. Even
the ropes are silk. The tent flexes easily when the wind changes. At
the same time, the center pole, signifying "the sureness of the soul,"
stands firmly in place and points toward heaven. The poem is one long
sentence that seems free to billow and shift like the tent in the wind.
In truth, the poem is tightly constructed in a traditional sonnet form,
which determines length, rhyme, and a regular rhythmic beat. The
countless ropes suggest that the woman is tied "To everything on earth
the compass round," yet her life is so in harmony that she is free.
Frost, both in meaning and in the poem's form, suggests that freedom
is achieved through attachment to important "ties."

Metaphors

Metaphors, like similes, connect unlike things having common qualities
that the poet wants to emphasize. How metaphor differs from simile is
subtle but crucial.

Simile: My joy is like a river.

Metaphor: My joy is a river.
    or: My joy, a river.

Poets use metaphor when they want a closer, more direct comparison between the two things. But metaphor is not simply the removal of *like*, *as*, or other connectives. The word *metaphor* comes from Greek roots which mean "to transfer." When Shakespeare says, "Juliet is the sun," he *transfers* the sun's qualities to Juliet. More is at stake than if he'd said, "Juliet is like the sun." Juliet's life-giving powers, brightness, and all-importance are intensified by the direct link. There is only one sun in our solar system. Perhaps other women could be "like the sun," but only one can *be* the sun.

Look at the difference:

No man is an island.   No man is like an island

John Donne

Like dilutes the assertive power of this image. Part of the reason for this is in the eye's response. Without the comparative word, the images have closer physical proximity on the page. *Like* and *as* call attention to themselves; we realize a comparison is taking place. Without them, a "transfer" occurs easily, almost automatically. Notice what happens when the Biblical quote "God is love" is changed to "God is like love."

The following poem uses metaphor to express the bodily changes a woman experiences during pregnancy. The nine-line structure, with nine syllables in each line, wittily reinforces Plath's pregnant subject.

METAPHORS

I'm a riddle in nine syllables,
An elephant, a ponderous house,
A melon strolling on two tendrils.
O red fruit; ivory, fine timbers!
This loaf's big with its yeasty rising.

> Money's new-minted in this fat purse.
> I'm a means, a stage, a cow in calf.
> I've eaten a bag of green apples,
> Boarded the train there's no getting off.

Sylvia Plath, 1932–1963

Suppose Plath had named the poem "Similes" and proceeded through her list using *like* or *as* or *resembles*. Read the poem again with that in mind and notice how different it feels.

In his *Poetics*, Aristotle said that metaphor is the "one thing that cannot be learned from others; and it is also a sign of genius, since a good metaphor implies an intuitive perception of the similarity in dissimilars." Metaphor is not simply a device writers use to ornament poems. William Butler Yeats wrote:

> God guard me from those thoughts men think
> In the mind alone;
> He that sings a lasting song
> Thinks in a marrow bone.

from "A Prayer for Old Age"

Metaphoric thinking constantly links the mind to the "marrow bone." Older civilizations than ours looked for signs all around them: fortunes in the leaves of tea, weather forecasts in the thickness of the goose's breastbone. Auspicious times for events were decided from the alignment of stars, flight patterns of birds, or droppings of animals. Augurs, the diviners of events, read these signs and made decisions or predictions from them. Although the use of metaphor is not as practically oriented as Roman augury, the this-is-that of metaphor touches the same core of thinking, the root that says unlike things have mysterious, informing links which we can discover. And not only discover, but analyze.

Though metaphor works first on an intuitive level, it also works on a logical level. We can know exactly *how* "Juliet is the sun." Figurative language jumps off into imaginative territory but usually does not cut free from connections to reality. When the poet pushes an image too far, this can happen:

The wild tulip, at the end of its tube, blows out its great red bell
Like a thin clear bubble of blood for the children to pick and sell.

Robert Browning

Children selling a bubble of blood? No. We don't *believe* that. Lovely as the first glass-blowing image is, the poor logic in the second line spoils the image.

When the metaphors are poorly conceived this kind of confusion results:

THE VINE

The wine of love is music,
   And the feast of love is song:
When love sits down to banquet,
   Love sits long:
Sits long and rises drunken,
   But not with the feast and the wine;
He reeleth with his own heart,
   That great rich Vine.

James Thomson, 1700–1748

If we remember Shakespeare's "If music be the food of love, play on" and similar treatments of the subject of love, we're ready to read this as a poem of that type. But these doubled-up metaphors get confusing. Vine, wine, feast, music, love—just which is the metaphor for what? None of the functions for figurative imagery are fulfilled; the tangle of imagery only obscures whatever significance that capital-letter "Vine" was supposed to have.

One step beyond vague metaphors are **mixed metaphors.** In these, the writer combines incompatible metaphors. If Shakespeare had written "If music be the fruit of love, play on, give me the whole nine yards," he would have run amuck with his metaphor. Mixed metaphors really do not occur much in poetry, except for comic effect.

Two Poems for Analysis

QUESTION

Body my house
my horse my hound
what will I do
when you are fallen

Where will I sleep   5
How will I ride
What will I hunt

Where can I go
without my mount
all eager and quick   10
How will I know
in thicket ahead
is danger or treasure
when Body my good
bright dog is dead   15

How will it be
to lie in the sky
without roof or door
and wind for an eye

With cloud for shift   20
how will I hide?

May Swenson, 1919–1989

Three metaphors for *body* work at once in "Question." The speaker's
body is her "house," "hound," and "horse." As the title indicates,
she is questioning the body's fate in terms of the three metaphors: What
will I do when my body fails me? What becomes of "I" when the body
fails? How does the "I" then sleep, ride, hunt? Questions are raised,
not answered.

What are the qualities of the body she evokes by the three metaphors? "House" connotes a sense of security, the place to be at ease;
"horse" links to quick mobility and liveliness; "hound" senses what's

ahead in the hunt—that is, in the process of living. These are some of the first connections the metaphors make.

Swenson's metaphors also. produce some more complex effects. Psychiatrist Carl Jung interpreted dreams of houses as a projection of the sense of self. A dream of wandering in a strange house, for instance, would be a metaphor for a quest within the self. In mythology, horses often represent the spiritual nature. In Greek legend, Pegasus, the winged horse who brought Zeus his thunderbolts, is associated with poetry. Hunting has many associations with quests and an intense, unpredictable pursuit of fate. Any discussion of a hunter brings up the old question, "Who is the hunter, who the hunted?"

May Swenson *may* have had some of these ideas in mind when she wrote "Question." For the reader, the metaphors are wide open to these and other interpretations. In the last stanza, *shift* means a dress. With only a cloud for a dress, how will "I" hide? With this final question, we see that all through the poem the speaker valued the body partly because some part of her is hidden within it. Without the protection of the body (with its attributes of security, liveliness, force) she questions the fate of the spirit which will "lie in the sky / without roof or door."

A JUST MAN

My eyes, you girls who milk the light,
turn over your pails.
Tongue, you tall handsome whooping young man,
leave your day-labour.
Breast, escape from me to Asia,   5
to the roots of sweating forests.
Backbone, collapse under the Eiffel Tower.
Nose, you sailing Greenland whaler,
keep your harpoon away from smells.
Hands, make a pilgrimage to Rome.   10
Legs, kick each other into a ditch.
Ears, surrender
your tympani, your tympani!
Leap over to Australia, my thigh,
you rose-pink marsupial.   15
Belly, you light balloon, soar
to Saturn, fly away!

Then I shall step out onto my lips,
with a curving shout jump into your ears,
and stopped clocks will start again,   20
and villages will shine like floodlights,
and the cities will be whitewashed,
and my vertebrae can scatter
in all directions of the globe,
because I'll be standing straight   25
among the crooked bodies of the dead.

Attila József, 1905–1937
(Translated by John Bátki)

József lists wild, impossible metaphors for parts of the body: eyes are
"girls who milk the light"; thigh, a "rose-pink marsupial"; belly, a
"light balloon." He instructs these parts to head for distant places:
Asia, Australia, the Eiffel Tower. As soon as he can get *out* of his body
(which is flying apart anyway) he'll be "standing straight" among the
dead.

What do you think József means by the last nine lines? Perhaps he
means that after his death we will hear his poems. When that happens,
the world will seem clean and new. He'll be both everywhere on the
globe *and* able to feel justified.

EXERCISE

Both "Question" and "A Just Man" travel far into the territory of the
imagination. Why? Why not choose literal descriptions of the body?
Refer to the four functions of figurative images listed earlier in the
chapter and discuss how they interconnect in these poems.

Other Tropes

As we've seen, metaphors and similes use words not literally, but
figuratively. The generic term for any figurative image is a **trope**. English has many other special function tropes including synesthesia, metonymy, synecdoche, personification, oxymoron, and conceits.

Synesthesia   One sensory perception is expressed in terms of a
different sense, doubling and interweaving the physical connections.

I know
the seven fragrances of the rainbow

May Swenson

. . . green wind . . .

Federico García Lorca

Light, chill and yellow
Bathes the serene
Foreheads of houses

Philip Larkin

A crinkled paper makes a brilliant sound.

Wallace Stevens

And the sabbath rang slowly
In the pebbles of the holy streams

Dylan Thomas

. . . blind mouths. . . .

John Milton

Metonymy An identifying emblem is substituted for the whole name. An "old salt" for a sailor, a "brown shirt" for a fascist, "red coats" for British soldiers. An *associated* quality speaks for the whole.

The pen is mightier than the sword.

Edward Bulwer-Lytton

Her voice is full of money.

F. Scott Fitzgerald

. . . doublet and hose
ought to show itself courageous to petticoat.

William Shakespeare

Synecdoche A piece or part of the whole represents the whole, as in "the long arm of the law," "Elvis the pelvis," "roof over one's head," "she's a brain." An active part, isolated, represents the whole more intensely. Someone who doesn't like "that look in your eye" probably finds your whole expression and demeanor disturbing; she emphasizes her objection by isolating the eye.

> Was this the face that launched a thousand ships?
>
> *Christopher Marlowe*

> Send home my long strayed eyes to me
> Which O! too long have dwelt on thee.
>
> *John Donne*

> Worcester, get thee gone for I do see
> Danger and disobedience in thine eye.
>
> *William Shakespeare*

The difference between synecdoche and metonymy is that synecdoche keeps *to itself* (face, eyes) for its representing image, while metonymy uses an emblem that is *outside itself* but associated, as salt is associated with the sea and therefore with sailors. When you disparagingly call someone a "redneck" (part of the person) you are using synecdoche; when you say "hayseed" (associated with farming) you're using metonymy. Although these distinctions among tropes seem like fine shadings, it's a pleasure to be able to identify the precise use of language a writer has chosen. Simile, metaphor, and synesthesia each use *comparisons* in different ways; synecdoche and metonymy both use closely identified *associations*.

Personification An emotion or something inhuman, such as a mountain or love or a tree, is given human qualities. Sometimes the personification is named directly, as in "Death be not proud. . . ." Other personifications:

> Some flakes have lost their way, and grope back upwards.
>
> *Thomas Hardy*

the speechless cities of the night

Randall Jarrell

whispers of wind in the listening sky

Stephen Spender

the sleeping sea

William Sharp

And in the soft ear of Spring, light voices sing.

Marcel du Bon

the last fingers of leaf
Clutch and sink into the wet bank.

T. S. Eliot

The primary purpose of personification is to make nature seem to extend the emotions of the speaker by reflecting them. Many nature personifications are clichés: weeping skies, smiling sun, dying sunset, angry seas, hopeful sunrises. When the waves are "happy" or the rain "weeps," the natural world is credited with human feelings. In old movies, the camera pans to the beautiful sunset as the lovers kiss; storms break out when danger approaches. The skies act out the emotions of the actors. This kind of nature personification is called a **pathetic fallacy.**

Personification is also used to give a quality or action or idea a "presence" by addressing it like a person: "Good morning Midnight," or "Truth settled an old score."

Oxymoron   Juxtaposes contrasting words in order to encompass contrary impressions or ideas. (The image of contradiction is reflected in the word itself: *oxymoron* comes from two Greek roots meaning "sharp" and "stupid.")

Mis-shapen chaos of well-seeming forms!
Feather of lead, bright smoke, cold fire, sick health!

William Shakespeare

                                          as cold
          And passionate as the dawn.

                              William Butler Yeats

Conceit   A bold and/or extended simile or metaphor, such as

          Let us go then you and I
          When the evening is spread out against the sky
          Like a patient etherized upon a table

                                    T. S. Eliot

The two images compared amuse, surprise, or disturb you by their
extreme contrast. "The Song of Solomon" in the Bible compares a
woman's lips to scarlet thread, her cheeks to the halves of a pomegranate, then daringly compares her neck to the tower of David and her
nose to the Tower of Lebanon, overlooking Damascus. Conceits involve risk: either captivating or repelling the reader. The conceit usually develops, making further connections between the two disparate
images. John Donne's likening of two lovers' souls to drawing compasses is a famous conceit:

          If they be two, they are two so
              As stiffe twin compasses are two,
          Thy soule the fixt foot, makes no show
              To move, but doth, if the 'other doe.

          And though it in the center sit,
              Yet when the other far doth rome,
          It leanes, and hearkens after it,
              and growes erect, as that comes home.

          Such wilt thou be to mee, who must
              Like th'other foot, obliquely runne;
          Thy firmnes drawes my circle just,
              And makes me end, where I begunne.

               from "A Valediction: Forbidding Mourning"

EXERCISES

1. For practice in recognizing effective similes, complete each phrase with a concrete image of your own. Try to think of a connection that performs one of the four functions listed on page 99. Look for a fresh image you've never seen in print before.
    a. The moon, broken off like
    b. A red flower, brilliant as
    c. Her fingers, delicate as
    d. The island stretches out from the coast like
    e. Your backbone ridged like
    f. Soft as
    g. That bicyclist, careening downhill like
    h. Crazy bird! Its song like
    i. His monotonous voice like
    j. She spun off like
    k. Days pass like

2. Identify the following tropes by type:
    a. honey-voiced
    b. the dark blue notes of the cello
    c. The flowers of the town are rotting away.

    C. Day Lewis

    d. Death, O Death! Can't you spare me over
        for another year?

    Kentucky Song

    e. When Poverty comes in the door,
        Love goes out the window.

    Georgia saying

    f. And winds went begging at each door.

    Geoffrey Hill

g. The sun, a demon's eye.

Edith Sitwell

h. I ran my heedless ways,
My wishes raced through the house high hay.

Dylan Thomas

i. In his devouring mind's eye. . . .

Washington Irving

j. Her jet appeared from nowhere,
A needle punched through blue linen.

Neal Bowers

3. Select a painting or a photograph and describe it so that you *show* the images. Use smell, touch, sound, taste, and motion as well as visual images.

4. Many metaphors are hidden in everyday speech. Once upon a time someone made the connection between the clock and the human face, between supports for the table and legs. These have long since become the face of the clock, the leg of the table. In the same way, it is natural to say the heart of the matter, the heel of Italy, the lip of the pitcher. Make a list of other metaphors embedded in everyday speech.

5. Describe the image on the next page. What is it? What is it *like?* A galaxy, a satellite photo of a weather front? What else? (Actually, it is a sonar scan of a three-month-old fetus in the womb.) Discuss the similes and metaphors one can make with this image.

6. "To Autumn" (see page 422) is one of the great examples of imagery in literature. Analyze Keats's use of literal imagery and tropes. Where does the personification of autumn begin? Is it effective—that is, does it enhance your perception? Does Keats use pathetic fallacies? Effectively? Is there any sense he does not use in his images?

7. In "Hope," do you find the personification convincing?

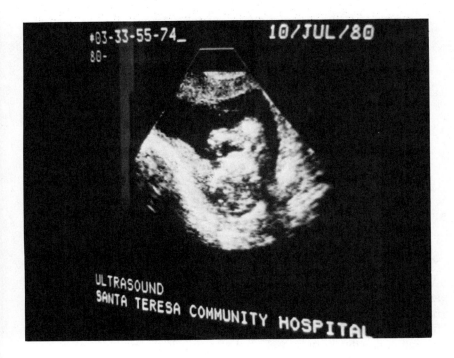

HOPE

Hope was but a timid friend—
She sat without[1] my grated den
Watching how my fate would tend
Even as selfish-hearted men.

She was cruel in her fear.   5
Through the bars, one dreary day,
I looked out to see her there
And she turned her face away!

[1] *without:* outside.

Like a false guard false watch keeping
Still in strife she whispered peace;   10
She would sing while I was weeping,
If I listened, she would cease.

False she was, and unrelenting.
When my last joys strewed the ground
Even Sorrow saw repenting   15
Those sad relics scattered round;

Hope—whose whisper would have given
Balm to all that frenzied pain—
Stretched her wings and soared to heaven;
Went—and ne'er returned again!   20

Emily Brontë, 1818–1848

Symbols

A **symbol** is an image or action that stands for more than itself. A black
and white mottled notebook may remind you of first grade, the teacher
named Miss Gray, the reading circle, your polished shoes, and the
line of alphabet letters around the blackboard. The black and white
notebook is actually only itself, but to you it is symbolic. The image
brings forth memories and ideas. Symbol comes from a Greek word
meaning "to put together." Whereas metaphor and simile *name* connections between seemingly dissimilar images, a symbol *suggests* a
range of connections.

A bare oak silhouetted against dark hills looks ominous, reminding
you of lonely nights, loss, winter. A photograph of a highway leading
away over rolling hills invites your imagination to go. The open road
symbolizes escape, adventure, perhaps reminding you of the time you
drove west alone. The notebook is a private symbol; the winter tree
and open road images are common to many, though certain nuances
may be particular to your experience. Some symbolic images cross
cultures and time; harvest, sunrise, the full moon, and many more
symbols are **archetypes,** images that have universal meaning. The connection between spring and rebirth belongs to everyone.

Poetry involves both kinds of symbolism, personal and universal.
A nightingale may mean nothing to you, but after you read "Ode To a
Nightingale" (page 415), Keats's own symbolic associations with the
"immortal" bird's song may become alive and full of meaning. The

meanings of a symbol gather as the poem develops. To awaken memories and associations, a symbol must join other qualities and perceptions. If you write about the notebook, no one will respond unless you cause the reader to experience some of the reasons this object has significance.

A knot in a piece of wood is the symbol working here:

THE KNOT

I've tried to seal it in,
that cross-grained knot
on the opposite wall,
scored in the lintel of my door,
but it keeps bleeding through   5
into the world we share.
Mornings when I wake,
curled in my web,
I hear it come
with a rush of resin   10
out of the trauma
of its lopping-off.
Obstinate bud,
sticky with life,
mad for the rain again,   15
it racks itself with shoots
that crackle overhead,
dividing as they grow.
Let be! Let be!
I shake my wings   20
and fly into its boughs.

Stanley Kunitz, 1905–

Kunitz's knot is a **private symbol;** readers do not come to it with symbolic associations of their own as they would if the subject were, say, a wedding ring or the evening star. He develops this context: he has painted over the knot trying to seal it in, but it persistently pushes its own life through these cover-ups. Kunitz never says so, but we begin to see that this knot is like something in the speaker's life which he has tried to obliterate but can't. A knot in wood results from the loss of a branch. We don't know the *exact* nature of the speaker's loss—which leaves the symbol open to our own associations—but we do know that something was lopped off. The symbol, in other words, isn't pinned down to *a* meaning, but the context establishes clear directions for meaning. Isn't there something you also try to push away which will not go away?

"The Knot" is straightforward. At times, symbolism gets extremely complex. Some poets have entire systems, secret cosmologies of symbols, which require extensive study. William Blake is one of these poets. The more familiar you are with his work, the richer Blake's symbols are, because the symbols interact among the poems. Two of his best-known lyrics will show how each one amplifies the other.

THE LAMB

> Little Lamb, who made thee?
> Dost thou know who made thee?
> Gave thee life, and bid thee feed,
> By the stream and o'er the mead;
> Gave thee clothing of delight,   5
> Softest clothing, woolly, bright;
> Gave thee such a tender voice,
> Making all the vales rejoice?
> Little Lamb, who made thee?
> Dost thou know who made thee?   10
>
> Little Lamb, I'll tell thee,
> Little Lamb, I'll tell thee:
> He is callèd by thy name,
> For he calls himself a Lamb.
> He is meek, and he is mild;   15
> He became a little child.
> I a child, and thou a lamb,
> We are callèd by his name.
> Little Lamb, God bless thee!
> Little Lamb, God bless thee!   20

William Blake, 1757–1827

THE TYGER

Tyger! Tyger! burning bright
In the forests of the night,
What immortal hand or eye
Could frame thy fearful symmetry?

In what distant deeps or skies   5
Burnt the fire of thine eyes?
On what wings dare he aspire?
What the hand dare seize the fire?

And what shoulder, and what art,
Could twist the sinews of thy heart?   10
And when thy heart began to beat,
What dread hand? and what dread feet?

What the hammer? what the chain?
In what furnace was thy brain?
What the anvil? what dread grasp   15
Dare its deadly terrors clasp?

When the stars threw down their spears,
And watered heaven with their tears,
Did he smile his work to see?
Did he who made the Lamb make thee?   20

Tyger! Tyger! burning bright
In the forests of the night,
What immortal hand or eye,
Dare frame thy fearful symmetry?

William Blake, 1757–1827

The lamb and the tiger symbolize opposites: innocence/experience, delight/terror, mildness/ferociousness. The lamb symbolizes *all* that is good, simple, gentle; the tiger, *all* that is predatory, mysterious, fearful. The first stanzas of both poems frame the question: Who is responsible for making you? Right away, we're shown that a large question is at stake; the poems are not just descriptions of animals. The speaker in "The Lamb" is child-like. The speaker in "The Tyger" is much more complex; the more sophisticated level of language reflects this difference. Considered alone, each poem loses some power because the poet is working with the idea that the creator who made the innocent lamb might have smiled also at his creation of the tiger. The pair of poems acknowledges the dual nature of creation and therefore of experience.

EXERCISES

1. Select an image from memory that is symbolic to you and write down all the images and ideas it brings to mind. It may be a red bike, a pencil box stenciled with your name, a sapphire pin your aunt wore at her throat, a pistol in a bedside drawer, the shape of a hill you could see from your window, a brown coat your mother wore to work every day.

2. The following poem begins with a metaphor: "My Life had stood—a Loaded Gun." The third line introduces the "Owner" of the gun. Both the gun and the owner, we quickly realize, are symbolic. (When a metaphor is extended, as it is in this poem, the distinction between metaphor and symbol blurs. The extended metaphor also becomes a symbol.) What does the "Owner" symbolize? Is he God? Could he be one part of the same person—body or soul? What other possibilities: Death? Sexuality? An internal conflict? This is a tough poem. The speaker seems perfectly secure in her logic, but no one can totally "explain" it. What are your ideas about the relationship of the gun and owner? About the last two lines?

754

My Life had stood—a Loaded Gun—
In Corners—till a Day
The Owner passed—identified—
And carried Me away—

And now We roam in Sovreign Woods—   5
And now We hunt the Doe—
And every time I speak for Him—
The Mountains straight reply—

And do I smile, such cordial light
Upon the Valley glow—   10
It is as a Vesuvian face
Had let its pleasure through—

And when at Night—Our good Day done—
I guard My Master's Head—
'Tis better than the Eider-Duck's   15
Deep Pillow—to have shared—

To foe of His—I'm deadly foe—
None stir the second time—
On whom I lay a Yellow Eye—
Or an emphatic Thumb—   20

Though I than He—may longer live
He longer must—than I—
For I have but the power to kill,
Without—the power to die—

Emily Dickinson, 1830–1886

3.   A memorial is overtly symbolic. In "Facing It," the poet makes
     rich use of the reader's awareness of the Vietnam Veterans Memo-
     rial in Washington, D.C. He assumes our common associations to
     a war memorial but uses in the poem only a personal experience
     of the memorial itself. The black marble surface both reflects and
     absorbs. It becomes symbolic of his consciousness and conveys to
     the reader a nonverbal, intense reaction to the memorial. The au-
     thor is black and the first two lines immediately call up both the
     statistics of black dead in the Vietnam War and the power of the
     memorial itself to pull this viewer inside. Where does he establish
     the first link between himself and the memorial? Discuss the images
     of light and black and white. What is the connection between "I'm
     stone" in the beginning and "I'm a window" near the end. Discuss
     the contrasts in the poem, such as the carved names of the dead,
     and the liveliness of the reflections in the stone. What is the effect

of the flashing brush strokes, the birds, the woman brushing the
boy's hair?

FACING IT

My black face fades,
hiding inside the black granite.
I said I wouldn't,
dammit: No tears.
I'm stone. I'm flesh.   5
My clouded reflection eyes me
like a bird of prey, the profile of night
slanted against morning. I turn
this way—the stone lets me go.
I turn that way—I'm inside   10
the Vietnam Veterans Memorial
again, depending on the light
to make a difference.
I go down the 58,022 names,
half-expecting to find   15
my own in letters like smoke.
I touch the name Andrew Johnson;
I see the booby trap's white flash.
Names shimmer on a woman's blouse
but when she walks away   20
the names stay on the wall.
Brushstrokes flash, a red bird's wings
cutting across my stare.
The sky. A plane in the sky.
A white vet's image floats   25
closer to me, then his pale eyes
look through mine. I'm a window.
He's lost his right arm
inside the stone. In the black mirror
a woman's trying to erase names: 30
No, she's brushing a boy's hair.

Yusef Komunyakaa, 1947–

4. Write a paper comparing "Reading the Names of the Vietnam War
    Dead" by Thomas McGrath (p. 438) with "Facing It."

Poems for Discussion

THIS LIVING HAND

This living hand, now warm and capable
Of earnest grasping, would, if it were cold
And in the icy silence of the tomb,
So haunt thy days and chill thy dreaming nights
That thou wouldst wish thine own heart dry of blood
So in my veins red life might stream again,
And thou be conscience-calm'd—see here it is—
I hold it towards you.

John Keats, 1795–1821

ALLEGRO

After a black day, I play Haydn,
and feel a little warmth in my hands.

The keys are ready. Kind hammers fall.
The sound is spirited, green, and full of silence.

The sound says that freedom exists   5
and someone pays no tax to Caesar.

I shove my hands in my haydnpockets
and act like a man who is calm about it all.

I raise my haydnflag. The signal is:
"We do not surrender. But want peace."   10

The music is a house of glass standing on a slope;
rocks are flying, rocks are rolling.

The rocks roll straight through the house
but every pane of glass is still whole.

Tomas Tranströmer, 1931–
(Translated by Robert Bly)

SAINT PUMPKIN

Somebody's in there.
Somebody's sealed himself up
in this round room,
this hassock upholstered in rind,
this padded cell.   5
He believes if nothing unbinds him
he'll live forever.

Like our first room
it is dark and crowded.
Hunger knows no tongue   10
to tell it.
Water is glad there.
In this room with two navels
somebody wants to be born again.

So I unlock the pumpkin.   15
I carve out the lid
from which the stem raises
a dry handle on a damp world.
Lifting, I pull away
wet webs, vines on which hang   20
the flat tears of the pumpkin,

like fingernails or the currency
of bats. How the seeds shine,
as if water had put out
hundreds of lanterns.   25
Hundreds of eyes in the windless wood
gaze peacefully past me,
hacking the thickets,

and now a white dew beads the blade.
Has the saint surrendered   30
himself to his beard?
Has his beard taken root in his cell?
    Saint Pumpkin, pray for me,
    because when I looked for you, I found nothing,
    because unsealed and unkempt, your tomb rots,   35
    because I gave you a false face
    and a light of my own making.

Nancy Willard, 1936–

TO ALTHEA, FROM PRISON

When Love with unconfinèd wings
Hovers within my gates,
And my divine Althea brings
To whisper at the grates;
When I lie tangled in her hair   5
And fettered to her eye,
The gods that wanton in the air
Know no such liberty.

When flowing cups run swiftly round,
With no allaying Thames,   10
Our careless heads with roses bound,
Our hearts with loyal flames;
When thirsty grief in wine we steep,
When healths and draughts go free,
Fishes, that tipple in the deep,   15
Know no such liberty.

When, like committed linnets, I
With shriller throat shall sing
The sweetness, mercy, majesty,
And glories of my King;   20
When I shall voice aloud how good
He is, how great should be,
Enlargèd winds, that curl the flood,
Know no such liberty.

Stone walls do not a prison make,   25
Nor iron bars a cage;
Minds innocent and quiet take
That for an hermitage.
If I have freedom in my love,
And in my soul am free,   30
Angels alone, that soar above,
Enjoy such liberty.

Richard Lovelace, 1618–1657

IN BACK OF THE REAL

railroad yard in San Jose
   I wandered desolate
in front of a tank factory
   and sat on a bench
near the switchman's shack.   5

A flower lay on the hay on
   the asphalt highway
—the dread hay flower
   I thought—It had a
brittle black stem and   10
   corolla of yellowish dirty
spikes like Jesus' inchlong
   crown, and a soiled
dry center cotton tuft
   like a used shaving brush   15
that's been lying under
   the garage for a year.

Yellow, yellow flower, and
   flower of industry,
tough spikey ugly flower,   20
   flower nonetheless,
with the form of the great yellow
   Rose in your brain!
This is the flower of the World.

Allen Ginsberg, 1926–

THE FORCE THAT THROUGH THE GREEN FUSE
DRIVES THE FLOWER

The force that through the green fuse drives the flower
Drives my green age; that blasts the roots of trees
Is my destroyer.
And I am dumb to tell the crooked rose
My youth is bent by the same wintry fever.   5

The force that drives the water through the rocks
Drives my red blood; that dries the mouthing streams
Turns mine to wax.

And I am dumb to mouth unto my veins
How at the mountain spring the same mouth sucks.   10

The hand that whirls the water in the pool
Stirs the quicksand; that ropes the blowing wind
Hauls my shroud sail.
And I am dumb to tell the hanging man
How of my clay is made the hangman's lime.   15

The lips of time leech to the fountain head;
Love drips and gathers, but the fallen blood
Shall calm her sores.
And I am dumb to tell a weather's wind
How time has ticked a heaven round the stars.   20

And I am dumb to tell the lover's tomb
How at my sheet goes the same crooked worm.

Dylan Thomas, 1914–1953

THE LOVER COMPARETH HIS STATE TO A SHIP
IN PERILOUS STORM TOSSED ON THE SEA

My galley chargèd with forgetfulness
   Through sharp seas in winter nights doth pass
   'Tween rock and rock; and eke[1] mine enemy,
alas,
   That is my lord, steereth with cruelness;
And every oar a thought in readiness,   5
   As though that death were light in such a case.
   An endless wind doth tear the sail apace,
   Of forcèd sighs and trusty fearfulness.
A rain of tears, a cloud of dark disdain,
   Hath done the wearied cords great hinderance,   10
   Wreathed with error and eke with ignorance.
The stars be hid that led me to this pain;
   Drownèd is reason that should me consort,
   And I remain despairing of the port.

Thomas Wyatt, 1503–1542

---

[1] *eke:* also.

from BODY POEMS

Big Toe

running running
running but clean
as a referee's whistle

& absolutely still
within my shoe
inside my sock:

he listens for mud.

Stomach

lunch paper sinking
into

the lake surface
the lake bottom

sleeping frogs
snapping turtles

Brain

a flashlight
looking through the empty
limbs

Appendix

one boxing glove
laced up
and ready

Bags Under the Eyes

the turnaround place
at the end of a lover's lane

why is that car coming back

Skeleton

on this jungle gym

Bruises

paint samples

Liver

a dripping locker room
full of older men

Yawn

(   )

Blood

the winery is on fire:

listen to the music

Coleman Barks, 1937–

THE THOUGHT-FOX

I imagine this midnight moment's forest:
Something else is alive
Beside the clock's loneliness
And this blank page where my fingers move.

Through the window I see no star: 5
Something more near
Though deeper within darkness
Is entering the loneliness:

Cold, delicately as the dark snow,
A fox's nose touches twig, leaf;   10
Two eyes serve a movement, that now
And again now, and now, and now

Sets neat prints into the snow
Between trees, and warily a lame

Shadow lags by stump and in hollow   15
Of a body that is bold to come

Across clearings, an eye
A widening deepening greenness,
Brilliantly, concentratedly,
Coming about its own business   20

Till with a sudden sharp hot stink of fox
It enters the dark hole of the head.
The window is starless still; the clock ticks,
The page is printed.

Ted Hughes, 1930–

MY MOTHER WOULD BE A FALCONRESS

My mother would be a falconress,
And I, her gay falcon treading her wrist,
would fly to bring back
from the blue of the sky to her, bleeding, a prize,
where I dream in my little hood with many bells   5
jangling when I'd turn my head.

My mother would be a falconress,
and she sends me as far as her will goes.
She lets me ride to the end of her curb
where I fall back in anguish.   10
I dread that she will cast me away,
for I fall, I mis-take, I fail in her mission.

She would bring down the little birds.
And I would bring down the little birds.
When will she let me bring down the little birds,   15
pierced from their flight with their necks broken,
their heads like flowers limp from the stem?

I tread my mother's wrist and would draw blood.
Behind the little hood my eyes are hooded.
I have gone back into my hooded silence,   20
talking to myself and dropping off to sleep.

For she has muffled my dreams in the hood she has made me,
sewn round with bells, jangling when I move.
She rides with her little falcon upon her wrist.
She uses a barb that brings me to cower.   25

She sends me abroad to try my wings
and I come back to her. I would bring down
the little birds to her
I may not tear into, I must bring back perfectly.

I tear at her wrist with my beak to draw blood,   30
and her eye holds me, anguisht, terrifying.
She draws a limit to my flight.
Never beyond my sight, she says.

She trains me to fetch and to limit myself in fetching.
She rewards me with meat for my dinner.   35
But I must never eat what she sends me to bring her.

Yet it would have been beautiful, if she would have carried me,
always, in a little hood with the bells ringing,
at her wrist, and her riding
to the great falcon hunt, and me   40
flying up to the curb of my heart from her heart
to bring down the skylark from the blue to her feet,
straining, and then released for the flight.

My mother would be a falconress,
and I her gerfalcon,[1] raised at her will,   45
from her wrist sent flying, as if I were her own
pride, as if her pride
knew no limits, as if her mind
sought in me flight beyond the horizon.

Ah, but high, high in the air I flew.   50
And far, far beyond the curb of her will,
were the blue hills where the falcons nest.
And then I saw west to the dying sun—
it seemd my human soul went down in flames.

I tore at her wrist, at the hold she had for me,   55
until the blood ran hot and I heard her cry out,
far, far beyond the curb of her will

to horizons of stars beyond the ringing hills of the world where
    the falcons nest
I saw, and I tore at her wrist with my savage beak.
I flew, as if sight flew from the anguish in her eye beyond her
    sight,   60

---

[1] *gerfalcon:* large falcon.

sent from my striking loose, from the cruel strike at her wrist,
striking out from the blood to be free of her.
My mother would be a falconress,
and even now, years after this,
when the wounds I left her had surely heald,   65
and the woman is dead,
her fierce eyes closed, and if her heart
were broken, it is stilld

I would be a falcon and go free.
I tread her wrist and wear the hood,   70
talking to myself, and would draw blood.

Robert Duncan, 1919–

NATURE, THAT WASHED HER HANDS IN MILK

Nature, that washed her hands in milk,
And had forgot to dry them,
Instead of earth took snow and silk,
At love's request to try them,
If she a mistress could compose   5
To please love's fancy out of those.

Her eyes he would should be of light,
A violet breath, and lips of jelly;
Her hair not black, nor overbright,
And of the softest down her belly;   10
As for her inside he'd have it
Only of wantonness and wit.

At love's entreaty such a one
Nature made, but with her beauty
She hath framed a heart of stone;   15
So as love, by ill destiny,
Must die for her whom nature gave him,
Because her darling would not save him.

But time (which nature doth despise,
And rudely gives her love the lie,   20
Makes hope a fool, and sorrow wise)
His hands do neither wash nor dry;
But being made of steel and rust,
Turns snow and silk and milk to dust.

The light, the belly, lips, and breath,   25
He dims, discolors, and destroys;
With those he feeds but fills not death,
Which sometimes were the food of joys.
Yea, time doth dull each lively wit,
And dries all wantonness with it.   30

Oh, cruel time! which takes in trust
Our youth, our joys, and all we have,
And pays us but with age and dust;
Who in the dark and silent grave
When we have wandered all our ways   35
Shuts up the story of our days.

Sir Walter Raleigh, 1554–1618

THE EVE OF ST. AGNES[1]

i

St. Agnes' Eve—Ah, bitter chill it was!
The owl, for all his feathers, was a-cold;
The hare limp'd trembling through the frozen grass,
And silent was the flock in woolly fold:
Numb were the Beadsman's fingers, while he told
His rosary, and while his frosted breath,
Like pious incense from a censer old,
Seem'd taking flight for heaven, without a death,
Past the sweet Virgin's picture, while his prayer he saith.

ii

His prayer he saith, this patient, holy man;   10
Then takes his lamp, and riseth from his knees,
And back returneth, meagre, barefoot, wan,
Along the chapel aisle by slow degrees:
The sculptur'd dead, on each side, seem to freeze,
Emprison'd in black, purgatorial rails: 15
Knights, ladies, praying in dumb orat'ries,
He passeth by; and his weak spirit fails
To think how they may ache in icy hoods and mails.

---

[1] *Eve of St. Agnes:* January 20, when a maiden who performed certain rituals (see stanza vi) would have a vision of her future lover or husband.

iii

Northward he turneth through a little door,
And scarce three steps, ere Music's golden tongue   20
Flatter'd to tears this aged man and poor;
But no—already had his deathbell rung:
The joys of all his life were said and sung:
His was harsh penance on St. Agnes' Eve:
Another way he went, and soon among   25
Rough ashes sat he for his soul's reprieve,
And all night kept awake, for sinners' sake to grieve.

iv

That ancient Beadsman heard the prelude soft;
And so it chanc'd, for many a door was wide,
From hurry to and fro. Soon, up aloft,   30
The silver, snarling trumpets 'gan to chide:
The level chambers, ready with their pride,
Were glowing to receive a thousand guests:
The carved angels, ever eager-eyed,
Star'd, where upon their heads the cornice rests,   35
With hair blown back, and wings put cross-wise on their breasts.

v

At length burst in the argent revelry,
With plume, tiara, and all rich array,
Numerous as shadows haunting faerily
The brain, new stuff'd, in youth, with triumphs gay   40
Of old romance. These let us wish away,
And turn, sole-thoughted, to one Lady there,
Whose heart had brooded, all that wintry day,
On love, and wing'd St. Agnes' saintly care,
As she had heard old dames full many times declare.   45

vi

They told her how, upon St. Agnes' Eve,
Young virgins might have visions of delight,
And soft adorings from their loves receive
Upon the honey'd middle of the night,
If ceremonies due they did aright;   50

As, supperless to bed they must retire,
And couch supine their beauties, lilly white:
Nor look behind, nor sideways, but require
Of Heaven with upward eyes for all that they desire.

vii

Full of this whim was thoughtful Madeline: 55
The music, yearning like a God in pain,
She scarcely heard: her maiden eyes divine,
Fix'd on the floor, saw many a sweeping train
Pass by—she heeded not at all: in vain
Came many a tiptoe, amorous cavalier,   60
And back retir'd: not cool'd by high disdain,
But she saw not: her heart was otherwhere:
She sigh'd for Agnes' dreams, the sweetest of the year.

viii

She danc'd along with vague, regardless eyes,
Anxious her lips, her breathing quick and short: 65
The hallow'd hour was near at hand: she sighs
Amid the timbrels,[2] and the throng'd resort
Of whisperers in anger, or in sport;
'Mid looks of love, defiance, hate, and scorn,
Hoodwink'd with faery fancy; all amort,   70
Save to St. Agnes and her lambs unshorn,[3]
And all the bliss to be before to-morrow morn.

ix

So, purposing each moment to retire,
She linger'd still. Meantime, across the moors,
Had come young Porphyro, with heart on fire   75
For Madeline. Beside the portal doors,
Buttress'd from moonlight, stands he, and implores
All saints to give him sight of Madeline,
But for one moment in the tedious hours,
That he might gaze and worship all unseen;   80
Perchance speak, kneel, touch, kiss—in sooth such things have
     been.

---

[2] *timbrels:* small drums.
[3] *lambs:* On St. Agnes's day two lambs were sacrificed and their wool was spun and
   woven into cloth by the nuns.

x

He ventures in: let no buzz'd whisper tell:
All eyes be muffled, or a hundred swords
Will storm his heart, Love's fev'rous citadel:
For him, those chambers held barbarian hordes,   85
Hyena foemen, and hot-blooded lords,
Whose very dogs would execrations howl
Against his lineage: not one breast affords
Him any mercy, in that mansion foul,
Save one old beldame, weak in body and in soul.   90

xi

Ah, happy chance! the aged creature came,
Shuffling along with ivory-headed wand,
To where he stood, hid from the torch's flame,
Behind a broad hall-pillar, far beyond
The sound of merriment and chorus bland: 95
He startled her; but soon she knew his face,
And grasp'd his fingers in her palsied hand,
Saying, "Mercy, Porphyro! hie thee from this place:
They are all here to-night, the whole blood-thirsty race!

xii

"Get hence! get hence! there's dwarfish Hildebrand;   100
He had a fever late, and in the fit
He cursed thee and thine, both house and land:
Then there's that old Lord Maurice, not a whit
More tame for his gray hairs—Alas me! flit!
Flit like a ghost away."—"Ah, Gossip dear,   105
We're safe enough; here in this arm-chair sit,
And tell me how"—"Good Saints! not here, not here;
Follow me, child, or else these stones will be thy bier."

xiii

He follow'd through a lowly arched way,
Brushing the cobwebs with his lofty plume,   110
And as she mutter'd "Well-a—well-a-day!"
He found him in a little moonlight room,
Pale, lattic'd, chill, and silent as a tomb.
"Now tell me where is Madeline," said he,

"O tell me, Angela, by the holy loom   115
Which none but secret sisterhood may see,
When they St. Agnes' wool are weaving piously."

xiv

"St. Agnes! Ah! it is St. Agnes' Eve—
Yet men will murder upon holy days:
Thou must hold water in a witch's sieve,[4]   120
And be liege-lord of all the Elves and Fays,
To venture so: it fills me with amaze
To see thee, Porphyro!—St. Agnes' Eve!
God's help! my lady fair the conjuror plays
This very night: good angels her deceive!   125
But let me laugh awhile, I've mickle[5] time to grieve."

xv

Feebly she laugheth in the languid moon,
While Porphyro upon her face doth look,
Like puzzled urchin on an aged crone
Who keepeth clos'd a wond'rous riddle-book,   130
As spectacled she sits in chimney nook.
But soon his eyes grew brilliant, when she told
His lady's purpose; and he scarce could brook
Tears, at the thought of those enchantments cold,
And Madeline asleep in lap of legends old.   135

xvi

Sudden a thought came like a full-blown rose,
Flushing his brow, and in his pained heart
Made purple riot: then doth he propose
A stratagem, that makes the beldame start:
"A cruel man and impious thou art: 140
Sweet lady, let her pray, and sleep, and dream
Alone with her good angels, far apart
From wicked men like thee. Go, go!—I deem
Thou canst not surely be the same that thou didst seem."

---

[4] *witch's sieve:* a sieve bewitched so that no water can run through it.
[5] *mickle:* much.

xvii

"I will not harm her, by all saints I swear,"   145
Quoth Porphyro: "O may I ne'er find grace
When my weak voice shall whisper its last prayer,
If one of her soft ringlets I displace,
Or look with ruffian passion in her face:
Good Angela, believe me by these tears;   150
Or I will, even in a moment's space,
Awake, with horrid shout, my foemen's ears,
And beard them, though they be more fang'd than wolves and
    bears."

xviii

"Ah! why wilt thou affright a feeble soul?
A poor, weak, palsy-stricken, churchyard thing,   155
Whose passing-bell may ere the midnight toll;
Whose prayers for thee, each morn and evening,
Were never miss'd"—Thus plaining, doth she bring
A gentler speech from burning Porphyro;
So woful, and of such deep sorrowing,   160
That Angela gives promise she will do
Whatever he shall wish, betide her weal or woe.

xix

Which was, to lead him, in close secrecy,
Even to Madeline's chamber, and there hide
Him in a closet, of such privacy   165
That he might see her beauty unespied,
And win perhaps that night a peerless bride,
While legion'd faeries pac'd the coverlet,
And pale enchantment held her sleepy-eyed.
Never on such a night have lovers met,   170
Since Merlin paid his Demon all the monstrous debt.[6]

xx

"It shall be as thou wishest," said the Dame:
"All cates and dainties shall be stored there
Quickly on this feast-night: by the tambour frame[7]

[6] *monstrous debt:* Merlin, son of a demon, paid the debt for his life by performing evil
    deeds.
[7] *tambour frame:* embroidery frame.

Her own lute thou wilt see: no time to spare,   175
For I am slow and feeble, and scarce dare
On such a catering trust my dizzy head.
Wait here, my child, with patience; kneel in prayer
The while: Ah! thou must needs the lady wed,
Or may I never leave my grave among the dead."   180

xxi

So saying, she hobbled off with busy fear.
The lover's endless minutes slowly pass'd;
The dame return'd, and whisper'd in his ear
To follow her; with aged eyes aghast
From fright of dim espial. Safe at last,   185
Through many a dusky gallery, they gain
The maiden's chamber, silken, hush'd, and chaste;
Where Porphyro took covert, pleas'd amain.
His poor guide hurries back with agues in her brain.

xxii

Her falt'ring hand upon the balustrade,   190
Old Angela was feeling for the stair,
When Madeline, St. Agnes' charmed maid,
Rose, like a mission'd spirit, unaware:
With silver taper's light, and pious care,
She turn'd, and down the aged gossip led   195
To a safe level matting. Now prepare,
Young Porphyro, for gazing on that bed;
She comes, she comes again, like ring-dove fray'd[8] and fled.

xxiii

Out went the taper as she hurried in;
Its little smoke, in pallid moonshine, died: 200
She clos'd the door, she panted, all akin
To spirits of the air, and visions wide:
No uttered syllable, or, woe betide!
But to her heart, her heart was voluble,
Paining with eloquence her balmy side;   205
As though a tongueless nightingale should swell
Her throat in vain, and die, heart-stifled, in her dell.

[8] *fray'd:* alarmed.

xxiv

A casement high and triple-arch'd there was,
All garlanded with carven imag'ries
Of fruits, and flowers, and bunches of knot-grass,   210
And diamonded with panes of quaint device,
Innumerable of stains and splendid dyes,
As are the tiger-moth's deep-damask'd wings;
And in the midst, 'mong thousand heraldries,
And twilight saints, and dim emblazonings,   215
A shielded scutcheon blush'd with blood of queens and kings.

xxv

Full on this casement shone the wintry moon,
And threw warm gules[9] on Madeline's fair breast,
As down she knelt for heaven's grace and boon;
Rose-bloom fell on her hands, together prest,   220
And on her silver cross soft amethyst,
And on her hair a glory, like a saint:
She seem'd a splendid angel, newly drest
Save wings, for heaven:—Porphyro grew faint:
She knelt, so pure a thing, so free from mortal taint.   225

xxvi

Anon his heart revives: her vespers done,
Of all its wreathed pearls her hair she frees;
Unclasps her warmed jewels one by one;
Loosens her fragrant boddice; by degrees
Her rich attire creeps rustling to her knees: 230
Half-hidden, like a mermaid in sea-weed,
Pensive awhile she dreams awake, and sees,
In fancy, fair St. Agnes in her bed,
But dares not look behind, or all the charm is fled.

xxvii

Soon, trembling in her soft and chilly nest,   235
In sort of wakeful swoon, perplex'd she lay,
Until the poppied warmth of sleep oppress'd
Her soothed limbs, and soul fatigued away;

[9] *gules:* red.

Flown, like a thought, until the morrow-day;
Blissfully haven'd both from joy and pain;   240
Clasp'd like a missal where swart Paynims[10] pray;
Blinded alike from sunshine and from rain,
As though a rose should shut, and be a bud again.

xxviii

Stol'n to this paradise, and so entranced,
Porphyro gazed upon her empty dress,   245
And listen'd to her breathing, if it chanced
To wake into a slumberous tenderness;
Which when he heard, that minute did he bless,
And breath'd himself: then from the closet crept,
Noiseless as fear in a wide wilderness,   250
And over the hush'd carpet, silent, stept,
And 'tween the curtains peep'd, where, lo!—how fast she slept.

xxix

Then by the bed-side, where the faded moon
Made a dim, silver twilight, soft he set
A table, and, half anguish'd, threw thereon   255
A cloth of woven crimson, gold, and jet:—
O for some drowsy Morphean[11] amulet!
The boisterous, midnight, festive clarion,
The kettle-drum, and far-heard clarinet,
Affray his ears, though but in dying tone:—   260
The hall door shuts again, and all the noise is gone.

xxx

And still she slept an azure-lidded sleep,
In blanched linen, smooth, and lavender'd,
While he from forth the closet brought a heap
Of candied apple, quince, and plum, and gourd;   265
With jellies soother than the creamy curd,
And lucent syrops, tinct with cinnamon;
Manna and dates, in argosy transferr'd
From Fez; and spiced dainties, every one,
From silken Samarcand to cedar'd Lebanon.   270

---

[10] *Paynims:* pagans.
[11] *Morphean:* refers to Morpheus, Greek god of sleep and dreams

xxxi

These delicates he heap'd with glowing hand
On golden dishes and in baskets bright
Of wreathed silver: sumptuous they stand
In the retired quiet of the night,
Filling the chilly room with perfume light.—   275
"And now, my love, my seraph fair, awake!
Thou art my heaven, and I thine eremite:[12]
Open thine eyes, for meek St. Agnes' sake,
Or I shall drowse beside thee, so my soul doth ache."

xxxii

Thus whispering, his warm, unnerved arm   280
Sank in her pillow. Shaded was her dream
By the dusk curtains:—'twas a midnight charm
Impossible to melt as iced stream:
The lustrous salvers in the moonlight gleam;
Broad golden fringe upon the carpet lies: 285
It seem'd he never, never could redeem
From such a stedfast spell his lady's eyes;
So mus'd awhile, entoil'd in woofed phantasies.

xxxiii

Awakening up, he took her hollow lute,—
Tumultuous,—and, in chords that tenderest be,   290
He play'd an ancient ditty, long since mute,
In Provence call'd, "La belle dame sans mercy:"
Close to her ear touching the melody;—
Wherewith disturb'd, she utter'd a soft moan:
He ceased—she panted quick—and suddenly   295
Her blue affrayed eyes wide open shone:
Upon his knees he sank, pale as smooth-sculptured stone.

xxxiv

Her eyes were open, but she still beheld,
Now wide awake; the vision of her sleep:
There was a painful change, that nigh expell'd   300
The blisses of her dreams so pure and deep

---

[12] *eremite:* hermit.

At which fair Madeline began to weep,
And moan forth witless words with many a sigh;
While still her gaze on Porphyro would keep;
Who knelt, with joined hands and piteous eye,   305
Fearing to move or speak, she look'd so dreamingly.

xxxv

"Ah, Porphyro!" said she, "but even now
Thy voice was at sweet tremble in mine ear,
Made tuneable with every sweetest vow;
And those sad eyes were spiritual and clear: 310
How chang'd thou art! how pallid, chill, and drear!
Give me that voice again, my Porphyro,
Those looks immortal, those complainings dear!
Oh leave me not in this eternal woe,
For if thou diest, my Love, I know not where to go."   315

xxxvi

Beyond a mortal man impassion'd far
At these voluptuous accents, he arose,
Ethereal, flush'd, and like a throbbing star
Seen mid the sapphire heaven's deep repose;
Into her dream he melted, as the rose   320
Blendeth its odour with the violet,—
Solution sweet: meantime the frost-wind blows
Like Love's alarum pattering the sharp sleet
Against the window-panes; St. Agnes' moon hath set.

xxxvii

'Tis dark: quick pattereth the flaw-blown sleet:[13]   ⁻ 325
"This is no dream, my bride, my Madeline!"
'Tis dark: the iced gusts still rave and beat:
"No dream, alas! alas! and woe is mine!
Porphyro will leave me here to fade and pine.—
Cruel! what traitor could thee hither bring?   330
I curse not, for my heart is lost in thine,
Though thou forsakest a deceived thing;—
A dove forlorn and lost with sick unpruned wing."

[13] *flaw-blown sleet:* gust-blown sleet.

xxxviii

"My Madeline! sweet dreamer! lovely bride!
Say, may I be for aye thy vassal blest?   335
Thy beauty's shield, heart-shap'd and vermeil[14] dyed?
Ah, silver shrine, here will I take my rest
After so many hours of toil and quest,
A famish'd pilgrim,—sav'd by miracle.
Thou I have found, I will not rob thy nest   340
Saving of thy sweet self; if thou think'st well
To trust, fair Madeline, to no rude infidel.

xxxix

"Hark! 'tis an elfin-storm from faery land,
Of haggard seeming, but a boon indeed:
Arise—arise! the morning is at hand;—   345
The bloated wassaillers will never heed:—
Let us away, my love, with happy speed;
There are no ears to hear, or eyes to see,—
Drown'd all in Rhenish[15] and the sleepy mead:
Awake! arise! my love, and fearless be,   350
For o'er the southern moors I have a home for thee."

xl

She hurried at his words, beset with fears,
For there were sleeping dragons all around,
At glaring watch, perhaps, with ready spears—
Down the wide stairs a darkling way they found.—   355
In all the house was heard no human sound.
A chain-dropp'd lamp was flickering by each door;
The arras,[16] rich with horseman, hawk, and hound,
Flutter'd in the besieging wind's uproar;
And the long carpets rose along the gusty floor.   360

[14] *vermeil:* vermillion.
[15] *Rhenish:* Rhine wine.
[16] *arras:* tapestry.

xli

They glide, like phantoms, into the wide hall;
Like phantoms, to the iron porch, they glide;
Where lay the Porter, in uneasy sprawl,
With a huge empty flaggon by his side:
The wakeful bloodhound rose, and shook his hide,   365
But his sagacious eye an inmate owns:
By one, and one, the bolts full easy slide:—
The chains lie silent on the footworn stones;—
The key turns, and the door upon its hinges groans.

xlii

And they are gone: aye, ages long ago   370
    These lovers fled away into the storm.
    That night the Baron dreamt of many a woe,
    And all his warrior-guests, with shade and form
    Of witch, and demon, and large coffin-worm,
    Were long be-nightmar'd. Angela the old   375
    Died palsy-twitch'd, with meagre face deform;
    The Beadsman, after thousand aves told,
For aye unsought for slept among his ashes cold.

John Keats, 1795–1821

FOG-HORN

Surely that moan is not the thing
That men thought they were making, when they
Put it there, for their own necessities.
That throat does not call to anything human
But to something men had forgotten,   5
That stirs under fog. Who wounded that beast
Incurably, or from whose pasture
Was it lost, full grown, and time closed round it
With no way back? Who tethered its tongue
So that its voice could never come   10
To speak out in the light of clear day,
But only when the shifting blindness
Descends and is acknowledged among us,
As though from under a floor it is heard,
Or as though from behind a wall, always   15
Nearer than we had remembered? If it
Was we that gave tongue to this cry

What does it bespeak in us, repeating
And repeating, insisting on something
That we never meant? We only put it there   20
To give warning of something we dare not
Ignore, lest we should come upon it
Too suddenly, recognize it too late,
As our cries were swallowed up and all hands lost.

W. S. Merwin, 1927–

AN EXCUSE OF ABSENCE[1]

You'le aske perhaps wherefore I stay,
Loving so much, so long away,
O doe not thinke t'was I did part,
It was my body, not my hearte,
For like a Compasse in your love,   5
One foote is fix'd and cannot moove,
The other may follow her blinde guide
Of giddy fortune, but not slide
Beyound your service, nor dares venture
To wander farre from you the Center.   10

Thomas Carew, 1595–1640

[1] *An Excuse of Absence:* Compare this with Donne's conceit (page 112). Carew's poem is not an imitation but a translation of an Italian poem by G. B. Guarini (1538–1612).

THE EXCHANGE

I am watching a woman swim below the surface
Of the canal, her powerful body shimmering,
Opalescent, her black hair wavering
Like weeds. She does not need to breathe. She faces

Upward, keeping abreast of our rented canoe.   5
Sweet, thick, white, the blossoms of the locust trees
Cast their fragrance. A redwing blackbird flies
Across the sluggish water. My children paddle.

If I dive down, if she climbs into the boat,
Wet, wordless, she will strangle my children   10
And throw their limp bodies into the stream.
Skin dripping, she will take my car, drive home.

When my husband answers the doorbell and sees
This magnificent naked woman, bits of sunlight
Glittering on her pubic fur, her muscular   15
Arm will surround his neck, once for each insult

Endured. He will see the blackbird in her eye,
Her drying mouth incapable of speech,
And I, having exchanged with her, will swim
Away, in the cool water, out of reach.   20

Alicia Ostriker, 1937–

UNIVERSITY OF IOWA HOSPITAL, 1976

The last time I walked into
Ward C-22 I was stoned,
it was evening, I was picking
up my final paycheck—

where to begin in this never   5
ending blasted field of corpses.
Men looking like they had been
attacked repeatedly by a succession

of wild animals, throats half gone,
eyes bleeding, raw meat heaped   10
in piles. One walks around
sniffing through his long tubes.

A woman in a private room lies
curled like a Cro-Magnon mummy
in the museum. Where are   15
doctors of love, love apples,

the supervisors of love, love
administrators? Pain is a steady
fall from a high place, one with
no view, no vision outside   20

itself. Pain is a weed more
beautiful to look at than
rooms of flowers next to it.
It lasts through no rain,

resists scissors, takes over.   25
Last Christmas in the back room
an intern sat putting a black
jigsaw puzzle together, one thousand

pieces, one very long night. I
took a boy who had shot his face   30
off six months earlier on a walk
around the hospital grounds. He

was still uninterested after all
that damage. Another showed me 200
miles of scars, sixty years of making   35
that road. I know fifty people who are

now dead. One I watched die, his blood
pressure dove to nothing, and I had
to stuff him with cotton, tie
string around his penis, glue a label   40

on his forehead. I became extremely
careful driving home each day, I ate
good foods, slept the right amount,
lived the short life of convalescence.

Edward Kleinschmidt, 1951–

FORK

This strange thing must have crept
Right out of hell.
It resembles a bird's foot
Worn around the cannibal's neck.

As you hold it in your hand,
As you stab with it into a piece of meat,
It is possible to imagine the rest of the bird:
Its head which like your fist
Is large, bald, beakless and blind.

Charles Simic, 1937–

THE BEAR

1

In late winter
I sometimes glimpse bits of steam
coming up from
some fault in the old snow
and bend close and see it is lung-colored   5
and put down my nose
and know
the chilly, enduring odor of bear.

2

I take a wolf's rib and whittle
it sharp at both ends   10
and coil it up
and freeze it in blubber and place it out
on the fairway of the bears.

And when it has vanished
I move out on the bear tracks,   15
roaming in circles
until I come to the first, tentative, dark
splash on the earth.

And I set out
running, following the splashes   20
of blood wandering over the world.
At the cut, gashed resting places
I stop and rest,
at the crawl-marks
where he lay out on his belly   25
to overpass some stretch of bauchy ice
I lie out
dragging myself forward with bear-knives in my fists.

3

On the third day I begin to starve,
at nightfall I bend down as I knew I would   30
at a turd sopped in blood,
and hesitate, and pick it up,

and thrust it in my mouth, and gnash it down,
and rise
and go on running.   35

4

On the seventh day,
living by now on bear blood alone,
I can see his upturned carcass far out ahead, a scraggled,
steamy hulk,
the heavy fur riffling in the wind.   40

I come up to him
and stare at the narrow-spaced, petty eyes,
the dismayed
face laid back on the shoulder, the nostrils
flared, catching   45
perhaps the first taint of me as he
died.

I hack
a ravine in his thigh, and eat and drink,
and tear him down his whole length   50
and open him and climb in
and close him up after me, against the wind,
and sleep.

5

And dream
of lumbering flatfooted   55
over the tundra,
stabbed twice from within,
splattering a trail behind me,
splattering it out no matter which way I lurch,
no matter which parabola of bear-transcendence,   60
which dance of solitude I attempt,
which gravity-clutched leap,
which trudge, which groan.

6

Until one day I totter and fall—
fall on this   65
stomach that has tried so hard to keep up,
to digest the blood as it leaked in,
to break up
and digest the bone itself: and now the breeze
blows over me, blows off   70
the hideous belches of ill-digested bear blood
and rotted stomach
and the ordinary, wretched odor of bear,

blows across
my sore, lolled tongue a song   75
or screech, until I think I must rise up
and dance. And I lie still.

7

I awaken I think. Marshlights
reappear, geese
come trailing again up the flyway.   80
In her ravine under old snow the dam-bear
lies, licking
lumps of smeared fur
and drizzly eyes into shapes
with her tongue. And one   85
hairy-soled trudge stuck out before me,
the next groaned out,
the next,
the next,
the rest of my days I spend   90
wandering: wondering
what, anyway,
was that sticky infusion, that rank flavor of blood, that poetry,
   by which I lived?

Galway Kinnell, 1927–

THE BEST DAYS

The sun was an old ball
in those days. The moon
was a dish of milk
in a blue night on sheets.
We were always thirsty   5
then. Wine flowed red
in our hearts. Love
was the way we felt
all over, every minute.
I'm not complaining   10
about now. I'm just lost
and not getting any help.
No one can break
the time we spent
together. We remember   15
the pink mud house,
startled cypresses
flickering in rain.
The morning we awoke
to the sound of summer   20
beating across the desert
driving clouds before it.
There is one half a red kiss
on your cup there
where you left it. It's still   25
warm because you just left.
This is a good day, maybe
one of the best. I don't know
for now. Those good days
are inside us, in heaven,   30
whatever you want to say.
They are more or less
gone, like you driving
to work, like me sitting here
with nothing to say   35
that isn't too ordinary or sad.

Quinton Duval, 1948–

ON TIME

Fly envious Time, till thou run out thy race,
Call on the lazy leaden-stepping hours,
Whose speed is but the heavy Plummet's[1] pace;
And glut thy self with what thy womb devours,
Which is no more than what is false and vain,   5
And merely mortal dross;
So little is our loss,
So little is thy gain.
For when as each thing bad thou hast entomb'd,
And last of all, thy greedy self consum'd,   10
Then long Eternity shall greet our bliss
With an individual kiss;
And Joy shall overtake us as a flood,
When every thing that is sincerely good
And perfectly divine,   15
With Truth, and Peace, and Love shall ever shine
About the supreme Throne
Of him, t'whose happy-making sight alone,
When once our heav'nly-guided soul shall climb,
Then all this Earthy grossness quit,   20
Attir'd with Stars, we shall for ever sit,
Triumphing over Death, and Chance, and thee O Time.

John Milton, 1608–1674

[1] *Plummet:* The weight that moves the works of a clock. A manuscript note indicates
that Milton intended the poem "to be set on a clock case."

WHAT RUSHES BY US

On the falling elevator trapped as the sixty-one floors blink
Like eyes in sequence, each possible resting place whipping by

Faster and faster, one after the other, Hello
Goodbye, my friends, yesterday we were talking, today we die

In our sleep, with the stars falling, surely it is the stars   5
In waterfalls of sparks, ribbons of light descending

With tennis racquets, Bibles, cars, violets, young men wearing hats
Ski lifts in winter, *The New York Times*, the Funnies,

All the intense conversations that will never end,
Your photograph on my wall, mine tucked in your billfold,   10

Do you know what you look like? Not now you don't,
Maybe one second ago you did, but the bits and pieces of yesterday

Are piling up, pushing (some even going on ahead),
There's Mother, there's Father, there's Edward from the first grade

And Beethoven's Ninth, and the Bach B Minor, each chord   15
Turns into a glissando, clusters of fireworks flying

With curses, cats wailing, the whine of the big guns
And desperate bombs going off, the little pot bellies

Of starved children, presidents, old beggars, vice-presidents,
Every newspaper headline, every last quarrel   20

We ever had, each hangover, each miraculous glass
Of the deep bourbon of love, even the pure silence of prayer

Is pouring past us like rain, like a blizzard of hard rice
Sliding by, sliding by, polished smooth as the ground

Each of us thinks he is standing on, certainly I do   25
Content, watching the world go by but suddenly

The bottom drops out, the stomach crazily catapults
Past the toes, the feet, the head follows, mountains

Exchange places with the back yard, even your face
Revolves in the sky, it's the Big Dipper, upside down   30

The wind roars in our ears, in the dizzy whirl of the blood
There's no turning back, on parallel tracks shooting

From the cliff of our birth we keep falling,
First you, then me, then me rushing by you.

Patricia Goedicke, 1931–

The Speaker:
The Eye of the Poem

I hear bravuras of birds, bustle of growing wheat, gossip of flames,
  clack of sticks cooking my meals,
I hear the sound I love, the sound of the human voice. . . .

Walt Whitman

A student wanted to write a poem about her friend's father's death.
Visiting the friend's house around Christmas, she imagined what the
family was feeling, tried to imagine death. How to approach such a
poem? She thought of describing the family, tried describing the event
of his death and her own feelings. Finally she decided to address the
father directly.

UNTITLED

You are dead now
your bones burning in the fire
cancer cells popping like oak
fine white oak your collar bone
and the branch from your leg   5
I think I see you
in the Christmas tree
smiling again like an ornament does
a red cardinal only for an instant

Your voice is the same voice but from back   10
far back in a line of ancestors
standing only briefly on the porch
faces outstretched into blanks
never moved since
They're all dead under the grass   15
and they're all still on the porch
with their reaching not grabbing faces

There was another picture of you happy
and not alone in the mountains
It's in somebody's wallet now   20
somebody who looks at it and wonders
how could you be a father
how could you smile like that with your hunting rifle

Ashley King, 1964–

King chose not to say that the father was her friend's. Why? She speaks
so that he seems almost present in the flash of the ornament twirling,
the crackle of the fire. The memory of the sound of his voice seems
as far removed as other long-dead ancestors who once gathered on a
porch, perhaps to pose for a photograph. The other picture of him is
in "somebody's" wallet. Probably she means her friend's wallet, but
in the poem she chose to leave this somebody anonymous. By addressing the father as "you" and by leaving the photo in the possession of
"somebody," King accomplishes two important things for the poem.
She lets the reader "overhear" the speaker, "I," talking to a "you."
Their connection is direct. What if at the end she'd said "in my friend's
wallet" instead of "somebody's wallet"? "Somebody" is the more
open choice; the reader feels included more than if the picture were
only the friend's. The discovery lines for the reader, and probably for
the writer, are "and they're all dead under the grass / and they're all
still on the porch." She realizes that the dead are both dead in the
earth *and* alive in memory, "reaching not grabbing." The choice of
"somebody" reflects this broad realization about the dead: anyone can
look at a photograph of the father and wonder at how present and yet
how irretrievable he is.

Of course the writer doesn't know all this in advance. The poet
finds the right speaker and the right listener, usually by trying out
several approaches.

The Invented "I"

Authority, that quality in a poem which makes it believable and real,
has the word *author* in it. The speaker the author selects establishes
the presence and authority we respond to as we read. Who is speaking?
And who is listening? Who is spoken about? The poet decides these
for definite reasons. These choices determine the poem's fundamental
orientation. The speaker's voice can have any number of tones, shades

of expression, pitches, and changes. All these choices reveal the speaker's attitude toward the subject and the audience.

The next title lets us know right away that this will be an emotional poem spoken by a shepherd to his love. He speaks directly to her and no one else.

THE PASSIONATE SHEPHERD TO HIS LOVE

Come live with me and be my love,
And we will all the pleasures prove
That valleys, groves, hills, and fields,
Woods, or steepy mountain yields.

And we will sit upon the rocks,   5
Seeing the shepherds feed their flocks,
By shallow rivers, to whose falls
Melodious birds sing madrigals.

And I will make thee beds of roses
And a thousand fragrant posies,   10
A cap of flowers, and a kirtle
Embroidered all with leaves of myrtle;

A gown made of the finest wool,
Which from our pretty lambs we pull;
Fair lined slippers for the cold,   15
With buckles of the purest gold;

A belt of straw and ivy buds
With coral clasps and amber studs:
And if these pleasures may thee move,
Come live with me and be my love.   20

The shepherd swains shall dance and sing
For thy delight each May morning:
If these delights thy mind may move,
Then live with me and be my love.

Christopher Marlowe, 1564–1593

The speaker's tone is gentle and persuasive but insistent: three times he entreats his love (but in the imperative voice) to live with him. We can imagine that she is not displeased to hear him; she seems to stay put while he promises quite a few beds of roses and coral clasps. We overhear. We're invisible to them. Marlowe chose the voice of the shepherd for his love poem instead of writing from his own personal voice. Why? The imaginary shepherd can freely propose an idyllic world where "swains shall dance and sing / for thy delight each May morning." Four hundred years later, the shepherd's world still evokes response; we still propose enduring passion to those we love, still wish for ideal circumstances. The shepherd is a **persona** (the Greek word for "mask") for Marlowe. Speaking through the voices of others gives poets wider possibilities than speaking always as a personal "I." In addition to increased freedom of expression, a character voice can heighten dramatic action. The character in "The Negress" is a runaway slave who managed to get to Massachusetts and now writes to her former mistress in the South:

THE NEGRESS: HER MONOLOGUE OF DARK CRÊPE WITH EDGES OF LIGHT:

Mistress Adrienne, I have been given a bed with a pink dresser
In the hot-house
Joining the Concord Public Library: the walls and roof are
Glass and my privacy comes from the apple-geraniums,
Violets, ferns, marigolds and white mayflags.   5
I get my meals
With the janitor and his wife and all of the books are mine
To use. I scour, sweep and dust.
I hope you don't think of me
As a runaway? I remember your kindness,   10
Your lessons in reading and writing on the piazza.
My journey was unusual. I saw some of the war
And it was terrible even far up into the North.
My first fright was at a train depot outside Memphis
Where some soldiers found me eating not yet ripened   15
Quinces and grapes, they took me prisoner: first
I helped some children carry tree limbs to the woodbox
Of the locomotive, then, I was shown to a gentleman
In the passenger car who was searching for his runaway
Negress in a purple dress; he wouldn't identify me,   20

And I was thrown in with about forty stray blacks into
An open boxcar and soon we were moving, next to me
A man was sucking on the small breasts of a girl

Maybe twelve years of age, across from them
A sad old woman smiled as she puffed on an old cigar end,   25
By afternoon she was dead, her two friends
Just kicked her out so that she rolled down into pasture
Frightening some hogs that ran off into a thicket.
The girl next to me whimpered and shook. Those quinces
Just ran straight through me and all I could do was   30
Squat in one corner that was supplied with ammonia-waters
And hay. We were given that night Confederate uniforms
To mend and when the others slept I dressed in three
Shirts and trousers and leapt from the moving train,
The padding helped some but I couldn't walk the next day.   35
I hid in a shack that seemed lonely but for a flock
Of turkeys, some young hens and a corn crib with tall
Split palings. The next morning from a hill
I watched field workers on a tobacco plantation, it took
Two men to carry a single leaf like a corpse from   40
A battle scene. That night I found a horse with a bit
In its mouth made of telegraph wire. He carried me up all

The way to Youngstown. *Chloe, you must*
Learn to swim in the pond and to ride the old sorrel.
I am grateful. I had to swim two rivers. I fished some   45
For perch, bream and trout and ate dried berries.
I stole a bushel of oysters from the porch of a farmhouse.
I treated my sores with blackgum from poplars. I witnessed
The hanging of three Confederate soldiers at a trestle:
Once they were done dancing, they settled in their greatcoats   50
Like dead folded birds. I have a hatred
Of men and I walked away from the trestle singing.
I spoke to The Concord Literary Club last Tuesday
About my experiences. I told them you never did
Abuse me. How we would sit out in the gazebo   55
And listen to the boys with their violins, tambourines,
Bones, drums and sticks. How we wept as girls
When the fox bit the head off our peahen and that
From that day how the peacock, missing his mate, would
See her in his reflection in a downstairs window   60
And fly at it increasing his iridescence with lacerations.
When I left you the windows were all missing and daubers
Were making their mud houses in the high corners
Of the hallway. With sugar-water and crêpe I have put a new
Hem on my purple dress.   65

At night I walk down the aisles
Of the library, the books climb twenty feet above me,

I just walk there naked with my tiny lamp.
I have the need to fling the lamp sometimes: but I resist it.
Mistress Adrienne, I saw three big cities burning!   70
Did you know ladies from Philadelphia rode for two days
In wagons to climb a hill where with spyglasses they watched
The war like a horse-pulling contest at a fair.
The man beside me on the train who was sucking the little
Girl's breasts, he was your stable boy, Napoleon. He said   75
He never had a bad word for you. His little mistress was
Still bare to the waist and before I leapt from the train,
And while he slept, I ran a rod into his eye. I stabbed him
In his brain. She stopped weeping.
Remember that French lullaby where two fleas in a gentleman's   80
Moustache die like a kiss between the lips of the gentleman
And his mistress. How we laughed at it!
I hope you were not long unconscious there beside the pond.
I just ran away from you, listening the whole night
For your father's hounds. I am   85
Afraid I split your parasol on your skull. If I
Don't hear from you I will try to understand. *Chloe.*

Norman Dubie, 1945–

In her own voice, Chloe tells Mistress Adrienne the story of her escape. This is a **dramatic monologue**, a poem spoken by a persona who tells someone else a story or an event of significance. The poem is also an **epistle**, a poem written as a letter. Chloe is a good letter writer. She recreates her experience with vivid language and exact imagery. We even know exactly what blooms outside her window in her new home. Her intimate tone partly comes from Dubie's decision to make the poem a letter. Letters are directed to *a* reader, almost guaranteeing a one-to-one tone. As Chloe tells the horrifying details of the train ride, we experience them as we expect Mistress Adrienne did when she read. However, the poem surprises us in the end. Chloe's apology for the way she escaped—a whack on dear Mistress Adrienne's head—makes us revise what we thought Mistress Adrienne was hearing all along. The poem is more complex than we thought. Chloe is both violent and heroic and perhaps a little crazed: she thinks of setting the library on fire. The image of the peacock flying at his reflection is an important one. The two women seemed to be close; but to get her freedom, Chloe had to throw herself against her owner.

What did Dubie gain by allowing Chloe to speak? He could have written:

> She has been given a bed with a pink dresser
> In the hot-house. . . .
> She gets her meals. . . .

By choosing Chloe's voice, Dubie lets us hear a live speaker instead of a third-person description of her experience. A character gives a first-hand account. Does "listening" to the voice of an escaped slave give you new insight into the Civil War era? This account has more vivacity than the history books' paragraphs on the underground rail-road routes and methods of escape.

In "My Last Duchess," the most famous dramatic monologue in English, Robert Browning speaks in the voice of the duke of Ferrara, Italy.

MY LAST DUCHESS

Ferrara

That's my last Duchess painted on the wall,
Looking as if she were alive. I call
That piece a wonder, now: Frà Pandolf's hands
Worked busily a day, and there she stands.
Will 't please you sit and look at her? I said   5
'Frà Pandolf' by design, for never read
Strangers like you that pictured countenance,
The depth and passion of its earnest glance,
But to myself they turned (since none puts by
The curtain I have drawn for you, but I)   10
And seemed as they would ask me, if they durst,
How such a glance came there; so, not the first
Are you to turn and ask thus. Sir, 't was not
Her husband's presence only, called that spot
Of joy into the Duchess' cheek: perhaps   15
Frà Pandolf chanced to say 'Her mantle laps
'Over my lady's wrist too much,' or 'Paint
'Must never hope to reproduce the faint
'Half-flush that dies along her throat:' such stuff
Was courtesy, she thought, and cause enough   20
For calling up that spot of joy. She had
A heart—how shall I say?—too soon made glad,

Too easily impressed; she liked whate'er
She looked on, and her looks went everywhere.
Sir, 't was all one! My favour at her breast,   25
The dropping of the daylight in the West,
The bough of cherries some officious fool
Broke in the orchard for her, the white mule
She rode with round the terrace—all and each
Would draw from her alike the approving speech,   30
Or blush, at least. She thanked men,—good! but thanked
Somehow—I know not how—as if she ranked
My gift of a nine-hundred-years-old name
With anybody's gift. Who'd stoop to blame
This sort of trifling? Even had you skill   35
In speech—(which I have not)—to make your will
Quite clear to such an one, and say, 'Just this
'Or that in you disgusts me; here you miss,
'Or there exceed the mark'—and if she let
Herself be lessoned so, nor plainly set   40
Her wits to yours, forsooth, and made excuse,
—E'en then would be some stooping; and I choose
Never to stoop. Oh sir, she smiled, no doubt,
Whene'er I passed her; but who passed without
Much the same smile? This grew; I gave commands;   45
Then all smiles stopped together. There she stands
As if alive. Will 't please you rise? We'll meet
The company below, then. I repeat,
The Count your master's known munificence
Is ample warrant that no just pretence   50
Of mine for dowry will be disallowed;
Though his fair daughter's self, as I avowed
As starting, is my object. Nay, we'll go
Together down, sir. Notice Neptune, though,
Taming a sea-horse, thought a rarity,   55
Which Claus of Innsbruck cast in bronze for me!

Robert Browning, 1812–1889

EXERCISES

1. To whom is the duke speaking? Why is the visitor there?

2. How does the duke see himself? How do we see him?

3. The primary effect of the poem is **ironic**: readers do not see the duke as he saw himself. Why? As the speaker reveals *his* sense of a situation, what makes you aware of the true nature of this drama?

4. Compare the tone of the duke's voice to that of Norman Dubie's Chloe. Which poem seems more immediate? Why?

The Personal "I" Speaker

Frequently the poem's "I" seems to be the actual voice of the author. When the first person is used this way, we respond to the immediacy of direct personal expression. Ideally the "I" voice, in developing the experience of the poem, also connects to the reader's experience, either internal or external. The poem's effect is not limited to the speaker.

The use of a character voice (Chloe's, for instance) has a very different dramatic impact from one's own voice telling an experience. Whereas with a character voice we keep some awareness of the fictional aspect of the poem, the personal "I" is more subjective. We feel near the voice of the poem. Poets adopt "I" because it conveys an often desired effect of immediacy, "as if" an experience were real. Although the "I" speaker in the poem and the author seem to be the same person, never assume the experience in the poem is an actual fact of the poet's life. "I" can be an invention as easily as any other voice. A poet can write about a morning in Barcelona in first person even if she has never been to Spain.

The choice of speaker is one of the big decisions the poet makes in determining the best stance for the poem. This choice focuses the poem in a particular way. Once the speaker is chosen, the poet still has infinite leeway in the tone of voice. Look at these two extremes in the use of "I":

I THINK CONTINUALLY OF THOSE
WHO WERE TRULY GREAT

I think continually of those who were truly great.
Who, from the womb, remembered the soul's history
Through corridors of light where the hours are suns,
Endless and singing. Whose lovely ambition
Was that their lips, still touched with fire,   5
Should tell of the spirit clothed from head to foot in song.
And who hoarded from the spring branches
The desires falling across their bodies like blossoms.

What is precious is never to forget
The delight of the blood drawn from ageless springs   10

Breaking through rocks in worlds before our earth;
Never to deny its pleasure in the simple morning light,
Nor its grave evening demand for love;
Never to allow gradually the traffic to smother
With noise and fog the flowering of the spirit.   15

Near the snow, near the sun, in the highest fields
See how those names are fêted by the waving grass,
And by the streamers of white cloud,
And whispers of wind in the listening sky;
The names of those who in their lives fought for life,   20
Who wore at their hearts the fire's centre.
Both of the sun they traveled a short while towards the sun,
And left the vivid air signed with their honour.

Stephen Spender, 1909–

AUTOBIOGRAPHIA LITERARIA

When I was a child
I played by myself in a
corner of the schoolyard
all alone.

I hated dolls and I   5
hated games, animals were
not friendly and birds
flew away.

If anyone was looking
for me I hid behind a   10
tree and cried out "I am
an orphan."

And here I am, the
center of all beauty!
writing these poems!   15
Imagine!

Frank O'Hara, 1926–1966

O'Hara's "I" is campy, playful. His off-beat, gee-whiz tone makes fun
of taking experience so seriously and, by implication, mocks those who
would presume to write a "literary autobiography." Spender's "I," in
contrast, venerates with deep seriousness the memory of those who

lived valuable lives. His poem has a great ambition: to define a valuable life. His tone is somber. We can imagine the speaker addressing a large audience. He speaks to us in a tone of high purpose and importance. The structured appearance of the poem and the repetition of words adds to the formality of the tone. Remembering the "author" in "authority," notice the absolutely unequivocal tone of the opening line and of "What is precious is never to forget. . . ," "Never to deny. . . ," and "Never to allow. . . ." The author is certain of his values and presents them unfalteringly.

Do you think to yourself in the same way you speak to others? Some "I" poems record the interior voice. We overhear the speaker's private perceptions as they occur.

THE PARTIAL EXPLANATION

Seems like a long time
Since the waiter took my order.
Grimy little luncheonette,
The snow falling outside.

Seems like it has grown darker   5
Since I last heard the kitchen door
Behind my back
Since I last noticed
Anyone pass on the street.

A glass of ice water   10
Keeps me company
At this table I chose myself
Upon entering.

And a longing,
Incredible longing   15
To eavesdrop
On the conversation
Of cooks.

Charles Simic, 1937–

The speaker's interior tone shows in the sentence fragments; he wouldn't speak like this to anyone but himself. He thinks in random observations which seem to float through his head. The glass of ice water keeping him company emphasizes his aloneness. This illogical thought is typical of the meanderings of someone musing to himself. No listener is implied. The speaker could be jotting notes on the napkin while we look over his shoulder.

Most "I" speakers do not assume a specific listener. The dramatic monologue is an exception. We experience the dramatic monologue as if we were standing with the intended listener. (In "My Last Duchess," for example, the reader "hears" with the visitor to whom the duke is showing his art works.) The **soliloquy**, also a solo voice, is another special use of "I." As in the dramatic monologue, a character is speaking. The speaker of a soliloquy usually is debating an action, not telling about an event. He or she is not aware of an audience: again, we overhear. Soliloquies are private, frequently used in plays to let the audience in on the inner thoughts of an actor, as in Hamlet's famous debate with himself.

from HAMLET

(Act III, scene i)

To be, or not to be, that is the question:	
Whether 'tis nobler in the mind to suffer	
The slings and arrows of outrageous fortune,	
Or to take arms against a sea of troubles,	
And by opposing end them. To die, to sleep—	5
No more; and by a sleep to say we end	
The heartache, and the thousand natural shocks	
That flesh is heir to. 'Tis a consummation	
Devoutly to be wished—to die, to sleep—	
To sleep, perchance to dream, ay there's the rub;	10
For in that sleep of death what dreams may come	
When we have shuffled off this mortal coil[1]	
Must give us pause—there's the respect[2]	
That makes calamity of so long life.[3]	
For who would bear the whips and scorns of time,	15
Th' oppressor's wrong, the proud man's contumely,	
The pangs of despised love, the law's delay,	
The insolence of office, and the spurns	

[1] *coil:* turmoil *or* rope ring, meaning flesh.
[2] *respect:* consideration.
[3] *so long life:* so long-lived.

That patient merit of th' unworthy takes,
When he himself might his quietus[4] make   20
With a bare bodkin?[5] Who would fardels[6] bear,
To grunt and sweat under a weary life,
But that the dread of something after death,
The undiscovered country, from whose bourn[7]
No traveller returns, puzzles the will,   25
And makes us rather bear those ills we have
Than fly to others that we know not of?
Thus conscience does make cowards of us all;
And thus the native hue of resolution
Is sicklied o'er with the pale cast of thought,   30
And enterprises of great pitch[8] and moment
With this regard their currents turn awry
And lose the name of action.—

William Shakespeare, 1564–1616

[4] *quietus:* legal term meaning full discharge.
[5] *bodkin:* dagger.
[6] *fardels:* burdens.
[7] *bourn:* region.
[8] *pitch:* height.

from PARADISE LOST

Book IX

Thus to herself she pleasingly began:
  "O sovran, virtuous, precious of all trees
In Paradise, of operation blest
To sapience,[1] hitherto obscured, infamed,[2]
And thy fair fruit let hang, as to no end   5
Created; but henceforth my early care,
Not without song, each morning, and due praise,
Shall tend thee, and the fertile burden ease
Of thy full branches offered free to all;
Till dieted by thee I grow mature   10
In knowledge, as the gods who all things know;
Though others envy what they cannot give;
For had the gift been theirs, it had not here
Thus grown. Experience, next to thee I owe,

[1] *sapience:* given the power to confer wisdom.
[2] *infamed:* misreputed.

Best guide; not following thee, I had remained   15
In ignorance; thou open'st wisdom's way,
And giv'st access, though secret she retire.
And I perhaps am secret; Heaven is high,
High and remote to see from thence distinct
Each thing on Earth; and other care perhaps   20
May have diverted from continual watch
Our great Forbidder, safe with all his spies
About him. But to Adam in what sort
Shall I appear? Shall I to him make known
As yet my change, and give him to partake   25
Full happiness with me, or rather not,
But keep the odds of knowledge in my power
Without copartner? so to add what wants
In female sex, the more to draw his love,
And render me more equal, and perhaps,   30
A thing not undesirable, sometime
Superior; for inferior who is free?
This may be well. But what if God have seen,
And death ensue? then I shall be no more,
And Adam wedded to another Eve,   35
Shall live with her enjoying, I extinct;
A death to think. Confirmed then I resolve,
Adam shall share with me in bliss or woe.
So dear I love him, that with him all deaths
I could endure, without him live no life.''   40

John Milton, 1608–1674

EXERCISE

In the soliloquy above, Eve debates whether or not to let Adam taste the forbidden fruit she has just tasted. From the Bible's creation story, we only know that Eve did offer Adam the apple. *Why* does she make the decision to share her knowledge with Adam? Is her logic sound or is she rationalizing? Is this an early note of feminism?

The Public Voice

When the speaker is "we," the poet presumes to speak for himself and others. "We" can be intimate, but usually "we" indicates that the poet will be concerned with a cultural or historical subject with broad scope

and conclusions. The U.S. Constitution begins, "We, the people. . . ,"
and "we" intends to represent all citizens. A poem that uses this kind
of "we" is a **public voice poem**. The public voice speaks for a group of
believers or participants in a common situation. The poet therefore
wants a larger platform than a personal voice would offer. The choice
of "we" stakes out a different territory than "I." Twentieth-century
poets are less willing to venture to speak from the broad, homogeneous
religious and political viewpoints that poets of earlier times took for
granted. The plurality of our culture makes "we" a difficult choice.

Wilfred Owen's "we" is a troop of World War I soldiers. Owen,
who died in that war, questions an ancient, accepted sentiment. The
purpose of his poem is **didactic**—a moral lesson is intended. The irony
here is that the poem disproves the lofty sentiment of the title. *Dulce
et decorum est pro patria mori* ("It is sweet and dignified to die for
one's country") is a common epitaph on the tombstones of European
soldiers.

DULCE ET DECORUM EST

Bent double, like old beggars under sacks,
Knock-kneed, coughing like hags, we cursed through sludge,
Till on the haunting flares we turned our backs,
And towards our distant rest began to trudge.
Men marched asleep. Many had lost their boots,   5
But limped on, blood-shod. All went lame, all blind;
Drunk with fatigue; deaf even to the hoots
Of gas-shells dropping softly behind.

Gas! Gas! Quick, boys!—An ecstasy of fumbling,
Fitting the clumsy helmets just in time,   10
But someone still was yelling out and stumbling
And flound'ring like a man in fire or lime.
Dim through the misty panes and thick green light,
As under a green sea, I saw him drowning.

In all my dreams before my helpless sight   15
He plunges at me, guttering, choking, drowning.
If in some smothering dreams, you too could pace
Behind the wagon that we flung him in,
And watch the white eyes wilting in his face,
His hanging face, like a devil's sick of sin,   20

If you could hear, at every jolt, the blood
Come gargling from the froth-corrupted lungs
Bitten as the cud
Of vile, incurable sores on innocent tongues,—
My friend, you would not tell with such high zest   25
To children ardent for some desperate glory,
The old lie: *Dulce et decorum est*
Pro patria mori.

                                        Wilfred Owen, 1893–1918

EXERCISES

1. At first, the soldier describes the experiences of "we." Midway,
    he uses "I," then begins to address "you" and "my friend." What
    is the effect of these switches?

2. Owen invites the reader to imagine war not as an abstract glory
    but as the muddy horror he experienced. Is he successful?

• • •

IF ON ACCOUNT OF THE POLITICAL SITUATION

If on account of the political situation,
There are quite a number of homes without roofs, and men,
Lying about in the countryside neither drunk nor asleep,
If all sailings have been cancelled till further notice,
If it's unwise now to say much in letters, and if,   5
Under the subnormal temperatures prevailing,
The two sexes are at the present the weak and the strong,
That is not at all unusual for this time of year.
If that were all, we should know how to manage. Flood, fire,
The destruction of grasslands, restraint of princes,   10
Piracy on the high seas, physical pain and fiscal grief,
These after all are our familiar tribulations,
And we have been through them all before, many, many, times.
As events which belong to the natural world where
The occupation of space is the real and final fact   15
And time turns round itself in an obedient circle,
They occur again and again but only to pass
Again and again into their formal opposites,

From sword to ploughshare, coffin to cradle, war to work,
So that, taking the bad with the good, the pattern composed   20
By the ten thousand odd things that can possibly happen
Is permanent in a general average way.

   Till lately we knew of no other, and between us we seemed
To have what it took—the adrenal courage of the tiger,
The chameleon's discretion, the modesty of the doe,   25
Or the fern's devotion to spatial necessity:
To practice one's peculiar civic virtue was not
So impossible after all; to cut our losses
And bury our dead was really quite easy: that was why
We were always able to say: we are the children of God,   30
And our father has never forsaken His people.

   But then we were children: that was a moment ago
Before an outrageous novelty had been introduced
Into our lives. Why were we never warned? Perhaps we were.
Perhaps that mysterious noise at the back of the brain   35
We noticed on certain occasions—sitting alone
In the waiting rooms of the country junction, looking
Up at the toilet window—was not indigestion
But this Horror starting already to scratch Its way in?
Just how, just when It succeeded we shall never know: 40
We can only say that now It is there and nothing
We learnt before It was there is now of the slightest use,
For nothing like It has happened before. It's as if
We had left our house for five minutes to mail a letter,
And during that time the living room had changed places   45
With the room behind the mirror over the fireplace;
It's as if, waking up with a start, we discovered
Ourselves stretched out flat on the floor, watching our shadow
Sleepily stretching itself at the window. I mean
That the world of space where events re-occur is still there.   50
Only now, it's no longer real; the real one is nowhere
Where time never moves and nothing can ever happen:
I mean that although there's a person we know all about
Still bearing our name and loving himself as before,
That person has become a fiction; our true existence   55
Is decided by no one and has no importance to love.

   That is why we despair; that is why we welcome
The nursery bogey or the winecellar ghost, why even
The violent howling of winter and war has become
Like a jukebox tune that we dare not stop. We are afraid   60
Of pain but more afraid of silence; for no nightmare

Of hostile objects could be as terrible as this void.
This is the abomination. This is the wrath of God.

W. H. Auden, 1907–1973

1. What are the common ("we") experiences in "If On Account of the Political Situation"?

2. How would you describe the tone of Auden's speaker?

3. Does Auden address the difficulty of writing from a broad cultural point of view? What is the "Horror"? What does he mean by "our true existence / Is decided by no one and has no importance to love"?

4. Do you accept the conclusion?

The Invisible Speaker

In a poem in the third person voice, the author acts as narrator, often not identifying himself at all except as a tone of voice. When a poem is about a "she" or "a woman" or "he" or "the people in apartment 4-C" or "a sparrow," the author-speaker intrudes on the subjects as little as possible. His voice sets the tone. This choice gives the poet a more objective stance than he has with "I," "we," or "you." The invisible speaker is close to the recording and accumulating camera eye.

AN ARUNDEL TOMB

Side by side, their faces blurred,
The earl and countess lie in stone,
Their proper habits vaguely shown
As jointed armor, stiffened pleat,
And that faint hint of the absurd—   5
The little dogs under their feet.

Such plainness of the pre-baroque
Hardly involves the eye, until

It meets his left-hand gauntlet, still
Clasped empty in the other: and   10
One sees, with a sharp tender shock,
His hand withdrawn, holding her hand.

They would not think to lie so long.
Such faithfulness in effigy
Was just a detail friends would see: 15
A sculptor's sweet commissioned grace
Thrown off in helping to prolong
The Latin names around the base.

They would not guess how early in
Their supine stationary voyage   20
The air would change to soundless damage,
Turn the old tenantry away;
How soon succeeding eyes begin
To look, not read. Rigidly they

Persisted, linked, through lengths and breadths   25
Of time. Snow fell, undated. Light
Each summer thronged the glass. A bright
Litter of birdcalls strewed the same
Bone-riddled ground. And up the paths
The endless altered people came.   30

Washing at their identity.
Now, helpless in the hollow of
An unarmorial age, a trough
Of smoke in slow suspended skeins
Above their scrap of history,   35
Only an attitude remains:

Time has transfigured them into
Untruth. The stone fidelity
They hardly meant has come to be
Their final blazon, and to prove   40
Our almost-instinct almost true:
What will survive of us is love.

Philip Larkin, 1922–1985

"An Arundel Tomb" describes the stone tomb carvings of the earl and
countess of Arundel at their twelfth-century castle in Sussex, England.
The invisible speaker presents the sculptures to the reader. He directs

our looking rather formally—"One sees, with a sharp tender shock"—but with an observant eye. The speaker notices that the figures are holding hands. Through centuries of change, "undated" snow, and generations of birdsong, with thousands of people filing by to see them, they've lain there, hands joined, unchanging. The last two lines make a jump. From describing the characters in third person, the speaker shifts to a public voice. The shift suddenly includes *us*. Larkin moves from the particular earl and countess to a general idea about the survival of love. The medieval figures confirm *our* "almost-instinct." What if he'd said "and to prove / Our instinct true / What will survive of us is love"? But Larkin's conclusion is qualified; he carefully does not claim that our instinct *is* true.

Larkin's formal tone suits his description of the stone sculptures and the contemplative mood they arouse. The poem is addressed to any reader. Larkin maintains formality by the use of "one." If his speaker addressed "you," he'd hit a folksy, less dignified note. But this author does not break the objectivity built into "one" and his cool third-person descriptions of the earl and countess. Each choice he makes fits his philosophical conclusion.

Poems for Discussion

CORINNA'S GOING A-MAYING

Get up! get up for shame! the blooming morn
Upon her wings presents the god unshorn.
  See how Aurora[1] throws her fair
  Fresh-quilted colors through the air:
  Get up, sweet slug-a-bed, and see   5
  The dew bespangling herb and tree.
Each flower has wept and bowed toward the east
Above an hour since, yet you not dressed;
  Nay, not so much as out of bed?
  When all the birds have matins said,   10
  And sung their thankful hymns, 'tis sin,
  Nay, profanation to keep in,
Whenas a thousand virgins on this day
Spring, sooner than the lark, to fetch in May.

---

[1] *Aurora:* goddess of dawn.

Rise, and put on your foliage, and be seen   15
To come forth, like the springtime, fresh and green,
    And sweet as Flora.[2] Take no care
    For jewels for your gown or hair;
    Fear not; the leaves will strew
    Gems in abundance upon you;   20
Besides, the childhood of the day has kept,
Against you come, some orient[3] pearls unwept;
    Come and receive them while the light
    Hangs on the dew-locks of the night,
    And Titan[4] on the eastern hill   25
    Retires himself, or else stands still
Till you come forth. Wash, dress, be brief in praying:
Few beads are best when once we go a-Maying.

Come, my Corinna, come; and, coming mark
How each field turns a street, each street a park   30
    Made green and trimmed with trees; see how
    Devotion gives each house a bough
    Or branch: each porch, each door ere this,
    An ark, a tabernacle is.
Made up of whitethorn neatly interwove,   35
As if here were those cooler shades of love.
    Can such delights be in the street
    And open fields, and we not see 't?
    Come, we'll abroad; and let's obey
    The proclamation made for May,   40
And sin no more, as we have done, by staying:
But, my Corinna, come, let's go a-Maying.

There's not a budding boy or girl this day
But is got up and gone to bring in May;
    A deal of youth, ere this, is come   45
    Back, and with whitethorn laden home.
    Some have dispatched their cakes and cream
    Before that we have left to dream;
And some have wept, and wooed, and plighted troth,
And chose their priest, ere we can cast off sloth.   50
    Many a green-gown has been given,
    Many a kiss, both odd and even,
    Many a glance, too, has been sent
    From out the eye, love's firmament;
Many a jest told of the keys betraying   55
This night, and locks picked; yet we're not a-Maying.

[2] *Flora:* goddess of flowers.
[3] *orient:* eastern.
[4] *Titan:* the sun.

Come, let us go while we are in our prime,
And take the harmless folly of the time.
   We shall grow old apace, and die
   Before we know our liberty.   60
   Our life is short, and our days run
   As fast away as does the sun;
And, as a vapor or a drop of rain
Once lost, can ne'er be found again;
   So when or you or I are made   65
   A fable, song, or fleeting shade,
   All love, all liking, all delight
   Lies drowned with us in endless night.
Then while time serves, and we are but decaying,
Come, my Corinna, come, let's go a-Maying.   70

Robert Herrick, 1591–1674

from MACBETH

(Act V, scene v)

Tomorrow, and tomorrow, and tomorrow,
Creeps in this petty pace from day to day
To the last syllable of recorded time,
And all our yesterdays have lighted fools
The way to dusty death. Out, out, brief candle!   5
Life's but a walking shadow, a poor player
That struts and frets his hour upon the stage
And then is heard no more; it is a tale
Told by an idiot, full of sound and fury,
Signifying nothing.   10

William Shakespeare, 1564–1616

RESEMBLANCE

You passed me today in your ugly form.
It was almost you, with eyes fifteen years older
and a drunkard's nose
shining out of your face.

He plodded from the Greyhound station   5
down the sidewalk swinging a small dirty bag.
He probably came to meet a death;
he would be the brother who drifts in
for funerals and no one
knows quite what to say.   10

He headed for the telephone booth
in front of Grandmother's old white house.
Her ten children skated down
that deep chicken-run hall, dodging bats.
Four interchangable cubicles, enough for everyone,   15
opened into that hall which bristled,
bled with our scabby knees. We shouted
that space to life.

So you walk by in your ugly form
and I end missing my grandmother and the bats.   20
Students live there now, they've painted
LOVE on every sagging window, LOVE
in every purple shade and shape, and they
will not repeal a contrast so complete.

I watched you, mister, I know you well   25
and I'm the only person in this town
glad to see you.

Rena Williams, 1940–

YOU

Sometimes in our sleep we touch
The body of another woman
And we wake up
And we know the first nights
With summer visitors   5
In the three storied house of our childhood.
Whatever we remember,
The darkest hair being brushed
In front of the darkest mirror
In the darkest room.   10

Frank Stanford, 1948–1978

THE RIVER MERCHANT'S WIFE: A LETTER

While my hair was still cut straight across my forehead
I played about the front gate, pulling flowers.
You came by on bamboo stilts, playing horse,
You walked about my seat, playing with blue plums.
And we went on living in the village of Chokan: 5
Two small people, without dislike or suspicion.

At fourteen I married My Lord you.
I never laughed, being bashful.
Lowering my head, I looked at the wall.
Called to, a thousand times, I never looked back.   10

At fifteen I stopped scowling
I desired my dust to be mingled with yours
Forever and forever and forever.
Why should I climb the look out?

At sixteen you departed,   15
You went into far Ku-to-en, by the river of swirling eddies,
And you have been gone five months.
The monkeys make sorrowful noise overhead.

You dragged your feet when you went out.
By the gate now, the moss is grown, the different mosses,   20
Too deep to clear them away!
The leaves fall early this autumn, in wind.
The paired butterflies are already yellow with August
Over the grass in the West garden;
They hurt me. I grow older.   25
If you are coming down through the narrows of the river Kiang,
Please let me know beforehand,
And I will come out to meet you
                    As far as Cho-fu-Sa.

Ezra Pound, 1885–1972
(Adaptation of Chinese poem by Li Po, 701–762)

FOR A NEW CITIZEN OF THESE UNITED STATES

Forgive me for thinking I saw
the irregular postage stamp of death;
a black moth the size of my left
thumbnail is all I've trapped in the damask.
There is no need for alarm. And 5

there is no need for sadness, if
the rain at the window now reminds you
of nothing; not even of that
parlor, long like a nave, where cloud-shadow,
wing-shadow, where father-shadow 10
continually confused the light. In flight,
leaf-throng and, later, soldiers and
flags deepened those windows to submarine.

But you don't remember, I know,
so I won't mention that house where Chung hid, 15
Lin wizened, you languished, and Ming—
Ming hush-hushed us with small song. And since you
don't recall the missionary
bells chiming the hour, or those words whose sounds
alone exhaust the heart—*garden,* 20
heaven, amen—I'll mention none of it.

After all, it was just our life,
merely years in a book of years. It was
1960, and we stood with
the other families on a crowded 25
railroad platform. The trains came, then
the rains, and then we got separated.
And in the interval between
familiar faces, events occurred, which
one of us faithfully pencilled 30
in a day-book bound by a rubber band.

But birds, as you say, fly forward.
So I won't show you letters and the shawl
I've so meaninglessly preserved.
And I won't hum along, if you don't, when 35
our mothers sing *Nights in Shanghai.*
I won't, each Spring, each time I smell lilac,
recall my mother, patiently
stitching money inside my coat lining,

if you don't remember your mother   40
preparing for your own escape.

After all, it was only our
life, our life and its forgetting.

Li-Young Lee, 1957–

AN EPITAPH

Interred beneath this marble stone,
Lie sauntering Jack and idle Joan.
While rolling threescore years and one
Did round this globe their courses run,
If human things went ill or well,   5
If changing empires rose or fell,
The morning passed, the evening came,
And found this couple still the same.
They walked and ate, good folks—what then?
Why then they walked and ate again.   10
They soundly slept the night away;
They did just nothing all the day;
And having buried children four,
Would not take pains to try for more.
Nor sister either had, nor brother;   15
They seemed just tallied for each other.
   Their moral and economy
Most perfectly they made agree;
Each virtue kept its proper bound,
Nor trespassed on the other's ground.   20
Nor fame nor censure they regarded;
They neither punished nor rewarded.
He cared not what the footmen did;
Her maids she neither praised, nor chid;
So every servant took his course.   25
And bad at first, they all grew worse.
Slothful disorder filled his stable,
And sluttish plenty decked her table.
Their beer was strong; their wine was port;
Their meal was large; their grace was short.   30
They gave the poor the remnant-meat,
Just when it grew not fit to eat.
   They paid the church and parish rate,
And took, but read not the receipt;
For which they claimed their Sunday's due,   35

Of slumbering in an upper pew.
  No man's defects sought they to know;
So never made themselves a foe.
No man's good deeds did they commend;
So never raised themselves a friend.   40
Nor cherished they relations poor,
That might decrease their present store;
Nor barn nor house did they repair,
That might oblige their future heir.
  They neither added nor confounded;   45
They neither wanted nor abounded.
Each Christmas they accompts did clear,
And wound their bottom[1] round the year.
Nor tear nor smile did they employ
At news of public grief or joy.   50
When bells were rung, and bonfires made,
If asked they ne'er denied their aid:
Their jug was to the ringers carried,
Whoever either died or married.
Their billet[2] at the fire was found,   55
Whoever was deposed, or crowned.
  Nor good, nor bad, nor fools, nor wise;
They would not learn, nor could advise:
Without love, hatred, joy, or fear,
They led—a kind of—as it were: 60
Nor wished, nor cared, nor laughed, nor cried;
And so they lived; and so they died.

                Matthew Prior, 1664–1721

[1] *wound their bottom:* wound up their thread.
[2] *billet:* firewood.

MUSÉE DES BEAUX ARTS

About suffering they were never wrong,
The Old Masters: how well they understood
Its human position; how it takes place
While someone else is eating or opening a window or just
    walking dully along;
How, when the aged are reverently, passionately waiting   5
For the miraculous birth, there always must be
Children who did not specially want it to happen, skating
On a pond at the edge of the wood:
They never forgot

That even the dreadful martyrdom must run its course   10
Anyhow in a corner, some untidy spot
Where the dogs go on with their doggy life and the torturer's horse
Scratches its innocent behind on a tree.
In Brueghel's *Icarus*,[1] for instance: how everything turns away
Quite leisurely from the disaster; the ploughman may   15
Have heard the splash, the forsaken cry,
But for him it was not an important failure; the sun shone
As it had to on the white legs disappearing into the green
Water; and the expensive delicate ship that must have seen
Something amazing, a boy falling out of the sky,   20
Had somewhere to get to and sailed calmly on.

W. H. Auden, 1907–1973

[1] Brueghel's *Icarus*: In "Landscape with the Fall of Icarus," Brueghel shows everyday
life continuing without anyone noticing Icarus falling into the sea.

THE ANNIVERSARY

You raise the ax,
the block of wood screams in half,
while I lift the sack of flour
and carry it into the house.
I'm not afraid of the blade   5
you've just pointed at my head.
If I were dead, you could take the boy,
hunt, kiss gnats, instead of my moist lips.
Take it easy, squabs are roasting,
corn, still in husks, crackles,   10
as the boy dances around the table:
old guest at a wedding party for two sad-faced clowns,
who together, never won a round of anything but hard times.
Come in, sheets are clean,
fall down on me for one more year   15
and we can blast another hole in ourselves without a sound.

Ai, 1947–

NANI

Sitting at her table, she serves
the sopa de arroz[1] to me
instinctively, and I watch her,
the absolute *mamá*, and eat words
I might have had to say more   5
out of embarrassment. To speak,
now-foreign words I used to speak,
too, dribble down her mouth as she serves
me albondigas.[2] No more
than a third are easy to me.   10
By the stove she does something with words
and looks at me only with her
back. I am full. I tell her
I taste the mint, and watch her speak
smiles at the stove. All my words   15
make her smile. Nani never serves
herself, she only watches me
with her skin, her hair. I ask for more.

I watch the *mamá* warming more
tortillas for me. I watch her   20
fingers in the flame for me.
Near her mouth, I see a wrinkle speak
of a man whose body serves
the ants like she serves me, then more words
from more wrinkles about children, words   25
about this and that, flowing more
easily from these other mouths. Each serves
as a tremendous string around her,
holding her together. They speak
Nani was this and that to me   30
and I wonder just how much of me
will die with her, what were the words
I could have been, was. Her insides speak
through a hundred wrinkles, now, more
than she can bear, steel around her,   35
shouting, then. What is this thing she serves?

[1] *sopa de arroz:* rice soup.
[2] *albondigas:* meatballs.

She asks me if I want more.
I own no words to stop her.
Even before I speak, she serves.

Alberto Ríos, 1953–

FOR DE LAWD

people say they have a hard time
understanding how I
go on about my business
playing my Ray Charles
hollering at the kids—   5
seem like my Afro
cut off in some old image
would show I got a long memory
and I come from a line
of black and going on women   10
who got used to making it through murdered sons
and who grief kept on pushing
who fried chicken
ironed
swept off the back steps   15
who grief kept
for their still alive sons
for their sons coming
for their sons gone
just pushing   20
in the inner city
or
like we call it
home
we think a lot about uptown   25
and the silent nights
and the houses straight as
dead men
and the pastel lights
and we hang on to our no place   30
happy to be alive
and in the inner city
or
like we call it
home   35

Lucille Clifton, 1936–

SNOW IN THE SUBURBS

Every branch big with it,
Bent every twig with it;
Every fork like a white web-foot;
Every street and pavement mute:
Some flakes have lost their way, and grope back upward, when   5
Meeting those meandering down they turn and descend again,
The palings are glued together like a wall,
And there is no waft of wind with the fleecy fall.

A sparrow enters the tree
Whereon immediately   10
A snow-lump thrice his own slight size
Descends on him and showers his head and eyes.
And overturns him,
And near inurns him,
And lights on a nether twig, when its brush   15
Starts off a volley of other lodging lumps with a rush.

The steps are a blanched slope,
Up which, with feeble hope,
A black cat comes, wide-eyed and thin;
And we take him in.   20

Thomas Hardy, 1840–1928

PROTOCOLS

(Birkenau, Odessa[1]; the children speak alternately.)

We went there on the train. *They had big barges that they towed,*
We stood up, there were so many I was squashed.
There was a smoke-stack, then they made me wash.
It was a factory, I think. *My mother held me up*
And I could see the ship that made the smoke.   5

When I was tired my mother carried me.
She said, "Don't be afraid." But I was only tired.
Where we went there is no more Odessa.
They had water in a pipe—like rain, but hot;
The water there is deeper than the world   10

---

[1] concentration camps

And I was tired and fell in in my sleep
And the water drank me. That is what I think.
And I said to my mother, "Now I'm washed and dried,"
My mother hugged me, and it smelled like hay.
And that is how you die. And that is how you die.   15

Randall Jarrell, 1914–1965

TO THE NIGHTINGALE

Exert thy voice, sweet harbinger of spring!
    This moment is thy time to sing,
    This moment I attend to praise,
And set my numbers to thy lays.
    Free as thine shall be my song,   5
    As thy music, short or long.
Poets, wild as thee, were born,
    Pleasing best when unconfined,
    When to please is least designed,
Soothing but their cares to rest;   10
    Cares do still their thoughts molest,
    And still the unhappy poet's breast,
Like thine, when best he sings, is placed against a thorn.
    She begins. Let all be still!
      Muse, thy promise now fulfil!   15
Sweet, oh sweet! still sweeter yet!
Can thy words such accents fit,
    Canst thou syllables refine,
    Melt a sense that shall retain
Still some spirit of the brain,   20
Till with sounds like these it join?
    'Twill not be! then change thy note,
    Let division shake thy throat.
Hark! division now she tries,
Yet as far the Muse outflies.   25
    Cease then, prithee, cease thy tune!
    Trifler, wilt thou sing till June!
Till thy business all lies waste,
And the time of building's past?
    Thus we poets that have speech,   30
Unlike what thy forests teach,
    If a fluent vein be shown
    That's transcendent to our own,
Criticize, reform, or preach,
Or censure what we cannot reach.   35

Anne Finch, Countess of Winchilsea, 1661–1720

INVITING A FRIEND TO SUPPER

Tonight, grave sir, both my poor house and I
   Do equally desire your company;
Not that we think us worthy such a guest,
   But that your worth will dignify our feast
With those that come, whose grace may make that seem   5
   Something, which else could hope for no esteem.
It is the fair acceptance, sir, creates
   The entertainment perfect, not the cates.[1]
Yet shall you have, to rectify your palate,
   An olive, capers, or some better salad   10
Ushering the mutton; with a short-legged hen,
   If we can get her, full of eggs, and then
Lemons, and wine for sauce; to these, a coney[2]
   Is not to be despaired of, for our money;
And, though fowl now be scarce, yet there are clerks,   15
   The sky not falling, think we may have larks.
I'll tell you of more, and lie, so you will come:
   Of partridge, pheasant, woodcock, of which some
May yet be there, and godwit, if we can:
   Knat, rail, and ruff[3] too. Howsoe'r, my man   20
Shall read a piece of Virgil, Tacitus,
   Livy, or of some better book to us,
Of which we'll speak our minds, amidst our meat;
   And I'll profess no verses to repeat.
To this, if aught appear which I not know of,   25
   That will the pastry, not my paper, show of.
Digestive cheese and fruit there sure will be;
   But that which most doth take my Muse and me,
Is a pure cup of rich Canary wine,
   Which is the Mermaid's[4] now, but shall be mine;   30
Of which had Horace,[5] or Anacreon[6] tasted,
   Their lives, as do their lines, till now had lasted.
Tobacco, nectar, or the Thespian spring,
   Are all but Luther's beer to this I sing.
Of this we will sup free, but moderately,   35
   And we will have no Pooley, or Parrot[7] by,
Nor shall our cups make any guilty men;

[1] *cates:* food.
[2] *coney:* rabbit.
[3] *godwit . . . knat . . . rail . . . ruff:* game birds considered delicacies in Jonson's time.
[4] *Mermaid:* a famous London pub and literary meeting place.
[5] *Horace* (65–8 B.C.): Roman poet and satirist.
[6] *Anacreon* (572–488 B.C.): Greek poet.
[7] *Pooley . . . Parrot:* spies.

But, at our parting we will be as when
We innocently met. No simple word
   That shall be uttered at our mirthful board,   40
Shall make us sad next morning or affright
   The liberty that we'll enjoy tonight.

Ben Jonson, 1573–1637

RIDE

It's not my world, I grant, but I made it.
It's not my ranch, lean oak, buzzard crow,
Not my fryers, mixmasters, well-garden.
And now it's down the road and I made it.

It's not your rackety car but you drive it.
It's not your four-door, top-speed, white-wall tires,
Not our state, not even, I guess, our nation,
But now it's down the road, and we're in it.

Josephine Miles, 1911–1985

5

Rhyme and Repetition

All deep things are Song. It seems somehow the very central essence of us, Song; as if all the rest were but wrappages and hulls! . . . See deep enough, and you see musically; the heart of Nature being *everywhere music, if you can only reach it.*

Thomas Carlyle

We take rhyme and repetition so much for granted in poetry that it seems odd even to question why they're used. The common property of both is recurrence of sound. Both give pleasure. We like sounds that strike and chime and slide by each other. We respond to the here-it-comes-again refrain.

In the Cockney section of London, people are so fond of rhyme that they incorporate it into their daily speech. A student remembers being carried up to bed by her father who said, "Up those apples," a phrase which makes perfect sense to Cockneys, who know that their rhyme for stairs is "apples and pears," gradually shortened to "apples." "I've got to go home to my trouble and strife," "Call the hot potato," "Pass the Aristotle," "Answer the dog and bone," and "I'm out of bees and honey" are all clear to those in the know: *wife, waiter, bottle, phone*, and *money* are the less colorful translations. Besides being fun, rhyming slang (as it's called) works as a disguise. Those who don't know can't understand. Guards from the Hampstead neighborhood, for instance, can't understand Cockney prisoners in London jails.

In America we have the black tradition of "rapping" (or "toasting," as it used to be called), the roots of which go back to African creation myths, initiation rites, and songs. As in rhyming slang, the rhyming adds get-up-and-go. It provokes improvisation. Certain words or phrases repeat, with humor or irony gathering force as the rap goes on. Repeating and rhyming also help stamp something in memory. In cultures without written language, songs and chants passed on history and values. Repetition connects with the cycles of weather and crops in this Navajo Indian song:

SONGS IN THE GARDEN OF THE HOUSE GOD

Now in the east
the white bean
& the great corn-plant
are tied with white lightning.
Listen! rain's drawing near!
The voice of the bluebird is heard.   5

     Now in the east
     the white bean
     & the great squash
     are tied with the rainbow.   10
     Listen! the rain's drawing near!
     The voice of the bluebird is heard.

From the top of the great corn-plant the water foams, I hear it.
Around the roots the water foams, I hear it.
Around the roots of the plant it foams, I hear it.   15
From their tops the water foams, I hear it.

     The corn grows up. The waters of the dark clouds drop, drop.
     The rain comes down. The waters from the corn leaves drop, drop.
     The rain comes down. The waters from the plants drop, drop.
     The corns grows up. The waters of the dark mists drop, drop.   20

     Shall I cull this fruit of the great corn-plant?
Shall you break it?
     Shall I break it?
Shall I break it?
     Shall you break it?   25
Shall I?
     Shall you?
Shall I cull this fruit of the great squash vine?
     Shall you pick it up?
Shall I pick it up?   30
     Shall I pick it up?
Shall you pick it up?
     Shall I?
Shall you?

     Speech and song uses of rhyme and repetition have everything to do with literary uses. All make rhymes and repeat words for surprise, for movement, for memory, for emphasis. Hopkins said, "Read with your ears,'' and we do. Along with word choice and sound patterns, the sound effects of rhyme and repetition help create the rhythm of the poem. The recurrence of a sound is itself a music. Like the chorus in a song, a refrain or rhyming pattern, once set up, rewards our antici-pation.

Square-dance callers improvise their calls, sending the dancers into various patterns but always returning them to the circle. Elza White used this call at dances in Texas in the 1880s:

> Salute your partner! Let her go!
> Balance all and do-si-do!
> Swing your gal, and all run away!
> Right and left, and gents sashay!
> Gents to the right and swing or cheat!
> On to the next gal and repeat!
> Balance to the next and don't be shy!
> Swing your partner and swing her high!
> Bunch the gals and circle around!
> Whack your feet until they sound!
> Form a basket! Break away!
> Swing and kiss and all git gay!
> All gents to the left and balance all!
> Lift your hoofs and let 'em fall!
> Swing your opp'sites! Swing again!
> Kiss the sage-hens if you can!
> Back to your partners, do-si-do!
> Gents salute your little sweets!
> Hitch up and promenade to your seats!

In "The Wheel," Wendell Berry draws us close to a deep unity of movement in dance. The title evokes the circular movement of the dance and also suggests the turning of the world, the clock, the wheel of fortune.

THE WHEEL

> At the first strokes of the fiddle bow
> the dancers rise from their seats.
> The dance begins to shape itself
> in the crowd, as couples join,
> and couples join couples, their movement   5
> together lightening their feet.

> They move in the ancient circle
> of the dance. The dance and the song
> call each other into being. Soon
> they are one—rapt in a single   10
> rapture, so that even the night
> has its clarity, and time
> is the wheel that brings it round.
> In this rapture the dead return.
> Sorrow is gone from them.   15
> They are light. They step
> into the steps of the living
> and turn with them in the dance
> in the sweet enclosure
> of the song, and timeless   20
> is the wheel that brings it round.

Wendell Berry, 1934–

Berry's repetition of single words keeps them in motion. The rhythm also comes from alliteration and consonance, especially the high incidence of -*s* sounds. Only five lines end with a period; the others run over to the next line. This sound flow adds to the endless circular motions of the dance. By implication, do you think Berry means that other formal patterns, perhaps the patterns in poetry, are also timeless? How do the dead "step / into the steps of the living"?

As in a square dance, the poem uses recurrence as an organizing principle. The dancers end in a circle; they end where they began—but meanwhile they have danced. Many poems begin and end with the same line. The ending line has accumulated meanings in the process; the reader comes full circle also. The patterns of rhymes resolve; nothing is left hanging over without its partnering rhyme. Rhyme and repetition unify the structure of the poem. Rhyming words resemble each other; repeating words and phrases, lines, or images are identical, though in succeeding contexts they often pick up different meanings and tones.

Reiteration gives balance and harmony. Along with the pleasure of hearing sounds echo, other subtle and distinct effects accrue through use of rhyme and repetition.

Rhyme

"Doesn't a poem have to rhyme?" students often ask. The question reveals the strong inheritance of traditional poetry. Most, though not all, English poetry between the twelfth and twentieth centuries rhymed. The earliest poetry was alliterative. As English poets began to hear the rhymed lyrics of the Provençal troubadors drift across the channel, rhyme slowly began to prevail over alliteration as a formal device. By now, rhyme is an *option*. Most poets use it on occasion but not as a regular practice. Why? Why not always use this tool that has pleased poets and readers for so many generations? The answer is part of the history of poetry, of course. There always was a parallel nonrhyming tradition in English poetry. In *Observations in the Art of English Poesie*, written in 1692, Thomas Campion said rhyme was "vulgar, unartificial, easy, rude, barbarous, shifting, sliding, and fat." Later, John Milton maintained that rhyme "is the invention of a barbarous Age, to set off wretched matter and lame meter." Rhyme, however, remained the strongest poetic convention until the twentieth century, when, with the breakup of other traditions, it became less common.

That World War I brought on a fragmentation of values and the breakdown of the coherent society in Western Europe is a concept most of us are familiar with. Certainly all the arts reflect this. But if the disharmony of the age is responsible for changes in poetry, that is no negative judgment. Change in art is healthy. Poets began to focus on imagery instead of rhyme or other poetic conventions. As emphasis shifted away from formal devices, it shifted *to* the sound of the natural speaking voice or to the rhythm of breath; it shifted *to* new uses and arrangements of the line. These changes too are not permanent; the only thing permanent in art is change. T. S. Eliot thought "excessive devotion to rhyme has thickened the modern ear" and hoped the "shift away from rhyme might be a liberation *of* rhyme." "Freed from its exacting task. . . ," he wrote, "it could be applied with greater effect where most needed."

Kinds of Rhyme

Rhyme is one of the strongest elements in the craft of poetry. It is simple—everyone knows what a rhyme is—but its effects are quite mysterious. At times it may seem merely ornamental, but a quick substitution of unrhyming synonyms shows how much intricate power the rhymes add to the meaning. Different kinds of rhymes cause different effects.

The most common rhymes are **pure rhymes**. In these, the initial sounds of the words differ and the rest of the sound is identical: hill/

still, pit/lit, form/storm, wrong/song. If you want a pure rhyme for *bell*, you can run through the alphabet: cell, dell, fell, hell, and so on. Pure rhymes are bold. They call attention to themselves by their clear likeness.

Words that almost rhyme are **slant rhymes**, also called **off rhymes** or **half rhymes**. Here, the sounds are closely related but not identical: fear/care, face/dress, gone/moan, dizzy/easy. In a poem with pure rhymes, we catch on to the sound quickly, wait for the rhyming sounds to recur. With slant rhymes, we hear the corresponding sounds, but they're less obviously matched than pure rhymes. Pure rhymes have the satisfying sound of a lock clicking shut; the effect of slant rhyming is more subtle.

Emily Dickinson was a great inventor of slant rhymes. Her poems are often written with a metronome regularity. Because of this, the reader expects to hear rhyming that is just as obvious. Obvious, Dickinson is not. Her poetry is totally unpredictable. You never know where her next line will take you. In almost every poem there's at least one strange word that makes you stare and question. Her poems are often cryptic, as was the poet herself. In a letter about her rhymes, she said, "I need the little bells to cool me." Her use of slant rhyme repeatedly emphasizes the surprise and complexity of her subject. Her favored punctuation mark is the dash, which often replaces a comma or period. Read the dash as she intended it—as a charged pause in timing.

1052

> I never saw a Moor—
> I never saw the Sea—
> Yet know I how the Heather looks
> And what a Billow be.
>
> I never spoke with God
> Nor visited in Heaven—
> Yet certain am I of the spot
> As if the Checks were given—

Emily Dickinson, 1830–1886

Rhymes at the ends of lines are called **end rhymes**. They link the line ends together by echoing sounds. If a word within the line rhymes with the end rhyme, or with another word within the line, this is called

internal rhyme. In the example below, internal rhyme tightens the sounds' unity. Also the end rhymes hit each other with force not only because they are pure but because their meanings collide.

> In autumn, the *mild* hunter brings down the *wild*
> *Boar*, the slow death *roar* sounds to the *child*

End rhymes with an accented last syllable (rĕ préss/uñ dréss) or a single syllable (gó/nó) are called **rising rhymes**. Those ending with an unaccented last syllable (párt lў/smárt lў) are **falling rhymes**. Formerly, these were dubbed "masculine" (strong, stressed ending) and "feminine" (soft, unstressed ending) but this terminology is outdated. A rising rhyme or falling rhyme indicates whether the line ends emphatically or softly.

Poets go to great lengths to make rhyming patterns. Consequently you will encounter several kinds of rhyme. The list below introduces the most pleasing and efficacious:

apocopated rhyme: a cut-off rhyme. The last syllable of one of the rhymes is missing: gain/painless, hot/potted, lean/cleaner.

linked rhyme: the first syllable of a line echoes the last syllable of the previous line. This has the same effect as internal rhyme:

> Night weighs down the roof*top*
> *stops* the flashlight of a scared *cop*.

triple rhyme: words of three rhyming syllables with the first syllable of each as the accented one. "Snow in the Suburbs" (p. 185) opens with a triple rhyme: "Every branch big with it / Bent every twig with it." Triples are often used for comic effect: higgledy/piggledy, Beelzebub/syllabub. Stevie Smith, however, uses triple rhyme (plus internal rhyme) somberly:

> For underneath the superscription lurked I knew
> With pulse quickening and the blood thickening
> For fear in every vein the deadly strychnine.

> from *"Death Came To Me"*

head rhyme: not really a rhyme but another name for **alliteration** (repetition of consonant sounds at the beginning of a word):

> Western *w*ind, *w*hen *w*ill thou blow?

eye rhyme: words that look similar though they are pronounced differently: ties/eternities, cough/rough, care/caress, wind/find.

unpatterned rhyme: randomly placed rhyming words. Unpatterned rhyme gives *some* unity and a sense of linguistic spontaneity. In "To a Chameleon," Marianne Moore matches her rhyming craft to her changeable subject:

> Hid by the august foliage and fruit
>   of the grape-vine
> twine
>   your anatomy
>   round the pruned and polished stem,   5
>   Chameleon.
>   Fire laid upon
>   an emerald as long as
>   the Dark King's massy
>   one,   10
> could not snap the spectrum up for food
>   as you have done.

identical rhyme: not rhyme at all but a repetition of the *same* word where you would expect the next rhyming word. The word is re-stated, therefore reemphasized.

ENVOY

(Vitae summa brevis spem nos vetat incohare longam)[1]

> They are not long, the weeping and the laughter,
>   Love and desire and hate;
> I think they have no portion in us after
>   We pass the gate.
>
> They are not long, the days of wine and roses:
>   Out of a misty dream
> Our path emerges for a while, then closes
>   Within a dream.

Ernest Dowson, 1867–1900

---

[1] *Vitae . . . longam:* Life's brevity prevents us from lengthy aspiration.

homonyms: not strictly rhymes but another unifying element like eye rhymes. Though the spelling differs, the same sound is repeated: time/thyme, sail/sale, praise/preys, pear/pair, reign/rain.

Rhyme Scheme

The **rhyme scheme** is the pattern of rhyme in an entire poem. To "read" the rhyme scheme give each new rhyme, as it appears, a letter. As a sound repeats, label it with the same letter as the word it rhymes with.

INFANT SORROW

My mother groaned, my father wept,	*a*
Into the dangerous world I leapt;	*a*
Helpless, naked, piping loud,	*b*
Like a fiend hid in a cloud.	*b*
Struggling in my father's hands,	*c*
Striving against my swaddling-bands,	*c*
Bound and weary, I thought best	*d*
To sulk upon my mother's breast.	*d*

William Blake, 1757–1828

Blake's rhyme scheme is aabb ccdd. If he had continued the poem, the pattern he set up would continue. "Infant Sorrow" is in two *stanzas*. In chapter 8 we will look in detail at different kinds of stanzas. For the moment, keep in mind that a stanza is a basic unit of thought and rhythm within a poem. The first stanza in a traditional poem establishes the rhythm, including the number of lines and the rhyme scheme which will be repeated in successive stanzas.

Occasionally you'll find a dangling rhyme or a disrupted rhyme scheme. Like a sudden shift in diction, this should alert you to something the poet wants you to notice. A broken-off, disjunctive, or incomplete rhyme will parallel a glitch or reversal in the poem's development.

Moon/June Rhymes

If rhyme casts a spell by binding sounds together, the spell should be a good one. No device can destroy a poem quicker than rhymes that clunk lifelessly down the right-hand edge of the poem. As an immediate test for hackneyed rhymes, see if you can predict the word coming up. If love/dove, sorrow/tomorrow, breath/death, moon/soon/June, true/blue, or pain/rain crop up, you know the poet got lazy and reached into the "poetry grab-bag" instead of working harder to sharpen the word choice. If the writer was satisfied with lazy rhymes, chances are the poem will be trite and imprecise. In such a poem, the rhyming word could be any number of choices:

> Seashell, seashell, what do you know?
> Tell your tale while the tide is [   ].
> Were you washed on a beach of pink.
> Where white caps sparkle and [   ].
> Did you witness a pirate's death
> Or swirl fast in a whale's deep [   ]
> *and so on*

The other hazard of rhyme is that a steady adherence to a rhyme scheme often forces extra, inappropriate words into the poem in order to fit the plan. Or it causes oddly twisted syntax, as in these lines about Lake Lemen:

> Lemen's is fair; but think not I forsake
> the sweet remembrance of a dearer shore:
> Sad havoc time must with my memory make,
> Ere *that* or *thou* can fade these eyes before;
>
> *George Gordon, Lord Byron*

Three of the four lines turn normal phrasing around. The last line has been so wrenched to find a rhyme for "shore" that it hardly makes sense.

Rhyme and Meaning

Good rhyme works with meaning. In this little stanza from "Upon Julia's Clothes," Robert Herrick's sounds are part of what he's saying:

> Whenas in silks my Julia goes,
> Then, then, methinks, how sweetly flows
> that liquefaction of her clothes.

Goes, flows, and *clothes* cohere closely. Further, they all end in *s*. Herrick uses four other *s* sounds in the stanza, all mimicking the swishing of Julia's silks. The sounds are mutually supportive, each enhancing the other. In contrast, the following poem makes rhyme work with meaning in an opposite way:

TWO IN AUGUST

Two that could not have lived their single lives
As can some husbands and wives
Did something strange: they tensed their vocal cords
And attacked each other with silences and words
Like catapulted stones and arrowed knives.   5

Dawn was not yet; night is for loving or sleeping,
Sweet dreams or safekeeping;
Yet he of the wide brows that were used to laurel
And she, the famed for gentleness, must quarrel.
Furious both of them, and scared, and weeping.   10

How sleepers groan, twitch, wake to such a mood
Is not well understood,
Nor why two entities grown almost one
Should rend and murder trying to get undone,
With individual tigers in their blood.   15

She in terror fled from the marriage chamber
Circuiting the dark rooms like a string of amber
Round and round and back,
And would not light one lamp against the black,
And heard the clock that clanged: Remember, Remember.   20

And he must tread barefooted the dim lawn,
Soon he was up and gone;
High in the trees and night-mastered birds were crying
With fear upon their tongues, no singing nor flying
Which are their lovely attitudes by dawn.   25

Whether those bird-cries were of heaven or hell
There is no way to tell;
In the long ditch of darkness the man walked
Under the hackberry trees where the birds talked
With words too sad and strange to syllable.   30

John Crowe Ransom, 1888–1974

"Two in August" concerns two warring people who are married. Ransom chooses rhymes that also rub uncomfortably against their mates. The rhyme scheme in each stanza is aabba. Like the two married people, the rhymes are linked in a formal arrangement. Notice the rhyming groups: lives/wives/knives;   one/undone;   mood/understood/blood; sleeping/safekeeping/weeping. How do these rhymes amplify the mood of the poem? One rhyme is abrasive in meaning to its partner, as in *sleeping* and *weeping, wives* and *knives*. The rhymes' simultaneous opposition in meaning and likeness in sound add drama and tension. This is unlike the Herrick stanza, where the rhyme is a force for harmony.

As you read rhymed poems, evaluate *how* the rhyme works. Is it a force for harmony, a reiteration of meaning? Or is it destabilizing, creating uncertainty, taking back with one hand what it gives with the other?

NOW WINTER NIGHTS ENLARGE

Now winter nights enlarge
　The number of their hours;
And clouds their storms discharge
　Upon the airy towers.
Let now the chimneys blaze　　　　　　　　　　　　　5
　And cups o'erflow with wine,
Let well-tuned words amaze
　With harmony divine.
Now yellow waxen lights
　Shall wait on honey love　　　　　　　　　　　　　10
While youthful revels, masques, and courtly sights
　Sleep's leaden spells remove.

This time doth well dispense
　With lover's long discourse;
Much speech hath some defense,　　　　　　　　　　　15
　Though beauty no remorse.
All do not all things well;
　Some measures comely tread,
Some knotted riddles tell,
　Some poems smoothly read.　　　　　　　　　　　　20

The summer hath his joys,
    And winter his delights;
Though love and all his pleasures are but toys,
    They shorten tedious nights.

Thomas Campion, 1567–1620

EXERCISES

1. The same Campion who complained about rhyme (page 193) was a master at it himself. To realize the precision and economy of his rhyming words, try rewriting this poem, substituting synonymous nonrhyming words for his.

2. One common rhyme scheme is ababbcc. It's called **rhyme royal** and first was used in English by Chaucer. Two effects happen in the seven lines. The sounds are staggered (abab) in the first lines, then closely linked in the last part of the stanza. Try your hand at a stanza in this rhyme scheme.

3. Look at John Webster's rhymes in "Hark, Now Everything Is Still" and Ransom's in "Two in August" (page 199). How do Webster's rhymes differ from Ransom's in the way they work with meaning?

HARK, NOW EVERYTHING IS STILL

Hark, now everything is still;
The screech owl and the whistler shrill
Call upon our dame aloud,
And bid her quickly don her shroud.
Much you had of land and rent;   5
Your length in clay's now competent.
A long war disturbed your mind;
Here your perfect peace is signed.
Of what is 't fools make such vain keeping?
Sin their conception, their birth weeping,   10
Their life a general mist of error,
Their death a hideous storm of terror.
Strew your hair with powders sweet,

Don clean linen, bathe your feet,
And, the foul fiend more to check,   15
A crucifix let bless your neck.
'Tis now full tide, 'tween night and day,
End your groan and come away.

John Webster, 1580–1625

Poems for Discussion

SONG

Go and catch a falling star,
  Get with child a mandrake root,[1]
Tell me where all past years are,
  Or who cleft the Devil's foot,
Teach me to hear mermaids singing,   5
Or to keep off envy's stinging,
        And find
        What wind
Serves to advance an honest mind.

If thou beest born to strange sights,   10
  Things invisible to see,
Ride ten thousand days and nights,
  Till age snow white hairs on thee.
Thou, when thou return'st, wilt tell me
All strange wonders that befell thee,   15
        And swear
        Nowhere
Lives a woman true, and fair.

If thou find'st one, let me know,
  Such a pilgrimage were sweet;   20
Yet do not, I would not go,
  Though at next door we might meet;
Though she were true when you met her,
And last till you write your letter,
        Yet she   25
        Will be
False, ere I come, to two, or three.

John Donne, 1572–1631

---

[1] *Mandrake root:* The forked root of the mandragora plant was associated with fertility.
It was said to shriek when pulled out of the ground. Its shape resembled a human form.

ON HER LOVING TWO EQUALLY

I

How strong does my passion flow,
Divided equally twixt two?
Damon had ne'er subdued my heart
Had not Alexis took his part;
Nor could Alexis powerful prove,   5
Without my Damon's aid, to gain my love.

II

When my Alexis present is,
Then I for Damon sigh and mourn;
But when Alexis I do miss,
Damon gains nothing but my scorn.   10
But if it chance they both are by,
For both alike I languish, sigh, and die.

III

Cure then, thou mighty wingéd god,
This restless fever in my blood;
One golden-pointed dart take back: 15
But which, O Cupid, wilt thou take?
If Damon's, all my hopes are crossed;
Or that of my Alexis, I am lost.

Aphra Behn, 1640–1689

MARRIAGE

No more alone sleeping, no more alone waking,
    Thy dreams divided, thy prayers in twain;
Thy merry sisters to-night forsaking,
    Never shall we see thee, maiden, again.

Never shall we see thee, thine eyes glancing,   5
    Flashing with laughter and wild in glee,
Under the mistletoe kissing and dancing,
        Wantonly free.

> There shall come a matron walking sedately,
>   Low-voiced, gentle, wise in reply.   10
> Tell me, O tell me, can I love her greatly?
>   All for her sake must the maiden die!

Mary Elizabeth Coleridge, 1861–1907

AN ANCIENT GESTURE

I thought, as I wiped my eyes on the corner of my apron:
Penelope[1] did this too.
And more than once: you can't keep weaving all day
And undoing it all through the night;
Your arms get tired, and the back of your neck gets tight;   5
And along towards morning, when you think it will never be light
And your husband has been gone, and you don't know where, for years,
Suddenly you burst into tears;
There is simply nothing else to do.

And I thought as I wiped my eyes on the corner of my apron: 10
This is an ancient gesture, authentic, antique,
In the very best tradition, classic, Greek;
Ulysses did this too.
But only as a gesture,—a gesture which implied
To the assembled throng that he was much too moved to speak.   15
He learned it from Penelope . . .
Penelope, who really cried.

Edna St. Vincent Millay, 1892–1950

[1] *Penelope:* the wife of Odysseus in Homer's *Odyssey*. While she waited for him to
return from the Trojan Wars, she wove all day. Since her suitors expected her to
remarry when the weaving was done, she unwove her work each night.

THE SONG OF ABSINTHE[1] GRANNY

Among some hills there dwelt in parody
A young woman; me.
I was that gone with child
That before I knew it I had three
And they hung whining and twisting.   5
Why I wasn't more than thirty-nine

[1] *Absinthe:* a liqueur made from wormwood.

And sparse as a runt fruit tree.
Three pips that plagued the life out of me.
Ah me. It wore me down,
The grubs, the grubbing.   10
We were two inches thick in dust
For lack of scrubbing.
Diapers and panty-shirts and yolk of eggs.
One day in the mirror I saw my stringy legs
And I looked around   15
And saw string on the floor,
And string on the chair
And heads like wasps' nests
Full of stringy hair.
"Well," I said, "if you have string, knit.   20
Knit something, don't just sit."
We had the orchard drops,
But they didn't keep.
The milk came in bottles
It came until the bottles were that deep   25
We fell over the bottles.
The milk dried on the floor.
"Drink it up," cried their papa,
And they all began to roar, "More!"
Well, time went on,   30
Not a bone that wasn't frayed.
Every chit was knicked and bit,
And nothing was paid.
We had the dog spayed.
"It looks like a lifetime,"   35
Their papa said.
"It's a good life, it's a good wife,
It's a good bed."
So I got the rifle out
To shoot him through the head.   40
But he went on smiling and sitting
And I looked around for a piece of string
To do some knitting.
Then I picked at the tiling
And the house fell down.   45
"Now you've done it," he said.
"I'm going to town.
Get them up out of there,
Put them to bed."
"I'm afraid to look," I whimpered,   50
"They might be dead."
"We're here, mama, under the shed."
Well, the winters wore on.
We had cats that hung around.

When I fed them they scratched.   55
How the little nippers loved them.
Cats and brats.
I couldn't see for my head was thatched
But they kept coming in when the door unlatched.
"I'll shave my head," I promised,   60
"I'll clip my mop.
This caterwauling has got to stop."
Well, all that's finished,
It's all been done.
Those were high kick summers,   65
It was bald galled fun.
Now the daft time's over
And the string is spun.
I'm all alone
To cull and be furry.   70
Not an extra page in the spanking story.
The wet britches dried
And the teeth came in.
The last one cried
And no new began.   75
Those were long hot summers,
Now the sun won't tarry.
My birds have flocked,
And I'm old and wary.
I'm old and worn and a cunning sipper,   80
And I'll outlive every little nipper.
And with what's left I'm chary,
And with what's left I'm chary.

Ruth Stone, 1915–

MAN AND WIFE

Tamed by *Miltown*,[1] we lie on Mother's bed;
the rising sun in war paint dyes us red;
in broad daylight her gilded bed-posts shine,
abandoned, almost Dionysian.
At last the trees are green on Marlborough Street,   5
blossoms on our magnolia ignite
the morning with their murderous five days' white.
All night I've held your hand,
as if you had

---

[1] *Miltown:* tranquilizers.

a fourth time faced the kingdom of the mad—   10
its hackneyed speech, its homicidal eye—
and dragged me home alive. . . . Oh my *Petite*,
clearest of all God's creatures, still all air and nerve:
you were in your twenties, and I,
once hand on glass   15
and heart in mouth,
outdrank the Rahvs in the heat
of Greenwich Village, fainting at your feet—
too boiled and shy
and poker-faced to make a pass,   20
while the shrill verve
of your invective scorched the traditional South.

Now twelve years later, you turn your back.
Sleepless, you hold
your pillow to your hollows like a child;   25
your old-fashioned tirade—
loving, rapid, merciless—
breaks like the Atlantic Ocean on my head.

Robert Lowell, 1917–1977

TO HER AGAINE, SHE BURNING IN A FEAVER

Now she burnes as well as I,
Yet my heat can never dye;
She burnes that never knew desire,
She that was yce, she now is fire,
Shee whose cold heart, chaste thoughts did arme   5
So, as Love flames could never warme
The frozen bosome where it dwelt,
She burnes, and all her beauties melt;
She burnes, and cryes, Loves fires are milde,
Feavers are Gods, and He's a childe.   10
Love; let her know the difference
Twixt the heat of soule, and sence.
Touch her with thy flames divine,
So shalt thou quench her fire, and mine.

Thomas Carew, 1595–1640

UPON A SPIDER CATCHING A FLY

Thou sorrow, venom elf:
  Is this thy play,
To spin a web out of thyself
  To catch a fly?
    For why?   5

I saw a pettish wasp
  Fall foul therein,
Whom yet thy whorl-pins did not clasp
  Lest he should fling
    His sting.   10

But as afraid, remote
  Didst stand hereat
And with thy little fingers stroke
  And gently tap
    His back.   15

Thus gently him didst treat
  Lest he should pet,
And in a froppish, waspish heat
  Should greatly fret
    Thy net.   20

Whereas the silly fly,
  Caught by its leg
Thou by the throat tookst hastily
  And hind the head
    Bite dead.   25

This goes to pot, that not
  Nature doth call.
Strive not above what strength hath got
  Lest in the brawl
    Thou fall.   30

This fray seems thus to us.
  Hell's spider gets
His entrails spun to whip-cords thus,
  And wove to nets.
    And sets.   35

To tangle Adam's race
    In's strategems
To their destructions, spoiled, made base
    By venom things,
        Damned sins.   40

But mighty, gracious Lord
    Communicate
Thy grace to break the cord, afford
    Us glory's gate
        And state.   45

We'll nightingale sing like
    When perched on high
In glory's cage, thy glory, bright,
    And thankfully,
        For joy.   50

Edward Taylor, 1642–1729

AUBADE

Jane, Jane,
Tall as a crane,
The morning light creaks down again;

Comb your cockscomb-ragged hair,
Jane, Jane, come down the stair.   5

Each dull blunt wooden stalactite
Of rain creaks, hardened by the light,

Sounding like an overtone
From some lonely world unknown.

But the creaking empty light   10
Will never harden into sight,

Will never penetrate your brain
With overtones like the blunt rain.

The light would show (if it could harden)
Eternities of kitchen garden,   15

Cockscomb flowers that none will pluck,
And wooden flowers that 'gin to cluck.

In the kitchen you must light
Flames as staring, red and white,

As carrots or as turnips, shining   20
Where the cold dawn light lies whining.

Cockscomb hair on the cold wind
Hangs limp, turns the milk's weak mind. . . .

    Jane, Jane,
    Tall as a crane,   25
    The morning light creaks down again!

        Edith Sitwell, 1887–1964

THE TEMPER (I)

How should I praise thee, Lord! how should my rhymes
    Gladly engrave thy love in steel,
    If what my soul doth feel sometimes,
        My soul might ever feel!

Although there were some forty heavens, or more,   5
    Sometimes I peer above them all;
    Sometimes I hardly reach a score;
        Sometimes to hell I fall.

O rack me not to such a vast extent;
    Those distances belong to thee: 10
    The world's too little for thy tent,
        A grave too big for me.

Wilt thou meet arms with man, that thou dost stretch
    A crumb of dust from heaven to hell?
    Will great God measure with a wretch?   15
        Shall he thy stature spell?

O let me, when thy roof my soul hath hid,
    O let me roost and nestle there;
    Then of a sinner thou art rid,
        And I of hope and fear.   20

Yet take thy way; for, sure, thy way is best:
   Stretch or contract me, thy poor debtor:
   This is but tuning of my breast,
     To make the music better.

Whether I fly with angels, fall with dust,   25
   Thy hands made both, and I am there.
   Thy power and love, my love and trust,
     Make one place everywhere.

                George Herbert, 1593–1633

THE CHANCES OF RHYME

The chances of rhyme are like the chances of meeting—
   In the finding fortuitous, but once found, binding:
They say, they signify and they succeed, where to succeed
   Means not success, but a way forward
If unmapped, a literal, not a royal succession;   5
   Though royal (it may be) is the adjective or region
That we, nature's royalty, are led into.
   Yes. We are led, though we seem to lead
Through a fair forest, an Arden (a rhyme
   For Eden)—breeding ground for beasts   10
Not bestial, but loyal and legendary, which is more
   Than nature's are. Yet why should we speak
Of art, of life, as if the one were all form
   And the other all Sturm-und-Drang?[1] And I think
Too, we should confine to Crewe or to Mow   15
   Cop, all those who confuse the fortuitousness
Of art with something to be met with only
   At extremity's brink, reducing thus
Rhyme to a kind of rope's end, a glimpsed grass
   To be snatched at as we plunge past it—   20
Nostalgic, after all, for a hope deferred.
   To take chances, as to make rhymes
Is human, but between chance and impenitence
   (A half-rhyme) come dance, vigilance
And circumstance (meaning all that is there   25
   Besides you, when you are there). And between
Rest-in-peace and precipice,
   Inertia and perversion, comes the varieties
Increase, lease, re-lease (in both

---

[1] *Sturm-und-Drang:* storm and stress (German).

Senses); and immersion, conversion—of inert   30
Mass, that is, into energies to combat confusion.
Let rhyme be my conclusion.

Charles Tomlinson, 1927–

MY LUTE, AWAKE!

My lute, awake! Perform the last
Labor that thou and I shall waste,
And end that I have now begun;
For when this song is sung and past,
My lute, be still, for I have done.   5

As to be heard where ear is none,
As lead to grave[1] in marble stone,
My song may pierce her heart as soon.
Should we then sigh or sing or moan?
No, no, my lute, for I have done.   10

The rocks do not so cruelly
Repulse the waves continually
As she my suit and affection.
So that I am past remedy,
Whereby my lute and I have done.   15

Proud of the spoil that thou has got
Of simple hearts, thorough love's shot;
By whom, unkind, thou hast them won,
Think not he hath his bow forgot,
Although my lute and I have done.   20

Vengeance shall fall on thy disdain
That makest but game on earnest pain.
Think not alone under the sun
Unquit[2] to cause thy lovers plain,
Although my lute and I have done.   25

Perchance thee lie withered and old
The winter nights that are so cold,
Plaining in vain unto the moon.

---

[1] *grave:* engrave.
[2] *unquit:* unrequited.

Thy wishes then dare not be told.
Care then who list,[3] for I have done.   30

And then may chance thee to repent
The time that thou hast lost and spent
To cause thy lovers sigh and swoon.
Then shalt thou know beauty but lent,
And wish and want as I have done.   35

Now cease, my lute. This is the last
Labor that thou and I shall waste,
And ended is that we begun.
Now is this song both sung and past;
My lute, be still, for I have done.   40

Thomas Wyatt, 1503–1542

[3] *list:* listen.

from FIVE SONGS

II

That night when joy began
Our narrowest veins to flush,
We waited for the flash
Of morning's levelled gun.

But morning let us pass,   5
And day by day relief
Outgrows his nervous laugh,
Grown credulous of peace,

As mile by mile is seen
No trespassers reproach,   10
And love's best glasses reach
No fields but are his own.

W. H. Auden, 1907–1973

Repetition

One of the most memorable speeches of World War II was Winston
Churchill's call to arms to the English people. He concluded:

> We shall not flag or fail. We shall go on to the end. We shall fight in France, we shall fight on the seas and oceans, we shall fight with growing strength in the air, we shall defend our island, whatever the cost may be, we shall fight on the beaches, we shall fight on the landing grounds, we shall fight in the field and in the streets, we shall fight in the hills; we shall never surrender.

The repetition of "we shall" and "we shall fight" insistently reinforces the commitment Churchill wanted to instill in the British people. "We shall" does not become simply a redundant sound but builds in intensity, gathering force and affirmation each time it occurs. No one who heard Churchill deliver this speech, or those who later heard a recording of it, will forget the message or the cadence.

Repetition allows the speaker, or writer, to emphasize what is important. Repetition is dramatic and rhythmic. Repetition can also have a hypnotic effect. In *The Act of Creation*, Arthur Koestler describes riding on a train at a time of confusion and self-blame in his life. In the sound of the wheels speeding along the rails Koestler heard, compulsively, *I* told *you so, I* told *you so, I* told *you so*, until he felt almost mad. In *Anna Karenina*, Leo Tolstoy uses repetition both for its emphatic and its hypnotic effects. Kitty sees Anna at a ball and realizes that the man she wants, Vronsky, is attracted to Anna instead of to her:

> Some supernatural force drew Kitty's eyes to Anna's face. She was fascinating in her simple black dress, fascinating were her round arms with their bracelets, fascinating was her firm neck with its thread of pearls, fascinating the straying curls of her loose hair, fascinating the graceful, light movements of her little feet and hands, fascinating was that lovely face in its eagerness, but there was something terrible and cruel in her fascination.

The recurring word marks each new aspect of Anna, and keeps our attention as rapt as Kitty's as she stares at her rival. The repetition becomes more emphatic at the end when Tolstoy reverses the sentence order, thereby giving the most emphasis to the words "terrible and cruel," which are Kitty's conclusions about Anna's beauty.

In chants and spells, prayers and songs, speeches and novels, as well as in poetry, repetition underscores, making what is said emphatic and memorable. Repetition is naturally rhythmic; words are set in motion by their recurrence. Waves breaking, a clock pendulum swinging, the pumping of bicycle pedals—regular patterns of sound create an expectation that the sound and pace will continue. And repetition is dramatic. That a line or word—or sometimes an image or idea—recurs signals that the writer thinks it bears repeating. For message or rhythm, or both, the writer wants our attention on the repeating elements. Unless the sound is repeated too often or goes on too long, our attention is held.

Types of Repetition

Single Word Repetition   When dethroned King Lear fantasizes taking revenge on those who usurped him, he said, "Then Kill, Kill, Kill, Kill, Kill, Kill." With each repetition, the word becomes more intense, a little wilder and more sinister. When Macbeth says:

> Tomorrow, and tomorrow, and tomorrow
> Creeps in this petty pace from day to day,
> To the last syllable of recorded time
> And all our yesterdays have lighted fools
> The way to dusty death. Out, out, brief candle!

the repetition of "tomorrow" sounds more and more weary each time the word occurs. The two commas and two conjunctions stretch out the sound even more. The short monosyllables "out, out" contrast with "tomorrow." Shakespeare made frequent use of the technique of repeating a single word, often with subtly different inflections depending on the context. "O Cressid! O false Cressid! false, false, false," from *Troilus and Cressida*, sounds childlike and petulant. In *Richard II*, the triple use of "little" sounds smaller with each use:

> And my large kingdom for a little grave,
> A little, little grave, an obscure grave

That "large" also begins with *l* heightens the contrast between the "large kingdom" and the "little grave."

Anaphora   The beginning word or words of a line repeat.

NIGHT SONG

Among rocks, I am the loose one,
among arrows, I am the heart,
among daughters, I am the recluse,
among sons, the one who dies young.

Among answers, I am the question,   5
between lovers, I am the sword,
among scars, I am the fresh wound,
among confetti, the black flag.

Among shoes, I am the one with the pebble,
among days, the one that never comes,   10
among the bones you find on the beach
the one that sings was mine.

Lisel Mueller, 1924–

Anaphora gives a songlike quality to "Night Song." Mueller interrupts
the repetition twice, once in the middle and again at the conclusion;
these lines break the pattern and keep the poem from becoming too
lulling.

The next poem not only uses anaphora but playfully piles on internal rhymes and end rhymes. Gertrude Stein is the queen of repetition;
for years she experimented in novels and poems with the myriad effects
of insistent repetition. This is a section from her longer work, "A Valentine for Sherwood Anderson":

A VERY VALENTINE

Very fine is my valentine.
Very fine and very mine.
Very mine is my valentine very mine and very fine.
Very fine is my valentine and mine, very fine very mine and
mine is my valentine.

Gertrude Stein, 1874–1946

Phrase or Line Repetition   Whole lines or parts of lines recur in a
regular or irregular pattern. Usually, when the repetition comes around
again, the reader has gained further knowledge, and the words are
enhanced or changed in meaning when they reappear.

FIFTEEN

South of the Bridge on Seventeenth
I found back of the willows one summer
day a motorcycle with the engine running
as it lay on its side, ticking over
slowly in the high grass. I was fifteen.   5

I admired all that pulsing gleam, the
shiny flanks, the demure headlights
fringed where it lay; I led it gently
to the road and stood with that
companion, ready and friendly. I was fifteen.   10

We could find the end of a road, meet
the sky on out Seventeenth. I thought about
hills, and patting the handle got back a
confident opinion. On the bridge we indulged
a forward feeling, a tremble. I was fifteen.   15

Thinking, back farther in the grass I found
the owner, just coming to, where he had flipped
over the rail. He had blood on his hand, was pale—
I helped him walk to his machine. He ran his hand
over it, called me good man, roared away.   20

I stood there, fifteen.

William Stafford, 1914–

Combined Repetition   Lines, phrases, and single words repeat extensively, tightly unifying the poem.

A RED, RED ROSE

O, my luve is like a red, red rose,
   That's newly sprung in June;
O, my luve is like the melodie
   That's sweetly play'd in tune.

As fair art thou, my bonnie lass,   5
   So deep in luve am I;
And I will luve thee still, my dear,
   Till a' the seas gang dry.

Till a' the seas gang dry, my dear,
And the rocks melt wi' the sun: 10
And I will love thee still, my dear,
While the sands o' life shall run.

And fare thee well, my only luve,
And fare thee well a while!
And I will come again, my luve, 15
Tho' it were ten thousand mile!

Robert Burns, 1759–1796

Refrains Whole stanzas, concluding lines of stanzas, or multiple lines recur. Folk poetry and songs, carols, and hymns often use this kind of repetition, which reiterates the primary emotion, lesson, or situation. Critic Justus Lawler, writing about a poem by Yeats, speculates that in "the repetition . . . there may be a clue to the fascination of all poetic refrains. Over and over, almost spirally, they proclaim the unity that awaits the faithful wayfarer at the end of each stanza of his journey and ultimately at journey's end itself."

LORD RANDAL

"O where hae ye been, Lord Randal, my son?
O where hae ye been, my handsome young man?"
"I hae been to the wild wood; mother, make my bed soon,
For I'm weary wi' hunting, and fain wald lie down."

"Where gat ye your dinner, Lord Randal, my son? 5
Where gat ye your dinner, my handsome young man?"
"I dined wi' my true-love; mother, make my bed soon,
For I'm weary wi' hunting, and fain wald lie down."

"What gat ye to your dinner, Lord Randal, my son?
What gat ye to your dinner, my handsome young man?" 10
"I gat eels boiled in broo; mother, make my bed soon,
For I'm weary wi' hunting, and fain wald lie down."

"What became of your bloodhounds, Lord Randal, my son?
What became of your bloodhounds, my handsome young man?"
"O they swelled and they died; mother, make my bed soon, 15
For I'm weary wi' hunting, and fain wald lie down."

"O I fear ye are poisoned, Lord Randal, my son!
O I fear ye are poisoned, my handsome young man!"
"O yes! I am poisoned; mother, make my bed soon,
For I'm sick at the heart, and I fain wald lie down."   20

Anonymous, fifteenth century(?)

Opening and Closing Repetition   When a poem ends with a line identical or similar to the opening line, the reader feels a sense of closure, as though the poem completes a full circle. If the poem is effective, the repeated line has gathered momentum and significance at the end. The ends of the short poems which follow repeat their openings with very different results.

BREAKFAST

We ate our breakfast lying on our backs
Because the shells were screeching overhead.
I bet a rasher to a loaf of bread
That Hull United would beat Halifax
When Jimmy Stainthorpe played full-back instead
Of Billy Bradford. Ginger raised his head
And cursed, and took the bet, and dropt back dead.
We ate our breakfast lying on our backs
Because the shells were screeching overhead.

Wilfrid Gibson, 1878–1962

SNAIL

They have brought me a snail.

Inside it sings
a map-green ocean.
My heart
swells with water,
with small fish
of brown and silver.

They have brought me a snail.

Frederico García Lorca, 1898–1936
(Translated by William Jay Smith)

Image Repetition The poet works with the repetition of an image or repeats a certain kind of imagery, such as smell or textures. For example, if you follow the sensuous color imagery in Keats's "The Eve of St. Agnes" (page 133), you can plot the lovers' emotions. Cool, silvery-white imagery heats to rich purple and red. If in a poem you find repeated images of wings, fire, roses, knives, any object or sensation, the repetition is integral to the meaning of the poem.

In the novel *Moby Dick*, Herman Melville made use of the color white in the same way image repetition works in poetry. Melville's narrator Ishmael says, "It was the whiteness of the whale that above all things appalled me" then launches into a nine-page catalogue of beautiful, then dreadful, images of whiteness: Japonicas, pearls, white-forked flame, brides, sacred snow-white bulls, ermine, milk-white steeds, then white sharks, bears, the pallor of the dead, an albatross, murderers in white hoods, a white squall, Antarctic seas, frost, and more. As we discover at the end of this meditation, Ishmael finds all colors a mask for white, the annihilation of color:

> . . . the sweet tinge of sunset skies and woods . . . gilded velvets of butterflies, and the butterfly cheeks of young girls; all these are but subtle deceits, not actually inherent in substances, but only laid on from without; so that all deified Nature absolutely paints like the harlot, whose allurements cover nothing but the charnel-house within; and when we proceed further, and consider that the mystical cosmetic which produces every one of her hues, the great principle of light, for ever remains white or colorless in itself, and it operating without medium upon matter, would touch all objects, even tulips and hoses, with its own blank tinge—pondering all this, the palsied universe lies before us a leper; and like wilful travellers in Lapland, who refuse to wear colored and coloring glasses upon their eyes, so the wretched infidel gazes himself blind at the monumental white shroud that wraps all the prospect around him. And all of these things the Albino whale was the symbol. Wonder ye then at the fiery hunt?

Anyone who reads *Moby Dick* remembers this central and powerful poetic section. The meditation on white reveals Ishmael's most basic relationship to nature and religion, in addition to his relationship to the great whale.

In poetry, this kind of repetition also causes the image to gather force and to achieve many of the effects of sound repetition: emphasis, memory, unity. It's beyond our scope here, but if you consider the repetition of images, even certain words, within a poet's whole body of work, you can identify that writer's major themes and concerns.

Often the cumulative power of the image is the main organizing principle of the poem. Adrienne Rich's images of diving into a wrecked ship never state exactly what the wreck means—history, one's own past, a relationship, or what. The wreck is *something* submerged and dangerous and important. Readers make different connections. Can you read this simply as a poem about deep sea diving? At what point does the image begin to seem symbolic to you?

DIVING INTO THE WRECK

First having read the book of myths,
and loaded the camera,
and checked the edge of the knife blade,
I put on
the body-armor of black rubber   5
the absurd flippers
the grave and awkward mask.
I am having to do this
not like Cousteau with his
assiduous team   10
aboard the sun-flooded schooner
but here alone.

There is a ladder.
The ladder is always there
hanging innocently   15
close to the side of the schooner.
We know what it is for,
we who have used it.
Otherwise
it's a piece of maritime floss   20
some sundry equipment.

I go down.
Rung after rung and still
the oxygen immerses me
the blue light   25
the clear atoms
of our human air.
I go down.

My flippers cripple me,
I crawl like an insect down the ladder   30
and there is no one
to tell me when the ocean
will begin.

First the air is blue and then
it is bluer and then green and then   35
black I am blacking out and yet
my mask is powerful
it pumps my blood with power
the sea is another story
the sea is not a question of power   40
I have to learn alone
to turn my body without force
in the deep element.

And now: it is easy to forget
what I came for   45
among so many who have always
lived here
swaying their crenellated fans
between the reefs
and besides   50
you breathe differently down here.

I came to explore the wreck.
The words are purposes.
The words are maps.
I came to see the damage that was done   55
and the treasures that prevail.
I stroke the beam of my lamp
slowly along the flank
of something more permanent
than fish or weed   60
the thing I came for:
the wreck and not the story of the wreck
the thing itself and not the myth
the drowned face always staring
toward the sun   65
the evidence of damage
worn by salt and sway into this threadbare beauty
the ribs of the disaster
curving their assertion
among the tentative haunters.   70

This is the place.
And I am here, the mermaid whose dark hair
streams black, the merman in his armored body
We circle silently
about the wreck   75
we dive into the hold.
I am she: I am he

whose drowned face sleeps with open eyes
whose breasts still bear the stress
whose silver, copper, vermeil cargo lies   80
obscurely inside barrels
half-wedged and left to rot
we are the half-destroyed instruments
that once held to a course
the water-eaten log   85
the fouled compass

We are, I am, you are
by cowardice or courage
the one who find our way
back to this scene   90
carrying a knife, a camera
a book of myths
in which
our names do not appear.

1972

Adrienne Rich, 1929–

Syntactical Repetition   A sentence structure or a part of a sentence
structure repeats. **Syntax** is the pattern of the word order in a sentence
or phrase. In Macbeth's speech quoted earlier (page 176), notice that
the repetition of "tomorrow" is followed by "in this petty pace,"
"from day," "to day," "to the last syllable," "of recorded time": five
prepositional phrases. Unlike verbs, which keep the sentence moving,
prepositional phrases are merely directional; they point our attention
toward the action. The repetition of this pattern is, like the "tomor-
rows," slow and weary.

Note the use of "if" and "you would" below:

IF YOU SAW ME WALKING

If you saw me walking one more time on the island
you would know how much the end of August meant to me;

and if you saw me singing as I slid over the wet stones
you would know I was carrying the secret of life in my hip pocket.

If my lips moved too much   5
you would follow one step behind to protect me;

if I fell asleep too soon
you would cover me in light catalpa or dry willow.

Oh if I wore a brace you would help me, if I stuttered
you would hold my arm, if my heart beat with fear   10

you would throw a board across the channel, you would put
out a hand to catch me, you would carry me on your back.

If you saw me swim back and forth through the algae
you would know how much I love the trees floating under me;

and if you saw me hold my leaf up to the sun   15
you would know I was still looking for my roots;

and if you saw me burning wood
you would know I was trying to remember the smell of maple.

If I rushed down the road buttoning my blue shirt—
if I left without coffee—if I forgot my chewed-up pen—   20

you would know there was one more day of happiness
before the water rose again for another year.

Gerald Stern, 1925–

Depending on the context, repetition of a grammatical construction can
be humorous, obsessive, insistent, or can portray other moods. For
instance, the repetition of ten short declarative sentences makes a
clipped, unequivocal sequence. Syntax has a psychological effect.
Stern's poem plays off our expectation of *if* constructions. *If* is usually
followed by a consequence—a *then*. We expect logic, but Stern steps

around logic into playful and personal consequence of *if*. He repeats a pattern but surprises us each time.

When a syntactical pattern is repeated, in poetry or prose, there's a reason. The writer wants to evoke a certain response. Sentences strung together with *and* and *but* and *or* have different impacts than four-word sentences. How many phrases are used, where verbs occur, what type they are—many syntactical choices are important to how the reader experiences the sentence. In prose as well as poetry, writers make psychological use of sentence structure. As an extreme, look at the movement of this wayward and wild sentence from the life of William Davenant in *Aubrey's Brief Lives:*

> He was a next servant (as I remember, a Page also) to Sir Fulke Grevil, Lord Brookes, with whom he lived to his death, which was that a servant of his (that had long wayted on him, and his Lordship had often told him that he would doe something for him, but did not, but still putt him off with delayes) as he was trussing up his Lord's pointes comeing from Stoole (for then their breeches were fastned to the doubletts with points; then came in hookes and eies; which not to have fastened was in my boy-hood a great crime) stabbed him.

The parentheses and phrases of mundane detail delay and delay (just like the servant was "putt off" by his master) the final revelation of violent death. The syntax of the sentence is revealing and funny.

EXERCISES

1. Choose a subject such as a hurricane, a robbery, a house, or a gift and write ten lines all in one continuous sentence. Then write ten sentences on the same subject, using (as Gerald Stern did) a repetitive sentence construction.

2. Compare the repeated use of imperatives (commands such as, "go to bed," "come here," "try this") in John Donne's "Song" (page 202) and "Corinna's Going A-Maying" (page 174) by Robert Herrick.

Dangers of Repetition

Repetition has pitfalls. If the recurring words do not continue to help the work progress, a terrible monotony can result. If you sing

> 99 bottles of beer on the wall
> 99 bottles of beer
> If one of those bottles should happen to fall
> 98 bottles of beer on the wall. . . .

through to its compulsive end, you may be ordered out of the car. Without variation, overuse deadens, especially in a long poem. Some poets seem immune to this truth. Turn-of-the-century schoolchildren memorized long sections of Robert Southey's "The Cataract of Lodore":

from THE CATARACT OF LODORE

Collecting, projecting,	
Receding and speeding,	
And shocking and rocking,	
And darting and parting,	
And threading and spreading,	5
And whizzing and hissing,	
And dripping and skipping,	
And hitting and splitting,	
And shining and twining,	
And rattling and battling,	10
And shaking and quaking,	
And pouring and roaring,	
And waving and raving,	
And tossing and crossing,	
And flowing and going,	15
And running and stunning,	
And foaming and roaming,	
And dinning and spinning,	
And dropping and hopping,	
And working and jerking,	20
And guggling and struggling,	
And heaving and cleaving,	
And moaning and groaning;	
And glittering and frittering,	
And gathering and feathering,	25
And whitening and brightening,	
And quivering and shivering,	
And hurrying and skurrying,	
And thundering and floundering;	
Dividing and gliding and sliding,	30
And falling and bawling and sprawling,	

And driving and riving and striving,
And sprinkling and twinkling and wrinkling,
And sounding and bounding and rounding,
And bubbling and troubling and doubling,   35
And grumbling and rumbling and tumbling,
And clattering and battering and shattering;

Retreating and beating and meeting and sheeting,
Delaying and straying and playing and spraying,
Advancing and prancing and glancing and dancing,   40
Recoiling, turmoiling and toiling and boiling,
And gleaming and streaming and steaming and beaming,
And rushing and flushing and brushing and gushing,
And flapping and rapping and clapping and slapping,
And curling and whirling and purling and twirling,   45
And thumping and plumping and bumping and jumping,
And dashing and flashing and splashing and clashing;
And so never ending, but always descending,
Sounds and motions forever and ever are blending,
All at once and all o'er, with a mighty uproar;   50
And this way the water comes down at Lodore.

Robert Southey, 1774–1843

How long can such crazy repeating go on? This is only a brief section.

With liveliness, with progression, however, a long repetitive form will sustain interest. "Jubilate Agno" (Rejoice in the Lamb) is over twelve hundred lines long. Christopher Smart repeats the words *let* and *for* throughout. He adapted the exhaulted form of the responsive readings in the Anglican Church liturgy to write, in part, about an ordinary subject, his cat Jeoffry. However Smart intended us to take his choice of liturgical form, if we're accustomed to responsive readings in a church, the antics of the cat running through that form add to the poem's humor. His sharp observation of the cat's personality and movement keeps this section of the poem lively. It seems that the reader almost can watch the cat.

from JUBILATE AGNO

For I will consider my Cat Jeoffry.

For he is the servant of the Living God duly and daily serving him.

For at the first glance of the glory of God in the East he worships in
his way.

For is this done by wreathing his body seven times round with
elegant quickness.

For then he leaps up to catch the musk, which is the blessing of God
upon his prayer.   5

For he rolls upon prank to work it in.

For having done duty and received blessing he begins to consider
himself.

For this he performs in ten degrees.

For first he looks upon his fore-paws to see if they are clean.

For secondly he kicks up behind to clear away there.   10

For thirdly he works it upon stretch with the fore-paws extended.

For fourthly he sharpens his paws by wood.

For fifthly he washes himself.

For Sixthly he rolls upon wash.

For Seventhly he fleas himself, that he may not be interrupted upon
the beat.   15

For Eighthly he rubs himself against a post.

For Ninthly he looks up for his instructions.

For Tenthly he goes in quest of food.

For having consider'd God and himself he will consider his
neighbour.

For if he meets another cat he will kiss her in kindness.   20

For when he takes his prey he plays with it to give it chance.

For one mouse in seven escapes by his dallying.

For when his day's work is done his business more properly begins.

For he keeps the Lord's watch in the night against the adversary.

For he counteracts the powers of darkness by his electrical skin &
glaring eyes.   25

For he counteracts the Devil, who is death, by brisking about the
life.

For in his morning orisons he loves the sun and the sun loves him.

For he is of the tribe of Tiger.

For the Cherub Cat is a term of the Angel Tiger.

For he has the subtlety and hissing of a serpent, which in goodness
he suppresses.   30

For he will not do destruction, if he is well-fed, neither will he spit
without provocation.

For he purrs in thankfulness, when God tells him he's a good Cat.

For he is an instrument for the children to learn benevolence upon.

For every house is incompleat without him & a blessing is lacking in
the spirit.

For the Lord commanded Moses concerning the cats at the
    departure of the Children of Israel from Egypt.   35
For every family had one cat at least in the bag.
For the English Cats are the best in Europe.
For he is the cleanest in the use of his fore-paws of any quadrupede.
For the dexterity of his defence is an instance of the love of God to
    him exceedingly.
For he is the quickest to his mark of any creature.   40
For he is tenacious of his point.
For he is a mixture of gravity and waggery.
For he knows that God is his Saviour.
For there is nothing sweeter than his peace when at rest.
For there is nothing brisker than his life when in motion.   45
For he is of the Lord's poor and so indeed is he called by
    benevolence perpetually—Poor Jeoffry! poor Jeoffry! the rat has
    bit thy throat.
For he can catch the cork and toss it again.
For he is hated by the hypocrite and miser.
For the former is afraid of detection.
For the latter refuses the charge.   50
For he camels his back to bear the first notion of business.
For he is good to think on, if a man would express himself neatly.
For he made a great figure in Egypt for his signal services.
For he killed the Icneumon-rat very pernicious by land.
For his ears are so acute that they sting again.   55
For from this proceeds the passing quickness of his attention.
For by stroaking of him I have found out electricity.
For I perceived God's light about him both wax and fire.
For the Electrical fire is the spiritual substance, which God sends
    from heaven to sustain the bodies both of man and beast.
For God has blessed him in the variety of his movements.   60
For, tho he cannot fly, he is an excellent clamberer.
For his motions upon the face of the earth are more than any other
    quadrupede.
For he can tread to all the measures upon the musick.
For he can swim for life.
For he can creep.   65

Christopher Smart, 1722–1771

Compare the repetition in "The Night Chant" and "I am of Ireland." The Navajo chant, addressed to a god, seems to invite us to
dance or sing. "I am of Ireland," which is an invitation to dance,
evokes a mixed response.

from THE NIGHT CHANT

In Tsegihi
In the house made of the dawn
In the house made of evening twilight
In the house made of dark cloud
In the house made of rain & mist, of pollen, of grasshoppers   5
Where the dark mist curtains the doorway
The path to which is on the rainbow
Where the zigzag lightning stands high on top
Where the he-rain stands high on top

O male divinity   10
With your moccasins of dark cloud, come to us
With your mind enveloped in dark cloud, come to us
With the dark thunder above you, come to us soaring
With the shapen cloud at your feet, come to us soaring
With the far darkness made of the dark cloud over your head,
    come to us soaring   15
With the far darkness made of the rain & mist over your head,
    come to us soaring
With the zigzag lightning flung out high over your head
With the rainbow hanging high over your head, come to us soaring
With the far darkness made of the rain & the mist on the ends of
    your wings, come to us soaring
With the far darkness of the dark cloud on the ends of your wings,
    come to us soaring   20
With the zigzag lightning, with the rainbow high on the ends of
    your wings, come to us soaring

With the near darkness made of the dark cloud of the rain & the
    mist, come to us
With the darkness on the earth, come to us

With these I wish the foam floating on the flowing water over the
    roots of the great corn
I have made your sacrifice   25
I have prepared a smoke for you
My feet restore for me
My limbs restore, my body restore, my mind restore, my voice
    restore for me
Today, take out your spell for me

Today, take away your spell for me   30
Away from me you have taken it

Far off from me it is taken
Far off you have done it
Happily I recover
Happily I become cool   35

My eyes regain their power, my head cools, my limbs regain their
   strength, I hear again

Happily the spell is taken off for me
Happily I walk, impervious to pain I walk, light within I walk,
   joyous I walk

Abundant dark clouds I desire
An abundance of vegetation I desire   40
An abundance of pollen, abundant dew, I desire

Happily may fair white corn come with you to the ends of the
   earth
Happily may fair yellow corn, fair blue corn, fair corn of all kinds,
   plants of all kinds, goods of all kinds, jewels of all kinds, come
   with you to the ends of the earth

With these before you, happily may they come with you
With these behind, below, above, around you, happily may they
   come with you   45
Thus you accomplish your tasks

Happily the old men will regard you
Happily the old women will regard you
The young men & the young women will regard you
The children will regard you   50
The chiefs will regard you

Happily as they scatter in different directions they will regard you
Happily as they approach their homes they will regard you
May their roads home be on the trail of peace
Happily may they all return   55

In beauty I walk
With beauty before me I walk
With beauty behind me I walk
With beauty above me I walk
With beauty above & about me I walk   60
It is finished in beauty
It is finished in beauty

I AM OF IRELAND

'I am of Ireland,
And the Holy Land of Ireland,
And time runs on,' cried she.
'Come out of charity,
Come dance with me in Ireland.'   5

One man, one man alone
In that outlandish gear,
One solitary man
Of all that rambled there
Had turned his stately head.   10
'That is a long way off,
And time runs on,' he said,
'And the night grows rough.'

'I am of Ireland,
And the Holy Land of Ireland,   15
And time runs on,' cried she.
'Come out of charity
Come dance with me in Ireland.'

'The fiddlers are all thumbs,
Or the fiddle-string accursed,   20
The drums and the kettledrums
And the trumpets all are burst,
And the trombone,' cried he,
'The trumpet and trombone,'
And cocked a malicious eye,   25
'But time runs on, runs on.'

'I am of Ireland,
And the Holy Land of Ireland,
And time runs on,' cried she.
'Come out of charity   30
And dance with me in Ireland.'

William Butler Yeats, 1865–1939

1. Analyze the uses of repetition in "The Night Chant" and "I Am of Ireland." Is the repeating used effectively in each? Identify the types of repetition (anaphora, syntactic, single word, image) at work.

2. Why is repetition used in each poem? What happens if you paraphrase these poems?

3. Read "The Night Chant" aloud together and then silently to yourself. Compare your responses to each way of reading. What role does repetition play in ritualistic activities you are involved in?

4. The repeating stanza in "I Am of Ireland" is Yeats's adaptation of a well-known Irish poem of the fourteenth century. The woman calls for a dancing partner. The man hears from "a long way off." Since he is "one man alone," perhaps he's a modern man listening to a voice from history. How does this information color your response? What do the two people agree on? Can the dance take place? How do you interpret the metaphor of dance?

• • •

TROOPSHIP: MID-ATLANTIC

Dark waters into crystalline brilliance break
About the keel as, through the moonless night,
The dark ship moves in its own moving lake
Of phosphorescent cold moon-coloured light;
And to the clear horizon all around   5
Drift pools of fiery beryl flashing bright,
As though unquenchably burning cold and white
A million moons in the night of waters drowned.

And staring at the magic with eyes adream
That never till now have looked upon the sea,   10
Boys from the Middle West lounge listlessly
In the unlanthorned[1] darkness, boys who go,
Beckoned by some unchallengeable dream,
To unknown lands to fight an unknown foe.

on the S.S. *Baltic*, July 1917
Wilfrid Gibson, 1878–1962

[1] *unlanthorned:* unlanterned.

EXERCISES

1. "Troopship: Mid-Atlantic" repeats extensive light and dark im-
    agery in stanza 1. What happens in stanza 2? Why?
2. What is the effect of the repetition of "unknown" in the last line?

Poems for Discussion

I HEAR AMERICA SINGING

I hear America singing, the varied carols I hear,
Those of mechanics, each one singing his as it should be blithe and
    strong,
The carpenter singing his as he measures his plank or beam,
The mason singing his as he makes ready for work, or leaves off work,
The boatman singing what belongs to him in his boat, the deckhand
    singing on the steamboat deck,   5
The shoemaker singing as he sits on his bench, the hatter singing as he
    stands,
The wood-cutter's song, the plowboy's on his way in the morning, or
    at noon intermission or at sundown,
The delicious singing of the mother, or of the young wife at work, or
    of the girl sewing or washing,
Each singing what belongs to him or her and to none else,
The day what belongs to the day—at night the party of young fellows,
    robust, friendly,   10
Singing with open mouths their strong melodious songs.

Walt Whitman, 1819–1892

SONG FOR THE LAST ACT

Now that I have your face by heart, I look.
Less at its features than its darkening frame
Where quince and melon, yellow as young flame,
Lie with quilled dahlias and the shepherd's crook.
Beyond, a garden. There, in insolent ease   5
The lead and marble figures watch the show
Of yet another summer loath to go
Although the scythes hang in the apple trees.

Now that I have your voice by heart, I look.

Now that I have your voice by heart, I read   10
In the black chords upon a dulling page
Music that is not meant for music's cage,
Whose emblems mix with words that shake and bleed.
The staves are shuttled over with a stark
Unprinted silence. In a double dream   15
I must spell out the storm, the running stream.
The beat's too swift. The notes shift in the dark.

Now that I have your voice by heart, I read.

Now that I have your heart by heart, I see
The wharves with their great ships and architraves;   20
The rigging and the cargo and the slaves
On a strange beach under a broken sky.
O not departure, but a voyage done!
The bales stand on the stone; the anchor weeps
Its red rust downward, and the long vine creeps   25
Beside the salt herb, in the lengthening sun.

Now that I have your heart by heart, I see.

Louise Bogan, 1897–1970

JAZZONIA

Oh, silver tree!
Oh, shining rivers of the soul!

In a Harlem cabaret
Six long-headed jazzers play.
A dancing girl whose eyes are bold   5
Lifts high a dress of silken gold.

Oh, singing tree!
Oh, shining rivers of the soul!

Were Eve's eyes
In the first garden   10
Just a bit too bold?
Was Cleopatra gorgeous
In a gown of gold?

Oh, shining tree!
Oh, silver rivers of the soul!   15

In a whirling cabaret
Six long-headed jazzers play.

Langston Hughes, 1902–1967

SOMNAMBULE[1] BALLAD

Green, how much I want you green.
Green wind. Green branches.
The ship upon the sea
and the horse in the mountain.
With the shadow on her waist   5
she dreams on her balcony,
green flesh, hair of green,
and eyes of cold silver.
Green, how much I want you green.
Beneath the gypsy moon,   10
all things look at her
but she cannot see them.

---
[1] *Somnambule:* sleepwalker.

Green, how much I want you green.
Great stars of white frost
come with the fish of darkness   15
that opens the road of dawn.
The fig tree rubs the wind
with the sandpaper of its branches,
and the mountain, a filching cat,
bristles its bitter aloes.   20
But who will come? And from where?
She lingers on her balcony,
green flesh, hair of green,
dreaming of the bitter sea.

—Friend, I want to change   25
my horse for your house,
my saddle for your mirror,
my knife for your blanket.
Friend, I come bleeding,
from the passes of Cabra.   30
—If I could, young man,
this pact would be sealed.
But I am no more I,
nor is my house now my house.
—Friend, I want to die   35
decently in my bed.
Of iron, if it be possible,
with sheets of fine holland.
Do you not see the wound I have
from my breast to my throat?   40
—Your white shirt bears
three hundred dark roses.
Your pungent blood oozes
around your sash.
But I am no more I,   45
nor is my house now my house.
—Let me climb at least
up to the high balustrades:
let me come! Let me come!
up to the green balustrades.   50
Balustrades of the moon
where the water resounds.

Now the two friends go up
towards the high balustrades.
Leaving a trail of blood,   55
leaving a trail of tears.

Small lanterns of tin
were trembling on the roofs.
A thousand crystal tambourines
were piercing the dawn.   60

Green, how much I want you green,
green wind, green branches.
The two friends went up.
The long wind was leaving
in the mouth a strange taste   65
of gall, mint and sweet-basil.
Friend! Where is she, tell me,
where is your bitter girl?
How often she waited for you!
How often did she wait for you,   70
cool face, black hair,
on this green balcony!

Over the face of the cistern
the gypsy girl swayed.
Green flesh, hair of green,   75
with eyes of cold silver.
An icicle of the moon
suspends her above the water.
The night became as intimate
as a little square.   80
Drunken civil guards
were knocking at the door.
Green, how much I want you green.
Green wind. Green branches.
The ship upon the sea.   85
And the horse on the mountain.

Federico García Lorca, 1898–1936
(Translated by Stephen Spender and J. L. Gili)

BREASTS

The day you came
this world got its hold on me.
Summer grass and the four of us pounding hell
out of each other for god knows what
green murder of the skull.   5
Swart nubbins, I noticed you then,
my mother shaking a gritty rag from the porch

to get my shirt on this minute. Brothers,
that was the parting of our ways, for then
you got me down by something else than flesh.   10
By the loose skin of a cotton shirt
you kept me to the ground
until the bloody gout hung in my face like a web.

Little mothers, I can't find your children.
I have looked in a man   15
who moved through the air like a god.
He brought me clouds
and the loose stars of his goings.
Another kissed me on a pier in Georgia
but there was blood on his hands,   20
bad whiskey in the wind. The last one,
he made me a liar until I stole
what I could not win. Loves,
what is this mirror you have left me in?

I could have told you at the start   25
there would be trouble
from other hands, how the sharp mouths
would find you where you slept.
But I have hurt you as certainly
with cold sorrowings as anyone,   30
have come the long way
over broken ground to this softness.
Good clowns, how could I know, all along
it was your blundering mercies kept me alive
when heaven was a luckless dream.   35

Tess Gallagher, 1943–

THE FORGOTTEN MADMEN OF MENILMONTANT

after Jacques Prevért

Do not look sadly at days gone by
days below days like a river running under the stars
Do not listen to the blues
or speak often with priests

Do not think the rich women enrolled in the college of nightfall   5
will always smell the same way

Everytime the tree works the leaves dream

Everytime I carve the dead wing my name
in the dark lamp of the outhouse
I said everytime I cut my name   10
in the old wood rotten as a tugboat
I know I am always with you

Everytime the schoolboy's bad moon
dowses blood from the virgin's stone thighs
I know I am handsome and young and drunk   15
eternal as a weed

It will not smell the same

Everytime I open a bottle of wine
and see a snake doctor[1] under my bed
I know there is something coming and eternal   20
like taking off a white coat over the body of the dead

Poets have done this before
Poets have made love and gathered at the cheap joints
they've cut their fingers toasting one another's death

Poets have made love   25
and remained thick
they've gotten cold feet at the crucial moments
when left alone with the students with sad eyes

Do not die in the wintertime
for there is no okra or sailboat   30

It will not smell the same
that twig of blood or the chiffonier

Do not listen to hunting dogs in autumn
or tie yellow flies for the small lips of desperate friends

---

[1] *snake doctor:* dragonfly.

Poets have done this before   35
and they've wandered off alone and unheard of
to bury the caul of their own still-born

Like a voice the odor has changed

Dust under the hooves of a horse
running side by side with the fog   40
a book in the hands of a fool

Frank Stanford, 1948–1978

RESIDUE

Of everything, a little stayed.
Of my fear. Of your temper.
Of stammered screams. Of the rose,
a little.

A little of the light stayed   5
pooled in the hat.
In the bully's eyes
a trace stayed, of gentleness
(only one).

A little of the dust   10
with which your white shoe
was covered. Random
clothes, some mass-veils, rotted,
a little, a little, a touch.

But of everything, a little stays.   15
Of the blasted bridge,
of two stalks of grass,
of the empty
box of cigarettes, a little stayed.

For of everything, a little stays.   20
The line of your chin stayed
in your daughter's.

Of your dry silence,
a little stayed, a little
in the angry walls,   25
in non-vocal leaves which spin.

A little of everything stayed
in the china saucer,
cracked dragon, pale flower;
the lines on your brow,   30
I mirror.

If a little stays of everything,
why shouldn't something mine stay,
too? in the train
running north, on a ship,   35
in newspaper ads;
a little of me in London,
some farther off?
in the consonant?
in the well?   40

A little buoys in the drift
at the river's mouth
and fish don't mind it,
a little, it's not in books.
Of everything a little stays.   45
Not much: from the faucet drips
this ludicrous drop
half alcohol, half salt,
this frog-leg that leaps,
this wrist watch lens   50
split in a thousand hopes,
this swan neck,
this secret, infantile . . .
Of everything, a little stays:
of me, of you; of Abelard.   55
Hair on my sleeve,
of everything a little stays,
wind in these ears,
buffoon burp, groan

from the abused entrails,   60
and tiny artifacts:
glass bell, honeycomb, shell
of revolver . . . aspirin.
Of everything, a little stays.

Oh, open the lotion bottles 65
and smother
the intolerable stench of memory.

But of everything terrible, a little stays,
and under the beating waves
and under the clouds and the winds 70
and under the bridges and the tunnels
and under the flames and under the sarcasm
and under the drool and under the vomit
and under the sob within the cell, the forgotten prisoner
and under the performances and the scarlet death 75
and under the libraries, the asylums, the triumphant churches
and under you yourself and under your feet, half stiff already,
and under the gross canopy of family and class,
a little something always stays.
A button, sometimes. Sometimes a rat. 80

Carlos Drummond de Andrade, 1902–1987
(Translated by Virginia de Araújo)

A LITANY IN TIME OF PLAGUE

Adieu, farewell earth's bliss,
This world uncertain is;
Fond are life's lustful joys,
Death proves them all but toys,
None from his darts can fly. 5
I am sick, I must die.
     Lord, have mercy on us!

Rich men, trust not in wealth,
Gold cannot buy you health;
Physic[1] himself must fade, 10
All things to end are made.
The plague full swift goes by;
I am sick, I must die.
     Lord, have mercy on us!

Beauty is but a flower 15
Which wrinkles will devour:
Brightness falls from the air,

---

[1] *physic:* medicine.

Queens have died young and fair,
Dust hath closed Helen's[2] eye.
I am sick, I must die.   20
          Lord, have mercy on us!

Strength stoops unto the grave,
Worms feed on Hector[3] brave,
Swords may not fight with fate.
Earth still holds ope her gate;   25
Come! come! the bells do cry.
I am sick, I must die.
          Lord, have mercy on us!

Wit with his wantonness
Tasteth death's bitterness;   30
Hell's executioner
Hath no ears for to hear
What vain art can reply.
I am sick, I must die.
          Lord, have mercy on us!   35

Haste, therefore, each degree,
To welcome destiny.
Heaven is our heritage,
Earth but a player's stage;
Mount we unto the sky.   40
I am sick, I must die.
          Lord, have mercy on us!

Thomas Nashe, 1567–1601

[2] *Helen:* Helen of Troy.
[3] *Hector:* great Trojan Hero.

LISTEN CHILDREN

listen children
keep this in the place
you have for keeping
always
keep it all ways   5

we have never hated black

listen
we have been ashamed
hopeless   tired   mad
but always   10
all ways
we loved us

we have always loved each other
children   all ways

pass it on   15

Lucille Clifton, 1936–

LUCKY LIFE

Lucky life isn't one long string of horrors
and there are moments of peace, and pleasure, as I lie in between the
    blows.
Lucky I don't have to wake up in Phillipsburg, New Jersey,
on the hill overlooking Union Square or the hill overlooking
Kuebler Brewery or the hill overlooking SS. Philip and James   5
but have my own hills and my own vistas to come back to.

Each year I go down to the island I add
one more year to the darkness;
and though I sit up with my dear friends
trying to separate the one year from the other,   10
this one from the last, that one from the former,
another from another,
after a while they all get lumped together,
the year we walked to Holgate,
the year our shoes got washed away,   15
the year it rained,
the year my tooth brought misery to us all.

This year was a crisis. I knew it when we pulled
the car onto the sand and looked for the key.
I knew it when we walked up the outside steps   20
and opened the hot icebox and began the struggle
with swollen drawers and I knew it when we laid out

the sheets and separated the clothes into piles
and I knew it when we made our first rush onto
the beach and I knew it when we finally sat   25
on the porch with coffee cups shaking in our hands.

My dream is I'm walking through Phillipsburg, New Jersey,
and I'm lost on South Main Street. I am trying to tell,
by memory, which statue of Christopher Columbus
I have to look for, the one with him slumped over   30
and lost in weariness or the one with him
vaguely guiding the way with a cross and globe in
one hand and a compass in the other.
My dream is I'm in the Eagle Hotel on Chamber Street
sitting at the oak bar, listening to two   35
obese veterans discussing Hawaii in 1942,
and reading the funny signs over the bottles.
My dream is I sleep upstairs over the honey locust
and sit on the side porch overlooking the stone culvert
with a whole new set of friends, mostly old and humorless.   40

Dear waves, what will you do for me this year?
Will you drown out my scream?
Will you let me rise through the fog?
Will you fill me with that old salt feeling?
Will you let me take my long steps in the cold sand?   45
Will you let me lie on the white bedspread and study
the black clouds with the blue holes in them?
Will you let me see the rusty trees and the old monoplanes one more year?
Will you still let me draw my sacred figures
and move the kites and the birds around with my dark mind?   50

Lucky life is like this. Lucky there is an ocean to come to.
Lucky you can judge yourself in this water.
Lucky the waves are cold enough to wash out the meanness.
Lucky you can be purified over and over again.
Lucky there is the same cleanliness for everyone.   55
Lucky life is like that. Lucky life. Oh lucky life.
Oh lucky lucky life. Lucky life.

Gerald Stern, 1925–

Meter: The Measured Flow

Poetry is nothing but time, rhythm perpetually creative.

Octavio Paz

Put your finger on your pulse. Feel the most basic rhythm we know: the tension/relaxation, tick/tock, yes/no, systole/diastole of our own circulation. All life on earth is rhythmic. Tides, breath, electromagnetic fields, sound waves, sleep, the moon's phases, the mating dance of mockingbirds, even traffic on the freeway—each has its own pulse rate. From the rapid rhythm of our hearts pumping seventy barrels of blood a day, to the seventeen-year cycle of cicadas, to the slow orbit of a comet sweeping by every ninety years, there is intrinsic periodicity to life and nature.

The heartbeat is the rhythm of our earliest experience. The fetus is close to the mother's heart. Once born, the baby is rocked back and forth. When the child can stand, he loves to bounce rhythmically in the crib and rattle the side slats. Long before the words make sense, the child holds up his hands to play Pat-a-Cake and moves his head to the beat of Mother Goose rhymes. The playground swing and seesaw: back and forth, up and down. Rhythm is pleasurable. Later, he learns that rhythm is a key to most sports. The tennis or golf swing is a whole flow of acts in one motion. In football, synchronization with teammates is crucial. To get a horse smoothly over a jump requires finding a rhythm which has to be set in motion long before the actual leap. Lovemaking, dancing, cooking, working on assembly lines—so much everyday living involves rhythm that we take its presence for granted.

Rhythm also has many practical uses. When a cheerleader shouts into a megaphone, it's usually a rhythmic slogan or chant. The fans join in. A regular beat, emphatic rhymes, and loud voices easily convey a crowd's passion.

From ancient times to the present, the song-stories of work, wars, and love have passed down the folk tradition in rhythmic forms. Chain gangs, field workers, railroaders, laborers of all kinds have joined the motions of their work to song and verse, both to facilitate the actual work motions and to lighten their labors.

LAMENT WHILE DESCENDING A SHAFT

Down in the hole we go, boys,
Down in the hole we go.
The nine hundred level
Is hot as the devil—
I envy the man with the hoe.

Wisconsin river drivers at the turn of the century sang:

STIRLING'S HOTEL

There's old Molly Hogan who cooks from a book,
She's the chief chambermaid and the past-e-ry cook,
The pies that she bakes us, good God, how they smell!
A dog wouldn't eat them at Stirling's Hotel.

There's old Jack McKissick who cuts wood for his board: 5
But fishes instead, wouldn't work if he could.
The fish that he catches, good God, how they smell!
A dog wouldn't eat them at Stirling's Hotel.

And old Ed Starkes who works in the saloon,
The drinks that he gives, you could hold in a spoon.   10
For these little drinks he charges like hell,
And he gets all the money 'round Stirling's Hotel.

All our beds they are crummy with bugs and with lice,
And holes in the walls seem to vomit the mice;
And the breeze from the pantry has an old rotten smell,   15
It revives all the boarders at Stirling's Hotel.

"Clementine," "I've Been Working on the Railroad," "Blow the Man Down," and countless other sea chanteys, field songs, schoolyard tunes, and other handed-down songs preserve the distant rhythms of our ancestors' lives. Most of the poems and songs we know "by heart" are rhythmic—with rhymes, repetitive beats, alliteration, and other patterns of sound.

Meter is a strong element of rhythm. **Meter**, or *measure*, is the organization of words' accents into a pattern. Like rhyme and other patterns of sound, meter aids our recall and helps keep our attention on the unfolding of the poem or song. That the same sound comes around again rewards our expectations.

What Is Meter?

Language is rhythmical. Our voices naturally rise and fall, pause for breath, accent some syllables more than others, and intensify tone for emphasis. We speak of the Irish "lilt," the Southern "drawl," the Midwestern "twang," "rapid-fire" French, "musical" Italian. All these characteristics are part of inflection and pace. Each aspect of rhythm you will study—rhyme, repetition, sound patterns, line, and meter—occurs in normal spoken and written English; as devices of poetry they are organized and heightened.

The unit of measurement in a metered poem is called a **foot**, reminding us that the original Greek rhythms were based on dance; some slow and steady, others ecstatic and wild. Much of the satisfaction of a regular beat stems from our breathing, turning, movement of muscles. If we no longer get up and and dance around a stone altar or even sing the poem, subtle effects of meter still appeal to primary origins.

No *single* effect makes the rhythm of a poem. The call of an auctioneer in a tobacco barn, the words you put to the swish-swish of the windshield wipers, or the hypnotically repeated prayer of an old man on a park bench can remind us that rhythm is a part of a complex, overall perception. As the Spanish poet García Lorca warned, "Beneath all the statistics, there's a drop of duck's blood." Beyond all analysis, there is a mystery to rhythm, an essence or an energy as simple and as unaccountable as our own heartbeat.

A poem is in meter if words are chosen and arranged so that accents (stresses) occur in a regular pattern. The meter of a poem works much like the beat of a song. It establishes a basic timing by organizing sounds. Of course absolute regularity of recurrence quickly gets monotonous. Poets usually vary meter or change it suddenly for emphasis. Musicians call this switch of timing **syncopation**. Some poets refer to it as *metrical tension* or *counterpoint*.

Listening carefully to the rise and fall of your own voice, say aloud:

> The splendor falls on castle walls
> And snowy summits old in story:
> The long light shakes across the lakes,
> And the wild cataract leaps in glory.

Alfred, Lord Tennyson

and:

> And time shall put them both to bed
> But she shall lie with earth above,
> And he beside another love.

A. E. Housman

Your voice quickly "hears" a meter. You naturally emphasize, or **accent**, some words more than others. These stronger accents alternate with "weaker" sounds.

A thorough study of meter could be a life's work. Scholars have devised complex systems for evaluating the relative time and sound duration of accents on syllables as well as musical schemes for plotting meter. Such specialized theories are not our concern now. What concerns us is understanding basic metrical structure. We look at meter to see *how* it works concurrently with the poem's subject. As Yeats asks, "How can we know the dancer form the dance?" How can we separate rhythm from the poem's significance? Ideally, we can't.

Scansion

Let's look at the easiest technique for discovering a poem's meter. In the Tennyson and Housman lines, if you mark the emphasized syllables with accents (´) and the unstressed syllables with the symbol ˘, you discover a pattern:

> The splen/dor falls/ on cas/tle walls
> And snow/y sum/mits old/ in story:
> The long/ light shakes/ across/ the lakes,
> And the wild/ cata/ract leaps /in glory.

and:

> Aňd tíme/ shǎll pút/ thěm bóth/ ǐo béd,
> But shě/ shǎll líe,/ wǐth eárth/ ǎbóve,
> Aňd hě/ běside/ ǎnóth/ěr lóve.

In the text, slashes (/) indicate where the metrical pattern starts to repeat; notice that the division can fall in the middle of a word. This process of noting accents and their intervals of recurrence is called **scansion.**

Scanning the lines above, we find the accents repeat in a two-syllable pattern: ˘´/˘´/˘´/˘´/. Each repeating set is called a foot. Both the Tennyson and Housman have four-foot patterns. (Poems with four-foot lines are called *tetrameter*, meaning "four measures.") But notice the variations. In the Tennyson lines a leftover *-y* hangs off *story* and *glory*. This kind of tag-end is metrically insignificant and is usually ignored. The fourth line departs radically from the pattern. Variations like these are important. In scanning a poem, first note the prevailing meter: that's the basic timing of the poem. Then see how the departures are working. "And the wild cataract leaps in glory" scrambles the lulling rhythm of the first three lines. "Wild cataract leaps" has four accents packed together. This intensifies the sudden motion of the cataract in contrast to the peace and quiet of the first lines.

Depending on the number of feet, lines are called: **monometer** (one foot), **dimeter** (two feet), **trimeter** (three feet), **tetrameter** (four feet), **pentameter** (five feet), **hexameter** or alexandrine, (six feet), **heptameter** (seven feet), **octameter** (eight feet).

Identifying the number of feet is half the process of scansion. The other half is determining the order of the accents. The most common order in English poetry is an unaccented syllable (˘) followed by an accented syllable (´). This pair (˘´) is called an **iamb**, or an **iambic foot.** The overall accent pattern of the Tennyson and Housman lines above is iambic tetrameter.

Other important syllable patterns in English are:

�’ ˘   **trochee:** óxfořd, áftěr, stágnǎnt, bóxěr

˘ ˘ ’   **anapest:** aňd thě móon, iňtertwíne

’ ’   **spondee:** deádheád, ríckráck, bíllboárd, póstcárd, "No, no"

Of course the spondee cannot be sustasined as a meter, since it consists of two strong stresses. It serves as a variation in a line for emphasis.

Other less common syllable patterns include:

´ ˘ ˘	dactyl
˘ ˘	pyrrhic
´ ˘ ´	cretic (also called amphimacer)
´ ´ ´	molossos
´ ˘ ˘ ´	choriamb
˘ ´ ˘	amphibrach
˘ ´ ´	bacchius
˘ ˘ ´ ´	ionic a minore
´ ´ ˘	antibacchius
˘ ´ ´ ´	epitrite
´ ´ ˘ ˘	ionic a majore
˘ ˘ ˘	tribrach

Of these, the **dactyl** (as in métrĭcăl, déspĕrăte) turns up occasionally. Except to a specialist, most of the others are not of significant importance in reading a poem. Being aware of this range, however, increases our sensitivity to the complex possibilities in metrical patterns.

Scanning is not a precise technique. If you scan a line of a poem and compare it with someone else's version, you'll see differences. You may hear *billboard* as a spondee; someone else may hear it as a trochee. You may hear phrases differently according to your mood or emotions, which can change the way you accent words. What is important is discovering the overall metrical scheme and where and why there are variations. Don't look for rigid adherence to a meter—too much evenness makes dull poetry. Many poems begin strongly stressed, then shift into another pattern. Poets frequently want opening words to be dramatic so the reader is drawn right into the poem. Even if you scan just as the poet did, the meter will have reversals and gaps in it—spondees, extra syllables, or other feet.

EXERCISES

1. Scan these words for practice in recognizing English accent patterns:

volume	difference	ornament
in a door	and the cat	interject
as they sang	blessing	under the
mystical	season	morning
endure	retire	lyrical
lexicon	tietack	family
heartbreak	dog food	along

2. Scan for the prevailing meter:

THE ARGUMENT OF HIS BOOK

I sing of brooks, of blossoms, birds, and bowers,
Of April, May, of June, and July flowers.
I sing of Maypoles, hock carts, wassails, wakes,
Of bridegrooms, brides, and of their bridal cakes.
I write of youth, of love, and have access   5
By these to sing of cleanly wantonness.
I sing of dews, of rains, and, piece by piece,
Of balm, of oil, of spice, and ambergris.
I sing of times trans-shifting, and I write
How roses first came red and lilies white.   10
I write of groves, of twilights, and I sing
The court of Mab and of the fairy king.
I write of hell; I sing (and ever shall)
Of heaven, and hope to have it after all.

Robert Herrick, 1591–1674

3. Practice scanning until it becomes familiar. Reading aloud will help you determine how accents fall. Count a poem's syllables per line for a clue to meter: If there are eight or ten, the poem probably is in one of the most common meters, tetrameter or pentameter. Then mark the accents. Begin with the lines in this exercise, then try whole poems at the end of the chapter. A comparison with others' scanning exercises will show differences. Discuss why the differ-

ences occur. Remember that meter is often a *prevailing* pattern, not a rigidly regular one.

a. It is, it is! Hie hence, be gone, away!
    It is the lark that sings so out of tune.

    Shakespeare

b. The curfew tolls the knell of parting day,
    The lowing herd winds slowly o'er the lea,
    The ploughman homeward plods his weary way,
    And leaves the world to darkness and to me.

    Thomas Gray

c. There's not a joy the world can give like that it takes away.

    George Gordon, Lord Byron

d. Would I were free from this restrain,
    Or else had hope to win her!
    Would she could make of me a saint,
    Or I of her a sinner!

    William Congreve

e. Speak roughly to your little boy,
    And beat him when he sneezes;
    He only does it to annoy,
    Because he knows it teases.
    Wow! Wow! Wow!

    Lewis Carroll

f. They flee from me, that sometime did me seek, . . .

    Sir Thomas Wyatt

g. The Assyrian came down like the wolf on the fold,
    And his cohorts were gleaming in purple and gold.

    George Gordon, Lord Byron

h. What lips my lips have kissed, and where, and why,
    I have forgotten, and what arms have lain
    Under my head till morning; but the rain
    Is full of ghosts tonight, that tap and sigh
    Upon the glass and listen for reply, . . .

    Edna St.Vincent Millay

   i. How like an angel came I down!
      How bright are all things here
  When first among his works I did appear,
    O how their glory did me crown!
  The world resembled his eternity,
    In which my soul did walk,
  And everything that I did see
    Did with me talk.

Thomas Traherne

Iambic Pentameter

Iambic pentameter is the most important meter in English. Five sets of two-syllable feet in the unaccented/accented pattern form the iambic pentameter line:

How cán/ wĕ knów/ thĕ dánc/ĕr fróm/ thĕ dánce?

Besides a connection to the heartbeat, the iamb and trochee (the other two-syllable foot), correspond to the back-and-forth movement of walking, sowing, and rowing—some of the most basic human activities. Possibly some of our pleasure in meter comes from these organic connections. Greek legend says that the iamb rhythm originated not from such fundamentals but from a dance imitating the motions of a crippled quail! Whatever the origin of the meter, the pattern suits our muscular English language with its many consonants and alternating accents.

Iambic pentameter proves especially flexible as a meter. The five-foot line corresponds to a common sentence length: It's long enough to accommodate subject, verb, and object or prepositional phrase and short enough to say in one breath. In skillful hands, this makes iambic pentameter adaptable to a believable approximation of natural speech, even though the language is artificially arranged. This is not to say, as is often claimed, that English is naturally iambic. We do not walk around speaking in prevailing iambs. If you scan a newspaper article or a conversation, you will find no pattern of accents.

Read "Once by the Pacific" aloud, noticing how with each new line you breathe out or in. Even with a tight aabbccddeeffgg rhyme scheme and iambic pentameter, Robert Frost's poem keeps the cadence of a speaking voice.

ONCE BY THE PACIFIC

The shattered water made a misty din,
Great waves looked over others coming in,
And thought of doing something to the shore
That water never did to land before.
The clouds were low and hairy in the skies   5
Like locks blown forward in the gleam of eyes.
You could not tell, and yet it looked as if
The sand was lucky in being backed by cliff,
The cliff in being backed by continent.
It looked as if a night of dark intent   10
Was coming, and not only a night, an age.
Someone had better be prepared for rage.
There would be more than ocean water broken
Before God's last *Put out the light* was spoken.

Robert Frost, 1874–1963

When iambic pentameter is not rhymed, we call it **blank verse**. Because blank verse is even more adaptable to speech than rhymed iambic pentameter, Shakespeare chose to write his plays in it, often alternating blank verse sections with prose. You may read poems and plays in blank verse without being conscious of meter at all. So subtle are the effects that Samuel Johnson, the eighteenth-century writer, remarked that blank verse was verse for the eye alone. He meant that the iambic pentameter retains the same visual appearance of metered poetry, but the inconspicuous modulations of sound without rhyme make blank verse seem closer to spoken English.

This discreet control gives blank verse power. The meter provides a light yoke of form without the appearance of artifice.

from AS YOU LIKE IT

(Act II, scene vii)

All the world's a stage,
And all the men and women merely players:
They have their exits and their entrances;
And one man in his time plays many parts,
His acts being seven ages. At first the infant,   5
Mewling and puking in the nurse's arms.
And then the whining schoolboy, with his satchel,

And shining morning face, creeping like snail
Unwilling to school. And then the lover,
Sighing like furnace, with a woeful ballad   10
Made to his mistress' eyebrow. Then a soldier,
Full of strange oaths, and bearded like the pard,[1]
Jealous in honour, sudden and quick in quarrel,
Seeking the bubble reputation
Even in the cannon's mouth. And then the justice,   15
In fair round belly with good capon lined,
With eyes severe and beard of formal cut,
Full of wise saws and modern instances;
And so he plays his part. The sixth age shifts
Into the lean and slippered pantaloon,   20
With spectacles on nose, and pouch on side;
His youthful hose, well saved, a world too wide
For his shrunk shank; and his big manly voice,
Turning again toward childish treble, pipes
And whistles in his sound. Last scene of all,   25
That ends this strange eventful history,
Is second childishness and mere oblivion,
Sans teeth, sans eyes, sans taste, sans everything.

William Shakespeare, 1564–1616

[1] *pard:* leopard.

An experienced actor can say these lines with naturalness. As you read aloud, you sense the alternating stresses in the sound of your voice—this alternation has a regularity prose lacks—but the meter hardly reveals itself otherwise. Rhyme makes a poem more noticeably a formal *object*. Blank verse, although capable of highly formal utterances, is closer to speech. Since meter is largely for the ear, not the eye, you catch it most readily when you read all poems aloud.

Blank verse provides poets with a distinctive, malleable tempo. In the seventeenth century, John Milton used blank verse for *Paradise Lost*, a long chronicle of Adam and Eve's fall from innocence. Blank verse accommodates itself to such extended works because it gives the poet a skeletal framework on which to build without making that framework invasive. John Dryden, a contemporary, was appalled by Milton's choice. Dryden wrote, ''For imagination in a poet is a faculty so wild and lawless that, like an high-ranging spaniel, it must have clogs tied to it, less it outrun the judgment. The great easiness of blank verse renders the poet too luxuriant.'' Even so, most poets, then and now, frequently loosen or vary even the "luxuriant" blank verse. Syncopation saves any meter from falling into a sing-song silliness or hypnotic monotony. In the next poem, blank verse is the base line for Wallace Stevens. If you scan the whole poem, you'll find other types of feet used in almost every line, but the overall movement of the poem keeps to blank verse—unrhymed iambic pentameter.

SUNDAY MORNING

I

Complacencies of the peignoir, and late
Coffee and oranges in a sunny chair,
And the green freedom of a cockatoo
Upon a rug mingle to dissipate
The holy hush of ancient sacrifice.   5
She dreams a little, and she feels the dark
Encroachment of that old catastrophe,
As a calm darkens among water-lights.
The pungent oranges and bright, green wings
Seem things in some procession of the dead,   10
Winding across wide water, without sound.
The day is like wide water, without sound.
Stilled for the passing of her dreaming feet
Over the seas, to silent Palestine,
Dominion of the blood and sepulchre.   15

II

Why should she give her bounty to the dead?
What is divinity if it can come
Only in silent shadows and in dreams?
Shall she not find in comforts of the sun,
In pungent fruit and bright, green wings, or else   20
In any balm or beauty of the earth,
Things to be cherished like the thought of heaven?
Divinity must live within herself:
Passions of rain, or moods in a falling snow;
Grievings in loneliness, or unsubdued   25
Elations when the forest blooms; gusty
Emotions on wet roads on autumn nights;
All pleasures and all pains, remembering
The bough of summer and the winter branch.
These are the measures destined for her soul.   30

III

Jove in the clouds had his inhuman birth.
No mother suckled him, no sweet land gave
Large-mannered motions to his mythy mind.
He moved among us, as a muttering king,
Magnificent, would move along his hinds,   35
Until our blood, commingling, virginal,
With heaven, brought such requital to desire
The very hinds discerned it, in a star.
Shall our blood fail? Or shall it come to be
The blood of paradise? And shall the earth   40
Seem all of paradise that we shall know?
The sky will be much friendlier then than now,
A part of labor and a part of pain,
And next in glory to enduring love,
Not this dividing and indifferent blue.   45

IV

She says, "I am content when wakened birds,
Before they fly, test the reality
Of misty fields, by their sweet questionings;
But when the birds are gone, and their warm fields
Return no more, where, then, is paradise?"   50
There is not any haunt of prophecy,
Nor any old chimera of the grave,
Neither the golden underground, nor isle
Melodious, where spirits gat them home,
No visionary south, nor cloudy palm   55
Remote on heaven's hill, that has endured
As April's green endures; or will endure
Like her remembrance of awakened birds,
Or her desire for June and evening, tipped
By the consummation of the swallow's wings.   60

V

She says, "But in contentment I still feel
The need of some imperishable bliss."
Death is the mother of beauty; hence from her,
Alone, shall come fulfilment to our dreams

And our desires. Although she strews the leaves   65
Of sure obliteration on our paths,
The path sick sorrow took, the many paths
Where triumph rang its brassy phrase, or love
Whispered a little out of tenderness,
She makes the willow shiver in the sun   70
For maidens who were wont to sit and gaze
Upon the grass, relinquished to their feet.
She causes boys to pile new plums and pears
On disregarded plate. The maidens taste
And stray impassioned in the littering leaves.   75

VI

Is there no change of death in paradise?
Does ripe fruit never fall? Or do the boughs
Hang always heavy in that perfect sky,
Unchanging, yet so like our perishing earth,
With rivers like our own that seek for seas   80
They never find, the same receding shores
That never touch with inarticulate pang?
Why set the pear upon those river-banks
Or spice the shores with odors of the plum?
Alas, that they should wear our colors there,   85
The silken weavings of our afternoons,
And pick the strings of our insipid lutes!
Death is the mother of beauty, mystical,
Within whose burning bosom we devise
Our earthly mothers waiting, sleeplessly.   90

VII

Supple and turbulent, a ring of men
Shall chant in orgy on a summer morn
Their boisterous devotion to the sun,
Not as a god, but as a god might be,
Naked among them, like a savage source.   95
Their chant shall be a chant of paradise,
Out of their blood, returning to the sky;
And in their chant shall enter, voice by voice,
The windy lake wherein their lord delights,
The trees, like serafin, and echoing hills,   100
That choir among themselves long afterward.

They shall know well the heavenly fellowship
Of men that perish and of summer morn.
And whence they came and whither they shall go
The dew upon their feet shall manifest.   105

VIII

She hears, upon that water without sound,
A voice that cries, "The tomb in Palestine
Is not the porch of spirits lingering.
It is the grave of Jesus, where he lay."
We live in an old chaos of the sun.   110
Or old dependency of day and night.
Or island solitude, unsponsored, free,
Of that wide water, inescapable.
Deer walk upon our mountains, and the quail
Whistle about us their spontaneous cries;   115
Sweet berries ripen in the wilderness;
And, in the isolation of the sky,
At evening, casual flocks of pigeons make
Ambiguous undulations as they sink,
Downward to darkness, on extended wings.   120

Wallace Stevens, 1879–1955

EXERCISE

Write a paper analyzing "Sunday Morning," bringing to bear all the elements you have covered so far: language, sound, speaker, imagery, meter.

More Key Meters

Iambic pentameter is the predominant choice of metrical poets writing in English. Though other meters are less flexible or harder to sustain, each has characteristics which are useful in different poetic situations.

The next poems illustrate different qualities of some standard meters. Meter, of course, determines line length. In each poem, notice how the metrical line length influences your reading pace: The line is a unit of time, and therefore has a major effect on the poem's rhythm.

Iambic Tetrameter (˘ ´/˘ ´/˘ ´/˘ ´)

With four feet, the iambic tetrameter line moves slightly faster than pentameter. The quickened tempo of a shorter line intensifies the rhythm and therefore the meaning. The shorter a line, the quicker the eye moves down the page. More vertical space is covered. The poem is falling, plunging, speeding rather than spreading across the page. Iambic tetrameter is a flexible meter. The line is shorter than pentameter, more compressed, a slightly rushed breath rhythm. It is still long enough to seem close to speech. "The Passionate Shepherd to His Love" (page 157) is a fine example of the meter's virtues. We hear the shepherd's voice; the speed of tetrameter adds to his urgency and passion. The following poem is another of the meter's great moments:

TO HIS COY MISTRESS

Had we but World enough, and Time,
This coyness Lady were no crime.
We would sit down, and think which way
To walk, and pass our long Loves Day.
Thou by the Indian Ganges side   5
Should'st Rubies find: I by the Tide
Of Humber[1] would complain. I would
Love you ten years before the Flood:
And you should, if you please, refuse
Till the Conversion of the Jews.   10
My vegetable Love should grow
Vaster than Empires, and more slow.
An hundred years should go to praise
Thine Eyes, and on thy Forehead Gaze.
Two hundred to adore each Breast: 15
But thirty thousand to the rest.
An Age at least to every part,
And the last Age should show your Heart.
For Lady you deserve this State;
Nor would I love at lower rate.   20
   But at my back I alwaies hear
Times winged Charriot hurrying near:
And yonder all before us lye
Deserts of vast Eternity.
Thy Beauty shall no more be found;   25

---

[1] *Humber:* a river in Marvell's native area of Hull, England.

Nor, in thy marble Vault, shall sound
My ecchoing Song: then Worms shall try
That long preserv'd Virginity:
And your quaint Honour turn to dust;
And into ashes all my Lust.   30
The Grave's a fine and private place,
But none I think do there embrace.
  Now therefore, while the youthful hew[2]
Sits on thy skin like morning glew,[3]
And while thy willing Soul transpires   35
At every pore with instant Fires,
Now let us sport us while we may;
And now, like am'rous birds of prey,
Rather at once our Time devour,
Than languish in his slow-chapt[4] pow'r.   40
Let us roll all our Strength, and all
Our sweetness, up into one Ball:
And tear our Pleasures with rough strife,
Thorough the Iron gates of Life.
Thus, though we cannot make our Sun   45
Stand still, yet we will make him run.

Andrew Marvell, 1621–1678

---

[2] *hew:* hue.
[3] *glew:* glow.
[4] *slow-chapt:* slow jawed.

Trochaic Trimeter (´˘/´˘/´˘)

A trochaic foot (´˘) reverses the iambic foot (˘´). Stress comes first.
The trochaic DA-da DA-da DA-da DA-da sound is called a **falling
rhythm,** whereas the iambic da-DA da-DA da-DA da-DA is a **rising
rhythm.** The sound falls off from the stress in the trochee and rises to
the stress in the iamb. In "To a Skylark," the short lines seem to "float
and run" like the bird. Each stanza ends with a stretched-out line. The
rhythm expands, contracts. This changes not only the rhythm but the
look of the poem on the page. Eye and ear respond to the sudden
overflow into the longer meter (usually iambic hexameter). Short meters are hard to maintain for long because they easily become monotonous. Shelley, by adding a longer line to each stanza and varying the
trochaic meter ensures against monotony.

TO A SKYLARK

Hail to thee, blithe spirit!
  Bird thou never wert,
That from heaven or near it
  Pourest thy full heart
In profuse strains of unpremeditated art.   5

Higher still and higher
  From the earth thou springest
Like a cloud of fire;
  The blue deep thou wingest,
And singing still dost soar, and soaring ever singest.   10

In the golden lightning
  Of the sunken sun,
O'er which clouds are brightening,
  Thou dost float and run;
Like an unbodied joy whose race is just begun.   15

The pale purple even
  Melts around thy flight;
Like a star of heaven,
  In the broad daylight
Thou art unseen, but yet I hear thy shrill delight,   20

Keen as are the arrows
  Of that silver sphere
Whose intense lamp narrows
  In the white dawn clear,
Until we hardly see, we feel that it is there.   25

All the earth and air
  With thy voice is loud,
As, when night is bare,
  From one lonely cloud
The moon rains out her beams, and heaven is overflowed.   30

What thou art we know not;
  What is most like thee?
From rainbow clouds there flow not
  Drops so bright to see,
As from thy presence showers a rain of melody: 35

Like a poet hidden
   In the light of thought,
Singing hymns unbidden,
   Till the world is wrought
To sympathy with hopes and fears it heeded not;   40

Like a high-born maiden
   In a palace tower,
Soothing her love-laden
   Soul in secret hour
With music sweet as love, which overflows her bower;   45

Like a glow-worm golden
   In a dell of dew,
Scattering unbeholden
   Its aërial hue
Among the flowers and grass which screen it from the view;   50

Like a rose embowered
   In its own green leaves,
By warm winds deflowered,
   Till the scent it gives
Makes faint with too much sweet those heavy-wingèd thieves.   55

Sound of vernal showers
   On the twinkling grass,
Rain-awakened flowers,
   All that ever was
Joyous and clear and fresh, thy music doth surpass.   60

Teach us, sprite or bird,
   What sweet thoughts are thine:
I have never heard
   Praise of love or wine
That panted forth a flood of rapture so divine.   65

Chorus hymeneal,
   Or triumphal chant,
Matched with thine would be all
   But an empty vaunt,
A thing wherein we feel there is some hidden want.   70

What objects are the fountains
   Of thy happy strain?
What fields, or waves, or mountains?
   What shapes of sky or plain?
What love of thine own kind? what ignorance of pain?   75

With thy clear keen joyance
   Languor cannot be;
Shadow of annoyance
   Never came near thee;
Thou lovest, but ne'er knew love's sad satiety.   80

Waking or asleep,
   Thou of death must deem
Things more true and deep
   Than we mortals dream,
Or how could thy notes flow in such a crystal stream?   85

We look before and after,
   And pine for what is not;
Our sincerest laughter
   With some pain is fraught;
Our sweetest songs are those that tell of saddest thought.   90

Yet if we could scorn
   Hate and pride and fear,
If we were things born
   Not to shed a tear,
I know not how thy joy we ever should come near.   95

Better than all measures
   Of delightful sound,
Better than all treasures
   That in books are found,
Thy skill to poet were, thou scorner of the ground!   100

Teach me half the gladness
   That thy brain must know;
Such harmonious madness
   From my lips would flow,
The world should listen then, as I am listening now.   105

Percy Bysshe Shelley, 1792–1822

Iambic Trimeter   ($\breve{~}\acute{~}/\breve{~}\acute{~}/\breve{~}\acute{~}$)

The three-foot iambic is also a brief line length. The meter and shortness of the next poem correspond to meaning. Frost laments the brevity of purity: the first tinge of green-gold in spring, the innocence of Eve, dawn—all end quickly.

NOTHING GOLD CAN STAY

Nature's first green is gold,
Her hardest hue to hold.
Her early leaf's a flower;
But only so an hour.
Then leaf subsides to leaf.
So Eden sank to grief,
So dawn goes down to day.
Nothing gold can stay.

Robert Frost, 1874–1963

Quite different is this poem by Arthur Gorges—perhaps the most imaginative use of iambic trimeter ever made. Or *is* it iambic trimeter? The poem can be read straight across as three feet in iambic meter. Since the poet arranges each line in columns, we can also read each one separately as three *monometers*, or one-foot lines. The spacing of the phrases invites cross and vertical reading. The opening line, which repeats within each stanza, also closes the poem. Everything seems connected to and equal to everything else.

HER FACE   HER TONGUE   HER WYTT

Her face	Her tongue	Her wytt	
So faier	So sweete	So sharpe	
first bent	then drewe	then hitt	
myne eye	myne eare	my harte	
Myne eye	Myne eare	My harte	5
to lyke	to learne	to love	
her face	her tongue	her wytt	
doth leade	doth teache	doth move	
Her face	Her tongue	Her wytt	
with beames	with sounde	with arte	10
doth blynd	doth charm	doth knitt	
myne eye	myne eare	my harte	
Myne eye	Myne eare	My harte	
with lyfe	with hope	with skill	
her face	her tongue	her witt	15
doth feede	doth feaste	doth fyll	

O face	O tongue	O wytt
with frownes	with cheeks	with smarte
wronge not	vex not	wounde not
myne eye	myne eare	my harte 20
This eye	This eare	This harte
shall Joye	shall yeald	shall swear
her face	her tongue	her witt

Arthur Gorges, 1557–1625

Iambic Dimeter (˘ ´/˘ ´)

Iambic dimeter consists of only two iambs. The line movement of "The Fly" suits a fly's motions and the poet's realization of his own life's brevity. Blake's poem is further unified by rhyme, which punctuates the quickness of the two-foot meter.

THE FLY

Little Fly,
Thy summer's play
My thoughtless hand
Has brush'd away.

Am not I   5
A fly like thee?
Or art not thou
A man like me?

For I dance,
And drink, & sing,   10
Till some blind hand
Shall brush my wing.

If thought is life
And strength & breath,
And the want   15
Of thought is death;

Then am I
A happy fly,
If I live
Or if I die.   20

William Blake, 1757–1827

Anapestic Tetrameter   ($\breve{}\breve{}\acute{}/\breve{}\breve{}\acute{}/\breve{}\breve{}\acute{}/\breve{}\breve{}\acute{}$)

The anapest ($\breve{}\breve{}\acute{}$), a triple-syllable foot, is another rising rhythm. Note how the three-syllable foot extends the line length in tetrameter. After reading Browning's "Good News," you'll see why poems in this meter are rare:

HOW THEY BROUGHT THE GOOD NEWS
FROM GHENT TO AIX

I sprang to the stirrup, and Joris, and he;
I galloped, Dirck galloped, we galloped all three;
'Good speed!' cried the watch, as the gate-bolts undrew;
'Speed!' echoed the wall to us galloping through;
Behind shut the postern, the lights sank to rest,   5
And into the midnight we galloped abreast.

Not a word to each other: we kept the great pace
Neck by neck, stride by stride, never changing our place;
I turned in my saddle and made its girths tight,
Then shortened each stirrup, and set the pique right,   10
Rebuckled the cheek-strap, chained slacker the bit,
Nor galloped less steadily Roland a whit.

'Twas moonset at starting; but while we drew near
Lokeren, the cocks crew and twilight dawned clear;
At Boom, a great yellow star came out to see;   15
At Düffeld, 'twas morning as plain as could be;
And from Mecheln church-steeple we heard the half-chime,
So Joris broke silence with, 'Yet there is time!'

At Aerschot, up leaped of a sudden the sun,
And against him the cattle stood black every one,   20
To stare thro' the mist at us galloping past,
And I saw my stout galloper Roland at last,
With resolute shoulders, each butting away
The haze, as some bluff river headland its spray.

And his low head and crest, just one sharp ear bent back   25
For my voice, and the other pricked out on his track;
And one eye's black intelligence,—ever that glance
O'er its white edge at me, his own master, askance!
And the thick heavy spume-flakes which aye and anon
His fierce lips shook upwards in galloping on.   30

By Hasselt, Dirck groaned; and cried Joris, 'Stay spur!
Your Roos galloped bravely, the fault's not in her,
We'll remember at Aix'—for one heard the quick wheeze
Of her chest, saw the stretched neck and staggering knees,
And sunk tail, and horrible heave of the flank,   35
As down on her haunches she shuddered and sank.

So we were left galloping, Joris and I,
Past Looz and past Tongres, no cloud in the sky;
The broad sun above laughed a pitiless laugh,
'Neath our feet broke the brittle bright stubble like chaff;   40
Till over by Dalhem a dome-spire sprang white,
And 'Gallop,' gasped Joris, 'for Aix is in sight!'

'How they'll greet us!'—and all in a moment his roan
Rolled neck and croup over, lay dead as a stone;
And there was my Roland to bear the whole weight   45
Of the news which alone could save Aix from her fate,
With his nostrils like pits full of blood to the brim,
And with circles of red for his eye-sockets' rim.

Then I cast loose my buffcoat, each holster let fall,
Shook off both my jack-boots, let go belt and all,   50
Stood up in the stirrup, leaned, patted his ear,
Called my Roland his pet-name, my horse without peer;
Clapped my hands, laughed and sang, any noise, bad or good,
Till at length into Aix Roland galloped and stood.

And all I remember is, friends flocking round   55
As I sat with his head 'twixt my knees on the ground;
And no voice but was praising this Roland of mine,
As I poured down his throat our last measure of wine,
Which (the burgesses voted by common consent)
Was no more than his due who brought good news from Ghent.   60

Robert Browning, 1812–1889

If Browning's gait seems familiar, that's because both "The Star Span-
gled Banner" and "The Night Before Christmas" are written in the
same meter. The outstanding characteristic of anapestic meter is a
tharumping gallop. For this reason, it's difficult to maintain; few poems
suit the pace. For example, William Wordsworth's anapests in "The
Reverie of Poor Susan" run immediately into sing-song:

THE REVERIE OF POOR SUSAN

At the corner of Wood Street, when daylight appears,
Hangs a thrust that sings loud, it has sung for three years;
Poor Susan has passed by the spot, and has heard
In the silence of morning the song of the bird.

'Tis a note of enchantment; what ails her? She sees   5
A mountain ascending, a vision of trees;
Bright volumes of vapor through Lothbury glide,
And a river flows on through the vale of Cheapside.

Green pastures she views in the midst of the dale,
Down which she so often has tripped with her pail;   10
And a single small cottage, a nest like a dove's,
The one only dwelling on earth that she loves.

She looks, and her heart is in heaven; but they fade,
The mist and the river, the hill and the shade;
The stream will not flow, and the hill will not rise,   15
And the colors have all passed away from her eyes!

William Wordsworth, 1770–1850

Dactylic Pentameter   (´˘˘ / ´˘˘ / ´˘˘ / ´˘˘ / ´˘˘)

The three-syllable dactyl becomes quite drawn-out in a pentameter line.
Impossible to maintain strictly, here the dactylic meter (´˘˘) prevails.
With their falling rhythm and triple-syllable pattern, dactyls are even
harder to sustain than anapests. They are used mainly as variation in
iambic poems or (as here) in combination with other meters.

TO THE DRIVING CLOUD

Gloomy and dark art thou, O chief of the mighty Omahas;
Gloomy and dark as the driving cloud, whose name thou hast taken!
Wrapped in thy scarlet blanket, I see thee stalk through the city's
Narrow and populous streets, as once by the margin of rivers
Stalked those birds unknown, that have left us only their foot–prints.   5
What, in a few short years, will remain of thy race but the
    foot–prints?

How canst thou walk these streets, who has trod the green turf
    of the prairies?
How canst thou breathe this air, who has breathed the sweet air
    of the mountains?
Ah! 'tis in vain that with lordly looks of disdain thou dost challenge
Looks of disdain in return, and question these walls and these
    pavements,   10
Claiming the soil for thy hunting-grounds, while down-trodden
    millions
Starve in the garrets of Europe, and cry from its caverns that they,
    too,
Have been created heirs of the earth, and claim its division!
Back, then, back to thy woods in the regions west of the Wabash!
There as a monarch thou reignest. In autumn the leaves of the maple 15
Pave the floor of thy palace-halls with gold, and in summer
Pine-trees waft through its chambers the odorous breath of their
    branches.
There thou art strong and great, a hero, a tamer of horses!
There thou chasest the stately stag on the banks of the Elkhorn.
Or by the roar of the Running-Water, or where the Omaha   20
Calls thee, and leaps through the wild ravine like a brave of the
    Blackfeet!

Hark! what murmurs arise from the heart of those mountainous
    deserts?
Is it the cry of the Foxes and Crows, or the mighty Behemoth,
Who, unharmed, on his tusks once caught the bolts of the thunder,
And now lurks in his lair to destroy the race of the red man?   25
Far more fatal to thee and thy race than the Crows and the Foxes,
Far more fatal to thee and thy race than the tread of Behemoth,
Lo! the big thunder-canoe, that steadily breasts the Missouri's
Merciless current! and yonder, afar on the prairies, the campfires
Gleam through the night; and the cloud of dust in the gray of the
    daybreak   30
Marks not the buffalo's track, nor the Mandan's dexterous horse-
    race;
It is a caravan, whitening the desert where dwell the Camanches!
Ha! how the breath of these Saxons and Celts, like the blast of the
    east-wind,
Drifts evermore to the west the scanty smokes of thy wigwams!

Henry Wadsworth Longfellow, 1807–1882

Two Other Metrical Options

The preceding meters are all **accentual-syllabic:** both the number of
syllables and the number of accents count. The other two metrical

systems are simpler. **Accentual** meter counts only the number of stresses per line. **Syllabic** meter counts only the number of syllables per line, with no attention paid to the stresses at all.

Accentual Meter

Accentual (or **strong-stress**) meter is the oldest formal metrical device in English. Anglo-Saxon poetry was based on a four-stress line. The stressed syllables were further linked by alliteration. The third element was a pause (called **caesura**, the Latin word for "cut") in the middle of the line. In the Middle Ages, Chaucer sometimes chose the old meter. He began his welcome to summer:

> Now welcom, somer, with thy sonne softe

The strongly stressed, alliterated line with a caesura still survives:

> he sang his didn't he danced his did

> *e.e. cummings*

A twentieth-century example, cummings's line has all the elements of its ancient forebears. Although this caesura isn't punctuated, you hear a definite midline pause.

In 1797 Coleridge wrote "Christabel," an unfinished poem about the pure Christabel's mysterious meeting with a supernatural, powerful woman in the woods. He noted, ". . . the meter of Christabel is not properly speaking, irregular, though it may seem so from its being founded on a new principle: namely that of counting in each line the accents, not the syllables." His "new" meter wasn't new, only rediscovered.

from CHRISTABEL

> 'Tis the middle of night by the castle clock,
> And the owls have awakened the crowing cock;
> Tu—whit!——Tu—whoo!
> And hark, again! the crowing cock,
> How drowsily it crew.   5

Sir Leoline, the Baron rich,
Hath a toothless mastiff bitch;
From her kennel beneath the rock
She maketh answer to the clock,
Four for the quarters, and twelve for the hour;   10
Ever and aye, by shine and shower,
Sixteen short howls, not over loud;
Some say, she sees my lady's shroud.

Is the night chilly and dark?
The night is chilly, but not dark.   15
The thin gray cloud is spread on high,
It covers but not hides the sky.
The moon is behind, and at the full;
And yet she looks both small and dull.
The night is chill, the cloud is gray: 20
'Tis a month before the month of May,
And the Spring comes slowly up this way.

The lovely lady, Christabel,
Whom her father loves so well,
What makes her in the wood so late,   25
A furlong from the castle gate?
She had dreams all yesternight
Of her own betrothed knight;
And she in the midnight wood will pray
For the weal of her lover that's far away.   30

She stole along, she nothing spoke,
The sighs she heaved were soft and low,
And naught was green upon the oak
But moss and rarest mistletoe:
She kneels beneath the huge oak tree,   35
And in silence prayeth she.

The lady sprang up suddenly,
The lovely lady, Christabel!
It moaned as near, as near can be,
But what it is she cannot tell.—   40
On the other side it seems to be,
Of the huge, broad-breasted old oak tree.

The night is chill; the forest bare;
Is it the wind that moaneth bleak?
There is not wind enough in the air   45

To move away the ringlet curl
From the lovely lady's cheek—
There is not wind enough to twirl
The one red leaf, the last of its clan,
That dances as often as dance it can,   50
Hanging so light, and hanging so high,
On the topmost twig that looks up at the sky.

Samuel Taylor Coleridge, 1772–1834

Poets are always rediscovering accentual meter. In the late nineteenth century, Gerard Manley Hopkins devised a system of rhythm derived from the early English roots. *Sprung rhythm*, as he named it, has as its strongest element the principle of accentual meter. Unaccented syllables are not taken into account. Hopkins's "Pied Beauty" (page 43), a litany of praise for all things "counter, original, spare, strange," hits four stresses in almost every line except for the suddenly shortened last line—where two words, equally stressed, bring the poem to an emphatic conclusion.

EXERCISE

Read "God's Grandeur" aloud, marking the strong stresses as you read. Is there a prevailing pattern? What other sound patterns does Hopkins rely on?

GOD'S GRANDEUR

The world is charged with the grandeur of God.
   It will flame out, like shining from shook foil;
   It gathers to a greatness, like the ooze of oil
Crushed. Why do men then now not reck[1] his rod?
Generations have trod, have trod, have trod;   5
   And all is seared with trade; bleared, smeared with toil;
   And wears man's smudge and shares man's smell: the soil
Is bare now, nor can foot feel, being shod.

[1] *reck:* reckon with.

And for all this, nature is never spent;
There lives the dearest freshness deep down things;   10
And though the last lights off the black West went
Oh, morning, at the brown brink eastward, springs—
Because the Holy Ghost over the bent
World broods with warm breast and with ah! bright wings.

Gerard Manley Hopkins, 1844–1889

Syllabic Meter

Syllabic meter is simple. Only the number of syllables in a line matters. Accents are not considered. The poet either maintains a constant number of syllables in each line throughout the poem or constructs a pattern of lines arranged by syllable count, as in this example:

10 syllables
3 syllables
5 syllables

10 syllables
3 syllables
5 syllables

Syllabic meter, occasional in English poetry, is awkward to handle; line endings are forced to fall where the syllable count ends. French and Japanese are friendlier languages for syllabics, since most syllables are equally weighted in those languages. Sometimes, however, the meter is used with felicity, even in English. Sylvia Plath manages to avoid pitfalls of dangling line endings in "Mushrooms." She allows herself five syllables per line and, with wit, gives mushrooms their first chance to "speak" their piece:

MUSHROOMS

Overnight, very
Whitely, discreetly,
Very quietly

Our toes, our noses
Take hold on the loam.   5
Acquire the air.

Nobody sees us,
Stops us, betrays us;
The small grains make room.

Soft fists insist on   10
Heaving the needles,
The leafy bedding,

Even the paving.
Our hammers, our rams,
Earless and eyeless,   15

Perfectly voiceless,
Widen the crannies,
Shoulder through holes. We

Diet on water,
On crumbs of shadow,   20
Bland-mannered, asking

Little or nothing.
So many of us!
So many of us!

We are shelves, we are   25
Tables, we are meek,
We are edible,

Nudgers and shovers
In spite of ourselves.
Our kind multiplies: 30

We shall by morning
Inherit the earth.
Our foot's in the door.

                    Sylvia Plath, 1932–1963

In "By Disposition of Angels," the syllable pattern of the first
stanza repeats in the second stanza. A casual reading of the poem
might not reveal this:

BY DISPOSITION OF ANGELS

Messengers much like ourselves? Explain it.
Steadfastness the darkness makes explicit?
Something heard most clearly when not near it?
    Above particularities,
these unparticularities praise cannot violate.   5
    One has seen, in such steadiness never deflected,
    how by darkness a star is perfected.

Star that does not ask me if I see it?
Fir that would not wish me to uproot it?
Speech that does not ask me if I hear it?   10
    Mysteries expound mysteries.
Steadier than steady, star dazzling me, live and elate,
    no need to say, how like some we have known; too like her,
    too like him, and a-quiver forever.

Marianne Moore, 1887–1972

Moore is a tricky writer—often hiding, or rather not emphasizing, some aspect which yields delight to the careful reader. Here she uses syllabics as a subtle underpinning to her poem. The syllabic structure becomes part of the idea of "how by darkness a star is perfected." By the almost hidden syllabic form, the poem is also made "steadfast." Like the "darkness," the hidden nature of the form "does not ask me if I see it" and "does not ask me if I hear it," but still provides a framework. Of the three metrical patterns, syllabics exert the least control over rhythm. The pattern gives, as Moore says, "steadfastness," a loose rein for a confident rider like Moore.

EXERCISE

Dylan Thomas's lyric poem "Fern Hill" (page 58) is about the ecstasy of childhood on a farm and about the inevitable fall into knowledge. On the first few readings, you might not recognize this as a syllabic poem. It is one of the most masterful uses of this form in the language because of the naturalness of the poem's movement and because of the way the meter works with the subject. Once you are aware of the syllabic control, you realize the triumph of the last line, "Though I sang in my chains like the sea"—that is exactly what the meter does. Though the poem appears to be free-wheeling and wild, it is, in fact, in check. Trace the syllabic pattern and discuss its effects on the subject.

Rhythm and Meaning

"The Dance" is one of the best-known modern examples of rhythm working in lockstep with the subject of the poem. "The Dance" is based on a sixteenth-century Flemish painting of peasants dancing:

THE DANCE

> In Breughel's great picture, The Kermess,
> the dancers go round, they go round and
> around, the squeal and the blare and the
> tweedle of bagpipes, a bugle and fiddles
> tipping their bellies (round as the thick-   5
> sided glasses whose wash they impound)
> their hips and their bellies off balance
> to turn them. Kicking and rolling about
> the Fair Grounds, swinging their butts, those
> shanks must be sound to bear up under such   10
> rollicking measures, prance as they dance
> in Breughel's great picture, The Kermess.

William Carlos Williams, 1883–1963

Scanning "The Dance" for a regular pattern of accents is impossible. Though the poem contains a large number of iambs and anapests, the meter is irregular. The vigorous, tharumping anapests and the quickly alternating iambs combine to make the poem itself kick and swing. Notice that the rhythm spills over from line to line; Williams uses only two sinuous sentences in all. The movement of the meter works with alliteration and participles (by expressing continuous action, *-ing* words seem to keep moving) to capture the rounded shapes of the dancers, the overall circular motions of dance, and the composition in the painting. Many of the words are short. This poem reads as fast as a jig.

When meter is working well with the subject of the poem, as it is above, there seems to be a seamless connection between both. However, rhythm is seldom as obvious as it is in "The Dance." And meter in itself does not deliver meaning. A single meter can accommodate racy, exuberant subjects as well as meditative and philosophical ones. The whole effect of a metered poem depends on the interlocking relationship of the subject with the poem's other components: rhyme, repetition, word choice and order, imagery, vowel and consonant relationships, *and* meter.

"Rhythm must have meaning," Ezra Pound insisted. Yes, and we must discover the meaning through analysis of the whole poem. The loose iambic pentameter of "Sunday Morning" (page 258), for instance, gives the impression of a voice meditating and describing and conjecturing. The low-key metrical pattern gives structure and formality without drawing much attention to itself. The luxurious, sprawling pentameter is the opposite of the don't-stop-for-a-moment movement in "The Dance." Stevens's occasional use of rhyme is also subtle: come/sun, sacrifice/water-light, else/herself. The quiet metrical framework acts as ballast for the rich words and imagery. In contrast, "The Dance" hypes the rhythm, piles on the short, quick words, and works the language to a froth in twelve quick lines.

MY PAPA'S WALTZ

The whiskey on your breath
Could make a small boy dizzy;
But I hung on like death:
Such waltzing was not easy.

We romped until the pans   5
Slid from the kitchen shelf;
My mother's countenance
Could not unfrown itself.

The hand that held my wrist
Was battered on one knuckle;   10
At every step you missed
My right ear scraped a buckle.

You beat time on my head
With a palm caked hard by dirt,
Then waltzed me off to bed   15
Still clinging to your shirt.

Theodore Roethke, 1908–1963

Scan "My Papa's Waltz." What is the meter? Compare the meter and meaning with "The Dance." Is "My Papa's Waltz" a light-hearted poem? Notice the images in the poem and discuss the contrast with the rhythm.

• • •

THE PASTURE

I'm going out to clean the pasture spring;
I'll only stop to rake the leaves away
(And wait to watch the water clear, I may):
I shan't be gone long.—You come too.

I'm going out to fetch the little calf
That's standing by the mother. It's so young,
It totters when she licks it with her tongue,
I shan't be gone long.—You come too.

Robert Frost, 1874–1963

EXERCISES

1. Scan "The Pasture." What is the basic meter? What happens at the end of each stanza? What effect does this have?
2. The best way to understand meter thoroughly is to try writing in a particular meter. Write several lines each of iambic dimeter, iambic pentameter, trochaic trimeter, and anapestic tetrameter. Try a few lines of accentual meter and a short syllabic poem. Don't be concerned about writing the perfect poem. This is practice in experiencing the meters first hand.

HIS RUNNING MY RUNNING

Mid-autumn late autumn
At dayfall in leaf-fall
A runner comes running.

How easy his striding
How light his footfall   5
His bare legs gleaming.

Alone he emerges
Emerges and passes
Alone, sufficient.

When autumn was early   10
Two runners came running
Striding together

Shoulder to shoulder
Pacing each other
A perfect pairing.   15

Out of leaves falling
Over leaves fallen
A runner comes running

Aware of no watcher
His loneness my loneness   20
His running my running.

Robert Francis, 1901–1987

Discuss the relationship of rhythm with the meaning of "His Running
My Running." Though extremely well-balanced, the poem is not in
meter. How does Francis get the strong rhythmic effects? Compare the
ways the lines are used with Williams's "The Dance." Which poem do
you prefer? Why?

Poems for Discussion

MNEMONIC

Trochee trips from long to short;
From long to long in solemn sort
Slow Spondee stalks; strong foot! yea ill able
Ever to come up with Dactyl's trisyllable.
Iambics march from short to long;
With a leap and a bound the swift Anapests throng.

Samuel Taylor Coleridge, 1772–1834

from ROMEO AND JULIET

(Act III, scene v)

JULIET
Wilt thou be gone? It is not yet near day.
It was the nightingale, and not the lark,
That pierced the fearful hollow of thine ear.
Nightly she sings on yond pomegranate tree.
Believe me, love, it was the nightingale.   5
ROMEO
It was the lark, the herald of the morn;
No nightingale. Look, love, what envious streaks
Do lace the severing clouds in yonder east.
Night's candles are burnt out, and jocund day
Stands tiptoe on the misty mountaintops.   10
I must be gone and live, or stay and die.
JULIET
Yond light is not daylight; I know it, I.
It is some meteor that the sun exhales
To be to thee this night a torchbearer
And light thee on thy way to Mantua.   15
Therefore stay yet; thou need'st not be gone.
ROMEO
Let me be ta'en, let me be put to death.
I am content, so thou wilt have it so.
I'll say yon gray is not the morning's eye,
'Tis but the pale reflex of Cynthia's brow[1]   20
Nor that is not the lark whose notes do beat
The vaulty heaven so high above our heads.

---

[1] *Cynthia's brow:* a reflection on the edge of the moon.

I have more care to stay than will to go.
Come death, and welcome! Juliet wills it so.
How is't, my soul? Let's talk; it is not day.   25
JULIET
It is, it is! Hie hence, be gone, away!
It is the lark that sings so out of tune,
Straining harsh discords and unpleasing sharps.
Some say the lark makes sweet division[2]
This doth not so, for she divideth us.   30
Some say the lark and loathèd toad change eyes;
O, now I would they had changed voices too,
Since arm from arm that voice doth us affray,[3]
Hunting thee hence with hunt's-up[4] to the day.
O, now be gone! More light and light it grows.   35
ROMEO
More light and light—more dark and dark our woes.

William Shakespeare, 1564–1616

[2] *division:* melody.
[3] *affray:* frighten.
[4] *hunt's up:* a morning song for hunters.

LINES

Composed a few miles above Tintern Abbey,
on revisiting the banks of the Wye during a tour.
July 13, 1798

Five years have passed; five summers, with the length
Of five long winters! and again I hear
These waters, rolling from their mountain springs
With a soft inland murmur. Once again
Do I behold these steep and lofty cliffs,   5
That on a wild secluded scene impress
Thoughts of more deep seclusion; and connect
The landscape with the quiet of the sky.
The day is come when I again repose
Here, under this dark sycamore, and view   10
These plots of cottage ground, these orchard tufts,
Which at this season, with their unripe fruits,
Are clad in one green hue, and lose themselves
'Mid groves and copses. Once again I see
These hedgerows, hardly hedgerows, little lines   15

Of sportive wood run wild—these pastoral farms,
Green to the very door; and wreaths of smoke
Sent up, in silence, from among the trees!
With some uncertain notice, as might seem
Of vagrant dwellers in the houseless woods,　　　　　　　　20
Or of some hermit's cave, where by his fire
The hermit sits alone.

　　　　　　　　These beauteous forms,
Through a long absence, have not been to me
As is a landscape to a blind man's eye;
But oft, in lonely rooms, and 'mid the din　　　　　　　25
Of towns and cities, I have owed to them
In hours of weariness, sensations sweet,
Felt in the blood, and felt along the heart;
And passing even into my purer mind,
With tranquil restoration; feelings too　　　　　　　　30
Of unremembered pleasure, such, perhaps,
As have no slight or trivial influence
On that best portion of a good man's life,
His little, nameless, unremembered, acts
Of kindness and of love. Nor less, I trust,　　　　　　35
To them I may have owed another gift,
Of aspect more sublime; that blessed mood,
In which the burthen of the mystery,
In which the heavy and the weary weight
Of all this unintelligible world,　　　　　　　　　　40
Is lightened: that serene and blessed mood,
In which the affections gently lead us on,
Until, the breath of this corporeal frame
And even the motion of our human blood
Almost suspended, we are laid asleep　　　　　　　45
In body, and become a living soul,
While with an eye made quiet by the power
Of harmony, and the deep power of joy,
We see into the life of things.
　　　　　　　　　　　　If this
Be but a vain belief, yet, oh! how oft—　　　　　　　50
In darkness and amid the many shapes
Of joyless daylight; when the fretful stir
Unprofitable, and the fever of the world,
Have hung upon the beatings of my heart—
How oft, in spirit, have I turned to thee,　　　　　　55
O sylvan Wye! thou wanderer through the woods,
How often has my spirit turned to thee!

And now, with gleams of half-extinguished thought,
With many recognitions dim and faint,
And somewhat of a sad perplexity,   60
The picture of the mind revives again:
While here I stand, not only with the sense
Of present pleasure, but with pleasing thoughts
That in this moment there is life and food
For future years. And so I dare to hope,   65
Though changed, no doubt, from what I was when first
I came among these hills; when like a roe
I bounded o'er the mountains, by the sides
Of the deep rivers, and the lonely streams,
Wherever nature led—more like a man   70
Flying from something that he dreads, than one
Who sought the thing he loved. For nature then
(The coarser pleasures of my boyish days,
And their glad animal movements all gone by)
To me was all in all. I cannot paint   75
What then I was. The sounding cataract
Haunted me like a passion; the tall rock,
The mountain, and the deep and gloomy wood,
Their colors and their forms, were then to me
An appetite; a feeling and a love,   80
That had no need of a remoter charm,
By thought supplied, nor any interest
Unborrowed from the eye. That time is past,
And all its aching joys are now no more,
And all its dizzy raptures. Not for this   85
Faint I, nor mourn nor murmur; other gifts
Have followed; for such loss, I would believe,
Abundant recompense. For I have learned
To look on nature, not as in the hour
Of thoughtless youth; but hearing oftentimes   90
The still, sad music of humanity,
Nor harsh nor grating, though of ample power
To chasten and subdue. And I have felt
A presence that disturbs me with the joy
Of elevated thoughts; a sense sublime   95
Of something far more deeply interfused,
Whose dwelling is the light of setting suns,
And the round ocean and the living air,
And the blue sky, and in the mind of man;
A motion and a spirit, that impels   100
All thinking things, all objects of all thought,
And rolls through all things. Therefore am I still
A lover of the meadows and the woods,

And mountains; and of all that we behold
From this green earth; of all the mighty world   105
Of eye, and ear—both what they half-create,
And what perceive; well pleased to recognize
In nature and the language of the sense,
The anchor of my purest thoughts, the nurse,
The guide, the guardian of my heart, and soul   110
Of all my moral being.
                              Nor perchance,
If I were not thus taught, should I the more
Suffer my genial spirits to decay;
For thou art with me here upon the banks
Of this fair river, thou my dearest friend,   115
My dear, dear friend; and in thy voice I catch
The language of my former heart, and read
My former pleasures in the shooting lights
Of thy wild eyes. Oh! yet a little while
May I behold in thee what I was once,   120
My dear, dear sister! and this prayer I make,
Knowing that Nature never did betray
The heart that loved her; 'tis her privilege,
Through all the years of this our life, to lead
From joy to joy; for she can so inform   125
The mind that is within us, so impress
With quietness and beauty, and so feed
With lofty thoughts, that neither evil tongues,
Rash judgments, nor the sneers of selfish men,
Nor greetings where no kindness is, nor all   130
The dreary intercourse of daily life,
Shall e'er prevail against us, or disturb
Our cheerful faith, that all which we behold
Is full of blessings. Therefore let the moon
Shine on thee in thy solitary walk;   135
And let the misty mountain winds be free
To blow against thee: and, in after years,
When these wild ecstasies shall be matured
Into a sober pleasure; when thy mind
Shall be a mansion for all lovely forms,   140
Thy memory be as a dwelling place
For all sweet sounds and harmonies; oh! then,
If solitude, or fear, or pain, or grief,
Should be thy portion, with what healing thoughts
Of tender joy wilt thou remember me,   145
And these my exhortations! Nor, perchance—
If I should be where I no more can hear
Thy voice, nor catch from thy wild eyes these gleams

Of past existence—wilt thou then forget
That on the banks of this delightful stream   150
We stood together; and that I, so long
A worshiper of Nature, hither came
Unwearied in that service; rather say
With warmer love—oh! with far deeper zeal
Of holier love. Nor wilt thou then forget,   155
That after many wanderings, many years
Of absence, these steep woods and lofty cliffs,
And this green pastoral landscape, were to me
More dear, both for themselves and for thy sake!

William Wordsworth, 1770–1850

THE PULLEY

When God at first made man,
Having a glass of blessings standing by;
"Let us" (said he) "pour on him all we can:
Let the world's riches, which dispersèd lie,
        Contract into a span."   5

So strength first made a way;
Then beauty flowed; then wisdom, honour, pleasure:
When almost all was out, God made a stay,
Perceiving that alone of all his treasure
        Rest in the bottom lay.   10

"For if I should" (said he)
"Bestow this jewel also on my creature,
He would adore my gifts instead of me,
And rest in nature, not the God of nature:
        So both should losers be.   15

"Yet let him keep the rest,
But keep them with repining restlessness:
Let him be rich and weary, that at least,
If goodness lead him not, yet weariness
        May toss him to my breast."   20

George Herbert, 1593–1633

ONE PERFECT ROSE

A single flow'r he sent me, since we met.
　　All tenderly his messenger he chose;
Deep-hearted, pure, with scented dew still wet—
　　One perfect rose.

I knew the language of the floweret;　　　　　　　　　　5
　　"My fragile leaves," it said, "his heart enclose."
Love long has taken for his amulet
　　One perfect rose.

Why is it no one ever sent me yet
　　One perfect limousine, do you suppose?　　　　　　　10
Ah no, it's always just my luck to get
　　One perfect rose.

Dorothy Parker, 1893–1967

THE DESTRUCTION OF SENNACHERIB

The Assyrian[1] came down like the wolf on the fold,
And his cohorts were gleaming in purple and gold;
And the sheen of their spears was like stars on the sea,
When the blue wave rolls nightly on deep Galilee.

Like the leaves of the forest when summer is green,　　　5
That host with their banners at sunset were seen:
Like the leaves of the forest when autumn hath blown,
That host on the morrow lay withered and strown.

For the Angel of Death spread his wings on the blast,
And breathed in the face of the foe as he passed;　　　　10
And the eyes of the sleepers waxed deadly and chill,
And their hearts but once heaved—and for ever grew still!

And there lay the steed with his nostril all wide,
But through it there rolled not the breath of his pride;
And the foam of his gasping lay white on the turf,　　　15
And cold as the spray of the rock-beating surf.

---

[1] *The Assyrian:* In the Old Testament (2 Kings: 19), King Sennacherib of Assyria is about to attack the Israelites when an angel slays his men.

And there lay the rider distorted and pale,
With the dew on his brow, and the rust on his mail;
And the tents were all silent, the banners alone,
The lances unlifted, the trumpet unblown.   20

And the widows of Ashur[2] are loud in their wail,
And the idols are broke in the temple of Baal;[3]
And the might of the Gentile, unsmote by the sword,
Hath melted like snow in the glance of the Lord!

George Gordon, Lord Byron, 1788–1824

[2] *Ashur:* god of the Assyrians.
[3] *Baal:* here represents a god foreign to the Israelites, though Baal was actually a Phoeni-
cian god, not an Assyrian god.

RENDEZVOUS

I have a rendezvous with Death
At some disputed barricade,
When Spring comes back with rustling shade
And apple-blossoms fill the air—
I have a rendezvous with Death   5
When Spring brings back blue days and fair.

It may be he shall take my hand
And lead me into his dark land
And close my eyes and quench my breath—
It may be I shall pass him still.   10
I have a rendezvous with Death
On some scarred slope of battered hill,
When Spring comes round again this year
And the first meadow-flowers appear.

God knows 'twere better to be deep   15
Pillowed in silk and scented down,
Where love throbs out in blissful sleep,
Pulse nigh to pulse, and breath to breath,
Where hushed awakenings are dear . . .
But I've a rendezvous with Death   20
At midnight in some flaming town,
When Spring trips north again this year,
And I to my pledged word am true,
I shall not fail that rendezvous.

Alan Seeger, 1888–1916

IN MEMORY OF W. B. YEATS

(d. January, 1939)

1

He disappeared in the dead of winter:
The brooks were frozen, the airports almost deserted,
And snow disfigured the public statues;
The mercury sank in the mouth of the dying day.
What instruments we have agree   5
The day of his death was a dark cold day.

Far from his illness
The wolves ran on through the evergreen forests,
The peasant river was untempted by the fashionable quays;
By mourning tongues   10
The death of the poet was kept from his poems.
But for him it was his last afternoon as himself,
An afternoon of nurses and rumors;
The provinces of his body revolted,
The squares of his mind were empty,   15
Silence invaded the suburbs,
The current of his feeling failed; he became his admirers.

Now he is scattered among a hundred cities
And wholly given over to unfamiliar affections,
To find his happiness in another kind of wood   20
And be punished under a foreign code of conscience.
The words of a dead man
Are modified in the guts of the living.

But in the importance and noise of tomorrow
When the brokers are roaring like beasts on the floor of the
    Bourse,[1]   25
And the poor have the sufferings to which they are fairly
    accustomed,
And each in the cell of himself is almost convinced of his freedom,
A few thousand will think of this day
As one thinks of a day when one did something slightly unusual.
What instruments we have agree   30
The day of his death was a dark cold day.

---

[1] *Bourse:* stock exchange.

2

You were silly like us; your gift survived it all:
The parish of rich women, physical decay,
Yourself. Mad Ireland hurt you into poetry.
Now Ireland has her madness and her weather still,   35
For poetry makes nothing happen: it survives
In the valley of its making where executives
Would never want to tamper, flows on south
From ranches of isolation and the busy griefs,
Raw towns that we believe and die in; it survives,   40
A way of happening, a mouth.

3

Earth, receive an honored guest;
William Yeats is laid to rest:
Let the Irish vessel lie
Emptied of its poetry.   45

Time that is intolerant
Of the brave and innocent,
And indifferent in a week
To a beautiful physique,

Worships language and forgives   50
Everyone by whom it lives;
Pardons cowardice, conceit,
Lays its honors at their feet.

Time that with this strange excuse
Pardoned Kipling and his views,   55
And will pardon Paul Claudel,
Pardons him for writing well.

In the nightmare of the dark
All the dogs of Europe bark,
And the living nations wait,   60
Each sequestered in its hate;

Intellectual disgrace
Stares from every human face,
And the seas of pity lie
Locked and frozen in each eye.   65

Follow, poet, follow right
To the bottom of the night,
With your unconstraining voice
Still persuade us to rejoice;

With the farming of a verse   70
Make a vineyard of the curse,
Sing of human unsuccess
In a rapture of distress:

In the deserts of the heart
Let the healing fountain start,   75
In the prison of his days
Teach the free man how to praise.

                                        W. H. Auden, 1907–1973

NATURE'S COOK

Death is the cook of nature, and we find
Creatures drest several ways to please her mind;
Some Death doth roast with fevers burning hot,
And some he boils with dropsies in a pot;
Some are consumed for jelly by degrees,   5
And some with ulcers, gravy out to squeeze;
Some, as with herbs, he stuffs with gouts and pains,
Others for tender meat he hangs in chains;
Some in the sea he pickles up to keep,
Others he, as soused brawn,[1] in wine doth steep;   10
Some flesh and bones he with the Pox chops small,
And doth a French fricassee make withall;
Some on grid-irons of calentures[2] are broiled,
And some are trodden down, and so quite spoiled:
But some are baked, when smothered they do die,   15
Some meat he doth by hectick fevers fry;
In sweat sometimes he stews with savory smell,
An hodge-podge of diseases he likes well;
Some brains he dresseth with apoplexy,
Or fawce[3] of megrims,[4] swimming plenteously;   20
And tongues he dries with smoak from stomachs ill,
Which, as the second course he sends up still;

[1] *soused brawn:* pickled hard.
[2] *calentures:* a tropical disease.
[3] *fawce:* sauce.
[4] *megrins:* migraines.

Throats he doth cut, blood puddings for to make,
And puts them in the guts, which cholicks rack;
Some hunted are by him for deer, that's red,   25
And some as stall-fed oxen knocked o'th' head;
Some singed and scald for bacon, seem most rare,
When with salt rheum and phlegm they powdered are.

Margaret, Duchess of Newcastle, 1625–1673

DRINK TO ME ONLY WITH THINE EYES

Drink to me only with thine eyes,
   And I will pledge with mine;
Or leave a kiss but in the cup,
   And I'll not look for wine.
The thirst that from the soul doth rise   5
   Doth ask a drink divine;
But might I of Jove's nectar sup,
   I would not change for thine.

I sent thee late a rosy wreath,
   Not so much honoring thee   10
As giving it a hope that there
   It could not withered be.
But thou thereon didst only breathe,
   And sent'st it back to me;
Since when it grows, and smells, I swear,   15
   Not of itself but thee.

Ben Jonson, 1573–1637

A HYMN TO GOD THE FATHER

Hear me, O God!
A broken heart,
Is my best part;
Use still thy rod,
That I may prove   5
Therein thy love.

If thou hadst not
Been stern to me,
But left me free,
I had forgot   10
Myself and thee.

For sin's so sweet,
As minds ill bent
Rarely repent,
Until they meet   15
Their punishment.

Who more can crave
Than thou has done,
That gav'st a Son,
To free a slave?   20
First made of naught,
With all since bought.

Sin, Death, and Hell,
His glorious Name
Quite overcame,   25
Yet I rebel,
And slight the same.

But I'll come in
Before my loss
Me farther toss,   30
As sure to win
Under his Cross.

Ben Jonson, 1573–1637

UPON HIS DEPARTURE HENCE

Thus I
Passe by,
And die:
As One,
Unknown,   5
And gon:
I'm made
A shade,
And laid
I'th grave,   10
There have
My Cave.
Where tell
I dwell,
Farewell.   15

Robert Herrick, 1591–1674

SAILING TO BYZANTIUM

That is no country for old men. The young
In one another's arms, birds in the trees
—Those dying generations—at their song,
The salmon-falls, the mackerel-crowded seas,
Fish, flesh, or fowl, commend all summer long   5
Whatever is begotten, born, and dies.
Caught in that sensual music all neglect
Monuments of unaging intellect.

An aged man is but a paltry thing,
A tattered coat upon a stick, unless   10
Soul clap its hands and sing, and louder sing
For every tatter in its mortal dress,
Nor is there singing school but studying
Monuments of its own magnificence;
And therefore I have sailed the seas and come   15
To the holy city of Byzantium.

O sages standing in God's holy fire
As in the gold mosaic of a wall,
Come from the holy fire, perne in a gyre,
And be the singing-masters of my soul.   20
Consume my heart away; sick with desire
And fastened to a dying animal
It knows not what it is; and gather me
Into the artifice of eternity.

Once out of nature I shall never take   25
My bodily form from any natural thing,
But such a form as Grecian goldsmiths make
Of hammered gold and gold enameling
To keep a drowsy Emperor awake;
Or set upon a golden bough to sing   30
To lords and ladies of Byzantium
Of what is past, or passing, or to come.

William Butler Yeats, 1865–1939

TO EARTHWARD

Love at the lips was touch
As sweet as I could bear;
And once that seemed too much;
I lived on air

That crossed me from sweet things,
The flow of—was it musk
From hidden grapevine springs
Down hill at dusk?   5

I had the swirl and ache
From sprays of honeysuckle   10
That when they're gathered shake
Dew on the knuckle,

I craved strong sweets, but those
Seemed strong when I was young;
The petal of the rose   15
It was that stung.

Now no joy but lacks salt
That is not dashed with pain
And weariness and fault;
I crave the stain   20

Of tears, the aftermark
Of almost too much love,
The sweet of bitter bark
And burning clove.

When stiff and sore and scarred   25
I take away my hand
From leaning on it hard
In grass and sand,

The hurt is not enough:
I long for weight and strength   30
To feel the earth as rough
To all my length.

Robert Frost, 1874–1963

RHYME

What laid, I said,
My being waste?
'Twas your sweet flesh
With its sweet taste,—

Which, like a rose,   5
Fed with a breath,
And at its full
Belied all death.

It's at springs we drink;
It's bread we eat,   10
And no fine body,
Head to feet,

Should force all bread
And drink together,
Nor be both sun   15
And hidden weather.

Ah no, it should not;
Let it be.
But once heart's feast
You were to me.   20

Louise Bogan, 1897–1970

I AM

I am: yet what I am none cares or knows,
    My friends forsake me like a memory lost:
I am the self-consumer of my woes.
    They rise and vanish in oblivious host,
Like shades in love and death's oblivion lost;   5
    And yet I am, and live with shadows tost

Into the nothingness of scorn and noise,
    Into the living sea of waking dreams,
Where there is neither sense of life nor joys,
    But the vast shipwreck of my life's esteems;   10
And e'en the dearest—that I loved the best—
And strange—nay, rather stranger than the rest.

I long for scenes where man has never trod.
    A place where woman never smiled or wept:
There to abide with my Creator, God,   15
    And sleep as I in childhood sweetly slept,
Untroubling and untroubled where I lie,
The grass below—above the vaulted sky.

John Clare, 1793–1864

BIRCHES

When I see birches bend to left and right
Across the lines of straighter darker trees,
I like to think some boy's been swinging them.
But swinging doesn't bend them down to stay
As ice-storms do. Often you must have seen them   5
Loaded with ice a sunny winter morning
After a rain. They click upon themselves
As the breeze rises, and turn many-colored
As the stir cracks and crazes their enamel.
Soon the sun's warmth makes them shed crystal shells   10
Shattering and avalanching on the snow-crust—
Such heaps of broken glass to sweep away
You'd think the inner dome of heaven had fallen.
They are dragged to the withered bracken by the load,
And they seem not to break; though once they are bowed   15
So low for long, they never right themselves:
You may see their trunks arching in the woods
Years afterwards, trailing their leaves on the ground
Like girls on hands and knees that throw their hair
Before them over their heads to dry in the sun.   20
But I was going to say when Truth broke in
With all her matter-of-fact about the ice-storm
I should prefer to have some boy bend them
As he went out and in to fetch the cows—
Some boy too far from town to learn baseball,   25
Whose only play was what he found himself,
Summer or winter, and could play alone.
One by one he subdued his father's trees
By riding them down over and over again
Until he took the stiffness out of them,   30
And not one but hung limp, not one was left
For him to conquer. He learned all there was
To learn about not launching out too soon
And so not carrying the tree away
Clear to the ground. He always kept his poise   35
To the top branches, climbing carefully
With the same pains you use to fill a cup

Up to the brim, and even above the brim.
Then he flung outward, feet first, with a swish,
Kicking his way down through the air to the ground.   40
So was I once myself a swinger of birches.
And so I dream of going back to be.
It's when I'm weary of considerations,
And life is too much like a pathless wood

Where your face burns and tickles with the cobwebs   45
Broken across it, and one eye is weeping
From a twig's having lashed across it open.
I'd like to get away from earth awhile
And then come back to it and begin over.
May no fate willfully misunderstand me   50
And half grant what I wish and snatch me away
Not to return. Earth's the right place for love:
I don't know where it's likely to go better.
I'd like to go by climbing a birch tree,
And climb black branches up a snow-white trunk   55
Toward heaven, till the tree could bear no more,
But dipped its top and set me down again.
That would be good both going and coming back.
One could do worse than be a swinger of birches.

Robert Frost, 1874–1963

STANZAS FOR MUSIC

There's not a joy the world can give like that it takes away,
When the glow of early thought declines in feelings' dull decay;
'Tis not on youth's smooth cheek the blush alone, which fades so fast,
But the tender bloom of heart is gone, ere youth itself be past.

Then the few whose spirits float above the wreck of happiness   5
Are driven o'er the shoals of guilt or ocean of excess:
The magnet of their course is gone, or only points in vain
The shore to which their shivered sail shall never stretch again.

Then the mortal coldness of the soul like death itself comes down;
It cannot feel for others' woes, it dare not dream its own;   10
That heavy chill has frozen o'er the fountain of our tears,
And though the eye may sparkle still, 'tis where the ice appears.

Though wit may flash from fluent lips, and mirth distract the breast,
Through midnight hours that yield no more their former hope of rest;
'Tis but as ivy-leaves around the ruined turret wreath,   15
All green and wildly fresh without, but worn and grey beneath.

Oh could I feel as I have felt,—or be what I have been,
Or weep as I could once have wept, o'er many a vanished scene:
As springs in deserts found seem sweet, all brackish though they be,
So, midst the withered waste of life, those tears would flow to me.   20

George Gordon, Lord Byron, 1788–1824

THE POPLAR FIELD

The poplars are felled, farewell to the shade
And the whispering sound of the cool colonnade,
The winds play no longer, and sing in the leaves,
Nor Ouse[1] on his bosom their image receives.

Twelve years have elapsed since I last took a view   5
Of my favourite field and the bank where they grew,
And now in the grass behold they are laid,
And the tree is my seat that once lent me a shade.

The blackbird has fled to another retreat
Where the hazels afford him a screen from the heat,   10
And the scene where his melody charmed me before,
Resounds with his sweet-flowing ditty no more.

My fugitive years are all hasting away,
And I must ere long lie as lowly as they,
With a turf on my breast, and a stone at my head,   15
Ere another such grove shall arise in its stead.

'Tis a sight to engage me; if any thing can,
To muse on the perishing pleasures of man;
Though his life be a dream, his enjoyments, I see,
Have a being less durable even than he.   20

William Cowper, 1731–1800

[1] *Ouse:* a river in England.

THE WHITE BIRDS

I would that we were, my beloved, white birds on the foam of
the sea!
We tire of the flame of the meteor, before it can fade and flee;
And the flame of the blue star of twilight, hung low on the rim
of the sky,
Has awakened in our hearts, my beloved, a sadness that may
not die.

A weariness comes from those dreamers, dew-dabbled, the
    lily and rose;   5
Ah, dream not of them, my beloved, the flame of the meteor
    that goes,
Or the flame of the blue star that lingers hung low in the fall
    of the dew:
For I would we were changed to white birds on the wandering
    foam: I and you!

I am haunted by numberless islands, and many a Danaan
    shore,
Where Time would surely forget us, and Sorrow come near us
    no more;   10
Soon far from the rose and the lily and fret of the flames
    would we be,
Were we only white birds, my beloved, buoyed out on the
    foam of the sea!

William Butler Yeats, 1865–1939

Free Verse

I have found the law of my own poems.

Walt Whitman

In the twentieth century, ways of making poems have multiplied. Poets felt dissatisfied with the restrictions of meter, set forms, and rhyme schemes that earlier poets took as the norm. They began to develop more diverse possibilities. Finding "the law of my own poems" means each poem is a "free verse," a new invention operating on its own terms instead of a marrying of subject, voice, and language to a pre-existing meter.

Meter, as the previous chapter discussed, plays a tremendous role when it is part of a poem. Mainly, it organizes the accents into an overall pattern and more or less evenly times the lines. Meter provides an underlying orderly structure on which the poet can play out innumerable variations. But meter does more than that. It's not just a taut line on which you can hang your words and thoughts like wash flapping in the breeze. In any poem, the poet aspires for form to *be* content, content to *be* form. The choice of a certain meter means the poet hears the music in that key. Free verse poets hear differently. For both ways of writing, Thomas Carlyle's insight is apt: "See deep enough, and you see musically; the heart of Nature *being* everywhere music, if only you can reach it." Poets are always reaching for the music at the heart of the poem.

Free verse is improvisational. Poets compose with an irregular line, the speaking voice, language and imagery as their primary instruments. In contemporary poems, lines do not necessarily follow the left margin; they may be placed in other arrangements. Blank space often is used for a pause within a line with or without punctuation. Some poems have no punctuation at all because the writer perceives it as an interruption. "I" is the most common speaker of the free verse poem; lines are broken to punctuate how the poet wants us to hear perceptions, individual speech, or breath rhythms.

No subject is taboo. In a contemporary poem, smog, rape, fallout, and cancer might meet waterfalls, birds of paradise, moonlight and papaya on the same page. Keats might be amazed to read about crime and other "ugly" subjects, as well as about utterly mundane subjects:

BETWEEN WALLS

the back wings
of the

hospital where
nothing

will grow lie   5
cinders

in which shine
the broken

pieces of a green
bottle   10

William Carlos Williams, 1883–1963

These are some of the touchstone developments of free verse. Not that all poets abandon the technical tools of traditional verse. A poem written tomorrow might well be at its best in trochaic tetrameter. Contemporary poems sometimes have the "ghost" of iambic pentameter or another meter working throughout the poem. And some poets, especially in England, still use the traditional meters entirely. Others use meter when particular poems benefit. Many, however, see meter as obsolete or as false to their purposes. American Charles Wright is not the only contemporary poet well-versed in metrics who scans his poems to make sure that they do *not* accidentally fall into regular meter.

The Genesis of Free Verse

The roots of this change are much older than the twentieth century. Walt Whitman, carpenter, newspaper editor, and hospital volunteer in the Civil War, broke decisively with the verse of his time. He wrote long, rising and falling lines with hypnotic repetition and rolling movement. He insisted on "including" rather than paring down. He wanted an American poetry "proportionate to our continent, with its powerful races of men, its tremendous historical events, its great oceans, its mountains and its illimitable prairies."

Emily Dickinson, Whitman's contemporary, was his opposite. While Whitman hung out around docks and took large-stride steps over as much of the American landscape as possible, Dickinson closed herself off in her father's house and wrote privately, tying her poems into neat fascicles with string. She heard her own music. At times she used no meter; often her rhythms were based on Protestant hymns. If you grew up singing songs such as "Amazing Grace" or "The God of Abraham Praise," you can often "sing" Dickinson's poems to those tunes. What is striking is how she surprises the reader's expectations constantly by the subversive contrast of these common meters with her wild imagination and subjects. She counters the simplicity of the beat with startling word choices, juxtaposition of perceptions that have never been near each other before, and dissonant off-rhymes that sound distinctly at odds with other nineteenth-century verse.

In Ralph Waldo Emerson we find another precursor of free verse. Two of his distinctly modern percepts were "Ask the fact for the form" and "Any word, every word in language, every circumstance, becomes poetic in the hands of a higher thought." In nineteenth-century Concord, Massachusetts, Emerson envisioned a new poetry shaped from within and capable of including any subject.

Early American poets often had a quirky sense of rhythm; English traditions did not migrate unscathed. Writing in isolation, American poets devised their own poetic variations on the models at hand. In end-of-the-century England, some poets grew "sick to death of Swinburne," the poet so well known for his flowing style of rhymes and meters that he sometimes even made fun of himself. Thomas Hardy, Gerard Manley Hopkins, and (to a lesser extent) A. E. Housman, all born in the mid-1800s, broke out of the pervasive gentility with new subjects and more percussive sounds. French poets had established a *vers libre* ("free verse"), and their influences began to blow fast across the waters.

The poets most receptive to the influence from France were a group in England including the Americans H. D. (Hilda Doolittle) and

Ezra Pound. By 1910, these poets were avidly reading Chinese poetry and discussing their own theories and values. The poetry they championed was based on clear, incisive images.

HEAT

O wind, rend open the heat,
cut apart the heat,
rend it to tatters.

Fruit cannot drop
through this thick air—   5
fruit cannot fall into heat
that presses up and blunts
the points of pears
and rounds the grapes.

Cut the heat—   10
plough through it,
turning it on either side
of your path.

H. D. (Hilda Doolittle), 1896–1961

An image, Pound said, "is that which presents an intellectual and emotional complex in an instant of time." His famous one-image poem on the faces he saw as he emerged from the metro at La Concorde was distilled from a thirty-line poem:

IN A STATION OF THE METRO

The apparition of these faces in the crowd;
Petals on a wet, black bough.

"In a poem of this sort," Pound explained, "one is trying to record the precise instant when a thing outward and objective transforms itself, or darts into a thing inward and subjective."

As a unified group of writers, the Imagists blazed only briefly on the scene, but their initial contributions provided, as T. S. Eliot noted, "the starting point of modern poetry." Their principles of concentration, precise diction, and composition in the "sequence of the musical phrase not the sequence of a metronome" (Pound's advice) deeply influenced the poets who followed.

Developments in the arts always connect to the broader context of history. The changes in poetry early in this century occurred as the English-speaking world shifted values. Historians pinpoint World War I as the time of irreconcilable fragmentation of society. This break-up of values and coherence erupted in all the arts. Musical composers began to include dissonance and cacophony in their work; painters multiplied their perspectives; dancers broke out of the classical repertoire into spontaneous, sometimes contorted movements. The powerful camera eye of photography and movies had strong impact on writers. At the same time, belief in *a* poetics broke open. Comparing meter with free verse, poet Robert Hass says:

> The difference is, in some ways, huge; the metrical poem begins with an assumption of human life which takes place in a pattern of orderly recurrence with which the poet must come to terms, the free verse poem with an assumption of openness or chaos in which an order must be discovered.

This is the basic fact of free verse: each poem is shaped from within. In a way, poets always had this goal. Coleridge sought an "organic" form; Keats thought poetry should come into being "as naturally as leaves to a tree"; Milton wanted a "simple, sensuous, and impassioned" poetry. These approaches, however, only varied existing meters. Poets of this century have made more decisive changes.

Without meter and rhyme scheme, what makes a poem a poem? When chloroform was invented, a famous doctor of the time remarked in dismay, "*Anyone* can be a surgeon now." When open forms began to strike a strong responsive chord in poets, many lamented like the good doctor. But the techniques of modern poetry, although different, are rigorous. A good poem remains difficult to achieve.

The Free Verse Craft of the Line

We know that the main difference between poetry and prose is that poetry is a line art and prose is a sentence art. Sentences run to the edge of the margin. Although lines of poems make sentences, the line lengths and breaks in poetry are crucial. (Prose poems are an exception to this. We'll study them later in the Open Forms chapter.) In both free verse and metered verse, lines are as important to the poem as rungs are to a ladder. Each line moves the poem along at a certain speed. A **line** is a unit of time; a line break is a punctuation, a slight halt in the flow. Where there is no comma or period, the line break indicates a slight pause, the equivalent of a half comma. The last word on a line always gets attention; that's where your eye stops before it returns to the beginning of the next line. You also attend to the first word in a line. Sometimes poets accentuate that first word more by capitalizing it. Whether short or long, free or metered, line length manages the flow of the poem and controls what words get the most attention. In free verse, therefore, lines often are irregular in length or are placed in arrangements on the page according to where the poet wants emphasis to fall. If the energy of one or a series of lines flags, the poem falls off in interest. What the line is *not*, necessarily, is a unit of sense. In all poetry, lines often **enjamb** (run on) to the next, as in these iambic tetrameter lines:

> The green catalpa tree has turned
> All white; the cherry blooms once more.
>
> *W. D. Snodgrass*

The second line is **end-stopped:** the sense of the line terminates with a period. Pauses and emphases are expressive of the poem's content.

Typed as conventional prose, an e. e. cummings poem reads:

> Buffalo Bill's defunct, who used to ride a water-smooth, silver stallion and break one, two, three, four, five pigeons just like that. Jesus, he was a handsome man. And what I want to know is, how do you like your blue-eyed boy, Mister Death?

These are lively words. But look at the increase of effect when they're arranged in lines:

from PORTRAITS

viii

Buffalo Bill's
defunct
    who used to
    ride a watersmooth-silver
                    stallion   5
and break onetwothreefourfive pigeonsjustlikethat
                            Jesus

he was a handsome man
                  and what i want to know is
how do you like your blueeyed boy   10
Mister Death

                       e. e. cummings, 1894–1962

The isolation of words on the short lines gives each word special importance. The long, jolting, run-together line speeds up the middle of the
poem violently, then drops off suddenly to exclaim "Jesus." We can
hear a speaking voice in the rhythm. When the voice concludes "how
do you like your blueeyed boy / Mister Death," we're surprised at the
shift from the exuberant descriptions of Buffalo Bill to a direct question
asked of Death. It is a surprise that works mainly because the line
break between "man" and "and what" downshifts from fast talk to a
question but also continues the conversational voice.

    Usually the use of the line is more subtly modulated than in "Buf-
falo Bill." In these cases, we have to look closely at how the line works
to reveal emotions or movements of thought.

THE ELDER SISTER

When I look at my elder sister now
I think how she had to go first, down through the
birth canal, to force her way
head-first through the tiny channel,
the pressure of Mother's muscles on her brain,   5
the tight walls scraping her skin.
Her face is still narrow from it, the long
hollow cheeks of a Crusader on a tomb,

and her inky eyes have the look of someone who has
been in prison a long time and   10
knows they can send her back. I look at her
body and think how her breasts were the first to
rise, slowly, like swans on a pond.
By the time mine came along, they were just
two more birds on the flock, and when the hair   15
rose on the white mound of her flesh, like
threads of water out of the ground, it was the
first time, but when mine came
they knew about it. I used to think
only in terms of her harshness, sitting and   20
pissing on me in bed, but now I
see I had her before me always
like a shield. I look at her wrinkles, her clenched
jaws, her frown-lines—I see they are
the dents on my shield, the blows that did not reach me. 25
She protected me, not as a mother
protects a child, with love, but as a
hostage protects the one who makes her
escape as I made my escape, with my sister's
body held in front of me.   30

Sharon Olds, 1942–

The poem starts quickly with "When I look at my elder sister now," which places the reader exactly where the speaker is: considering the older sister. Each line of the poem is strong, a ladder rung taking us decisively through ways the speaker regards her sister. All but three lines are enjambed. These run-on lines, plus the use of several conjunctions, emphasize midsentence words and the forceful flow of the speaker's voice. A few lines end with *the* or in the middle of an infinitive ("to / rise"). These give a dangling or suspended quality to the line, as though we hear an odd pause in the speaker's voice. The third end-stopped line (". . . the blows that did not reach me") marks the end of the story of the sister. The next five lines summarize what the younger sister now realizes. Throughout the poem, the lines seem close to the pace of breathing. They slightly expand and contract in length, slowing and speeding the pace as you read. Note the internal rhymes (now/how/down) and other intensifying, unifying sound patterns (pressure/muscles/scraping/skin) throughout the poem.

In e. e. cummings's poem, the line use establishes an individual speech rhythm: we hear a voice speaking and we listen to it. In Olds's poem, the fierce lines seem almost deployed, fired down onto the page. "The Elder Sister" is a **continuous form:** it proceeds without stanza breaks. This uninterrupted form intensifies the urgent all-at-onceness of the enjambed lines.

A break for a stanza is a break in timing, a big pause. William Carlos Williams chose continuous lines for the rhythm of "The Great Figure." He wanted lines to *go* at the speed of the truck:

THE GREAT FIGURE

Among the rain
and lights
I saw the figure 5
in gold
on a red   5
firetruck
moving
tense
unheeded
to gong clangs   10
siren howls
and wheels rumbling
through the dark city.

William Carlos Williams, 1883–1963

Williams's line becomes the movement of the action in the poem.

Lines can rush like a fuse burning, drop down like a rock in water, drift about musically, or curve as though the writer were hemming a circular skirt. The line is *expressive* of the content. In free verse, rhythm is individualized. A subtle poem, laid out to reveal the motions of the mind in the process of perception, will not strike you with its movement. You must judge each poem's way of using the line.

Although we're looking at functions of lines separately, remember that usually several forces are working together. cummings's Buffalo Bill poem, for example, uses a speech rhythm, but also at work is the passionate rush of fear and wonder at death. The next poem's short lines are restless like the wind; they also seem to reflect the quick movement of the poet's perception. *Scirocco* is a seasonal, harsh wind.

SCIROCCO

In Rome, at 26
    Piazza di Spagna,
at the foot of a long
    flight of
stairs, are rooms   5
    let to Keats

in 1820,
    where he died. Now
you can visit them,
    the tiny terrace,   10
the bedroom. The scraps
    of paper

on which he wrote
    lines
are kept behind glass,   15
    some yellowing,
some xeroxed or
    mimeographed. . . .

Outside his window
    you can hear the scirocco   20
working
    the invisible.
Every dry leaf of ivy
    is fingered,

refingered. Who is   25
    the nervous spirit
of this world
    that must go over and over
what it already knows,
    what is it   30

so hot and dry
    that's looking through us,
by us,
    for its answer?
In the arbor   35
    on the terrace

the stark hellenic
    forms

of grapes have appeared.
 They'll soften   40
till weak enough
 to enter

our world, translating
 helplessly
from the beautiful   45
 to the true. . . .
Whatever the spirit,
 the thickening grapes

are part of its looking,
 and the slow hands   50
that made this mask
 of Keats
in his other life,
 and the old woman,

the memorial's   55
 custodian,
sitting on the porch
 beneath the arbor
sorting chick-peas
 from pebbles   60

into her cast-iron
 pot.
See what her hands
 know—
they are its breath,   65
 its mother

tongue, dividing,
 discarding.
There is light playing
 over the leaves,   70
over her face,
 making her

abstract, making
 her quick
and strange. But she   75
 has no care
for what speckles her,
 changing her,

she is at
    her work. Oh how we want   80
to be taken
    and changed,
want to be mended
    by what we enter.

Is it thus   85
    with the world?
Does it wish us
    to mend it,
light and dark,
    green   90

and flesh? Will it
    be free then?
I think the world
    is a desperate
element. It would have us   95
    calm it,

receive it. Therefore this
    is what I
must ask you
    to imagine: wind;   100
the moment
    when the wind

drops; and grapes,
    which are nothing,
which break   105
    in your hands.

Jorie Graham, 1951–

The very short lines of "Scirocco" work *for* the complex subjects of
the poem. Keats died at 25; his brief life ended in Rome, where he'd
gone to escape the English climate. The brief lines—fleeting, delicate—break on important words. The additional attention the eye gives
to the end words and to the single-word lines emphasizes more words
than we would in longer lines.

Notice the old woman sorting peas. We see her on the porch under
the arbor—a wide focus. Then she's sorting peas into her pot. Then
the focus narrows further: we're shown her hands, the light on her face

as the wind moves the leaves. The lines both present and time the image by zooming in closer and closer on the woman. We see her in stages, as the poet saw.

"Scirocco" is a speculative poem with no single meaning, certainly no easily paraphrasable meaning. In "Ode on a Grecian Urn," Keats wrote:

> "Beauty is truth, truth beauty,"—that is all
> Ye know on earth, and all ye need to know.

Graham's speaker echoes this famous quote as she looks out Keats's window "from the beautiful / to the true. . . ." All that is past and present seems to be part of the restless impulse of the inquiring spirit personified by the wind. We're invited in to hear the speaker's meditation and, lastly, to imagine simultaneously the constant wind and the perfect "hellenic" forms of the grapes which cannot endure.

Did Graham decide on the form in advance? Probably not. In writing, a poet may notice a shape starting to form in the rough draft; here, a contracting and expanding line might have determined the form. Once the shape emerges, the poet starts to work with it, just as Michelangelo claimed to have *released* the shapes of his sculptures from giant blocks of marble.

A vastly different line rhythm is used by C. K. Williams. His books are sometimes printed in a wide format to accommodate his very long lines—longer than most prose. This book isn't wide enough to print his lines without breaking them. Imagine each indented line as part of the line above it. Although many poets occasionally work with a long line, no one else since Whitman has consistently used this stretched-to-the-limit length. Williams's poems have stories to tell. He uses lines in layers to build his story gradually. The eye must travel all the way across the page. Further, he uses many conjunctions. The rhythm may remind you of the Old Testament, with its rolling *ands* and *thens* gathering cumulative power. Williams's poems expand. They do not pare down, compress. They are twentieth-century urban poems that combine fact, memory, and imagination with a landscape that is *inclusive* like Whitman's, but inclusive of squad cars, urban renewal, and winos.

BLADES

When I was about eight, I once stabbed somebody, another kid,
   a little girl.
I'd been hanging around in front of the supermarket near our house
and when she walked by, I let her have it, right in the gap between
   her shirt and her shorts
with a piece of broken-off car antenna I used to carry around in
   my pocket.
It happened so fast I still don't know how I did it: I was as
   shocked as she was   5
except she squealed and started yelling as though I'd plunged a
   knife in her
and everybody in the neighborhood gathered around us, then they
   called the cops,
then the girl's mother came running out of the store saying "What
   happened? What happened?"
and the girl screamed, "He stabbed me!" and I screamed back,
   "I did not!" and she you did too
and me I didn't and we were both crying hysterically by that time.   10
Somebody pulled her shirt up and it was just a scratch but we
   went on and on
and the mother, standing between us, seemed to be absolutely
   terrified.
I still remember how she watched first one of us and then the other
   with a look of complete horror—
You did too! I did not!—as though we were both strangers,
   as though it was some natural disaster
she was beholding that was beyond any mode of comprehension
   so all she could do   15
was stare speechlessly at us, and then another expression came
   over her face,
one that I'd never seen before, that made me think she was going
   to cry herself
and sweep both of us, the girl and me, into her arms to hold us
   against her.
The police came just then, though, quieted everyone down,
   put the girl and the mother
into a squad-car to take to the hospital and me in another to take
   to jail   20
except they really only took me around the corner and let me go
   because the mother and daughter were black
and in those days you had to do something pretty terrible to get
   into trouble that way.

I don't understand how we twist these things or how we get them
    straight again
but I relived that day I don't know how many times before I
    realized I had it all wrong.
The boy wasn't me at all, he was another kid: I was just there.   25
And it wasn't the girl who was black, but him. The mother was
    real, though.
I really had thought she was going to embrace them both
    and I had dreams about her for years afterwards: that I'd be
    being born again
and she'd be lifting me with that same wounded sorrow or she
    would suddenly appear out of nowhere,
blotting out everything but a single, blazing wing of holiness.   30
Who knows the rest? I can still remember how it felt the old way.
How I make my little thrust, how she crushes us against her, how
    I turn and snarl
at the cold circle of faces around us because something's torn in
    me,
some ancient cloak of terror we keep on ourselves because we'll
    do anything,
anything, not to know how silently we knell in the mouth of
    death   35
and not to obliterate the forgivenesses and the lies we offer
    one another and call innocence.
This is innocence. I touch her, we kiss.
And this. I'm here or not here. I can't tell. I stab her. I stab her
    again. I still can't.

                                  C. K. Williams, 1936–

    A metrical line is easy to grasp. We hear the harmony of the repeating pattern of syllables and line length. Without metrical standards, you learn to pay attention to the poet's sense of how rhythm works in each poem—whether it captures speech rhythms, underscores meaning, mirrors the motion of the mind as it perceives, or captures an actual physical motion. Read the Williams and Graham poems aloud, pausing (a half-comma pause) at the line breaks. Listen to the difference in the lines' shaping of the poems' progress and movement.

    Beginning readers of free verse often ask, "What's the difference in these modern poems and a bunch of chopped-up sentences?" The timing and attention we pay to *words* in important positions is not as important in prose as it is in poetry. Rhythm is often at work in prose, of course, but it is the rhythm of sentences building up, a rhythm that comes from word choice and syntax. Poetry adds the additional control of line breaks and spacing.

In crafting a poem in free verse, the writer is not "free" just because the conventions of meter and rhyme scheme are abandoned. Free verse challenges the poet to make imaginative and expressive use of the line. The free verse line is like the sensitive needle on the seismograph, tracing the movement and tremors of the earth.

Remember that the way a line is crafted constantly interacts with other elements. Line use is inseparable in its effect from elements such as sound patterns, imagery, repetition. All of these elements merge with the voice of the poem.

Voice

We convince by our presence.

Walt Whitman

Someone's voice is mysterious. You can get a call from someone you haven't talked to in years and recognize her just from the way she says your name. If you're familiar with a writer's work, you can recognize the author's voice in even a few unsigned lines. If you know Mozart well, you'll spot even unfamiliar works as his. These recognitions have to do with characteristic sounds and tones. When a parent says, "Don't speak to me in that tone of voice," you know what is meant. You also know the difference in the way you sound speaking to someone and the more fragmented way you think, muse, and imagine to yourself. A poem's tone of voice is similarly revealing. The forceful, direct tone in "The Elder Sister" tells you that the poem's message is unequivocal. The voice leaves nothing ambiguous. It is an outside, direct-address voice. In contrast, the voice in "Scirocco" moves back and forth from an outer voice addressing "you" to an inner, contemplative voice thinking to itself. This poem requires more participation from the reader. The voice in "Blades" is casual at first. The speaker says "about eight," "another kid," and "hanging around." He could be telling you this over coffee. His storyteller mode (this happened, then this, then this) continues until the break. The last section shifts: he realizes the story did not happen that way at all. Reality and fantasy change places in memory. In the last seven lines, Williams speeds up the rhythm, drops the casual words and writes about "holiness," "death," "forgiveness." The language shift indicates an opening of the speaker's perception into larger questions: what is the truth of memory, how do we protect ourselves, what is innocence? The last line of the poem contains six clipped, contradictory sentences. In dramatic complement to their meaning, the truncated, blurted last sentences also contradict the leisurely syntax of the long lines.

Free Verse and the Tradition

After free verse took hold, poetry changed irrevocably. By now, free verse has evolved into a complex craft and tradition in itself, with criteria as rigorous as metrical verse.

What makes a poem good applies to both free verse and metered poetry. What's good seems new; it is not predictable. The language is precise and fresh. The ideas or emotions develop. The craft holds our interest as the development takes place. There are compelling reasons for the poem to exist.

Open forms and metrics are not an either/or choice. Poets in any age use whatever tool is available to forge the poems they want to write. Someone right now, given the right subject, can use trochees or anapests to make a memorable contemporary poem. In someone else's hand, a metered poem will seem dated, dressed up in a bustle and high-buttoned shoes. The forms and techniques of traditional poetry are alive. They're here, along with later craft developments, available for the right use.

YOUNG DEER

> That it looks out at us,
>   from
> that thicket, front legs planted
> in the dry gold of leaves,
>   ears standing up   5
>
> alerted into fans of listening to what may be
> coming,   eyes huge in
> that narrow head, mouth tender.

How that look pierces us, innocent
                            (in a sense)   10
but not ignorant of hurt, of all
baleful cruelties in the world outside and

inside the autumn forest,
                    how it holds us,
that look so knowing of us,   of   15
our hurtfulness, of what the deer tells us

is irreparable, never
to be restored, so that his fearfulness
is more than fear,
                    is a knowledge   20

like that which children seem to show, weeping
for the unredeemable,   shocking us
into guilt. This young deer with his eyes

equal to the eyes of homeless children
                            looking out at us   25
& knowing the forest, cruelty
of the life there,   glimpsing us only

in these moments,
                    he sees enough not to
forgive,   bounding away,   30
neck stretched, hind legs bent for

lightness.

                                        Hilda Morley, 1921–

PSALM

Veritas sequitur . . . [1]

In the small beauty of the forest
The wild deer bedding down—
That they are there!

---

[1] *Veritus sequitur:* Truth follows.

Their eyes
Effortless, the soft lips   5
Nuzzle and the alien small teeth
Tear at the grass

The roots of it
Dangle from their mouths
Scattering earth in the strange woods.   10
They who are there.

Their paths
Nibbled thru the fields, the leaves that shade them
Hang in the distances
Of sun   15

The small nouns
Crying faith
In this in which the wild deer
Startle, and stare out.

George Oppen, 1908–1984

EXERCISES

1. Analyze "Young Deer" and "Psalm," which have similar subjects. Are the voices alike? The conclusions? How are these two poets using lines?

2. What happens if you rewrite "Psalm" in long lines?

3. You can experience the power of line breaks by rewriting prose paragraphs as free verse. Try different line arrangements with this paragraph from Arlene Blum's book about mountain climbers in the Himalayas, *Annapurna: A Woman's Place*. After you find the line arrangement that best emphasizes the motion and drama of the paragraph, edit the words for further intensification.

   I was just beginning to cross the mounds of avalanche debris when I saw, but didn't hear, a great cloud of snow and ice coming down from the right side of the Sickle. It looked as though the three members ahead of me were directly in its path. I turned around and ran, occasionally looking back at its progress. I got so winded running full speed with my pack that I had to slow to a fast walk. When I felt

I was out of the way, I looked around for the others. All I saw was a great cloud of snow engulfing the area where they'd been. I knelt down, breathing fast and hard. I didn't know what to do. Should I probe for them? What if another avalanche came down? Should I run back to Camp II for help? What if I forgot the place where I'd last seen them? . . . What should I do?

4. Rewrite this passage from Wright Morris's novel *Ceremony at Lone Tree* as free verse. Try two versions, one with longer lines and one with shorter.

> Come to the window. The one at the rear of the Lone Tree Hotel. The view is to the west. There is no obstruction but the sky. Although there is no one outside to look in, the yellow blind is drawn low at the window, and between it and the pane a fly is trapped. He has stopped buzzing. Only the crawling shadow can be seen. Before the whistle of the train is heard the loose pane rattles like a simmering pot, then stops, as if pressed by a hand, as the train goes past. The blind sucks inward and the dangling cord drags in the dust on the sill.

5. Here Laurie Sheck's poem "Bluefish" is typed as prose. Arrange the words in lines you think suit the words. Compare your lines to those in the original (page 330).

> Opened by the knife it is beautiful archeology, abstract as desires the body has abandoned. Its eyes a milky blue. Its scales prisms that break light. Its whole body arched toward death the way a woman having placed a stone in each pocket enters the still water. We wrap it in plastic, take it to the car. But once beneath sunlight and a knife, its body, opened, was strangely undiminished. Intricate cage.

Poems for Discussion

SNOW

The room was suddenly rich and the great bay-window was
Spawning snow and pink roses against it
Soundlessly collateral and incompatible:
World is suddener than we fancy it.

World is crazier and more of it than we think,   5
Incorrigibly plural. I peel and portion
A tangerine and spit the pips and feel
The drunkenness of things being various.

And the fire flames with a bubbling sound for world
Is more spiteful and gay than one supposes—   10
On the tongue on the eyes on the ears in the palm of one's hands—
There is more than glass between the snow and the huge roses.

Louis MacNeice, 1907–1963

STARLIGHT

My father stands in the warm evening
on the porch of my first house.
I am four years old and growing tired.
I see his head among the stars,
the glow of his cigarette, redder   5
than the summer moon riding
low over the old neighborhood. We
are alone, and he asks me if I am happy.
"Are you happy?" I cannot answer.
I do not really understand the word,   10
and the voice, my father's voice, is not
his voice, but somehow thick and choked,
a voice I have not heard before, but
heard often since. He bends and passes
a thumb beneath each of my eyes.   15
The cigarette is gone, but I can smell
the tiredness that hangs on his breath.
He has found nothing, and he smiles
and holds my head with both his hands.
Then he lifts me to his shoulder,   20
and now I too am there among the stars,
as tall as he. Are you happy? I say.
He nods in answer, Yes! oh yes! oh yes!
And in that new voice he says nothing,
holding my head tight against his head,   25
his eyes closed up against the starlight,
as though those tiny blinking eyes
of light might find a tall, gaunt child
holding his child against the promises
of autumn, until the boy slept   30
never to awaken in that world again.

Philip Levine, 1928–

THE CENTURY QUILT

for Sarah Mary Taylor, Quilter

My sister and I were in love
with Meema's Indian blanket.
We fell asleep under army green
issued to Daddy by Supply.
When Meema came to live with us   5
she brought her medicines, her cane,
and the blanket I found on my sister's bed
the last time I visited her.
I remembered how I'd planned to inherit
that blanket, how we used to wrap ourselves   10
at play in its folds and be chieftains
and princesses.

Now I've found a quilt
I'd like to die under:
Six Van Dyke brown squares,   15
two white ones, and one square
the yellowbrown of Mama's cheeks.
Each square holds a sweet gum leaf
whose fingers I imagine
would caress me into the silence.   20

I think I'd have good dreams
for a hundred years under this quilt,
as Meema must have, under her blanket,
dreamed she was a girl again in Kentucky
among her yellow sisters,   25
their grandfather's white family
nodding at them when they met.
When their father came home from his store
they cranked up the pianola
and all of the beautiful sisters   30
giggled and danced.
She must have dreamed about Mama
when the dancing was over:
a lanky girl trailing after her father
through his Oklahoma field.   35

Perhaps under this quilt
I'd dream of myself,
of my childhood of miracles,
of my father's burnt umber pride,

my mother's ochre gentleness.   40
Within the dream of myself
perhaps I'd meet my son
or my other child, as yet unconceived.
I'd call it The Century Quilt,
after its pattern of leaves.   45

Marilyn Nelson Waniek, 1946–

CAT & THE WEATHER

Cat takes a look at the weather:
snow;
puts a paw on the sill;
his perch is piled, is a pillow.

Shape of his pad appears: 5
will it dig? No,
not like sand,
like his fur almost.

But licked, not liked:
too cold.   10
Insects are flying, fainting down.
He'll try

to bat one against the pane.
They have no body and no buzz,
and now his feet are wet;   15
it's a puzzle.

Shakes each leg,
then shakes his skin
to get the white flies off;
looks for his tail,   20

tells it to come on in
by the radiator.
World's turned queer
somehow: all white,

no smell. Well, here   25
inside it's still familiar.
He'll go to sleep until
it puts itself right.

May Swenson, 1919–1989

POEM

As the cat
climbed over
the top of

the jamcloset
first the right   5
forefoot

carefully
then the hind
stepped down

into the pit of   10
the empty
flowerpot

William Carlos Williams, 1883–1963

COLLOQUY

In the broken light, in owl weather,
Webs on the lawn where the leaves end,
I took the thin moon and the sky for cover
To pick the cat's brains and descend
A weedy hill. I found him groveling   5
Inside the summerhouse, a shadowed bulge,
Furred and somnolent.—"I bring,"
I said, "besides this dish of liver, and an edge
Of cheese, the customary torments,
And the usual wonder why we live   10
At all, and why the world thins out and perishes
As it has done for me, sieved
As I am toward silences. Where
Are we now? Do we know anything?"
—Now, on another night, his look endures.   15
"Give me the dish," he said.
I had his answer, wise as yours.

Weldon Kees, 1914–1955?

LONG RANGE PATROL

Tense
again there as a
cat and sure   I
can see in the dark
this blanket bulletproof   5
the attack will come
on the other side
they won't
get me they don't   I am
home   it is   10
daylight
     then
our sentry blows
his claymore   we
all let go and I wish   15
I had dug deeper or it
wasn't me or
my friends hold me
I am home   it is
daylight   20

D. F. Brown, 1949–

I KNOW A MAN

As I sd to my
friend, because I am
always talking,—John, I

sd, which was not his
name, the darkness sur-   5
rounds us, what

can we do against
it, or else, shall we &
why not, buy a goddamn big car,

drive, he sd, for   10
christ's sake, look
out where yr going.

Robert Creeley, 1926–

MEDITATION AT LAGUNITAS

All the new thinking is about loss.
In this it resembles all the old thinking.
The idea, for example, that each particular erases
the luminous clarity of a general idea. That the clown-
faced woodpecker probing the dead sculpted trunk   5
of that black birch is, by his presence,
some tragic falling off from a first world
of undivided light. Or the other notion that,
because there is in this world no one thing
to which the bramble of *blackberry* corresponds,   10
a word is elegy to what it signifies.
We talked about it late last night and in the voice
of my friend, there was a thin wire of grief, a tone
almost querulous. After a while I understood that,
talking this way, everything dissolves: *justice*,   15
pine, *hair*, *woman*, *you* and *I*. There was a woman
I made love to and I remembered how, holding
her small shoulders in my hands sometimes,
I felt a violent wonder at her presence
like a thirst for salt, for my childhood river   20
with its island willows, silly music from the pleasure boat,
muddy places where we caught the little orange-silver fish
called *pumpkinseed*. It hardly had to do with her.
Longing, we say, because desire is full
of endless distances. I must have been the same to her.   25
But I remember so much, the way her hands dismantled bread,
the thing her father said that hurt her, what
she dreamed. There are moments when the body is as numinous
as words, days that are the good flesh continuing.
Such tenderness, those afternoons and evenings,   30
saying *blackberry*, *blackberry*, *blackberry*.

Robert Hass, 1941–

BLACKBERRYING

Nobody in the lane, and nothing, nothing but blackberries,
Blackberries on either side, though on the right mainly,
A blackberry alley, going down in hooks, and a sea
Somewhere at the end of it, heaving. Blackberries
Big as the ball of my thumb, and dumb as eyes   5
Ebon in the hedges, fat
With blue-red juices. These they squander on my fingers.

I had not asked for such a blood sisterhood; they must love
    me.
They accommodate themselves to my milkbottle, flattening
    their sides.

Overhead go the choughs in black, cacophonous flocks—   10
Bits of burnt paper wheeling in a blown sky.
Theirs is the only voice, protesting, protesting.
I do not think the sea will appear at all.
The high, green meadows are glowing, as if lit from within.
I come to one bush of berries so ripe it is a bush of flies,   15
Hanging their bluegreen bellies and their wing panes
    in a Chinese screen.

The honey-feast of the berries has stunned them; they believe
    in heaven.
One more hook, and the berries and bushes end.

The only thing to come now is the sea.
From between two hills a sudden wind funnels at me,   20
Slapping its phantom laundry in my face.
These hills are too green and sweet to have tasted salt.
I follow the sheep path between them. A last hook brings me
To the hills' northern face, and the face is orange rock
That looks out on nothing, nothing but a great space   25
Of white and pewter lights, and a din like silversmiths
Beating and beating at an intractable metal.

Sylvia Plath, 1932–1963

TO A POOR OLD WOMAN

    munching a plum on
    the street a paper bag
    of them in her hand

    They taste good to her
    They taste good   5
    to her. They taste
    good to her

    You can see it by
    the way she gives herself
    to the one half   10
    sucked out in her hand

Comforted
a solace of ripe plums
seeming to fill the air
They taste good to her   15

William Carlos Williams, 1883–1963

BLUEFISH

Opened by the knife
it is beautiful
archeology,
abstract as desires
the body has abandoned.   5

Its eyes a milky blue.
Its scales prisms
that break light.
Its whole body arched
toward death   10
the way a woman
having placed a stone
in each pocket
enters the still water.

We wrap it in plastic,   15
take it to the car.
But once beneath sunlight
and a knife,
its body, opened,
was strangely undiminished.   20
Intricate cage.

Laurie Sheck, 1953–

THIRTEEN WAYS OF LOOKING AT A BLACKBIRD

i

Among twenty snowy mountains,
The only moving thing
Was the eye of the blackbird.

ii

I was of three minds,
Like a tree   5
In which there are three blackbirds.

iii

The blackbird whirled in the autumn winds.
It was a small part of the pantomime.

iv

A man and a woman
Are one.   10
A man and a woman and a blackbird
Are one.

v

I do not know which to prefer,
The beauty of inflections
Or the beauty of innuendoes,   15
The blackbird whistling
Or just after.

vi

Icicles filled the long window
With barbaric glass.
The shadow of the blackbird   20
Crossed it, to and fro.
The mood
Traced in the shadow
An indecipherable cause.

vii

O thin men of Haddam,   25
Why do you imagine golden birds?
Do you not see how the blackbird
Walks around the feet
Of the women about you?

viii

I know noble accents   30
And lucid, inescapable rhythms;
But I know, too,
That the blackbird is involved
In what I know.

ix

When the blackbird flew out of sight,   35
It marked the edge
Of one of many circles.

x

At the sight of blackbirds
Flying in a green light,
Even the bawds of euphony   40
Would cry out sharply.

xi

He rode over Connecticut
In a glass coach.
Once, a fear pierced him,
In that he mistook   45
The shadow of his equipage
For blackbirds.

xii

The river is moving.
The blackbird must be flying.

xiii

It was evening all afternoon.   50
It was snowing
And it was going to snow.
The blackbird sat
In the cedar-limbs.

Wallace Stevens, 1879–1955

FOR THE ANNIVERSARY OF MY DEATH

Every year without knowing it I have passed the day
When the last fires will wave to me
And the silence will set out
Tireless traveller
Like the beam of a lightless star   5
Then I will no longer
Find myself in life as in a strange garment
Surprised at the earth
And the love of one woman
And the shamelessness of men   10
As today writing after three days of rain
Hearing the wren sing and the falling cease
And bowing not knowing to what

W. S. Merwin, 1927–

FROM THE ROOF

This wild night, gathering the washing as if it were flowers
          animal vines twisting over the line and
          slapping my face lightly, soundless merriment
          in the gesticulations of shirtsleeves,
I recall out of my joy a night of misery   5
walking in the dark and the wind over broken earth,
          halfmade foundations and unfinished
          drainage trenches and the spaced-out circles of glaring light
          marking streets that were to be,
walking with you but so far from you,   10

and now alone in October's
first decision towards winter, so close to you—
          my arms full of playful rebellious linen, a freighter
          going down-river two blocks away, outward bound,
          the green wolf-eyes of the Harborside Terminal glittering on
              the Jersey shore,   15
and a train somewhere under ground bringing you towards me
to our new living-place from which we can see

a river and its traffic (the Hudson and the
hidden river, who can say which it is we see, we see
something of both. Or who can say   20
the crippled broom-vendor yesterday, who passed

just as we needed a new broom, was not
one of the Hidden Ones?)
        Crates of fruit are unloading
        across the street on the cobbles,   25
        and a brazier flaring
        to warm the men and burn trash. He wished us
luck when we bought the broom. But not luck
brought us here. By design

clear air and cold wind polish   30
the river lights, by design
we are to live now in a new place.

Denise Levertov, 1923–

PACHUTA, MISSISSIPPI / A MEMOIR

        I too
      once lived
    in the country

        Incandescent
          fruits   5
       in moonlight
     whispered to me
      from trees
       of
      1950   10
     swishing
    in the green nights

        wavelengths away
         from
        tongue-red meat   15
         of melon

      wounded squash
    yellow as old afternoons

        chicken
         in love   20
          with calico

hiss & click of flit gun

juice music
    you suck up
lean stalks of field cane   25

            Cool as sundown
            I lived there too

        Al Young, 1939–

Traditional and Open Forms

> *In poetry you have a form looking for a subject and a subject looking for a form. When they come together successfully you have a poem.*
>
> W. H. Auden

Form is the first thing you notice about a poem. At a glance, your eye picks up many subtle clues that orient you. Is the poem dense, or is it surrounded by a lot of white space? Do words appear scattered, or are they justified along the left margin? Any irregular spacing attracts the eye, alerts you to listen to the poem's particular music. Stanzas indicate a formal coherence. If the stanzas are couplets (two lines) or quatrains (four lines), the unrolling of those equally formed verses down the page contributes right away to a sense of harmony and order.

How does form relate to the poem's overall impact? And why? Does form contribute meaning? What is it exactly?

Form doesn't hold a poem like a pitcher holds milk. Form is more like a satin dress that fits tight as a second skin. That's the right fit, but form can't come off like a dress. Although the accepted wisdom, "Form follows function," works for architecture, it isn't quite accurate for poetry. "Sound must seem an echo to the sense," the famous dictum of Alexander Pope, also just misses. "Echo" and "follow" are misleading words. They imply that the inside and the outside of the poem are separable.

The poem's form and content are totally interactive systems. Form without balanced content is hollow; content without form is chaos. The poem *is* the form; the form *is* the poem.

The American Heritage Dictionary lists many meanings for form. First, "the contour and structure of something as distinguished from its substance." Second, "the body or outward appearance (of a person or animal) considered separately from the face or head." Those definitions won't do for our purposes. If all parts of a poem work together as a whole, form cannot be "separated" or "distinguished from" other elements. We read at definition 8: "fitness, as of an athlete or animal, with regard to health or training." This is getting close. Certainly the life of the poem depends on a strong form, but this definition too misses something. Form is not simply a well-trained body which gets the poem over the finish line. All these are helpful, but we're after the precise relationship of form and substance.

All the way down at definition number 19, we find "the resting place of a hare." The resting place and the hare give a good figurative image for the intertwining of form and substance in poetry: the live animal and the moment of its shaping the grass. The resting place of the rabbit, a swirl of grasses, occurs simultaneously with the wild animal settling into it. The form of a good poem occurs simultaneously with the meaning, not as separate phenomenon. The better the poem, the more natural the form seems.

Yeats makes interesting use of the same image:

MEMORY

One had a lovely face,
And two or three had charm,
But charm and face were in vain
Because the mountain grass
Cannot but keep the form
Where the mountain hare has lain.

William Butler Yeats, 1865–1939

Yeats's metaphor of the hare and grass reveals that because of his identity with the woman, he cannot help but retain within himself a place for her presence: he is formed *only* for her. The poem's form, ideally, has the same inevitability.

Looking at Forms

What first impressions do you get from a shape?

EASTER WINGS

Lord, who createdst man in wealth and store,
Though foolishly he lost the same,
Decaying more and more,
Till he became
Most poor:
With thee
O let me rise
As larks, harmoniously,
And sing this day thy victories:
Then shall the fall further the flight in me.

My tender age in sorrow did begin;
And still with sicknesses and shame
Thou didst so punish sin,
That I became
Most thin.
With thee
Let me combine,
And feel this day thy victory;
For, I imp my wing on thine,
Affliction shall advance the flight in me.

George Herbert, 1593–1633

Written in the seventeenth century, "Easter Wings" represents an extreme use of form. The shape of the poem actually makes a visual image of wings. Poets since the Greeks have experimented with portraying graphically the relationship of subject and form. **Concrete poetry** (or *shaped* poetry) is the name for poetry with this intent. In "Easter Wings," notice how the expansion and contraction of the line lengths works. The line expands for God, contracts for mankind and "I." Herbert's subject is, broadly, the possibility of resurrection inspired by Easter. The term *imp* in the next-to-last line means "to graft." Falconers imped extra feathers on wings so their birds could be more powerful. Herbert uses the term as a metaphor for attaching his spirit to God's. The poem's concrete image of wings underscores this metaphor.

Poems have been constructed, often with wit, in the shape of crosses, swans, lambs, hourglasses, and apples. Sometimes the concrete poem is *only* shape; the image or typographical arrangement *is* the poem:

eyeye

Aram Saroyan, 1943–

Generally, concrete poems surprise us with novelty. After the first reaction to the typography wears off, however, the poem might not be very interesting. The shape can seem to call too much attention to itself, overshadowing content. But some concrete poems, like "Easter Wings," offer more than a quick impression; even though the balance is somewhat tipped, our interest in the content isn't overwhelmed by the visual impact.

For most poets, shaped or concrete poems are merely occasional pieces. Not every poem about a tulip benefits from the tulip shape. But often the desire to make the poem into an image of content influences the form. Just as line placement is expressive, a poem's overall shape subtly expresses something too.

The form of "The Shape of Death" borrows some of the impact of a concrete poem. The appearance is disturbing. A white, jagged shape runs down the middle. With the title in mind, we begin reading the poem with a sense of intrigue: Is death this ghostly hole down the middle? Do we read straight across or down? Does the gap in each line work as a long caesura? As we read, the white space becomes an imaginative blank which counterpoises love (small as a cell that can't be split) and death (large as a nuclear blast). Central to the poem is a questioning, which the mysterious, shifting white space actively reinforces. The hole down the middle remains ambiguous. Unlike concrete poems, which make a visual image such as an apple or a flower, this internal shaping uses the line and the stanza to express important tension in the poem.

THE SHAPE OF DEATH

What does love look like?
Death is a cloud, immense
lid is lifted from the
clap of sound. A white
jaw of fright. A
white to gray, like a
and burns—then turns
away, filling the whole
Thickly it wraps, between
moon, the earth's green
cocoon, its choking
of death. Death is a

We know the shape of death.
and awesome. At first a
eye of light. There is a
blossom belches from the
pillared cloud churns from   5
monstrous brain that bursts
sickly black, spilling
sky with ashes of dread.
the clean seas and the
head. Trapped in its   10
breath, we know the shape
cloud. What does love look

like? Is it a particle,
beyond the microscope and
the length of hope? Is
that we shall never dare
color, and its alchemy?
can it be dug? Or
it be bought? Can it be
a shy beast to be caught?
a clap of sound. Love is
nests within each cell,
is a ray, a seed, a note,
our air and blood. It is
our very skin, a sheath

a star, invisible entirely,
Palomar? A dimension past
it a climate far and fair,   15
discover? What is its
Is it a jewel in the earth,
dredged from the sea? Can
sown and harvested? Is it
Death is a cloud—immense   20
little and not loud. It
and it cannot be split. It
a word, a secret motion of
not alien—it is near—
to keep us pure of fear.   25

May Swenson, 1919–

"The Shape of Death" is an **open form:** the shape is unique to this particular poem. Open forms sometimes are called **nonce forms,** nonce meaning "for an occasion."

A poem's form doesn't always make a visual statement. Most poems line up in blocks or move straight down the page. A practiced reader of poetry recognizes right away if a poem is one of the traditional forms of English poetry. The next poem is a **sonnet.** Unless you already know the form, its shape offers little immediate information. The sonnet has fourteen lines and is the great English poetic form. There is some choice about how these lines are divided into stanzas; but basically, when a reader spots a fourteen-line poem, most probably a sonnet is at hand.

BRIGHT STAR

Bright star, would I were stedfast as thou art—
    Not in lone splendour hung aloft the night
And watching, with eternal lids apart,
    Like nature's patient, sleepless Eremite,[1]
The moving waters at their priestlike task   5
    Of pure ablution round earth's human shores,
Or gazing on the new soft-fallen mask
    Of snow upon the mountains and the moors—
No—yet still stedfast, still unchangeable,
    Pillow'd upon my fair love's ripening breast,   10
To feel for ever its soft fall and swell,
Awake for ever in a sweet unrest,
Still, still to hear her tender-taken breath,
And so live ever—or else swoon to death.

John Keats, 1795–1821

[1] *Eremite:* hermit.

    A poet who chooses the sonnet form is committed to a meter and rhyme scheme, and to a small space and fast development. The usual rhyme scheme of the sonnet demands a strong closing rhyme, which tends toward a resolved ending. The end bangs shut. These "givens" offer some advantages to the writer, but also some dangers. Since so many great poems exist in the form, just choosing it reminds the reader of other sonnets and invites comparisons. Obviously, using the inherited form becomes a rich complement when the poem is good and a tremendous liability otherwise. This is one of the challenges of all traditional forms. Another is that when the writer tries the sonnet, or other traditional forms, often ideas come from the set form. The sonnet possesses a momentum of its own and may channel the poet's mind in new directions.

    The poems above represent three approaches to structure: making a concrete visual image out of words, developing an expressive shape, and using an inherited form. In a good poem, no matter what its structure, *the form is the content.*

Traditional Forms

Stanzas

In Italian, *stanza* means "room"; a stanza is to the poem as a room is to the house. Each stanza does different work and each is necessary to the poem's whole structure. Like verses in a song, a stanza follows a set pattern, stops, then starts the pattern again. Usually there's a line space between stanzas.

Why is a poem written in stanzas? Think of the stanza as a *section of development*. A stanza works like a paragraph. New paragraph, new viewpoint or subject. The same holds for poetry, although the change is sometimes subtle.

Stanzas, like meters, have no inherent significance. They are plastic, accommodating themselves to massacres as well as love songs, to nonsense as well as high seriousness. As with each other element in poetry, we must always look to the whole for meaning, not to any one part.

These are examples of stanzas commonly used in English. Stanzas may, of course, be unrhymed, although in traditional poetry we expect a rhyme scheme.

Couplet: two lines. Sometimes the couplet is set off in stanzas but, rhymed, the couplet is often employed for long uninterrupted verse. An aa rhyme identifies the couplet. The **heroic couplet** is rhymed iambic pentameter:

> The hungry judges soon the sentence sign,
> And wretches hang that jurymen may dine.
>
> *Alexander Pope*

Tercet (also called **triplet**): three lines. Usual rhyme schemes are aaa (all end words rhyme) or aba.

> O wild West Wind, thou breath of Autumn's being,
> Thou, from whose unseen presence the leaves dead
> Are driven, like ghosts from an enchanter fleeing,
>
> *Percy Bysshe Shelley*

Tercets that are rhyme-linked (aba, bcb, cdc, and so on) are called **terza rima**. This is the stanza used in one of the great works of world literature, Dante's *Divine Comedy*.

Quatrain: four lines. Ballads and many hymns are written in quatrains. Many types of quatrains exist, with varied meters and rhyme schemes. A quatrain called **common measure** alternates a four-foot iambic line with a three-foot iambic line, rhyming abcb. Quatrains are the most frequently used of all the types of stanzas.

> I strove with none, for none was worth my strife;
>   Nature I loved; and next to Nature, Art.
> I warm'd both hands against the fire of life;
>   It sinks, and I am ready to depart.

>> *Walter Savage Landor,*
>> from "Dying Speech
>> of an Old Philosopher"

Quintet: five lines with no prescribed rhyme. This example rhymes ababb:

> How can the bird that is born for joy
> Sit in a cage and sing?
> How can a child, when fears annoy,
> But droop his tender wing,
> And forget his youthful spring?

> *William Blake,* from "The School Boy"

Sestet: six lines variously rhymed, or unrhymed

> For oft, when on my couch I lie
> in vacant or in pensive mood,
> They flash upon that inward eye
> Which is the bliss of solitude;
> And then my heart with pleasure fills,
> And dances with the daffodils.

> *William Wordsworth,* from "I Wandered Lonely as a Cloud"

Septet (or **Chaucerian stanza** or **rhyme royal**): seven lines. Chaucer was the first to write septets (rhyming ababbcc) in English, but because King James I of Scotland once wrote the same stanza form, it is sometimes called rhyme royal. When used with other rhyme schemes, this stanza is simply called a septet.

With so glad cheere his gestes° she receyveth,	*guests*
And so konnyngly° everich° in his degree,	*adeptly, each one*
That no defaute° no man aperceyveth°	*fault, perceived*
But ay they wondren what she myghte be	
That in so poure array was for to se	
And koude° swich honour and reverence,	*was familiar with*
And worthily they preysen° hir prudence.	*praised*

Geoffrey Chaucer, from *The Canterbury Tales*

Octave: eight lines. An octave may have any rhyme scheme, or none. **Ottava rima** is a special form of the octave rhyming abababcc.

But sweeter still than this, than these, than all,
   Is first and passionate love—it stands alone,
Like Adam's recollection of his fall;
   The tree of knowledge has been plucked—all's known—
And life yields nothing further to recall
   Worthy of this ambrosial sin, so shown,
No doubt in fable, as the unforgiven
Fire which Prometheus filched for us from heaven.

George Gordon, Lord Byron, from "Don Juan"

Spenserian Stanza: nine lines with an ababbcbcc rhyme. An unusual stanza because eight lines in iambic pentameter are followed by a longer hexameter (six-foot) line. This makes an effective visual and rhythmic break in a long poem.

And they are gone: aye, ages long ago
These lovers fled away into the storm.
That night the Baron dreamt of many a woe,
And all his warrior-guests, with shade and form
Of witch, and demon, and large coffin-worm,
Were long be-nightmared. Angela the old
Died palsy-twitched, with meager face deform;
The Beadsman, after thousand aves told,
For aye unsought-for slept among his ashes cold.

John Keats, from "The Eve of St. Agnes"

These nine lengths are the major building blocks of stanzaic poetry. Poets often combine several types of stanzas in one poem. For instance, notice that the sonnets in the next section are made of quatrains and couplets or octaves and sestets. Shelley's "Ode to the West Wind" (page 366) combines the terza rima stanza with a couplet at the end of each section.

A thorough study of stanza combinations, variations, and the traditional forms used in poetry could fill several volumes. For this introductory study, we will look in detail at four forms with distinctly different qualities: the sonnet, the villanelle, the sestina, and the ballad.

Sonnet

Sonneto means "little song" in Italian. The **sonnet** is a lyric with fourteen rhyming lines in iambic pentameter. Before the twentieth century, almost every major writer, along with thousands of minor ones, selected this form at some time. Early poets were partial to the **sonnet sequence** (a group of sonnets on a theme) and to **sonnet crowns** (seven linked sonnets in which the last line of one becomes the first line of the next, and the last line of the final poem repeats the first line of the first poem). Because the sonnet form is short, it lends itself to such groupings. But short also means difficult. Many poets write sonnets about the sonnet, revealing their love/hate feelings for the requirements of the form. The form is exacting, particularly at the end. Early sonnets are primarily love poems but every subject finds a home in the form. Hundreds of experiments and adaptations have bent and continue to bend the form to various ends.

Why is the sonnet the great traditional English form? Partly because English poets fell in love with the sonnets of the Italian Renaissance and wanted to write their own versions. Fortunately, the imported form adapted to our language. Once on English soil, the form naturalized. Iambic pentameter conducts a seemingly effortless flow of English, and the short form seems conducive to English also, like the usual length of a prose paragraph.

The three major types of sonnet are Shakespearean, Petrarchan, and Spenserian. Each is a tight structure. Their challenging rhyme schemes all produce a coherent, packed, and therefore charged form.

The **Shakespearean sonnet** (also called the **English sonnet**) consists of three quatrains rhyming abab, cdcd, and efef, followed by a concluding couplet rhyming gg. The action of the poem proceeds, then, like three quick spins and a sudden leap. The final rhyme, coming so close to its partner, closes the poem. with finality; there is no doubting the end. Therefore, this kind of sonnet suits subjects that need strong closure. If the subject does not, the form can sound forced toward a conclusion not demanded by the quatrains.

SONNET XCVIII

From you have I been absent in the spring,
When proud-pied April, dress'd in all his trim,
Hath put a spirit of youth in every thing,
That heavy Saturn laugh'd and leap'd with him.
Yet nor the lays of birds, nor the sweet smell   5
Of different flowers in odour and in hue,
Could make me any summer's story tell,
Or from their proud lap pluck them where they grew:
Nor did I wonder at the lily's white,
Nor praise the deep vermilion in the rose;   10
They were but sweet, but figures of delight,
Drawn after you, you pattern of all those.
Yet seem'd it winter still, and, you away,
As with your shadow I with these did play.

William Shakespeare, 1564–1616

The **Petrarchan sonnet** form, named after the fourteenth-century Italian poet Petrarch, is in two parts: an octave rhyming abbaabba and a sestet of varying rhyme schemes, often cdcdcd. Between the octave and sestet, where the rhyme break occurs, there is usually a psychological break called the *turn*. Here, after the rather leisurely eight-line opening where the subject is laid forth, the poem changes course. Words such as *but, thus, so,* or *because* often further pinpoint the change in thought or direction which this turn signals. After the turn, the sestet resolves or consolidates or reflects on the concerns of the octave. The subject of the poem must lend itself to this kind of resolution in order for the form to fit.

The Petrarchan is hard to sustain because the writer works with only four different rhymes instead of the six of the Shakespearean sonnet; thus four words must rhyme with each other instead of only two. Some poets object to this tighter rhyme scheme; Keats called it "pouncing rhyme."

ON FIRST LOOKING INTO CHAPMAN'S HOMER[1]

Much have I traveled in the realms of gold,
   And many goodly states and kingdoms seen;
   Round many western islands have I been
Which bards in fealty to Apollo hold.
Oft of one wide expanse had I been told   5
   That deep-browed Homer ruled as his demesne[2];
   Yet did I never breathe its pure serene
Till I heard Chapman speak out loud and bold:
Then felt I like some watcher of the skies
   When a new planet swims into his ken;   10
Or like stout Cortez[3] when with eagle eyes
   He stared at the Pacific—and all his men
Looked at each other with a wild surmise—
   Silent, upon a peak in Darien.

John Keats, 1795–1821

[1] *Chapman's Homer:* George Chapman, Elizabethan poet, translated Homer.
[2] *demesne:* realm.
[3] *Cortez:* Keats mistakes Cortez for Balboa, the explorer who first reached the Pacific in 1513.

The **Spenserian sonnet** is the least used of the three major types. Like the Spenserian stanza, this sonnet is named for the innovative sixteenth-century poet, Edmund Spenser. His abab, bcbc, cdcd, ee rhyme scheme links even the quatrains together. These interwoven rhymes give an intensely lyrical effect, blending the lines together.

SONNET LXXV

One day I wrote her name upon the strand,
   But came the waves and washed it away;
   Again I wrote it with a second hand.
   But came the tide and made my pains his prey.
"Vain man," said she, "that dost in vain assay   5
   A mortal thing so to immortalize,
   For I myself shall like to this decay,
   And eke my name be wiped out likewise."

"Not so," quod I, "let baser things devise
  To die in dust, but you shall live by fame;   10
  My verse your virtues rare shall eternize
  And in the heavens write your glorious name,
Where, whenas death shall all the world subdue,
  Our love shall live, and later life renew."

Edmund Spenser, 1522–1599

Villanelle

Although imported to England from France, the villanelle also originated in Italy, where it was a folk song form in the late fifteenth century.
In English, as in Italian, it is primarily a lyric form.

IF I COULD TELL YOU

Time will say nothing but I told you so,
Time only knows the price we have to pay;
If I could tell you I would let you know.

If we should weep when clowns put on their show,
If we should stumble when musicians play,   5
Time will say nothing but I told you so.

There are no fortunes to be told, although,
Because I love you more than I can say,
If I could tell you I would let you know.

The winds must come from somewhere when they blow,   10
There must be reasons why the leaves decay;
Time will say nothing but I told you so.

Perhaps the roses really want to grow,
The vision seriously intends to stay;
If I could tell you I would let you know.   15

Suppose the lions all get up and go,
And all the brooks and soldiers run away;
Will Time say nothing but I told you so?
If I could tell you I would let you know.

W. H. Auden, 1907–1973

Understanding the structure of this appealing form becomes easier after reading and hearing the repeating lines. The **villanelle** consists of nineteen lines: five tercets and a concluding quatrain. Each tercet rhymes aba. The quatrain at the end rhymes abaa. The first line of the poem repeats as the end of stanzas 2 and 4; it also repeats in the penultimate line. The last line of stanza 1 repeats as the last line of stanzas 3 and 5, and also at the last line of the poem. No set metrical pattern is required, though lines usually are close to the same syllabic length.

The repetition cannot be static. Each time a repeating line reappears, it should have added significance. Rhythmically, the repetition seems to push the poem forward, like waves breaking behind waves. The repetition of both recurrent lines at the end seems to deliver all the rhythm of the poem to the closing.

Sestina

The most mysterious form used in English is the **sestina** (see page 353). As the word suggests, the form is based on sixes. Six six-line stanzas end with a tercet. The last words on each line in the first stanza are repeated as the last words in the following stanzas, in a defined order. All six key words also appear in the tercet, three as end words and one in the middle of each line. Notice too that the last word of a stanza ends the first line in the next stanza. Finally, the last word of the poem repeats the last word of the first line. In this example by the author, trace these recurrences.

SESTINA FOR THE OWL

	True, I am afraid of birds, but the <u>owl</u>	A
	has yellow round eyes that open and <u>close</u>	B
	like a human's. I'm fixed in that <u>stare</u>.	C
	Every day at Mother's table, the owl is <u>over</u>	D
5	me, blinking. I do not hear her <u>fly</u>	E
	in, flatten quietly against the wall. <u>Terror</u>	F
	of her gleaming talons as I blow the soup. <u>Terror</u>	F
	of her feathers ruffling. In the frame she's "The Snowy <u>Owl</u>,"	A
	pretending. I sip the soup. She spots prey, <u>flies</u>.	E
10	Devours on the spot and I <u>close</u>	B

my fists, vomit fur tooth bone. Over and <u>over</u>	D
at dinner she calls, oooo . . . eee. I run <u>upstairs</u>.	C
I won't sleep. I won't sleep because she <u>stares</u>	C
down from the high rafters above my bed. <u>Terror</u>	F
15 of her cry, you . . . me. . . . In the dark, <u>over</u>	D
my body she is waiting. If I sleep, the <u>owl</u>	A
will fall, rake out my palms with her talons, <u>close</u>	B
my sharp eyes. If I slowly drift, she <u>flies</u>	E
at me, my mouth fills with feathers, <u>flies</u>	E
20 down, hard beak gouging. Wild, she <u>stares</u>	C
flapping until I scream for Mother, Hold me <u>close!</u>	B
There's no such thing! I can't trust her, my <u>terror</u>	F
chattering my teeth, her snowy gown white as <u>owl's</u>.	A
The night will never be <u>over</u>.	D
25 Now, in the dream the old woman in a coat hunches <u>over</u>	D
the hill, returns, turns fierce, turns owl, <u>flies</u>	E
for me. And at the museum I see the very <u>owl's</u>	A
soft plumage, the angel bird, immovable eyes. I <u>stare</u>	C
a long time deeply stirred. Could I feel the <u>terror</u>	F
30 of the field mouse lifted high in my hooks, <u>close</u>	B
to my breast, smothering, thrilled. The stuffed owl <u>closes</u>	B
her eyes. No it will never be <u>over</u>.	D
In the field she is always circling, her shadow a <u>terror</u>	F
over small creatures. My red coat draws her eye. She <u>flies</u>	E
35 around and around me, narrowing my chances. I <u>stare</u>	C
up at the sky where she sails in wide rings. The <u>owl</u>	A
swoops <u>close</u> and flies, swoops close. <u>Flies</u>	(B) E
into the body of a woman and <u>over</u> the child running <u>downstairs</u>	(D) C
wings spreading <u>terror</u>. You, me, you, me, sings the <u>owl</u>.	(F) A

If the end words in stanza one are lettered ABCDEF, the pattern for repeating the words is:

1. ABCDEF

2. FAEBDC

3. CFDABE

4. ECBFAD

5. DEACFB

6. BDFECA

7. ECA (with BDF midline)

When the sestina was first used in the early twelfth century, the numerology of the sixes probably had a mystical meaning that is lost to us now. What is still fascinating, on inspection of the form, is that each end word is positioned next to every other end word twice in the poem. If we make a hexagon of end words (called ABCDEF) and connect each end word as it touches all the other end words in every stanza, we see that the poem is indeed graphically complete (see figure next page).

This locked network, along with the incantatory effect of the return of the word in different contexts in each stanza, *creates* the sestina's closed, web-like structure. Subjects must call for intricacy in order for the form to fit. The sestina especially suits exploring compulsive subjects, problems without solution, obsessions, or dream states. Possibly these are the reasons the sestina remains a popular form in contemporary poetry.

Ballad

The folk **ballad** is the most familiar and enduring form in English poetry. Ballads were made to be sung and to tell a story. Inspiration for a ballad can come from a lost love, a cup of poison, the ghostly return of someone dead, a battle, a rivalry—romantic or heroic subjects, uncanny or dramatic events. As part of oral folk culture, the songs change with the teller and time. Amazingly, ballads from fifteenth-century Scotland and England survive in the Southern Appalachians among people who never read them in books but heard them from their families and neighbors.

Usually the form simply repeats the **ballad stanza,** a quatrain with four metrical feet in lines 1 and 2 and three feet in lines 3 and 4. The quatrain usually rhymes abcb. Actually ballads vary tremendously in their metrical and rhyme pattern. Many have a refrain stanza.

"The Elfin Knight" is centuries old. Like most anonymous ballads, it survives in a number of different versions. You may recognize in this early-twentieth-century version the roots of "Scarborough Fair," a once-popular song performed by Simon and Garfunkel.

The Sestina

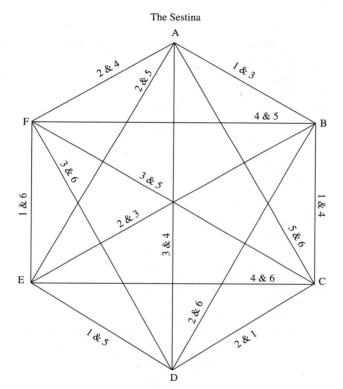

Letters = end words
Numbers = stanzas where words
are next to each other; for example,
E is next to D in stanzas 1 and 5

THE ELFIN KNIGHT

"Go tell him to clear me one acre of ground,
Setherwood, sale, rosemary and thyme,
Betwixt the sea and the sea-land side,
And then he'll be a true lover of mine.

"Tell him to plough it all up with an old leather plough,   5
Setherwood, sale, rosemary and thyme,
And hoe it all over with a pea-fowl's feather,
And then he'll be a true lover of mine.

"Go tell him to plant it all over with one grain of corn,
And reap it all down with an old ram's horn.   10

"Go tell him to shock it in yonder sea,
And return it back to me all dry."

"Go tell her to make me a cambric shirt,
Without any needle or needle's work.

"Go tell her to wash it in yonders well,   15
Setherwood, sale, rosemary and thyme,
Where rain nor water never fell,
And then she'll be a true lover of mine.

"Go tell her to hang it on yonders thorn,
Setherwood, sale, rosemary and thyme,   20
Where man nor thorn was never seen born,
And then she'll be a true lover of mine."

Along with hundreds of other ballads by regional singers, "Fair
Margaret and Sweet William" was taped for the Library of Congress
archives. This version was recorded from the song of Bascom Lamar
Lunsford of South Turkey Creek, North Carolina, in 1946. In stanza
8, the word *corpy* catches our attention. Because of the similarity to
corpse, we can deduce the meaning. But why *corpy*? The *Oxford English Dictionary* lists *corp* as the Scottish spelling before 1500 for a
dead body. *Corpy* would be an adjective form. A word that started to
die out in Scotland around 500 years ago survives in the North Carolina
oral tradition.

FAIR MARGARET AND SWEET WILLIAM

(Little Marg'et)

Little Marg'et sitting in her high hall door,
A-combing back her long yellow hair,
Saw sweet William and his new-made bride
A-riding up the road so near.

She throwed down her ivory comb, 5
She throwed back her long yellow hair,
Said, "I'll go out and bid 'em farewell
And never more go there."

'Twas all lately in the night
When they were fast asleep, 10
Little Marg'et appeared all dressed in white
Standing at their bed feet.

"How do you like that snow-white pillow?
How do you like your sheet?
How do you like that fair young lady 15
That lies in your arms asleep?"

"Oh, well do I like my snow-white pillow,
Oh, well do I like my sheet,
Much better do I like that fair young lady
That stands at my bed feet." 20

He called on serving men to go
And saddle the dapple roan,
He went to her father's house and knocked
And he knocked at the door alone.

"Is little Marg'et in the house 25
Or is she in the hall?"
"Little Marg'et's in her coal-black coffin
With her face turned to the wall."

"Unfold, unfold them snow-white robes,
Be they ever so fine, 30
And let me kiss them cold corpy lips
For I know they'll never kiss mine."

> Once he kissed her lily-white hands,
> Twice he kissed her cheeks,
> Three times he kissed her cold corpy lips,   35
> And he fell in her arms asleep.

Three Lyric Forms

Three similar French forms that made their way into the repertoire of English poetry are the triolet, the rondeau, and the rondel. All are light lyrics. Although each is of slight importance in our tradition, their concentrated repetition and lyric qualities demonstrate both the difficulty and the felicity of these highly wrought forms.

The **triolet** is one octave rhyming abaaabab. The first line repeats at lines 4 and 7. The second line is repeated as the last line of the poem. Sometimes the triolet is written in two stanzas, a quintet and a triplet, with the same rhyme and repeat pattern.

FIRST PHOTOS OF FLU VIRUS

> Viruses, when the lens is right,
> change into a bright bouquet.
> Are such soft forms of pure delight
> viruses? When the lens is right,
> instead of swarms of shapeless blight,
> we see them in a Renoir way.
> Viruses when the lens is right
> change into a bright bouquet.

Harold Witt, 1923–

"Early Supper" skillfully triples the triolet form.

EARLY SUPPER

> Laughter of children brings
>   The kitchen down with laughter.
> While the old kettle sings
> Laughter of children brings
> To a boil all savory things.   5
>   Higher than beam or rafter,
> Laughter of children brings
>   The kitchen down with laughter.

So ends an autumn day,
    Light ripples on the ceiling,   10
Dishes are stacked away;
So ends an autumn day,
The children jog and sway
    In comic dances wheeling.
So ends an autumn day,   15
    Light ripples on the ceiling.

They trail upstairs to bed,
    And night is a dark tower.
The kettle calls: instead
They trail upstairs to bed,   20
Leaving warmth, the coppery-red
    Mood of their carnival hour.
They trail upstairs to bed,
    And night is a dark tower.

Barbara Howes, 1914–

Of several possible choices, the most common—**rondeau**—consists of fifteen lines arranged in a quintet, quatrain, and sestet. The first few words of the first line act as a refrain in lines 9 and 15. These refrain lines do not rhyme, but repeating the fragment seems to imply the rest of the line, including the rhyme. The rhyme, therefore, acts invisibly. The rondeau's usual rhyme scheme is aabba, aab*Refrain*, aabba*Refrain*. An eight-syllable line is traditional.

DEATH OF A VERMONT FARM WOMAN

Is it time now to go away?
July is nearly over; hay
Fattens the barn, the herds are strong,
Our old fields prosper; these long
Green evenings will keep death at bay.   5

Last winter lingered; it was May
Before a flowering lilac spray
Barred cold for ever. I was wrong.
          Is it time now?

Six decades vanished in a day!   10
I bore four sons: one lives; they
Were all good men; three dying young
Was hard on us. I have looked long
For these hills to show me where peace lay. . .
Is it time now?   15

Barbara Howes, 1914–

Rondels are similar to rondeaux. Thirteen or fourteen lines use two refrains. Line 1 comes back at 7; line 2 repeats a 8. The first two lines close the poem. The chosen rhyme scheme determines which will be the last line. Two quatrains followed by a quintet or sestet is the usual structure. The rhyme scheme varies: often it is abba, abab, abbaa.

TOO HARD IT IS TO SING

(Too hard it is to sing
In these untuneful times,
When only coin can ring,
And no one cares for rhymes!

Alas! for him who climbs   5
To Aganippe's spring:[1]
Too hard it is to sing
In these untuneful times!

His kindred clip his wing;
His feet the critic limes: 10
If Fame her laurel bring,
Old age his forehead rimes:
Too hard it is to sing
In these untuneful times!)

Austin Dobson, 1840–1921

[1] *Aganippe's spring:* spring on Mount Helicon, sacred to the muses.

Other Traditions: Haiku and Pantoum

The forms we've considered so far all evolved in England and western Europe. Haiku and pantoum are two forms from more exotic sources.

Japanese **haikus** appear to be simple. Many of us learned to write them in grade school. The form is only seventeen syllables, arranged in three lines of 5-7-5 syllables. The form may have originated as long ago as the thirteenth century in the linked verses of medieval Japan. The haiku is related to the **tanka,** a slightly longer poem of 31 syllables in five lines, arranged 5-7-5-7-7. The haiku construction corresponds to the first three lines of the tanka form. Traditional Japanese poetry is based on the alternation of 5-7-5 lines, the short length corresponding to the culture's appreciation for simplicity. In the twentieth century, the haiku form became extraordinarily popular in English. Technically it is next to impossible to write a true haiku in our language. Japanese is a language without stresses and with different grammatical constructions. English cannot condense, without wrenching the meaning, to the extent Japanese can.

We can sense the compression possible in Japanese by looking at the word-for-word translation of a haiku: 'bell fading out flower's scent as for strike evening.'' A translator wanting to make this meaningful to an English reader has to keep the economy of the original while supplying more connectives. We might write:

> As bell tones fade,
> flower scents take up the ringing—
> evening breeze.

With these difficulties in mind, the English approximations of haikus can be satisfying on their own terms. Often, because of the language differences, translators of haiku sacrifice the correct syllable count in an attempt to keep to the economical compression of the original. Haiku composed in English keeps closer to the 5-7-5 form.

Whether a haiku is a translation or an English original, the form must work as quickly as the brush stroke in a Japanese ink sketch. The immediacy of a single image—bell notes, cherry blossoms, birds—joined to a seasonal allusion suggests a time passing or a change in a human condition.

These translations are by R. H. Blyth:

> The silence!
> The voice of the cicada
> Penetrates the rocks.

Basho

The coolness:
The voice of the bell
As it leaves the bell!

Buson

It is deep autumn
My neighbor—
How does he live?

Buson

The wind-bells ringing,
While the leeks
Sway.

Shosei

New Year's Day;
The hut just as it is,
Nothing to ask for.

Nanshi

Ah, grief and sadness!
The fishing-line trembles
In the autumn breeze.

Buson

How long the day:
The boat is talking
With the shore.

Shiki

The snake slid away,
But the eyes that glared at me,
Remained in the grass.

Kyoski

For an imported form to take root, it must fill a need for a certain kind of expression. Before the haiku was adopted, English had nothing like it in size or intent. Closest in tone and length was the **epigram,** a rhyming couplet or quatrain such as:

> But when to mischief mortals bend their will,
> How soon they find fit instruments of ill!
>
> *Alexander Pope*

But epigrams have very different qualities. An anonymous Latin epigram describes itself:

> Three things must epigrams, like bees, have all,
> A sting, and honey, and a body small.

Epigrams *comment.* Though often funny or ironic, their primary function is to impart wisdom.* The haiku may be wise also, but the chief purpose is to reveal a momentary, often quite complex perception. Writers in English adopted the haiku because they responded to the delicate sensibility inherent in the form.

The **pantoum** also has qualities not found in English. The form is a Malayan one from the fifteenth century, with older roots in Chinese and Persian poetry. The sound effect is close to chanting, with extensive use of repetition. A pantoum consists of an indefinite number of quatrains of any line length. The second and fourth lines of each stanza become the first and third lines of the next stanza. Sometimes the pantoum is rhymed abab, bcbc, cdcd (and so on), but usually in English it is unrhymed. The pantoum circles back. Like some of the French lyric forms, it ends where it began: the last line of the poem repeats the first line. The second line of the last stanza repeats the third line of stanza 1. Often the pantoum develops two ideas. The first starts in the first two lines of the poem and the second starts in the last two lines of stanza 1. Because of the pattern of the repeating lines, the two subjects work their way down the poem in a back-and-forth, push-pull movement. The poem progresses much like the children's game "Mother, May I?" where one of the instructions is to take two steps forward and one backward.

---

* *Note:* Don't confuse *epigram* with *epitaph* (the inscription on a tombstone) or with *epigraph* (a quote at the beginning of a poem or story).

ATOMIC PANTOUM

In a chain reaction
the neutrons released
split other nuclei
which release more neutrons

The neutrons released   5
blow open some others
which release more neutrons
and start this all over

Blow open some others
and choirs will crumble   10
and start this all over
with eyes burned to ashes

And choirs will crumble
the fish catch on fire
with eyes burned to ashes   15
in a chain reaction

The fish catch on fire
because the sun's force
in a chain reaction
has blazed in our minds   20

Because the sun's force
with plutonium trigger
has blazed in our minds
we are dying to use it

With plutonium trigger   25
curled and tightened
we are dying to use it
torching our enemies

Curled and tightened
blind to the end   30
torching our enemies
we sing to Jesus

Blind to the end
split up like nuclei
we sing to Jesus   35
in a chain reaction

Peter Meinke, 1932–

SONNET REVERSED

Hand trembling towards hand; the amazing lights
Of heart and eye. They stood on supreme heights.

Ah, the delirious weeks of honeymoon!
   Soon they returned, and, after strange adventures,
Settled at Balham by the end of June.   5
   Their money was in Can. Pacs. B. Debentures,
And in Antofagastas. Still he went
   Cityward daily; still she did abide
At home. And both were really quite content
   With work and social pleasures. Then they died.   10
They left three children (besides George, who drank):
   The eldest Jane, who married Mr Bell,
William, the head-clerk in the County Bank,
   And Henry, a stock-broker, doing well.

Rupert Brooke, 1887–1915

EXERCISES

1. Not quite a traditional love sonnet, ''Sonnet Reversed'' begins with the couplet, which usually closes a sonnet. What point does this reversal of form make?

2. Discuss the change in language as the poem progresses. What does it imply about the speaker's judgment of the marriage?

● ● ●

OZYMANDIAS[1]

I met a traveller from an antique land
Who said: Two vast and trunkless legs of stone
Stand in the desert. Near them, on the sand,
Half sunk, a shattered visage lies, whose frown,
And wrinkled lip, and sneer of cold command,   5
Tell that its sculptor well those passions read
Which yet survive, stamped on these lifeless things,

[1] Greek name for the Egyptian ruler Ramses II, thirteenth century B.C.

The hand that mocked them and the heart that fed;
And on the pedestal these words appear:
"My name is Ozymandias, king of kings: 10
Look on my works, ye Mighty, and despair!"
Nothing besides remains. Round the decay
of that colossal wreck, boundless and bare,
The lone and level sands stretch far away.

Percy Bysshe Shelley, 1792–1822

THE PILLAR OF FAME

Fames pillar here, at last, we set,
Out-during *Marble*, *Brasse*, or *Jet*,
    Charm'd and enchanted so,
    As to withstand the blow
        Of   overthrow: 5
        Nor shall the seas,
          Or OUTRAGES
        Of storms orebear
        What we up-rear,
        Tho Kingdoms fal,   10
This   pillar   never   shall
    Decline or waste at all;
But stand for ever by his owne
Firme and well fixt foundation.

To his Book's end this last line he'd have plac't,   15
Jocond his Muse was; but his life was chast.

Finis.

Robert Herrick, 1591–1674

EXERCISES

1. "The Pillar of Fame" and "Ozymandias," seventeenth- and nine-teenth-century poems, both have the endurance of fame as their subject. Compare the way form and subject work together in the two poems.

2. Is the content of "The Pillar of Fame" overwhelmed by its shape? What happens metrically as the shape changes?

3. What type of sonnet is "Ozymandias"?

4. Try writing about an object (such as a loaf of bread, apple, tree, or star) in the shape of the object.

• • •

JULY 19, 1979

I'll write a sonnet just to get in form,
allowing fifteen minutes by the clock
to build gratuitously block by block
of quatrains. Almost six, pale sunlight, warm
(last night we thought there'd be a thunderstorm).   5
The crickets fiddle buzz-saws without vowels.
I've had thrice-daily bouts of runny bowels,
which seems, on travels south, to be the norm.
I must avoid the self-indulgent stance
of lovesick troubadours—that isn't wise,   10
in spite of being in the South of France
with a capricious woman whose blue eyes
invest the genre with some relevance.
She says they're green. I've done my exercise.

Marilyn Hacker, 1942–

EXERCISE

Keats and his friends often had fifteen-minute sonnet competitions. "July 19, 1979" is a contemporary sonnet written as a warm-up exercise in fifteen minutes. Choose a rhyme scheme, set the timer, and try your own.

ODE TO THE WEST WIND

I

O wild West Wind, thou breath of Autumn's being,
Thou, from whose unseen presence the leaves dead
Are driven, like ghosts from an enchanter fleeing,

Yellow, and black, and pale, and hectic red,
Pestilence-stricken multitudes! O thou   5
Who chariotest to their dark wintry bed

The winged seeds, where they lie cold and low,
Each like a corpse within its grave, until
Thine azure sister of the spring shall blow

Her clarion o'er the dreaming earth, and fill   10
(Driving sweet buds like flocks to feed in air)
With living hues and odours plain and hill:

Wild spirit, which art moving everywhere;
Destroyer and preserver; hear, O hear!

II

Thou on whose stream, 'mid the steep sky's commotion,   15
Loose clouds like earth's decaying leaves are shed,
Shook from the tangled boughs of heaven and ocean,

Angels of rain and lightning: there are spread
On the blue surface of thine airy surge,
Like the bright hair uplifted from the head   20

Of some fierce Maenad,[1] even from the dim verge
Of the horizon to the zenith's height,
The locks of the approaching storm. Thou dirge

Of the dying year, to which this closing night
Will be the dome of a vast sepulchre,   25
Vaulted with all thy congregated might

---

[1] *Maenad:* wild, frenzied woman; originally a member of the cult of Dionysus, Greek
god of wine and fertility.

Of vapours, from whose solid atmosphere
Black rain, and fire, and hail will burst: O hear!

III

Thou who didst waken from his summer dreams
The blue Mediterranean, where he lay.   30
Lulled by the coil of his crystalline streams,

Beside a pumice isle in Baiae's bay,[2]
And saw in sleep old palaces and towers
Quivering within the wave's intenser day,

All overgrown with azure moss and flowers   35
So sweet, the sense faints picturing them! Thou
For whose path the Atlantic's level powers

Cleave themselves into chasms, while far below
The sea-blooms and the oozy woods which wear
The sapless foliage of the ocean, know   40

Thy voice, and suddenly grow gray with fear,
And tremble and despoil themselves: O hear!

IV

If I were a dead leaf thou mightest bear;
If I were a swift cloud to fly with thee;
A wave to pant beneath thy power, and share   45

The impulse of thy strength, only less free
Than thou, O uncontrollable! if even
I were as in my boyhood, and could be

The comrade of thy wanderings over heaven,
As then, when to outstrip thy skiey speed   50
Scarce seemed a vision; I would ne'er have striven

As thus with thee in prayer in my sore need.
O! lift me as a wave, a leaf, a cloud!
I fall upon the thorns of life! I bleed!

[2] *Baiàe's bay:* northwestern part of the Bay of Naples.

A heavy weight of hours has chained and bowed   55
One too like thee: tameless, and swift, and proud.

                                V

Make me thy lyre, even as the forest is:
What if my leaves are falling like its own?
The tumult of thy mighty harmonies

Will take from both a deep autumnal tone,   60
Sweet though in sadness. Be thou, spirit fierce,
My spirit! Be thou me, impetuous one!

Drive my dead thoughts over the universe,
Like withered leaves, to quicken a new birth;
And, by the incantation of this verse,   65

Scatter, as from an unextinguished hearth
Ashes and sparks, my words among mankind!
Be through my lips to unawakened earth

The trumpet of a prophecy! O wind,
If winter comes, can spring be far behind?   70

                              Percy Bysshe Shelley, 1792–1822

EXERCISES

1. How does the terza rima stanza (aba, bcb, cdc, etc.) work with the
    subject of "Ode to the West Wind"? What other elements of craft
    contribute to the "windiness" and the beautiful running form of
    the poem? Notice the verbs.

2. What is the effect of closing each section with a couplet?

3. Writing in forms is a good way to understand their power. Try
    writing a sestina. Select six words related to a subject you'd like
    to explore—a specific activity such as sailing or dancing or an
    emotion such as jealousy or joy. Following the pattern for the
    sestina, map your six end words along a right margin, then work
    with the lines. You may want to change words after you get started.
    Or try other forms, perhaps haiku, pantoum, or villanelle.

Open Forms

A poem is in open form when the shape is invented for the particular poem. No *set* pattern of stanzas is selected. No pre-existing formal structure is adhered to. But each poem does have a form. It may present a striking appearance, like May Swenson's poem at the beginning of this chapter. It may have verse paragraphs of two-, six-, four-, and seven-line sections. Or it could be a continuous long poem in free verse with no breaks at all. The shape is made anew for each poem.

Let's clarify an important distinction. Although the terms usually are used interchangeably, verse paragraphs and stanzas are different. The stanza is a unit of a *set* number of lines. The **verse paragraph** has no such regularity. The verse paragraphs of a poem could be of two, five, eight, and six lines whereas a poem in stanzas is a series or patterned mix of quatrains, octaves, or whatever the poet chooses. Both verse paragraphs and stanzas may rhyme or be metrical, though this is much more expected in stanzaic poems. The important thing to note is simply that verse paragraphs keep to no established repeating pattern or number of lines. Despite this difference, stanzas and verse paragraphs have similar functions. Like a stanza, a new verse paragraph indicates a change in perspective, action, or subject.

Verse paragraphs, continuous form (uninterrupted by breaks), and one-of-a-kind shapes such as concrete poems are all *open forms*. Although many free verse poems are in open form, it would be a mistake to lump all free verse into this category because sometimes free verse is arranged in regular stanzas.

Much of the free verse you read in chapter 7 was in open forms. There the focus was on the use of voice and line. Now we'll concentrate on the overall shapes of some interesting cases of poems in open form.

EFFORT AT SPEECH BETWEEN TWO PEOPLE

```
 :   Speak to me.    Take my hand.     What are you now?
     I will tell you all.     I will conceal nothing.
     When I was three, a little child read a story about a rabbit
     who died, in the story, and I crawled under a chair   :
     a pink rabbit  :   it was my birthday, and a candle                5
     burnt a sore spot on my finger, and I was told to be happy.
```

:   Oh, grow to know me.   I am not happy.   I will be open:
    Now I am thinking of white sails against a sky like music,
    like glad horns blowing, and birds tilting, and an arm about me.
    There was one I loved, who wanted to live, sailing.   10

:   Speak to me.   Take my hand.   What are you now?
    When I was nine, I was fruitily sentimental,
    fluid   :   and my widowed aunt played Chopin,
    and I bent my head on the painted woodwork, and wept.
    I want now to be close to you.   I would   15
    link the minutes of my days close, somehow, to your days.

:   I am not happy.   I will be open.
    I have liked lamps in evening corners, and quiet poems.
    There has been fear in my life.   Sometimes I speculate
    On what a tragedy his life was, really.   20

:   Take my hand.   Fist my mind in your hand.   What are you now?
    When I was fourteen, I had dreams of suicide,
    and I stood at a steep window, at sunset, hoping toward death   :
    if the light had not melted clouds and plains to beauty,
    if light had not transformed that day, I would have leapt.   25
    I am unhappy.   I am lonely.   Speak to me.

:   I will be open.   I think he never loved me:
    he loved the bright beaches, the little lips of foam
    that ride small waves, he loved the veer of gulls:
    he said with a gay mouth: I love you.   Grow to know me.   30

:   What are you now?   If we could touch one another,
    if these our separate entities could come to grips,
    clenched like a Chinese puzzle . . . yesterday
    I stood in a crowded street that was live with people,
    and no one spoke a word, and the morning shone.   35
    Everyone silent, moving. . . . Take my hand.   Speak to me.

Muriel Rukeyser, 1913–1980

The first thing to notice about "Effort at Speech Between Two People" is the odd line of colons along the left margin. Other colons appear within the verse paragraphs, as does staggered white space within the lines. The grammatical function of a colon is to indicate an addition to what has just been written. Rukeyser's choice of this punctuation mark does not just separate the two "efforts at speech." The section breaks could do that. She indicates by the colon that there is a connection *between* the sections. The isolation of one speaker emphasizes the isolation of the other. Though the two lone voices speak back and forth, the two speakers seem not to hear each other. The halting progression of the speech and the short sentences and phrases with wide spacing remind us of the word *effort* in the title. The form incorporates the silent pauses, the irregular movement of thought changing into speech. The poem ends with the words which began it: "Speak to me." The last image is of a crowd (an expanded version of the two speakers) where "no one spoke a word."

THE HOWLING OF WOLVES

Is without world.

What are they dragging up and out on their long leashes of sound

That dissolve in the mid-air silence?

Then crying of a baby, in this forest of starving silences,
Brings the wolves running.   5
Tuning of a violin, in this forest delicate as an owl's ear,
Brings the wolves running—brings the steel traps clashing and slavering,
The steel furred to keep it from cracking in the cold,
The eyes that never learn how it has come about
That they must live like this,   10

That they must live

Innocence crept into minerals.

The wind sweeps through and the hunched wolf shivers.
It howls you cannot say whether out of agony or joy.

The earth is under its tongue,   15
A dead weight of darkness, trying to see through its eyes.
The wolf is living for the earth.
But the wolf is small, it comprehends little.

It goes to and fro, trailing its haunches and whimpering horribly.

It must feed its fur.   20

The night snows stars and the earth creaks.

Ted Hughes, 1930–

"The Howling of Wolves" has two powerful fragment lines. The beginning, "Is without world," actually completes the title; but set on its own line, it starts the poem with a sense of dangling. The eerie sounds of the wolves are outside our world. They call up dark forces, primitive instincts. In the middle of the poem the author isolates the line "That they must live," the completion being "Innocence crept into minerals." That is, the animals living for basic survival can have no innocence. Innocence belongs to what is inanimate. Other plaintive sounds—the baby's cry, the tuning up of a violin—bring back to mind the wolves' cry underneath everything. The language is dramatic and elemental, like the subject. The single-line verse paragraphs put white space above and below many lines. This adds to their importance by focusing our attention. White space functions as punctuation. The eye must pause for it. What did Hughes want when he used this form? Why not construct the poem in quatrains or couplets? As it is, the form seems to move as thoughts occur: slowly then quickly, long then short. We "hear" a person thinking. A stanza would have impressed us with its order, undercutting the awareness of the bestial undercurrents which this dark poem brings to us.

WOLVES

Last night I heard wolves howling,
their voices coming from afar
over the wind-polished ice—so much
brave solitude in that sound.

They are death's snowbound sailors: 5
they know only a continual
drifting between moonlit islands,
their tongues licking the stars.

But they sing as good seamen should,
and tomorrow the sun will find them   10
yawning and blinking
the snow from their eyelashes.

Their voices rang through the frozen
water of my human sleep,
blown by the night wind   15
with the moon for an icy sail.

John Haines, 1924–

1. Discuss the figurative imagery in "Wolves." Does it seem accurate and evocative?

2. Compare the form and subject relationship in "Wolves" with "The Howling of Wolves" by Ted Hughes. Which poem brings the reality of the wolves' howls closer? How?

3. In terms of development, how do the poems differ? Does the fragmentary, illogical process at work in Hughes's poem affect you?

Prose Poems

In poetry there are exceptions to every rule. One useful rule we've learned is that poetry is written in lines and prose is written in sentences. But prose poems are not written in lines, and still they are poems.

Not everyone agrees. Some critics maintain that the writer of prose poems didn't take the trouble to find a form; it's some aberration, like the fish in Florida that crawls out of water and walks.

But the short block of prose *is* the form. Line breaks aside, the prose poem keeps the craft tools of free verse working as hard as in other forms. Density can give an implosive quality to a subject; the lack of white space intensifies the impression that everything is happening at once. Some prose poems have a relaxed appearance, skipping lines or including conversation. Because of the prose appearance, the writer, at times, seems freed from the serious idea of Poetry with a capital *P* and admits more humor, conversation, description, or irony into the poem.

Look at the unexpected effects of prose in this poem set in El Salvador during its recent war:

THE COLONEL

What you have heard is true. I was in his house. His wife carried a tray of coffee and sugar. His daughter filed her nails, his son went out for the night. There were daily papers, pet dogs, a pistol on the cushion beside him. The moon swung bare on its black cord over the house. On the television was a cop show. It was in English. Broken bottles were embedded in the walls around the house to scoop the kneecaps from a man's legs or cut his hands to lace. On the windows there were gratings like those in liquor stores. We had dinner, rack of lamb, good wine, a gold bell was on the table for calling the maid. The maid brought green mangoes, salt, a type of bread. I was asked how I enjoyed the country. There was a brief commercial in Spanish. His wife took everything away. There was some talk then of how difficult it had become to govern. The parrot said hello on the terrace. The colonel told it to shut up, and pushed himself from the table. My friend said to me with his eyes: say nothing. The colonel returned with a sack used to bring groceries home. He spilled many human ears on the table. They were like dried peach halves. There is no other way to say this. He took one of them in his hands, shook it in our faces, dropped it into a water glass. It came alive there. I am tired of fooling around he said. As for the rights of anyone, tell your people they can go fuck themselves. He swept the ears to the floor with his arm and held the last of his wine in the air. Something for your poetry, no? he said. Some of the ears on the floor caught this scrap of his voice. Some of the ears on the floor were pressed to the ground.

Carolyn Forché, 1950–

The narrative in this poem is highly dramatic. The poet makes a wise choice for her form. The flat tone of statement, at war with the violence within the poem, maintains tension. Line breaks would increase that tension, pushing the poem too far toward the melodramatic. It's easy to see the poetic craft at work in "The Colonel": the intimate tone of the voice speaking directly to you, the repetition of the same declarative sentence structure, the compressed event. The deliberate plainness of the statements is important. (As Forché says, "There is no other way to say this.") The cumulative effect of the simple style emphasizes the growing horror of what is revealed.

We widen our conception of poetry a bit to admit the prose poem. When is a piece of prose a prose poem? No exact definition exists. A prose poem may use any or all of the assets of poetry except the line. Primarily, the form must be needed: the margin-to-margin line, the density and concentration should be part of the effect necessary to the subject.

We could lift whole prose poems out of novels by James Joyce, Virginia Woolf, Herman Melville, Thomas Wolfe, or Colette. Prose poems also have links to fairy tales and parables. Sections of the Bible could be called prose poems. In mid-nineteenth-century France, Charles Baudelaire codified the modern poets' version of the form. In the preface to his *Little Poems in Prose*, Baudelaire asks, "Which of us, in his ambitious moments, has not dreamed of the miracle of a poetic prose. . . ?" As with haiku and pantoum, the prose poem offers a mode of writing unavailable in other forms. As with all others, this form's special characteristics are part of what is being said.

THE SILENT ANGEL

As I sat down by the bus window in the gate of Verona, I looked over my left shoulder. A man was standing in one of the pink marble arches at the base of the great Roman Arena. He smiled at me, a gesture of the utmost sweetness, such as a human face can rarely manage to shine with, even a beloved face that loves you in return.

He seemed dressed like a musician, as well he might have been, emerging for a moment into the sunlight from one of the secluded and cool rehearsal chambers of the upper tiers of the Arena.

As the bus driver powered his motor and drew us slowly around the great public square, the Piazza Bra, the man in the half-golden rose shadow of the Arena kept his gaze on my face. He waved goodbye to me, his knowing eyes never leaving me as long as he could still see any of me at all, though how long that was I don't precisely know.

He raised his hand at the last moment to wave me out of Verona as kindly as he could. He held in his right hand what seemed to be a baton, and it hung suspended for a long instant in the vast petals of rose shadows cast down by the marble walls. Even after he had vanished back into the archway, I could still see his hand.

James Wright, 1927–1980

EXERCISE

What are the predominant elements of poetic craft at work in "The Silent Angel"? Compare the poem with Forché's "The Colonel." What tone does the voice have in each? How do the endings compare? Is there a sense of strong closure? Compare the syntax used in each.

Poems for Discussion

SONNET CXVI

Let me not to the marriage of true minds
Admit impediments. Love is not love
Which alters when it alteration finds,
Or bends with the remover to remove:
O, no! it is an ever-fixed mark,   5
That looks on tempests and is never shaken;
It is the star to every wandering bark,
Whose worth's unknown, although his height be taken.
Love's not Time's fool, though rosy lips and cheeks
Within his bending sickle's compass come;   10
Love alters not with his brief hours and weeks,
But bears it out even to the edge of doom.
If this be error and upon me proved,
I never writ, nor no man ever loved.

William Shakespeare, 1564–1616

THE WORLD IS TOO MUCH WITH US; LATE AND SOON

The world is too much with us; late and soon,
Getting and spending, we lay waste our powers:
Little we see in Nature that is ours;
We have given our hearts away, a sordid boon!
This Sea that bares her bosom to the moon;   5
The winds that will be howling at all hours,
And are up-gathered now like sleeping flowers;
For this, for everything, we are out of tune;
It moves us not.—Great God! I'd rather be
A Pagan suckled in a creed outworn;   10
So might I, standing on this pleasant lea,
Have glimpses that would make me less forlorn;
Have sight of Proteus[1] rising from the sea;
Or hear old Triton[2] blow his wreathèd horn.

William Wordsworth, 1770–1850

---

[1] *Proteus:* sea god who changed his shape at will.
[2] *Triton:* another sea god.

SONNET XCVII

How like a winter hath my absence been
From thee, the pleasure of the fleeting year!
What freezings have I felt, what dark days seen!
What old December's bareness every where!
And yet this time removed was summer's time;   5
The teeming autumn, big with rich increase,
Bearing the wanton burthen of the prime,
Like widowed wombs after their lord's decease:
Yet this abundant issue seem'd to me
But hope of orphans and unfather'd fruit;   10
For summer and his pleasures wait on thee,
And, thou away, the very birds are mute;
Or, if they sing, 'tis with so dull a cheer
That leaves look pale, dreading the winter's near.

William Shakespeare, 1564–1616

PRAISE IN SUMMER

Obscurely yet most surely called to praise,
As sometimes summer calls us all, I said
The hills are heavens full of branching ways
Where star-nosed moles fly overhead the dead;
I said the trees are mines in air, I said   5
See how the sparrow burrows in the sky!
And then I wondered why this mad *instead*
Perverts our praise to uncreation, why
Such savor's in this wrenching things awry.
Does sense so stale that it must needs derange   10
The world to know it? To a praiseful eye
Should it not be enough of fresh and strange
That trees grow green, and moles can course in clay,
And sparrows sweep the ceiling of our day?

Richard Wilbur, 1921–

ON HIS BLINDNESS

When I consider how my light is spent,
Ere half my days, in this dark world and wide,
And that one talent which is death to hide
Lodged with me useless, though my soul more bent
To serve therewith my Maker, and present   5
My true account, lest he returning chide,
"Doth God exact day labor, light denied?"
I fondly ask; but Patience, to prevent
That murmur, soon replies: "God doth not need
Either man's work or his own gifts; who best   10
Bear his mild yoke, they serve him best. His state
Is kingly: thousands at his bidding speed
And post o'er land and ocean without rest.
They also serve who only stand and wait."

John Milton, 1608–1674

from HOLY SONNETS

Sonnet 7

At the round earth's imagined corners, blow
Your trumpets, angels, and arise, arise
From death, you numberless infinities
Of souls, and to your scattered bodies go;
All whom the flood did, and fire shall o'erthrow;   5
All whom war, dearth, age, agues, tyrannies,
Despair, law, chance, hath slain, and you whose eyes
Shall behold God, and never taste death's woe.
But let them sleep, Lord, and me mourn a space,
For if above all these my sins abound,   10
'Tis late to ask abundance of thy grace
When we are there; here on this lowly ground
Teach me how to repent; for that's as good
As if thou hadst sealed my pardon with thy blood.

John Donne, 1572–1631

SESTINA: OF THE LADY PIETRA[1] DEGLI SCROVIGNI

To the dim light and the large circle of shade
I have clomb, and to the whitening of the hills,
There where we see no color in the grass.
Natheless my longing loses not its green,
It has so taken root in the hard stone   5
Which talks and hears as though it were a lady.

Utterly frozen is this youthful lady,
Even as the snow that lies within the shade;
For she is no more moved than is the stone
By the sweet season which makes warm the hills   10
And alters them afresh from white to green,
Covering their sides again with flowers and grass.

When on her hair she sets a crown of grass
The thought has no more room for other lady;
Because she weaves the yellow with the green   15
So well that Love sits down there in the shade,—
Love who has shut me in among low hills
Faster than between walls of granite-stone.

She is more bright than is a precious stone;
The wound she gives may not be healed with grass: 20
I therefore have fled o'er plains and hills
For refuge from so dangerous a lady;
But from her sunshine nothing can give shade,—
Not any hills, nor wall, nor summer-green.

A while ago, I saw her dressed in green,—   25
So fair, she might have wakened in a stone
This love which I do feel even for her shade;
And therefore, as one woos a graceful lady,
I wooed her in a field that was all grass
Girdled about with very lofty hills.   30

Yet shall the streams turn back and climb the hills
Before Love's flame in this damp wood and green
Burn, as it burns within a youthful lady,
For my sake, who would sleep away in stone

---

[1] *Pietra:* This is known as Dante's "stony sestina." The woman's name is the source of wordplay: *pietra* means "stone."

My life, or feed like beasts upon the grass,   35
Only to see her garments cast a shade.

How dark soe'er the hills throw out their shade,
Under her summer-green the beautiful lady
Covers it, like a stone covered in grass.

Dante Alighieri, 1265–1321
(Translated by D. G. Rossetti)

SESTINA: VANISHING POINT

A city, alive with sleeping people. Awake, the man
feels in his pockets. A roll of film, loose change,
ticket stubs, a book of matches. All he owns
can be quickly summarized. The drift of moonlight
across the dark floor is more to the point   5
here. Some things don't pin down. The woman

he thought was his is now another woman
in another city. Luminous, she leaves the man
his own flesh, a roll of film. The vanishing point
is that moment when the phone's ringing changes   10
to silence, and we are vibrant and alone, and moonlight
seems like the only thing that's left worth owning

and we attend its shifting configuration, own it
by our attention. His fist is empty. The woman
is on the move. Like many lovers the moonlight   15
waxes, illumines her, and wanes, and the man's
heart will beat until it stops. We are a cellchange,
we vanish and reappear, and there's a point

at which you are not who you were. At some point—
but where? She knows no location, only her own   20
shifting configuration, the play of loose change
in Heisenberg's pocket, nude descending a staircase. A woman
dies but her fingernails grow after death. The man
caught her once, asleep beside a shaft of moonlight

but he moved: the photo's blurred, moonlight   25
and flesh in slow fog, through their point
of vanishing and gone. There's not a man
on earth or moon can claim to own

white clarity for long. Or was it the woman
dreaming an earthquake, buckling rock changing   30

the lay of the land? At some point she wakes, changes
cities, names, cuts her hair. Like moonlight
we occur and reoccur. He's not wrong, but the woman
in the photo is dead, the moon's set. What's the point
of trying to buy time? What this man owns   35
isn't what he needs in the dark. This is the man

who wanted to remember the point at which he fell
asleep. But he's awake, without moonlight or a plan,
on his own, on the move, changing like a woman leaving a man.

Marilyn Krysl, 1942–

SESTINA

September rain falls on the house.
In the failing light, the old grandmother
sits in the kitchen with the child
beside the Little Marvel Stove,
reading the jokes from the almanac,   5
laughing and talking to hide her tears.

She thinks that her equinoctial tears
and the rain that beats on the roof of the house
were both foretold by the almanac,
but only known to a grandmother.   10
The iron kettle sings on the stove.
She cuts some bread and says to the child,

It's time for tea now; but the child
is watching the teakettle's small hard tears
dance like mad on the hot black stove,   15
the way the rain must dance on the house.
Tidying up, the old grandmother
hangs up the clever almanac

on its string. Bird-like, the almanac
hovers half open above the child,   20
hovers above the old grandmother
and her teacup full of dark brown tears.
She shivers and says she thinks the house
feels chilly, and puts more wood in the stove.

It was to be, says the Marvel Stove.   25
I know what I know, says the almanac.
With crayons the child draws a rigid house
and a winding pathway. Then the child
puts in a man with buttons like tears
and shows it proudly to the grandmother.   30

But secretly, while the grandmother
busies herself about the stove,
the little moons fall down like tears
from between the pages of the almanac
into the flower bed the child   35
has carefully placed in the front of the house.

Time to plant tears, says the almanac.
The grandmother sings to the marvellous stove
and the child draws another inscrutable house.

Elizabeth Bishop, 1911–1979

DO NOT GO GENTLE INTO THAT GOOD NIGHT

Do not go gentle into that good night,
Old age should burn and rave at close of day;
Rage, rage against the dying of the light.

Though wise men at their end know dark is right,
Because their words had forked no lightning they   5
Do not go gentle into that good night.

Good men, the last wave by, crying how bright
Their frail deeds might have danced in a green bay,
Rage, rage against the dying of the light.

Wild men who caught and sang the sun in flight,   10
And learn, too late, they grieved it on its way,
Do not go gentle into that good night.

Grave men, near death, who see with blinding sight
Blind eyes could blaze like meteors and be gay,
Rage, rage against the dying of the light.   15

And you, my father, there on the sad height,
Curse, bless, me now with your fierce tears, I pray.
Do not go gentle into that good night.
Rage, rage against the dying of the light.

Dylan Thomas, 1914–1953

THE WAKING

I wake to sleep, and take my waking slow.
I feel my fate in what I cannot fear.
I learn by going where I have to go.

We think by feeling. What is there to know?
I hear my being dance from ear to ear.   5
I wake to sleep, and take my waking slow.

Of those so close beside me, which are you?
God bless the Ground! I shall walk softly there,
And learn by going where I have to go.

Light takes the Tree; but who can tell us how?   10
The lowly worm climbs up a winding stair;
I wake to sleep, and take my waking slow.

Great Nature has another thing to do
To you and me; so take the lively air,
And, lovely, learn by going where to go.   15

This shaking keeps me steady. I should know.
What falls away is always. And is near.
I wake to sleep, and take my waking slow.
I learn by going where I have to go.

Theodore Roethke, 1908–1963

THE FREAKS AT SPURGIN ROAD FIELD

The dim boy claps because the others clap.
The polite word, handicapped, is muttered in the stands.
Isn't it wrong, the way the mind moves back.

One whole day I sit, contrite, dirt, L.A.
Union Station, 46, sweating through last night.   5
The dim boy claps because the others clap.

Score, 5 to 3. Pitcher fading badly in the heat.
Isn't it wrong to be or not be spastic?
Isn't it wrong, the way the mind moves back.

I'm laughing at a neighbor girl beaten to scream   10
by a savage father and I'm ashamed to look.
The dim boy claps because the others clap.

The score is always close, the rally always short.
I've left more wreckage than a quake.
Isn't is wrong, the way the mind moves back.   15

The afflicted never cheer in unison.
Isn't it wrong, the way the mind moves back
to stammering pastures where the picnic should have worked.
The dim boy claps because the others clap.

Richard Hugo, 1923–1982

WHAT IS AN EPIGRAM?

What is an epigram? a dwarfish whole,
Its body brevity, and wit its soul.

Samuel Taylor Coleridge, 1772–1834

WHEN FIRST WE MET

When first we met we did not guess
That Love would prove so hard a master;
Of more than common friendliness
When first we met we did not guess.
Who could foretell this sore distress   5
This irretrievable disaster
When first we met?—We did not guess
That Love would prove so hard a master.

Robert Bridges, 1844–1930

ULYSSES

It little profits that an idle king,
By this still hearth, among these barren crags,
Matched with an aged wife, I mete and dole
Unequal laws unto a savage race,
That hoard, and sleep, and feed, and know not me.   5
I cannot rest from travel; I will drink
Life to the lees. All times I have enjoyed
Greatly, have suffered greatly, both with those
That loved me, and alone; on shore, and when
Thro' scudding drifts the rainy Hyades   10
Vext the dim sea. I am become a name;
For always roaming with a hungry heart
Much have I seen and known,—cities of men
And manners, climates, councils, governments,
Myself not least, but honored of them all,—   15
And drunk delight of battle with my peers,
Far on the ringing plains of windy Troy.
I am a part of all that I have met;
Yet all experience is an arch wherethro'
Gleams that untravelled world whose margin fades   20
For ever and for ever when I move.
How dull it is to pause, to make an end,
To rust unburnished, not to shine in use!
As tho' to breathe were life! Life piled on life
Were all too little, and of one to me   25
Little remains; but every hour is saved
From that eternal silence, something more,
A bringer of new things; and vile it were
For some three suns to store and hoard myself,
And this gray spirit yearning in desire   30
To follow knowledge like a sinking star,
Beyond the utmost bound of human thought.
      This is my son, mine own Telemachus,
To whom I leave the sceptre and the isle,—
Well-loved of me, discerning to fulfil   35
This labor, by slow prudence to make mild
A rugged people, and thro' soft degrees
Subdue them to the useful and the good.
Most blameless is he, centred in the sphere
Of common duties, decent not to fail   40
In offices of tenderness, and pay
Meet adoration to my household gods,
When I am gone. He works his work, I mine.
      There lies the port; the vessel puffs her sail;

There gloom the dark broad seas. My mariners,   45
Souls that have toiled, and wrought, and thought with me,—
That ever with a frolic welcome took
The thunder and the sunshine, and opposed
Free hearts, free foreheads,—you and I are old;
Old age hath yet his honor and his toil.   50
Death closes all; but something ere the end,
Some work of noble note, may yet be done,
Not unbecoming men that strove with Gods.
The lights begin to twinkle from the rocks;
The long day wanes; the slow moon climbs; the deep   55
Moans round with many voices. Come, my friends.
'Tis not too late to seek a newer world.
Push off, and sitting well in order smite
The sounding furrows; for my purpose holds
To sail beyond the sunset, and the baths   60
Of all the western stars, until I die.
It may be that the gulfs will wash us down;
It may be we shall touch the Happy Isles,
And see the great Achilles, whom we knew.
Tho' much is taken, much abides; and tho'   65
We are not now that strength which in old days
Moved earth and heaven, that which we are, we are,—
One equal temper of heroic hearts,
Made weak by time and fate, but strong in will
To strive, to seek, to find, and not to yield.   70

Alfred, Lord Tennyson, 1809–1892

SOLDIERS BATHING

The sea at evening moves across the sand.
Under a reddening sky I watch the freedom of a band
Of soldiers who belong to me. Stripped bare
For bathing in the sea, they shout and run in the warm air;
Their flesh worn by the trade of war, revives   5
And my mind towards the meaning of it strives.

All's pathos now. The body that was gross,
Rank, ravenous, disgusting in the act or in repose,
All fever, filth and sweat, its bestial strength
And bestial decay, by pain and labour grows at length   10
Fragile and luminous. 'Poor bare forked animal,'
Conscious of his desires and needs and flesh that rise and fall,
Stands in the soft air, tasting after toil

The sweetness of his nakedness: letting the sea-waves coil
Their frothy tongues about his feet, forgets   15
His hatred of the war, its terrible pressure that begets
A machinery of death and slavery,
Each being a slave and making slaves of others: finds that he
Remembers his old freedom in a game
Mocking himself, and comically mimics fear and shame.   20

He plays with death and animality;
And reading in the shadows of his pallid flesh, I see
The idea of Michelangelo's cartoon
Of soldiers bathing, breaking off before they were half done
At some sortie of the enemy, an episode   25
Of the Pisan wars with Florence. I remember how he showed
Their muscular limbs that clamber from the water,
And heads that turn across the shoulder, eager for the slaughter,
Forgetful of their bodies that are bare,
And hot to buckle on and use the weapons lying there.   30
—And I think too of the theme another found
When, shadowing men's bodies on a sinister red ground,
Another Florentine, Pollaiuolo,
Painted a naked battle: warriors, straddled, hacked the foe,
Dug their bare toes into the ground and slew   35
The brother-naked man who lay between their feet and drew
His lips back from his teeth in a grimace.

They were Italians who knew war's sorrow and disgrace
And showed the thing suspended, stripped: a theme
Born out of the experience of war's horrible extreme   40
Beneath a sky where even the air flows
With lacrimae Christi.[1] For that rage, that bitterness, those blows,
That hatred of the slain, what could they be
But indirectly or directly a commentary
On the Crucifixion? And the picture burns   45
With indignation and pity and despair by turns,
Because it is the obverse of the scene
Where Christ hangs murdered, stripped, upon the Cross. I mean,
That is the explanation of its rage.

And we too have our bitterness and pity that engage   50
Blood, spirit, in this war. But night begins,
Night of the mind: who nowadays is conscious of our sins?
Though every human deed concerns our blood,

---

[1] *lacrimae Christi:* tears of Christ.

And even we must know, what nobody has understood,
That some great love is over all we do,   55
And that is what has driven us to this fury, for so few
Can suffer all the terror of that love:
The terror of that love has set us spinning in this groove
Greased with our blood.
                       These dry themselves and dress,   60
Combing their hair, forget the fear and shame of nakedness.
Because to love is frightening we prefer
The freedom of our crimes. Yet, as I drink the dusky air,
I feel a strange delight that fills me full,
Strange gratitude, as if evil itself were beautiful,   65
And kiss the wound in thought, while in the west
I watch a streak of red that might have issued from Christ's breast.

F. T. Prince, 1912–

DOVER BEACH

The sea is calm to-night,
The tide is full, the moon lies fair
Upon the Straits;—on the French coast, the light
Gleams, and is gone; the cliffs of England stand,
Glimmering and vast, out in the tranquil bay.   5
Come to the window, sweet is the night air!
Only, from the long line of spray
Where the ebb meets the moon-blanch'd sand,
Listen! you hear the grating roar
Of pebbles which the waves suck back, and fling,   10
At their return, up the high strand,
Begin, and cease, and then again begin,
With tremulous cadence slow, and bring
The eternal note of sadness in.

Sophocles long ago   15
Heard it on the Aegean, and it brought
Into his mind the turbid ebb and flow
Of human misery; we
Find also in the sound a thought,
Hearing it by this distant northern sea.   20

The sea of faith
Was once, too, at the full, and round earth's shore
Lay like the folds of a bright girdle furl'd;
But now I only hear

Its melancholy, long, withdrawing roar,   25
Retreating to the breath
Of the night-wind down the vast edges drear
And naked shingles of the world.

Ah, love, let us be true
To one another! for the world, which seems   30
To lie before us like a land of dreams,
So various, so beautiful, so new,
Hath really neither joy, nor love, nor light,
Nor certitude, nor peace, nor help for pain;
And we are here as on a darkling plain   35
Swept with confused alarms of struggle and flight,
Where ignorant armies clash by night.

Matthew Arnold, 1822–1888

LOVE AMONG THE RUINS

I

Where the quiet-coloured end of evening smiles
    Miles and miles
On the solitary pastures where our sheep
    Half-asleep
Tinkle homeward through the twilight, stray or stop   5
    As they crop
Was the site once of a city great and gay,
    (So they say)
Of our country's very capital, its prince
    Ages since   10
Held his court in, gathered councils, wielding far
    Peace or war.

II

Now,—the country does not even boast a tree,
    As you see,
To distinguish slopes of verdure, certain rills   15
    From the hills
Intersect and give a name to, (else they run
    Into one)
Where the domed and daring palace shot its spires
    Up like fires   20
O'er the hundred-gated circuit of a wall
    Bounding all,

Made of marble, men might march on nor be pressed,
    Twelve abreast.

III

And such plenty and perfection, see, of grass
    Never was!
Such a carpet as, this summer-time, o'er-spreads   25
    And embeds
Every vestige of the city, guessed alone,
    Stock or stone—
Where a multitude of men breathed joy and woe
    Long ago;   30
Lust of glory pricked their hearts up, dread of shame
    Struck them tame;
And that glory and that shame alike, the gold
    Bought and sold.

IV

Now,—the single little turret that remains   35
    On the plains,
By the caper overrooted, by the gourd
    Overscored,
While the patching houseleek's head of blossom winks
    Through the chinks—   40
Marks the basement whence a tower in ancient time
    Sprang sublime,
And a burning ring, all round, the chariots traced
    As they raced,
And the monarch and his minions and his dames   45
    Viewed the games.

V

And I know, while thus the quiet-colored eve
    Smiles to leave
To their folding, all our many-tinkling fleece
    In such peace,   50
And the slopes and rills in undistinguished grey
    Melt away—
That a girl with eager eyes and yellow hair
    Waits me there
In the turret whence the charioteers caught soul   55
    For the goal,
When the king looked, where she looks now, breathless, dumb
    Till I come.

VI

But he looked upon the city, every side,
    Far and wide,   60
All the mountains topped with temples, all the glades'
    Colonnades,
All the causeys, bridges, aqueducts,—and then,
    All the men!
When I do come, she will speak not, she will stand,   65
    Either hand
On my shoulder, give her eyes the first embrace
    Of my face,
Ere we rush, ere we extinguish sight and speech
    Each on each.   70

VII

In one year they sent a million fighters forth
    South and North,
And they built their gods a brazen pillar high
    As the sky,
Yet reserved a thousand chariots in full force—   75
    Gold, of course.
Oh heart! oh blood that freezes, blood that burns!
    Earth's returns
For whole centuries of folly, noise and sin!
    Shut them in,   80
With their triumphs and their glories and the rest!
    Love is best.

Robert Browning, 1812–1889

TULIPS

The tulips are too excitable, it is winter here.
Look how white everything is, how quiet, how snowed-in.
I am learning peacefulness, lying by myself quietly
As the light lies on these white walls, this bed, these hands.
I am nobody; I have nothing to do with explosions.   5
I have given my name and my day-clothes to the nurses
And my history to the anaesthetist and my body to surgeons.

They have propped my head between the pillow and the sheet-cuff
Like an eye between two white lids that will not shut.
Stupid pupil, it has to take everything in.   10
The nurses pass and pass, they are no trouble,

They pass the way gulls pass inland in their white caps,
Doing things with their hands, one just the same as another,
So it is impossible to tell how many there are.

My body is a pebble to them, they tend it as water   15
Tends to the pebbles it must run over, smoothing them gently.
They bring me numbness in their bright needles, they bring me sleep.
Now I have lost myself I am sick of baggage—
My patent leather overnight case like a black pillbox,
My husband and child smiling out of the family photo;   20
Their smiles catch onto my skin, little smiling hooks.

I have let things slip, a thirty-year-old cargo boat
Stubbornly hanging on to my name and address.
They have swabbed me clear of my loving associations.
Scared and bare on the green plastic-pillowed trolley   25
I watched my tea-set, my bureaus of linen, my books
Sink out of sight, and the water went over my head.
I am a nun now, I have never been so pure.

I didn't want any flowers, I only wanted
To lie with my hands turned up and be utterly empty.   30
How free it is, you have no idea how free—
The peacefulness is so big it dazes you,
And it asks nothing, a name tag, a few trinkets.
It is what the dead close on, finally; I imagine them
Shutting their mouths on it, like a Communion tablet.   35

The tulips are too red in the first place, they hurt me.
Even through the gift paper I could hear them breathe
Lightly, through their white swaddlings, like an awful baby.
Their redness talks to my wound, it corresponds.
They are subtle: they seem to float, though they weigh me down,   40
Upsetting me with their sudden tongues and their color,
A dozen red lead sinkers round my neck.

Nobody watched me before, now I am watched.
The tulips turn to me, and the window behind me
Where once a day the light slowly widens and slowly thins,   45
And I see myself, flat, ridiculous, a cut-paper shadow
Between the eye of the sun and the eyes of the tulips,
And I have no face, I have wanted to efface myself.
The vivid tulips eat my oxygen.

Before they came the air was calm enough,   50
Coming and going, breath by breath, without any fuss.

Then the tulips filled it up like a loud noise.
Now the air snags and eddies round them the way a river
Snags and eddies round a sunken rust-red engine.
They concentrate my attention, that was happy   55
Playing and resting without committing itself.

The walls, also, seem to be warming themselves.
The tulips should be behind bars like dangerous animals;
They are opening like the mouth of some great African cat,
And I am aware of my heart: it opens and closes   60
Its bowl of red blooms out of sheer love of me.
The water I taste is warm and salt, like the sea,
And comes from a country far away as health.

Sylvia Plath, 1932–1963

NOW

I park the car because I'm happy,
because if everyone parked we'd have a street party,
because the moon is full—
it is orange, the sky is closer
and it would be wrong to drive into it.   5
This is the first day of summer—
everyone is hanging out,
women walk by in their bodies so mellow
I feel I'm near a friend's house.

The small white flakes of the headlights   10
sweat for a second on the storefronts.
In the windows, darkened afterhours,
a reflection stares back
looking more like me than me.
I reach to touch   15
and the reflection touches me.
Everything is perfect—
even my skin fits.

Hanging out,
the taillights of the turning cars   20
are fires, going out—
are the spaces of roses flowered
deeper in themselves. I close my eyes
and am flowered deeper in myself.
Further up the street a walking figure   25

I can't make out, a face
behind a bag of groceries, free arm swinging
in the air the wave of a deep red
fluid shifting to and fro.

At the vegetarian restaurant   30
I see it's Michael the Conga Drummer—
been looking for him 2 months.
He asks me, "what's happening?"
I love his fingers.
When we shake hands I mix his grip   35
with the curve of my father's
toting cantaloup in the house from the market.
We are two griots at an intersection.
I answer him in parable:

the orange that I've been carrying   40
is some luminous memory, bursting,
bigger than my hand can hold,
so I hand him half.

Christopher Gilbert, 1949–

LIVING

If this is Wednesday, write Lazartigues, return library books,
pick up passport form, cancel the paper.

If this is Wednesday, mail B her flyers and K her shirts. Last
thing I asked as I walked K to her car, "You sure you have
everything?" "Oh yes," she smiled, as she squalled off. Whole
wardrobe in front closet.

Go to Morrison's for paint samples, that's where
housepainter has account (near Pier One), swing by Gano St.
for another bunch of hydroponic lettuce. Stop at cleaners if
there's parking.

Pap smear at 4. After last month with B's ear infections, can't
bear sitting in damn doctor's office. Never a magazine or
picture on the wall worth looking at. Pack a book.

Ever since B born, nothing comes clear. My mind like a
mirror that's been in a fire. Does this happen to the others.

If this is Wednesday, meet Moss at the house at noon. Pick B
up first, call sitter about Friday evening. If she prefers, can bring
B to her (hope she keeps the apartment warmer this year).

Need coat hooks and picture hangers for office. Should take
car in for air filter, oil change. F said one of back tires low.
Don't forget car payment, late last two months in a row.

If this is Wednesday, there's a demo on the green at 11. Took
B to his first down at Quoinset Point in August. Blue skies.
Boston collective provided good grub for all. Long column of
denims and flannel shirts. Smell of Patchouli made me so
wistful, wanted to buy a wood stove, prop my feet up, share a J
and a pot of Constant Comment with a friend. Maybe some
zucchini bread.

Meet with honors students from 1 to 4. At the community
college I tried to incite them to poetry. Convince them this line
of work beats the bejesus out of a gig as gizzard splitter at the
processing plant or cleaning up after a leak at the germ warfare
center. Be all you can be, wrap a rubber band around your
trigger finger until it drops off.

Don't forget to cancel the goddamned paper. At the very least
quit reading editorials and police reports—local boys caught
throwing sewer caps off the overpass again, not to mention
recreational violence in the park next to our cashew-colored
house every night of the year.

Swim at 10:00 before picking up B, before demo on the
green, and before meeting Moss, if it isn't too crowded. Only
three old women talking about their daughters-in-law last
Wednesday at 10:00.

Phone hardware to see if radon test arrived.

Keep an eye out for a new yellow blanket. Left B's on the
plane, though he seems over it already. Left most recent issue of
Z in the seat. That will make a few businessmen boil. I liked the
man who sat next to me, he was sweet to B. Hated flying, said
he never let all of his weight down.

Need to get books in the mail today. Make time pass in line at
the p.o. imagining man in front of me butt naked. Fellow in the
good-preacher-blue suit, probably has a cold, hard bottom.

Call N for green tomato recipe. Have to get used to the
yankee growing season. If this is Wednesday, N goes in hospital
today. Find out how long after marrow transplant before
can visit.

Mother said she read in paper that Pete was granted a divorce.
His third. My highschool boyfriend. Meanest thing I could have
done, I did to him, returning the long-saved-for engagement
ring in a band-aid box, while he was stationed in Danang.

Meant to tell F this morning about dream of eating
grasshoppers, fried but happy. Our love a difficult instrument
we are learning to play. Practice, practice.

No matter where I call home anymore, feel like a boat under
the trees. Living is strange.

This week only: bargain on laid paper at East Side
Copy Shop.

Woman picking her nose at the stoplight. Shouldn't look,
only privacy we have anymore in the car. Isn't that the woman
from the colloquium last fall, who told me she was a stand-up
environmentalist. What a wonderful trade, I said, because the
evidence of planetary wrongdoing is overwhelming. Because
because because of the horrible things we do.

If this is Wednesday, meet F at Health Department at 10:45
for AIDS test.

If this is Wednesday, it's trash night.

C. D. Wright, 1949–

GIRL

   Wash the white clothes on Monday and put them on the stone
heap; wash the color clothes on Tuesday and put them on the clothes-
line to dry; don't walk barehead in the hot sun; cook pumpkin fritters
in very hot sweet oil; soak your little cloths right after you take them
off; when buying cotton to make yourself a nice blouse, be sure that
it doesn't have gum in it, because that way it won't hold up well after
a wash; soak salt fish overnight before you cook it; is it true that you
sing benna in Sunday School?; always eat your food in such a way

that it won't turn someone else's stomach; on Sundays try to walk like a lady and not like the slut you are so bent on becoming; don't sing benna in Sunday school; you mustn't speak to wharf-rat boys, not even to give directions; don't eat fruits on the street—flies will follow you; *but I don't sing benna on Sundays at all and never in Sunday school;* this is how to sew on a button; this is how to make a buttonhole for the button you have just sewed on; this is how to hem a dress when you see the hem coming down and so to prevent yourself from looking like the slut I know you are so bent on becoming; this is how you iron your father's khaki shirt so that it doesn't have a crease; this is how you iron your father's khaki pants so that they don't have a crease; this is how you grow okra—far from the house, because okra tree harbors red ants; when you are growing dasheen, make sure it gets plenty of water or else it makes your throat itch when you are eating it; this is how you sweep a corner; this is how you sweep a whole house; this is how you sweep a yard; this is how you smile to someone you don't like too much; this is how you smile to someone you don't like at all; this is how you smile to someone you like completely; this is how you set a table for tea; this is how you set a table for dinner; this is how you set a table for dinner with an important guest; this is how you set a table for lunch; this is how you set a table for breakfast; this is how to behave in the presence of men who don't know you very well, and this way they won't recognize immediately the slut I have warned you against becoming; be sure to wash every day, even if it is with your own spit; don't squat down to play marbles—you are not a boy, you know; don't pick people's flowers—you might catch something; don't throw stones at blackbirds, because it might not be a blackbird at all; this is how to make a bread pudding; this is how to make doukona; this is how to make pepper pot; this is how to make a good medicine for a cold; this is how to make a good medicine to throw away a child before it even becomes a child; this is how to catch a fish; this is how to throw back a fish you don't like, and that way something bad won't fall on you; this is how to bully a man; this is how a man bullies you; this is how to love a man, and if this doesn't work there are other ways, and if they don't work don't feel too bad about giving up; this is how to spit up in the air if you feel like it, and this is how to move quick so that it doesn't fall on you; this is how to make ends meet; always squeeze bread to make sure it's fresh; *but what if the baker won't let me feel the bread?;* you mean to say that after all you are really going to be the kind of woman who the baker won't let near the bread?

Jamaica Kincaid, 1949–

9

Subject and Style

All the fun's in how you say a thing.

Robert Frost

While one great poem begins with a philosophical speculation on the vicissitudes of history, another may start with someone sitting in the sun clipping her toenails. Fleas and angels, ecstasy and flowers, rain and potatoes, war and pinball—anything is a potential subject for a poem.

By now you've read dozens of poems on many subjects and in many forms and voices. It may surprise you to hear Chilean poet Pablo Neruda's opinion that there are only eleven subjects for poetry. Neruda didn't say exactly what the eleven are. His point was that all poetry revolves around a few basic human situations and universal concerns.

Various lists of eleven subjects—or nine or eighteen—might exist; surely some common denominators are love, death, conflict, identity, politics, memory, art, nature, spirituality. What else? Perhaps loss, joy, time, power, mortality, beginnings. Quickly the subjects begin to blur together—perhaps loss is an aspect of memory or death, joy an aspect of love. The categories don't matter. What matters is that poems have essential concerns which people of any time recognize as important to their own living. In contrast to the old saw "There's nothing new under the sun," each subject becomes new to new generations. The ancient Greek tragedy of Medea killing her own children still hits the modern reader with force. A contemporary poem on the fear of war or the pleasure of petting a horse in a meadow would have moved someone living centuries ago.

Types of Poems

Some subjects written about over and over have been codified into types of poems. A **pastoral**, for example, features a rural landscape.

"Write about dogs!"
Drawing by Booth; © 1976 The New Yorker Magazine, Inc.

The pastoral often involves the lives or loves of nymphs and shepherds. Writers choose this setting because of a special effect: the idyllic landscape releases the subject from the real world of complex, mundane situations. No petty details, class differences, or world events can get to the lovers. For the space of the poem, they're together in an Eden-like landscape. In "Michael," the shepherd knows "the meaning of all winds." The last four lines of this excerpt make clear what the fields and hills of Michael's home meant to him. In pastorals, the setting takes on the same role as a person: it is an active force in the poem.

from MICHAEL, A PASTORAL

Of shepherds, dwellers in the valleys, men
Whom I already loved; not verily
For their own sakes, but for the fields and hills
Where was their occupation and abode.
And hence this tale, while I was yet a boy   5
Careless of books, yet having felt the power
Of Nature, by the gentle agency
Of natural objects, led me on to feel
For passions that were not my own, and think
(At random and imperfectly indeed)   10
On man, the heart of man, and human life.
Therefore, although it be a history
Homely and rude, I will relate the same
For the delight of a few natural hearts;
And, with yet fonder feeling, for the sake   15
Of youthful poets, who among these hills
Will be my second self when I am gone.

Upon the forest side in Grasmere Vale
There dwelt a shepherd, Michael was his name;
An old man, stout of heart, and strong of limb.   20
His bodily frame had been from youth to age
Of an unusual strength; his mind was keen,
Intense, and frugal, apt for all affairs,
And in his shepherd's calling he was prompt
And watchful more than ordinary men.   25
Hence had he learned the meaning of all winds,
Of blasts of every tone; and, oftentimes,
When others heeded not, he heard the south
Make subterraneous music, like the noise
Of bagpipers on distant Highland hills.   30

The shepherd, at such warning, of his flock
Bethought him, and he to himself would say,
"The winds are now devising work for me!"
And, truly, at all times, the storm, that drives
The traveler to a shelter, summoned him   35
Up to the mountains; he had been alone
Amid the heart of many thousand mists,
That came to him, and left him, on the heights.
So lived he till his eightieth year was past.
And grossly that man errs, who should suppose   40
That the green valleys, and the streams and rocks,
Were things indifferent to the shepherd's thoughts.
Fields, where with cheerful spirits he had breathed
The common air; hills, which with vigorous step
He had so often climbed; which had impressed   45
So many incidents upon his mind
Of hardship, skill or courage, joy or fear;
Which, like a book, preserved the memory
Of the dumb animals, whom he had saved,
Had fed or sheltered, linking to such acts   50
The certainty of honorable gain;
Those fields, those hills—what could they less? had laid
Strong hold on his affections, were to him
A pleasurable feeling of blind love,
The pleasure which there is in life itself.   55

William Wordsworth, 1770–1850

The pastoral tradition goes back to the third century B.C. poems of
Theocritus, who described the Sicilian landscape of his childhood.
Today, since nymphs and shepherds are in short supply, we use the
term *pastoral* for any poem describing a rural scene. Briefly, other
common subject-types of poems are:

Ars poetica (the art of poetry): a poem written on the subject of the
poetic art, usually to explain the poet's reasons for writing.

ARS POETICA?

I have always aspired to a more spacious form
that would be free from the claims of poetry or prose
and would let us understand each other without exposing
the author or reader to sublime agonies.

In the very essence of poetry there is something indecent: 5
a thing is brought forth which we didn't know we had in us,

so we blink our eyes, as if a tiger had sprung out
and stood in the light, lashing his tail.

That's why poetry is rightly said to be dictated by a daimonion,
though it's an exaggeration to maintain that he must be an angel.   10
It's hard to guess where that pride of poets comes from,
when so often they're put to shame by the disclosure of their frailty.

What reasonable man would like to be a city of demons,
who behave as if they were at home, speak in many tongues,
and who, not satisfied with stealing his lips or hand   15
work at changing his destiny for their convenience?

It's true that what is morbid is highly valued today,
and so you may think that I am only joking
or that I've devised just one more means
of praising Art with the help of irony.   20

There was a time when only wise books were read
helping us to bear our pain and misery.
This, after all, is not quite the same
as leafing through a thousand works fresh from psychiatric clinics.

And yet the world is different from what it seems to be   25
and we are other than how we see ourselves in our ravings.
People therefore preserve silent integrity
thus earning the respect of their relatives and neighbors.

The purpose of poetry is to remind us
how difficult it is to remain just one person,   30
for our house is open, there are no keys in the doors,
and invisible guests come in and out at will.

What I'm saying here is not, I agree, poetry,
as poems should be written rarely and reluctantly,
under unbearable duress and only with the hope   35
that good spirits, not evil ones, choose us for their instrument.

Czeslaw Milosz, 1911–
(Translated by the author and Lillian Vallee)

Aubade (or **alba**): a poem composed at dawn, usually in the voice of a departing lover.

ALBA

Dawn breaking as I woke,
With the white sweat of the dew
On the green, new grass.
I walked in the cold, quiet as
If it were the world beginning;   5
Peeling and eating a chilled tangerine.
I may have many sorrows,
Dawn is not one of them.

Derek Walcott, 1930–

Carpe diem: a poem urging one to live in the moment because time
passes quickly. Named from a poem by Horace which begins, *"Carpe
diem, quam minimum credula postero"* ("Seize today, and trust tomorrow little").

TO THE VIRGINS, TO MAKE MUCH OF TIME

Gather ye rosebuds while you may,
   Old time is still a-flying;
And this same flower that smiles today
   Tomorrow will be dying.

The glorious lamp of heaven, the sun,   5
   The higher he's a-getting,
The sooner will his race be run,
   And nearer he's to setting.

That age is best which is the first,
   When youth and blood are warmer;   10
But being spent, the worse, and worst
   Times still succeed the former.

Then be not coy, but use your time,
   And, while ye may, go marry;
For, having lost but once your prime,   15
   You may forever tarry.

Robert Herrick, 1591–1674

Dithyramb: originally a poem about Dionysus, the Greek god of
fertility and procreation. The subject gradually widened to include any

poem about the adventures of the gods. In modern times *dithyramb* has come to mean a poem of revelry or praise, or any exaggerated, passionate composition.

A SMART* DITHYRAMB

(Christopher Smart 1722–1771)*

Let us consider the Great Gray Whale
For his skin is a mystery to our fingers and on those we can count
   his blessings
For first he has adopted a medium where all movement is graceful
For secondly, in that darkness, he opens his great harp mouth
and gives us sidelong smiles as small fish enter his belly to pray   5
For thirdly he is forty tons heavy
For fourthly he can stand on his tail
For fifthly he likes company and when the temperature drops
travels in cheap charters to southern lagoons
For sixthly he is blessed with very close friends, barnacles and lice   10
For seventhly when he rises to the surface and blows
God lifts himself from the deep and becomes noise
For eighthly are we moved to awe when he mates
seeing only fin and fluke, conjuring the rest
For ninthly he is playful, Heaven's great child   15
For tenthly his language is inaudible
For he is bored by encounters with our elite
No sparrow falls where he might notice it
The credentials of colour slide easily past his grey back
For he has an archbishop's dignity   20
One moment solid as land, the next only a slick
glossing the water's surface, our breath floundering in his wake

For praise is in his eye, which sights land and remembers

For his long journey is a meditation
The stippled hinds of his cow and calf glittering in the evening
   sun   25
Let us give thanks for there is no meanness in him
For our spirits soar with his breach which cracks the world's rim

He dives beyond reach, takes with him the remnants of our
   imagination

Susan MacDonald, 1937–

Elegy: a poem written for or about someone dead. The poet usually contemplates the meaning of death and often finds some consolation.

ON MY FIRST SON

Farewell, thou child of my right hand,[1] and joy;
My sin was too much hope of thee, loved boy:
Seven years thou wert lent to me, and I thee pay,
Exacted by thy fate, on the just day.[2]
O could I lose all father now! for why   5
Will man lament the state he should envy,
To have so soon 'scaped world's and flesh's rage,
And, if no other misery, yet age?
Rest in soft peace, and asked, say, "Here doth lie
Ben Jonson his best piece of poetry."   10
For whose sake henceforth all his vows be such
As what he loves may never like too much.

Ben Jonson, 1573–1637

[1] *child of my right hand:* Jonson's son's name was Benjamin, which means "child of my right hand" in Hebrew.
[2] *the just day:* the child died on his birthday.

Encomium: originally a celebration for a hero or heroine, now a laudatory poem for a legendary or real person.

TO TOUSSAINT L'OUVERTURE[1]

Toussaint, the most unhappy man of men!
Whether the whistling rustic tend his plough
Within thy hearing, or thy head be now
Pillowed in some deep dungeon's earless den—
O miserable chieftain! where and when   5
Wilt thou find patience! Yet die not; do thou
Wear rather in thy bonds a cheerful brow:
Though fallen thyself, never to rise again,
Live, and take comfort. Thou hast left behind
Powers that will work for thee; air, earth, and skies;   10

[1] *Toussaint L'Ouverture:* Black Haitian revolutionary who declared independence from France. He was defeated and sent to a French prison, where he died in 1803.

There's not a breathing of the common wind
That will forget thee: thou hast great allies;
Thy friends are exultations, agonies,
And love, and man's unconquerable mind.

William Wordsworth, 1770–1850

Epithalamium: a celebration for a wedding.

from EPITHALAMIUM

	Wake, now my love, awake; for it is time,	
	The Rosy Morne long since left Tithones[1] bed,	
	All ready to her silver coche° to clyme,	*coach*
	And Phoebus[2] gins° to shew his glorious hed.	*begins*
5	Hark how the cheerefull birds do chaunt theyr laies°	*lays, songs*
	And carroll of loves praise.	
	The merry Larke hir mattins sings aloft,	
	The thrust replyes, the Mavis° descant° playes,	*thrush, accompaniment*
	The Ouzell° shrills, the Ruddock° warbles soft,	*blackbird, robin*
10	So goodly all agree with sweet consent,	
	To this dayes merriment.	
	Ah my deere love why doe ye sleepe thus long,	
	When meeter were that ye should now awake,	
	T' awayt the comming of your joyous make,°	*mate*
15	And hearken to the birds lovelearnèd song,	
	The deawy leaves among.	
	For they of joy and pleasance to you sing,	
	That all the woods them answer and theyr eccho ring.	
	My love is now awake out of her dreame,	
20	And her fayre eyes like stars that dimmèd were	
	With darksome cloud, now shew theyr goodly beams	
	More bright then Hesperus[3] his head doth rere.	
	Come now ye damzels, daughters of delight,	
	Helpe quickly her to dight,	
25	But first come ye fayre houres which were begot	
	In Joves sweet paradice, of Day and Night,	
	Which doe the seasons of the yeare allot,	
	And al that ever in this world is fayre	

[1] *Tithones:* a mortal loved by the goddess of dawn.
[2] *Phoebus:* the sun god, also called Apollo.
[3] *Hesperus:* evening star, also called Venus.

Doe make and still repayre.
30   And ye three handmayds of the Cyprian Queene,[4]
The which doe still adorne her beauties pride,
Helpe to addorne my beautifullest bride:
And as ye her array, still throw betweene
Some graces to be seene,
35   And as ye use to Venus, to her sing,
The whiles the woods shal answer and your eccho ring.

Now is my love all ready forth to come,
Let all the virgins therefore well awayt,
And ye fresh boyes that tend upon her groome
40   Prepare your selves; for he is comming strayt.
Set all your things in seemely good aray
Fit for so joyfull day,
The joyfulst day that ever sunne did see.
Faire Sun, shew forth thy favourable ray,
45   And let thy lifull° heat not fervent be   *lifeful, vital*
For feare of burning her sunshyny face,
Her beauty to disgrace.
O fayrest Phoebus, father of the Muse,
If ever I did honour thee aright,
50   Or sing the thing, that mote° thy mind delight,   *might*
Doe not thy servants simple boone° refuse,   *prayer*
But let this day let this one day be myne,
Let all the rest be thine.
Then I thy soverayne prayses loud wil sing,
55   That all the woods shal answer and theyr eccho ring.

Harke how the Minstrels gin to shrill aloud
Their merry Musick that resounds from far,
The pipe, the tabor,° and the trembling Croud,°   *drum, fiddle*
That well agree withouten breach or jar.°   *discord*
60   But most of all the Damzels doe delite,
When they their tymbrels smyte,
And thereunto doe daunce and carrol sweet,
That all the sences they doe ravish quite,
The whyles° the boyes run up and downe the street,   *while*
65   Crying aloud with strong confusèd noyce,
As if it were one voyce.
Hymen iô Hymen, Hymen[5] they do shout,
That even to the heavens they'r shouting shrill
Doth reach, and all the firmament doth fill,

[4] *Cyprian queen:* Venus, associated in myth with the island of Cyprus.
[5] *Hymen, Hymen:* ritual cry of ancient marriage procession.

70	To which the people standing all about,
	As in approvance doe thereto applaud
	And loud advaunce her laud,° *praise*
	And everymore they *Hymen Hymen* sing,
	That al the woods them answer and theyr eccho ring.

75 Loe where she comes along with portly pace
Lyke Phoebe[6] from her chamber of the East,
Arysing forth to run her mighty race,
Clad all in white, that seemes° a virgin best.   *becomes*
So well it her beseemes that ye would weene
80 Some angell she had beene.
Her long loose yellow locks lyke golden wyre,
Sprinckled with perle, and perling° flowres a tweene,   *winding*
Doe lyke a golden mantle her attyre,
And being crownèd with a girland greene,
85 Seeme lyke some mayden Queene.
Her modest eyes abashèd to behold
So many gazers, as on her do stare,
Upon the lowly ground affixèd are.
Ne dare lift up her countenance too bold,
90 But blush to heare her prayses sung so loud,
So farre from being proud.
Nathlesse° doe ye still loud her prayses sing.   *nevertheless*
That all the woods may answer and your eccho ring.

Tell me ye merchants daughters did ye see
95 So fayre a creature in your towne before,
So sweet, so lovely, and so mild as she,
Adorned with beautyes grace and vertues store,
Her goodly eyes lyke Saphyres shining bright,
Her forehead yvory white,
100 Her cheekes lyke apples which the sun hath rudded,°   *reddened*
Her lips lyke cherryes charming men to byte,
Her brest like to a bowle of creame uncrudded,°   *uncurdled*
Her paps lyke lyllies budded,
Her snowie necke lyke to a marble towre,
105 And all her body lyke a pallace fayre,
Ascending uppe with many a stately stayre,
To honors seat and chastities sweet bowre.
Why stand ye still ye virgins in amaze,
Upon her so to gaze,
110 Whiles ye forget your former lay to sing,
To which the woods did answer and your eccho ring.

---

[6] *Phoebe:* moon goddess, also called Diana.

But if ye saw that which no eyes can see,
The inward beauty of her lively spright,°   *spirit*
Garnisht with heavenly guifts of high degree,
115   Much more then would ye wonder at that sight,
And stand astonisht lyke to those which red°   *saw*
Medusaes mazeful hed.
There dwels sweet love and constant chastity,
Unspotted fayth and comely womanhood,
120   Regard of honour and mild modesty,
There vertue raynes as Queene in royal throne,
And giveth lawes alone.
The which the base° affections doe obay,   *lower*
And yeeld theyr services unto her will,
125   Ne thought of thing uncomely ever may
Thereto approach to tempt her mind to ill.
Had ye once seene these her celestial threasures,
And unrevealèd pleasures,
Then would ye wonder and her prayses sing,
130   That al the woods should answer and your eccho ring.

Open the temple gates unto my love,
Open them wide that she may enter in,
And all the postes adorne as doth behove,°   *behoove*
And all the pillours deck with girlands trim,
135   For to recyve this Saynt with honour dew,
That commeth in to you.
With trembling steps and humble reverence,
She commeth in, before th' almighties vew,
Of her ye virgins learne obedience,
140   When so ye come into those holy places,
To humble your proud faces:
Bring her up to th' high altar, that she may
The sacred ceremonies there partake,
The which do endlesse matrimony make,
145   And let the roring Organs loudly play
The praises of the Lord in lively notes,
The whiles with hollow throates
The Choristers the joyous Antheme sing,
That al the woods may answere and their eccho ring.

Edmund Spenser, 1522–1599

Palinode: a poem retracting a regretted derogatory or negative statement or retracting a previous poem. In a lighter moment, Edmund Bolton wrote a more positive poem; here he takes a gloomy position on the transience of praise, pomp, glory, and joy.

A PALINODE

As withereth the primrose by the river,
As fadeth summer's sun from gliding fountains,
As vanisheth the light-blown bubble ever,
As melteth snow upon the mossy mountains:
So melts, so vanisheth, so fades, so withers   5
The rose, the shine, the bubble, and the snow
Of praise, pomp, glory, joy—which short life gathers—
Fair praise, vain pomp, sweet glory, brittle joy.
The withered primrose by the morning river,

The faded summer's sun from weeping fountains,   10
The light-blown bubble vanishèd forever,
The molten snow upon the naked mountains,
    Are emblems that the treasures we up-lay
    Soon wither, vanish, fade, and melt away.

For as the snow, whose lawn did overspread   15
The ambitious hills, which giant-like did threat
To pierce the heaven with their aspiring head,
Naked and bare doth leave their craggy seat;
Whenas the bubble, which did empty fly
The dalliance of the undiscernèd wind,   20
On whose calm rolling waves it did rely,
Hath shipwreck made, where it did dalliance find;

And when the sunshine which dissolved the snow,
Coloured the bubble with a pleasant vary,
And made the rathe and timely primrose grow.   25
Swarth clouds withdrawn (which longer time do tarry)—
    Oh, what is praise, pomp, glory, joy, but so
    As shine by fountains, bubbles, flowers, or snow?

Edmund Bolton, 1575?–1633?

Other less common types are the **madrigal**, a short poem (12 or 13 lines, usually with a rhyming couplet at the end) about nature and love; and the **rune**, a magical chant or incantation.

These types of poems are not forms but simply the names of common subjects. An aubade, pastoral or other type may be in any shape or meter. Thousands of poems, of course, do not fall neatly into any subject category.

"What are your poems about?" must be the question poets hate most.

A profound, brilliant writer may have to answer, "Blackbirds, childhood in Ohio, and weather." A terrible writer might answer, "Traveling through the Yucatan on foot and serving time in an Arab jail." So what? As poet William Matthews notes, "It is not, of course, the subject that is or isn't dull but the quality of attention we do or do not pay to it, and the strength of our will to transform."

How does the writer *transform* a subject? Besides craft, besides choice of speaker and subject, what connective tissue in the poem holds it together?

Style

Writers often feel that everything that could be said on any subject has been said before—and better—by other writers. A young poet comparing his new poem to one by Yeats is bound to fear at some point that the new work, so engrossing while he was writing it, hardly bears considering. Yeats is great! But what keeps writers sharpening their pencils is a hope that one's own *way* with the subject, one's own poem on spring or love, will stand out. The art of poetry is largely the art of *revisioning*, in one's own time and style, the subjects that always have concerned writers.

The interplay of everything the poet brings to the art comprises **style**. *Style* is an elusive term; we can recognize style more easily than we can describe it. When you say that a friend "really has style," you mean not only her looks and dress but her whole way of talking, walking, expressing herself, and regarding life. When someone tells you, "That sounds like something only you would think of," *your* way of being is recognized, something of your essential style noticed.

A poet's style is made up of characteristic words and images, prevalent concerns, tone of voice, patterns of syntax, and form. When we read enough of an author, we begin to know the kind of power he has over language and the resources of language at his disposal. What makes us recognize the author, even if a poem is not identified, is style. In a long career, style changes. Early Yeats is different from late Yeats. We can trace his growth in power, the enlargement of his subjects. Still, Yeats is Yeats. Certain traits—a trace in the phrasing here, an identifying word there—mark the style, as, at times, in an old face you glimpse the younger person.

Sometimes a writer grows overly aware of his style and begins to sound too much like himself. The reader says, "Oh no, there he goes again, pressing the same set of buttons." He has gone lazy on himself, doing too easily what he knows how to do. The work becomes a parody of itself.

The poet who keeps evolving is the one who pays new attention to the subject of each poem, essentially starting over with each attempt to write. To find out what only *he* could say is to find—and keep—a singular, unmistakable style. "Make it new" was Ezra Pound's advice to poets. This requires delving into one's own unique imagination, intellect, and experience and forging from those a piece of art. "Finding your own voice" isn't like looking for the proverbial needle in the haystack; it is being able to hear yourself clearly. One test of style is to ask whether someone else could have written the poem. If not, why? That *why* is the key to the poem's style.

Keats's Style

Like fine paper held up to the light, a good poem is stamped with the poet's watermark, a distinctive complex of qualities that make up the writer's style. Read, for example, several poems by John Keats. Keats's watermarks are a richness and complexity of imagery and an honest, clear voice full of life. His constant subjects are ordinary ones: love, death, seasons, the transience of life. He was interested in myth and dramatic narratives. In frustration with the sonnet form, he developed the ten-line stanza to use in his odes. This stanza compresses the fourteen-line sonnet length and uses a metrically longer last line. Keats found a form that was adaptable to his exploring, speculative mode.

Because Keats died at 25, he did not have long to try his skills; but by experimenting constantly, he pushed into new areas to an astonishing degree. In his letters, Keats wrote: "We hate poetry that has a palpable design upon us. . . . Poetry should be great and unobtrusive, a thing which enters into one's soul, and does not startle it or amaze it with itself but with its subject." And: "I think Poetry should surprise by a fine excess and not by singularity—it should strike the Reader as a wording of his own highest thoughts, and appear almost a Remembrance." Keats's own work meets these standards. The poems seem to unfold naturally, with sincerity and without dogmatism. A Keats poem always has a sense of newness, as though the ink is still wet.

Keats also wrote that he valued *gusto*—there's the word most appropriate to his own vitality with language. The texture of a Keats poem is crowded with fully formed images and surprising juxtapositions of words, as in "nervy knees," "listening fear," "pleasant pain," "icy trance." He also gives an ongoing and present quality to the poems through frequent use of participle endings: *tasting, winding, opening, passing.* Assonance, consonance, and alliteration are hard at work to unify the images by sound. No writer except Shakespeare uses imagery as sensuously as Keats. Recall his description of Madeline kneeling under the stained glass window in "The Eve of St. Agnes" (page 133):

> A casement high and triple-arch'd there was,
> All garlanded with carven imag'ries
> Of fruits, and flowers, and bunches of knot-grass,
> And diamonded with panes of quaint device,
> Innumerable of stains and splendid dyes,
> As are the tiger-moth's deep damask'd wings;
> And in the midst, 'mong thousand heraldries,
> And twilight saints, and dim emblazonings,
> A shielded scutcheon blush'd with blood of queens and kings.
>
> Full on this casement shone the wintry moon,
> and threw warm gules[1] on Madeline's fair breast,
> As down she knelt for heaven's grace and boon;
> Rose-bloom fell on her hands, together presst,
> And on her silver cross soft amethyst,
> And on her hair a glory, like a saint:
> She seem'd a splendid angel, newly dresst,
> Save wings, for heaven:—Porphyro grew faint:
> She knelt, so pure a thing, so free from mortal taint.

[1] *gules:* reds.

Keats often doubles the impact of his imagery by using *synesthesia* (one sense experienced in terms of another) or by using a second image to reinforce the first.

> Forlorn! the very word is like a bell

> convuls'd with scarlet pain

> moist scent of flowers

> hushed, cool rooted flowers, fragrant eyed

But here is no light
Save what from heaven is with the breezes blown

. . . the small warm rain
Melts out the frozen incense from all flowers

Music's golden tongue

the silver snarling trumpets

Sudden a thought came like a full-blown rose
Flushing his brow, and in his pained heart
Made purple riot

thine own soft-conched ear

•   •   •

ODE TO A NIGHTINGALE

My heart aches, and a drowsy numbness pains
  My sense, as though of hemlock I had drunk,
Or emptied some dull opiate to the drains
  One minute past, and Lethe-wards[1] had sunk:
'Tis not through envy of thy happy lot,   5
  But being too happy in thy happiness,—
    That thou, light wingèd Dryad[2] of the trees,
      In some melodious plot
Of beechen green, and shadows numberless,
  Singest of summer in full-throated ease.   10

O for a draught of vintage! that hath been
  Cooled a long age in the deep-delvèd earth,
Tasting of Flora[3] and the country green,
  Dance, and Provençal song, and sunburnt mirth!
O for a beaker full of the warm South,   15
  Full of the true, the blushful Hippocrene,[4]
    With beaded bubbles winking at the brim,

[1] *Lethe-wards:* towards Lethe, river in Hades whose water induces forgetfulness.
[2] *Dryad:* wood nymph.
[3] *Flora:* goddess of flowers.
[4] *Hippocrene:* fountain of the muses.

And purple-stainèd mouth;
  That I might drink, and leave the world unseen,
  And with thee fade away into the forest dim: 20

Fade far away, dissolve, and quite forget
  What thou among the leaves hast never known,
The weariness, the fever, and the fret
  Here, where men sit and hear each other groan;
Where palsy shakes a few, sad, last grey hairs,   25
  Where youth grows pale, and spectre-thin, and dies;
    Where but to think is to be full of sorrow
      And leaden-eyed despairs,
  Where Beauty cannot keep her lustrous eyes,
    Or new Love pine at them beyond to-morrow.   30

Away! away! for I will fly to thee,
  Not charioted by Bacchus[5] and his pards,
But on the viewless wings of Poesy,
  Though the full brain perplexes and retards:
Already with thee! tender is the night,   35
  And haply the Queen-Moon is on her throne,
    Clustered around by all her starry Fays,[6]
      But here there is no light,
  Save what from heaven is with the breezes blown
    Through verdurous glooms and winding mossy ways.   40

I cannot see what flowers are at my feet,
  Nor what soft incense hangs upon the boughs,
But, in embalmèd darkness, guess each sweet
  Wherewith the seasonable month endows
The grass, the thicket, and the fruit tree wild;   45
  White hawthorn, and the pastoral eglantine;
    Fast fading violets covered up in leaves;
      And mid-May's eldest child,
  The coming musk rose, full of dewy wine,
    The murmurous haunt of flies on summer eves.   50

Darkling I listen; and, for many a time
  I have been half in love with easeful Death,
Called him soft names in many a musèd rhyme,
  To take into the air my quiet breath;
Now more than ever seems it rich to die,   55

[5] *Bacchus:* god of wine and fertility. His chariot was pulled by leopards.
[6] *Fays:* fairies.

To cease upon the midnight with no pain,
   While thou art pouring forth thy soul abroad
      In such an ecstasy!
Still wouldst thou sing, and I have ears in vain—
   To thy high requiem become a sod.   60

Thou wast not born for death, immortal Bird!
   No hungry generations tread thee down;
The voice I hear this passing night was heard
   In ancient days by emperor and clown:
Perhaps the self-same song that found a path   65
   Through the sad heart of Ruth,[7] when, sick for home,
      She stood in tears amid the alien corn;
         The same that oft-times hath
   Charmed magic casements, opening on the foam
   Of perilous seas, in faery lands forlorn.   70

Forlorn! the very word is like a bell
   To toll me back from thee to my sole self!
Adieu! the fancy cannot cheat so well
   As she is famed to do, deceiving elf.
Adieu! adieu! thy plaintive anthem fades   75
   Past the near meadows, over the still stream,
      Up the hillside; and now 'tis buried deep
         In the next valley glades:
   Was it a vision, or a waking dream?
   Fled is that music:—Do I wake or sleep?   80

John Keats, 1795–1821

---

[7] *Ruth:* faithful Biblical wife who followed her husband's family to a foreign country.

EXERCISES

1. What does the speaker know that the nightingale "hast never known"? How can the speaker attain the "full throated ease" of the bird? Discuss these questions in relation to Keats's concerns in his other poems.

2. Discuss the use of sound imagery. What other senses predominate?

3. Read all the poems by Keats in this text (see index). Can you now recognize a Keats poem? How?

4. Read all the poems in this book by Dylan Thomas. What are some hallmarks of his style?

5. When you hear the first few bars of music by a group you like, you recognize their style immediately. Read all the poems by Emily Dickinson in this book. What enables you to recognize her style?

6. Other poets with high-profile styles are Gerard Manley Hopkins, William Butler Yeats, and Walt Whitman. Review poems by each and discuss their distinctive aspects and differences.

• • •

THE WINDHOVER[1]

To Christ Our Lord

I caught this morning morning's minion, kingdom of daylight's
    dauphin, dapple-dawn-drawn Falcon, in his riding
      Of the rolling level underneath him steady air, and striding
High there, how he rung upon the rein of a wimpling wing
In his ecstasy! then off, off forth on swing,
    As a skate's heel sweeps smooth on a bow-bend: the hurl
      and gliding   5
    Rebuffed the big wind. My heart in hiding
Stirred for a bird,—the achieve of, the mastery of the thing!

Brute beauty and valor and act, oh, air, pride, plume, here
    Buckle! And the fire that breaks from thee then, a billion
Times told lovelier, more dangerous, O my chevalier!   10

    No wonder of it: shéer plód makes plough down sillion
Shine, and blue-bleak embers, ah my dear,
    Fall, gall themselves, and gash gold-vermilion.

---

[1] *Windhover:* a small hawk.

THE BARE TREE

The bare cherry tree
higher than the roof
last year produced
abundant fruit. But how
speak of fruit confronted   5
by that skeleton?
Though live it may be
there is no fruit on it.
Therefore chop it down
and use the wood   10
against this biting cold.

William Carlos Williams, 1883–1963

EXERCISE

Compare the styles of "The Windhover" and "The Bare Tree." Rewrite each poem, imagining first that you are Hopkins getting his hands
on Williams's poem and then that you are Williams rewriting "The
Windhover." The differences in each writer will become quickly ap-
parent.

● ● ●

TO A STEAM ROLLER

The illustration
is nothing to you without the application.
    You lack half wit. You crush all the particles down
        into close conformity, and then walk back and forth on them.

Sparkling chips of rock   5
are crushed down to the level of the parent block.
    Were not "impersonal judgment in aesthetic
        matters, a metaphysical impossibility," you

might fairly achieve
it. As for butterflies, I can hardly conceive   10
   of one's attending upon you, but to question
     the congruence of the complement is vain, if it exists.

Marianne Moore, 1887–1972

TO A LOCOMOTIVE IN WINTER

Thee for my recitative,
Thee in the driving storm even as now, the snow, the winter-day
   declining,
Thee in thy panoply, thy measur'd dual throbbing and thy beat
   convulsive,
Thy black cylindric body, golden brass and silvery steel,
Thy ponderous side-bars, parallel and connecting rods, gyrating,
   shuttling at thy sides,   5
Thy metrical, now swelling pant and roar, now tapering in the
   distance.
Thy great protruding head-light fix'd in front,
Thy long, pale, floating vapor-pennants, tinged with delicate purple,
The dense and murky clouds out-belching from thy smokestack,
Thy knitted frame, thy springs and valves, the tremulous twinkle
   of thy wheels,   10
Thy train of cars behind, obedient, merrily following,
Through gale or calm, now swift, now slack, yet steadily careering;
Type of the modern—emblem of motion and power—pulse of the
   continent
For once come serve the Muse and merge in verse, even as here I
   see thee,
With storm and buffeting gusts of wind and falling snow,   15
By day thy warning ringing bell to sound its notes,
By night thy silent signal lamps to swing.

Fierce-throated beauty!
Roll through my chant with all thy lawless music, thy swinging
   lamps at night,
Thy madly-whistled laughter, echoing, rumbling like an earthquake,
   rousing all,   20
Law of thyself complete, thine own track firmly holding,
(No sweetness debonair of tearful harp or glib piano thine,)
Thy trills of shrieks by rocks and hills return'd,
Launch'd o'er the prairies wide, across the lakes,
To the free skies unpent and glad and strong.   25

Walt Whitman, 1819–1892

1. In "To a Steam Roller" and "To a Locomotive in Winter," the machines are addressed directly. How do the poets' tones differ? Are these poems typical of each author's style? Reread other poems by Moore and Whitman.
2. Is Moore's steamroller metaphorical? Do the butterfly and steamroller "complement" each other? How do you interpret the last line?
3. Rewrite "To a Steam Roller" in Whitman's style.
4. Rewrite "To a Locomotive in Winter" in Moore's style.

Poems on Five Subjects

With Pound's "Make it new" in mind, read the following groups of poems on ordinary subjects. How do the poets' approaches to the same subject differ? Compare styles, keeping in mind that the style includes voice, craft, and subject. A writer's style in a whole body of work may differ from your impression in a particular poem, but it is useful to look at single poems and ask what is distinctive about each.

Autumn

Almost every poet at some time writes on the subject of autumn. The change of summer into fall stirs all of us to consider how the year is passing, how time is passing, how one's own life is changing and moving toward death, how each time in life and each season are unique.

GRAPPA[1] IN SEPTEMBER

The mornings run their course, clear and deserted
along the river's banks, which at dawn turn foggy,
darkening their green, while they wait for the sun.
In the last house, still damp, at the field's edge,
they sell tobacco, which is blackish in color   5
and tastes of sugar: it gives off a bluish haze.
They also have grappa there, the color of water.

---

[1] *grappa:* a strong drink distilled from grape husks after the juice has been pressed for wine.

There comes a moment when everything stands still
and ripens. The trees in the distance are quiet,
their darkness deepens, concealing fruit so ripe   10
it would drop at a touch. The occasional clouds
are swollen and ripe. Far away, in city streets,
every house is mellowing in the mild air.

This early, you see only women. The women don't smoke,
or drink. All they can do is stand in the sunlight,   15
letting it warm their bodies, as if they were fruit.
The air, raw with fog, has to be swallowed in sips,
like grappa. Everything here distills its own fragrance.
Even the water in the river has absorbed the banks,
steeping them to their depths in the soft air. The streets   20
are like the women. They ripen by standing still.

This is the time when every man should stand
still in the street and see how everything ripens.
There's even a breeze, which doesn't move the clouds
but somehow succeeds in maneuvering the bluish haze   25
without scattering it. The smell drifting by is a new smell,
the tobacco is tinged with grappa. So it seems
the women aren't the only ones who enjoy the morning.

Cesare Pavese, 1908–1950
(Translated by William Arrowsmith)

TO AUTUMN

i

Season of mists and mellow fruitfulness,
    Close bosom friend of the maturing sun,
Conspiring with him how to load and bless
    With fruit the vines that round the thatch-eaves run:
To bend with apples the mossed cottage-trees,   5
And fill all fruit with ripeness to the core;
    To swell the gourd, and plump the hazel shells
    With a sweet kernel; to set budding more,
And still more, later flowers for the bees,
Until they think warm days will never cease,   10
    For summer has o'er-brimmed their clammy cells.

ii

Who hath not seen thee oft amid thy store?
  Sometimes whoever seeks abroad may find
Thee sitting careless on a granary floor,
  Thy hair soft-lifted by the winnowing wind;   15
Or on a half-reaped furrow sound asleep,
  Drowsed with the fume of poppies, while thy hook
    Spares the next swath and all its twinèd flowers;
And sometimes like a gleaner thou dost keep
Steady thy laden head across a brook.   20
Or by a cider-press, with patient look,
  Thou watchest the last oozings hours by hours.

iii

Where are the songs of spring? Aye, where are they?
  think not of them, thou hast thy music too—
While barrèd clouds bloom the soft-dying day,   25
  And touch the stubble-plains with rosy hue.
Then in a wailful choir the small gnats mourn
  Among the river sallows, borne aloft
    Or sinking as the light wind lives or dies;
And full-grown lambs loud bleat from hilly bourn;   30
  Hedge-crickets sing; and now with treble soft
The red-breast whistles from a garden-croft;
  And gathering swallows twitter in the skies.

John Keats, 1795–1821

THE WILD SWANS OF COOLE

The trees are in their autumn beauty,
The woodland paths are dry,
Under the October twilight the water
Mirrors a still sky;
Upon the brimming water among the stones   5
Are nine-and-fifty swans.

The nineteenth autumn has come upon me
Since I first made my count;
I saw, before I had well finished,
All suddenly mount   10
And scatter wheeling in great broken rings
Upon their clamorous wings.

I have looked upon those brilliant creatures,
And now my heart is sore.
All's changed since I, hearing at twilight,   15
The first time on this shore,
The bell-beat of their wings above my head,
Trod with a lighter tread.

Unwearied still, lover by lover,
They paddle in the cold   20
Companionable streams or climb the air;
Their hearts have not grown old;
Passion or conquest, wander where they will,
Attend upon them still.

But now they drift on the still water,   25
Mysterious, beautiful;
Among what rushes will they build,
By what lake's edge or pool
Delight men's eyes when I awake some day
To find they have flown away?   30

William Butler Yeats, 1865–1939

THE END OF AUTUMN

In the end, autumn is no more than a cold infusion. Dead leaves of all essences steep in the rain. No fermentation, no resulting alcohol: the effect of compresses applied to a wooden leg will not be felt till spring.

The stripping is messily done. All the doors of the reading room fly open and shut, slamming violently. Into the basket, into the basket! Nature tears up her manuscripts, demolishes her library, furiously thrashes her last fruits.

She suddenly gets up from her work table; her height at once immense. Unkempt, she keeps her head in the mist. Arms dangling, she rapturously inhales the icy wind that airs her thoughts. The days are short, night falls fast, there is no time for comedy.

The earth, amid the other planets in space, regains its seriousness. Its lighted side is narrower, infiltrated by valleys of shadow. Its shoes, like a tramp's, slosh and squeak.

In this frog pond, this salubrious amphibiguity, everything regains strength; hops from rock to rock, and moves on to another meadow. Rivulets multiply.

That is what is called a thorough cleaning, and with no respect for conventions! Garbed in nakedness, drenched to the marrow.

And it lasts, does not dry immediately. Three months of healthy reflection in this condition; no vascular reaction, no bathrobe, no scrubbing brush. But its hearty constitution can take it.

And so, when the little buds begin to sprout again, they know what they are up to and what is going on—

Francis Ponge, 1899–1988
(Translated by Beth Brombert)

EXERCISES

1. Are any of the autumn poems simply descriptions of the season? What characterizes the style of each?

2. Compare each poem's treatment of change as a subject.

3. Would you say that "The End of Autumn" is radically different from the other poems? What is Ponge's tone of voice? Compare his diction (for example, "The stripping is messily done") with Keats's.

4. Discuss the personification (autumn as "she") in Keats's and Ponge's poems.

5. Compare the imagery in "To Autumn" and "Grappa in September."

6. Compare the styles of three vastly different spring poems: "Spring and All" by William Carlos Williams (page 20), "chanson innocente" by e.e. cummings (page 21), and "The Soote Season" by Henry Howard, Earl of Surrey (page 63). What do the poems have in common?

7. Write a poem exploring your personal connotations of October.

Four Love Poems

somewhere i have never travelled

somewhere i have never travelled, gladly beyond
any experience, your eyes have their silence:
in your most frail gesture are things which enclose me,
or which i cannot touch because they are too near

your slightest look easily will unclose me   5
though i have closed myself as fingers,
you open always petal by petal myself as Spring opens
(touching skilfully, mysteriously) her first rose

or if your wish be to close me, i and
my life will shut very beautifully, suddenly,   10
as when the heart of this flower imagines
the snow carefully everywhere descending;

nothing which we are to perceive in this world equals
the power of your intense fragility whose texture
compels me with the colour of its countries,   15
rendering death and forever with each breathing

(i do not know what it is about you that closes
and opens; only something in me understands
the voice of your eyes is deeper than all roses)
nobody, not even the rain, has such small hands   20

e.e. cummings, 1894–1962

I WILL ENJOY THEE NOW

I will enjoy thee now, my Celia, come,
And fly with me to Love's Elysium.
The giant, Honour, that keeps cowards out
Is but a masquer, and the servile rout
Of baser subjects only bend in vain   5
To the vast idol; whilst the nobler train
Of valiant lovers daily sail between
The huge Colossus' legs, and pass unseen
Unto the blissful shore. Be bold and wise,
And we shall enter; the grim Swiss denies   10
Only to tame fools a passage, that not know
He is but form and only frights in show
The duller eyes that look from far; draw near
And thou shalt scorn what we were wont to fear.
We shall see how the stalking pageant goes   15
With borrow'd legs, a heavy load to those
That made and bear him; not, as we once thought,
The seed of gods, but a weak model wrought
By greedy men, that seek to enclose the common,
And within private arms empale free woman.   20

Come, then, and mounted on the wings of Love
We'll cut the flitting air and soar above
The monster's head, and in the noblest seats
Of those blest shades quench and renew our heats.
There shall the queens of love and innocence,   25
Beauty and Nature, banish all offence
From our close ivy-twines; there I'll behold
Thy baréd snow and thy unbraided gold;
There my enfranchised hand on every side
Shall o'er thy naked polish'd ivory slide.   30
No curtain there, though of transparent lawn,
Then, as the empty bee that lately bore
Into the common treasure all her store,
Flies 'bout the painted field with nimble wing,
Deflow'ring the fresh virgins of the spring,   35
So will I rifle all the sweets that dwell
In my delicious paradise, and swell
My bag with honey, drawn forth by the power
Of fervent kisses from each spicy flower.
I'll seize the rose-buds in their perfumed bed,   40
The violet knots, like curious mazes spread
Shall be before thy virgin-treasure drawn;
But the rich mine, to the enquiring eye
Exposed, shall ready still for mintage lie,

And we will coin young Cupids. There a bed   45
Of roses and fresh myrtles shall be spread,
Under the cooler shades of cypress groves;
Our pillows of the down of Venus' doves,
Whereon our panting limbs we'll gently lay,
In the faint respites of our active play;   50
That so our slumbers may in dreams have leisure
To tell the nimble fancy our past pleasure,
And so our souls, that cannot be embraced,
Shall the embraces of our bodies taste.
Meanwhile the bubbling stream shall court the shore,   55
Th' enamour'd chirping wood-choir shall adore
In varied tunes the deity of love;
The gentle blasts of western winds shall move
The trembling leaves, and through their close boughs breathe
Still music, whilst we rest ourselves beneath   60
Their dancing shade; till a soft murmur, sent
From souls entranced in amorous languishment,
Rouse us, and shoot into our veins fresh fire,
Till we in their sweet ecstasy expire.

O'er all the garden, taste the ripen'd cherry,   65
The warm firm apple, tipp'd with coral berry;
Then will I visit with a wand'ring kiss
The vales of lilies and the bower of bliss;
And where the beauteous region doth divide
Into two milky ways, my lips shall slide   70
Down those smooth alleys, wearing as they go
A track for lovers on the printed snow;
Thence climbing o'er the swelling Apennine,
Retire into thy grove of eglantine,
Where I will all those ravish'd sweets distill   75
Through Love's alembic, and with chemic skill
From the mix'd mass one sovereign balm derive,
Then bring that great elixir to thy hive.

Thomas Carew, 1595–1640

NON SUM QUALIS ERAM BONAE SUB REGNO CYNARAE[1]

Last night, ah, yesternight, betwixt her lips and mine
There fell thy shadow, Cynara! thy breath was shed
Upon my soul between the kisses and the wine;
And I was desolate and sick of an old passion,
  Yea, I was desolate and bowed my head: 5
I have been faithful to thee, Cynara! in my fashion.

All night upon mine heart I felt her warm heart beat,
Night-long within mine arms in love and sleep she lay;
Surely the kisses of her bought red mouth were sweet;
But I was desolate and sick of an old passion,   10
  When I awoke and found the dawn was gray:
I have been faithful to thee, Cynara! in my fashion.

I have forgot much, Cynara! gone with the wind,
Flung roses, roses riotously with the throng,
Dancing, to put thy pale, lost lilies out of mind;   15
But I was desolate and sick of an old passion,

---

[1] *Non . . . Cynarae:* "I am not as I was under reign of the good Cynara" (quoted from
Horace's Odes: IV, i, lines 3 and 4). Dowson borrows the romantic name for his
beloved.

Yea, all the time, because the dance was long:
I have been faithful to thee, Cynara! in my fashion.

I cried for madder music and for stronger wine,
But when the feast is finished and the lamps expire,   20
Then falls thy shadow, Cynara! the night is thine;
And I am desolate and sick of an old passion,
    Yea hungry for the lips of my desire:
I have been faithful to thee, Cynara! in my fashion.

Ernest Dowson, 1867–1900

EVERY DAY YOU PLAY

Every day you play with the light of the universe.
Subtle visitor, you arrive in the flower and the water.
You are more than this white head that I hold tightly
as a cluster of fruit, every day, between my hands.

You are like nobody since I love you.   5
Let me spread you out among yellow garlands.
Who writes your name in letters of smoke among the stars of the
    south?
Oh let me remember you as you were before you existed.

Suddenly the wind howls and bangs at my shut window.
The sky is a net crammed with shadowy fish.   10
Here all the winds let go sooner or later, all of them.
The rain takes off her clothes.

The birds go by, fleeing.
The wind. The wind.

I can contend only against the power of men.   15
The storm whirls dark leaves
and turns loose all the boats that were moored last night to the sky.

You are here. Oh, you do not run away. You will answer me to
    the last cry.
Cling to me as though you were frightened.   20
Even so, at one time a strange shadow ran through your eyes.

Now, now too, little one, you bring me honeysuckle,
and even your breasts smell of it.

While the sad wind goes slaughtering butterflies
I love you, and my happiness bites the plum of your mouth.   25

How you must have suffered getting accustomed to me,
my savage, solitary soul, my name that sends them all running.
So many times we have seen the morning star burn, kissing our
    eyes,
and over our heads the grey light unwind in turning fans.

My words rained over you, stroking you.   30
A long time I have loved the sunned mother-of-pearl of your body.
I go so far as to think that you own the universe.
I will bring you happy flowers from the mountains, bluebells,
dark hazels, and rustic baskets of kisses.
I want   35
to do with you what spring does with the cherry trees.

Pablo Neruda, 1904–1973
(Translated by W. S. Merwin)

EXERCISES

1. All of these love poems have in common a tone of intimacy. They are written to or about a person, not about love as a subject. How do they differ in their approaches to the other person? Discuss the role of the person addressed in each poem.

2. Which poem would you like to have written? Why?

3. The next poem, "Proclamation," suffers in comparison with the poems above. Why? With a common subject such as love, written about in thousands of poems, how did the other poets avoid these problems?

PROCLAMATION

I love you though 'tis wrong to say.
My thoughts are with you every day.

You are on my mind and in my heart.
It's hard to bear that we're apart.

For I will love you as long as day   5
turns from blue to black, I say.

And if it does not please you,
Even then I will still be true.

Though you lie in the arms of another,
with love over your soul always I hover.   10

4. Write a poem that expresses love. Try to find the precise language
    that touches the unmistakable source of feelings you have for
    someone. Your poem can be about any kind of love, not necessar-
    ily romantic love.
5. For pleasure, read other love poems in the text, then analyze each
    poem's style and content. For example: "The River Merchant's
    Wife: A Letter," Ezra Pound's adaptation of Li Po (page 178),
    and "If I Could Tell You" by W. H. Auden (page 349).
6. The love poems listed above and those given as examples are ad-
    dressed to the loved one. Turn to poems whose *subject* is love,
    such as the selection from "From Pent-up Aching Rivers" by Walt
    Whitman (page 464). "An Arundel Tomb" by Philip Larkin (page
    172), and "On Her Loving Two Equally" by Aphra Behn (page
    203). To whom are these poems addressed and how does this
    change the tone?

Poems on a Painting

Three poets look at the same painting by Pieter Brueghel, Flemish
painter of the sixteenth century.

THE HUNTERS IN THE SNOW

The over-all picture is winter
icy mountains
in the background the return

from the hunt it is toward evening
from the left   5
sturdy hunters lead in

their pack the inn-sign
hanging from a
broken hinge is a stag a crucifix

Pieter Brueghel, *The Hunters in the Snow (January)*, 1565.

between his antlers the cold   10
inn yard is
deserted but for a huge bonfire

that flares wind-driven tended by
women who cluster
about it to the right beyond   15

the hill is a pattern of skaters
Brueghel the painter
concerned with it all has chosen

a winter-struck bush for his
foreground to
complete the picture   20

William Carlos Williams, 1883–1963

WINTER LANDSCAPE

The three men coming down the winter hill
In brown, with tall poles and a pack of hounds
At heel, through the arrangement of the trees,
Past the five figures at the burning straw,
Returning cold and silent to their town,   5

Returning to the drifted snow, the rink
Lively with children, to the older men,
The long companions they can never reach,
The blue light, men with ladders, by the church
The sledge and shadow in the twilit street,   10

Are not aware that in the sandy time
To come, the evil waste of history
Outstretched, they will be seen upon the brow
Of that same hill: when all their company
Will have been irrecoverably lost,   15

These men, this particular three in brown
Witnessed by birds will keep the scene and say
By their configuration with the trees,
The small bridge, the red houses and the fire,
What place, what time, what morning occasion   20

Sent them into the wood, a pack of hounds
At heel and the tall poles upon their shoulders,
Thence to return as now we see them and
Ankle-deep in snow down the winter hill
Descend, while three birds watch and the fourth flies.   25

John Berryman, 1914–1972

HUNTERS IN THE SNOW: BRUEGHEL

Quail and rabbit hunters with tawny hounds,
Shadowless, out of late afternoon
Trudge toward the neutral evening of indeterminate form.
Done with their blood-annunciated day
Public dogs and all the passionless mongrels   5
Through deep snow
Trail their deliberate masters
Descending from the upper village home in hovering light.

Sooty lamps
Glow in the stone-carved kitchens.   10

This is the fabulous hour of shape and form
When Flemish children are grey-black-olive
And green-dark-brown
Scattered and skating informal figures
On the mill ice pond.   15
Moving in stillness
A hunched dame struggles with her bundled sticks,
Letting her evening's comfort cudgel her
While she, like jug or wheel, like a wagon cart
Walked by lazy oxen along the old snowlanes,   20
Creeps and crunches down the dusky street.

High in the fire-red dooryard
Half unhitched the sign of the Inn
Hangs in wind
Tipped to the pitch of the roof.   25
Near it anonymous parents and peasant girl,
Living like proverbs carved in the alehouse walls,
Gather the country evening into their arms
And lean to the glowing flames.

Now in the dimming distance fades   30
The other village; across the valley
Imperturbable Flemish cliffs and crags
Vaguely advance, close in, loom,
Lost in nearness. Now
The night-black raven perched in branching boughs   35
Opens its early wing and slipping out
Above the grey-green valley
Weaves a net of slumber over the snow-capped homes.
And now the church, and then the walls and roofs
Of all the little houses are become   40
Close kin to shadow with small lantern eyes.
And now the bird of evening
With shadows streaming down from its gliding wings
Circles the neighboring hills
Of Hertogenbosch, Brabant.   45

Darkness stalks the hunters,
Slowly sliding down,
Falling in beating rings and soft diagonals.
Lodged in the vague vast valley the village sleeps.

Joseph Langland, 1917–

1. The subject of each poem is "The Hunters in the Snow." How does each poem use Brueghel's painting? Are the poems able to stand alone? How does seeing the painting influence your reaction?
2. Compare the tone in each poem. Does it correspond in any way to the style of the painting?
3. Does one poem "paint" images more vividly than the others?
4. Read Keats's "Ode on a Grecian Urn" (page 440). Was Berryman influenced by Keats's ideas?
5. Discuss the effect of Williams's lack of punctuation.

War

WAR MOVIE IN REVERSE

Holes close to smooth skin
when the shrapnel flashes out.
The shores of burns recede,
and flames leap with their hot metal
back into the bomb that rises,   5
whole and air-borne again,
with its gathered blast.
Leading the plane perfectly,
the bomb arcs back slowly
through the open gates   10
and disappears into the waiting belly.
The bombardier lifts
his peering eye from the sight.
Swallowing its wake,
the plane returns to base   15
with its countermanded mission.
The pilot, irresolute now, faces
his commandant, who marches,
brisk and backward
to the general's lair.   20
The general takes back the orders.
But into what deep and good and hidden
recess of the will
go his thoughts of not bombing?

Mark Johnston, 1945–

CHANNEL FIRING

That night your great guns, unawares,
Shook all our coffins as we lay,
And broke the chancel window-squares,
We thought it was the Judgment-day

And sat upright. While drearisome   5
Arose the howl of wakened hounds:
The mouse let fall the altar-crumb,
The worms drew back into the mounds,

The glebe cow drooled. Till God called, 'No;
It's gunnery practice out at sea   10
Just as before you went below;
The world is as it used to be:

'All nations striving strong to make
Red war yet redder. Mad as hatters
They do no more for Christés sake   15
Than you who are helpless in such matters.

'That this is not the judgment-hour
For some of them's a blessed thing,
For if it were they'd have to scour
Hell's floor for so much threatening. . . .   20

'Ha, ha. It will be warmer when
I blow the trumpet (if indeed
I ever do; for you are men,
And rest eternal sorely need.)'

So down we lay again. 'I wonder,   25
Will the world ever saner be,'
Said one, 'than when He sent us under
In our indifferent century!'

And many a skeleton shook his head.
'Instead of preaching forty year,'   30
My neighbour Parson Thirdly said,
'I wish I had stuck to pipes and beer.'

Again the guns disturbed the hour,
Roaring their readiness to avenge,
As far inland as Stourton Tower,   35
And Camelot, and starlit Stonehenge.

Thomas Hardy, 1840–1928

AT THE BOMB TESTING SITE

At noon in the desert a panting lizard
waited for history, its elbows tense,
watching the curve of a particular road
as if something might happen.

It was looking at something farther off   5
than people could see, an important scene
acted in stone for little selves
at the flute end of consequences.

There was just a continent without much on it
under a sky that never cared less.   10
Ready for a change, the elbows waited.
The hands gripped hard on the desert.

William Stafford, 1914–

A COMPLICATED DUST

When it gets dark, I feel as though I'm dying.
                    —Claude Monet

This is the surface of a planet.
It is after the war.
Bougainvillea climb the sky.
As if they were exotic.
Survivors look for their names   5
in the newspaper. Perhaps
they're missing after all.
They've been practicing forever
in the cellar, the door locked—
no key, no matter,   10
behind the door a wall, possibly
clay, and behind it, who knows?

The ground grows smoke
inviting romance. A telephone
rings in the distance,   15
the woman says, "let it go,
it's only birds." She says
"it's all so bent and bending,
it's all so damn humble—this
must be what Jesus had in mind."   20

The backyard might be complicated dust,
pale green light settling on char,
the sky boiling like last night's supper,
the ground too tired to weep; everything
is here, all the letters in your name   25
all the songs ever sung, it is after
the last bar has closed but someone
looking for souvenirs stays to
wash the glasses.

One more round, the air   30
as sober as death, the clouds vacillating
waiting for the tornado,
waiting for a favorite god, all things are
pushed into other things, not by magic
but by words. All that's left, Delia's   35
gone, it is after the war
the growing season ends in
dung heaps in autumn crumbling gray.
Perhaps wheat will spring from brain
like Athena from Zeus, perhaps not.   40
The sunsets don't seem human,
still, the woman says, "I know
sundown when I see it."

Bernard Gershenson, 1947–

READING THE NAMES OF THE VIETNAM WAR DEAD

For a long day and a night we read the names:
Many thousand brothers fallen in the green and distant land . . .

Sun going south after the autumn equinox.
By night the vast moon: "Moon of the Falling Leaves";

Our voices hoarse in the cold of the first October rains.   5
And the long winds of the season to carry our words away.

The citizens go on about their business.
By night sleepers condense in the houses grown cloudy with
    dreams.

By day a few come to hear us and leave, shaking their heads
Or cursing. On Sunday the moral animal prays in his church.   10

It is Fall; but a host of dark birds flies toward the cold North.
Thousands of dense black stones fall forever through the darkness
    under the earth.

Thomas McGrath, 1916–1990

EXERCISES

1. "At the Bomb Testing Site," "A Complicated Dust," and "Channel Firing" begin with ordinary creatures, people, or events. Discuss the movement toward larger realization in each poem.

2. In "Channel Firing," how is "you" used? Who are "we"? What connotations does Stonehenge add to the end? Consider Hardy's "I wonder, / will the world ever saner be." Does he think so? What is your opinion?

3. Why do you think Stafford chose to write about a lizard?

4. Compare "Reading the Names of the Vietnam War Dead" with *"Dulce et Decorum Est"* (page 169).

5. Compare the endings of each war poem.

6. Which poem connects most strongly with your own feelings about war? Why?

Looking at Objects

"The Red Wheelbarrow," the first poem in this group, is one of the most famous twentieth century poems—a plain presentation of a simple image. On a farm much *does* depend on a wheelbarrow, of course, but by showing it to us carefully, line by line, timing the images by his line breaks, Williams makes a subtle case that an object itself is worth close attention. We see almost a watercolor image: the red wheelbarrow glazed with rain beside white chickens. No comments are attached, aside from "so much depends." The poem exemplifies Williams' belief, "No ideas but in things."

In contrast, Keats's and Neruda's objects provoke them to profound thoughts. The objects are present *and* are points of departure. Stein's piano may already be playing music. The poem is both verbal music and a way of seeing—Stein's way. Influenced by the Cubist painters, who fractured "normal" visual images to create new angular forms, Stein broke up the continuity of language in the interest of creating new patterns of seeing. Her poem doesn't "mean" in the conventional sense; instead, it breaks up and rearranges our straight-on view of an object.

THE RED WHEELBARROW

so much depends
upon

a red wheel
barrow

glazed with rain
water

beside the white
chickens.

William Carlos Williams, 1883–1963

ODE ON A GRECIAN URN

1

Thou still unravished bride of quietness,
    Thou foster-child of silence and slow time,
Sylvan historian, who canst thus express
    A flowery tale more sweetly than our rhyme:

What leaf-fringed legend haunts about thy shape   5
  Of deities or mortals, or of both,
    In Tempe or the dales of Arcady?
  What men or gods are these? What maidens loth?
What mad pursuit? What struggle to escape?
    What pipes and timbrels? What wild ecstasy?   10

2

Heard melodies are sweet, but those unheard
  Are sweeter; therefore, ye soft pipes, play on;
Not to the sensual ear, but, more endeared,
  Pipe to the spirit ditties of no tone:
Fair youth, beneath the trees, thou canst not leave   15
  Thy song, nor ever can those trees be bare;
    Bold Lover, never, never canst thou kiss,
Though winning near the goal—yet, do not grieve;
    She cannot fade, though thou hast not thy bliss,
  Forever wilt thou love, and she be fair!   20

3

Ah, happy, happy boughs! that cannot shed
  Your leaves, nor ever bid the Spring adieu;
And, happy melodist, unwearied,
  Forever piping songs forever new;
More happy love! more happy, happy love!   25
  Forever warm and still to be enjoyed,
    Forever panting, and forever young;
All breathing human passion far above,
  That leaves a heart high-sorrowful and cloyed,
    A burning forehead, and a parching tongue.   30

4

Who are these coming to the sacrifice?
  To what green altar, O mysterious priest,
Lead'st thou that heifer lowing at the skies,
  And all her silken flanks with garlands dressed?
What little town by river or sea shore,   35
  Or mountain-built with peaceful citadel,
    Is emptied of this folk, this pious morn?
And, little town, thy streets forevermore
  Will silent be; and not a soul to tell
    Why thou art desolate, can e'er return.   40

5

O Attic shape! Fair attitude! with brede
  Of marble men and maidens overwrought,
With forest branches and the trodden weed;
  Thou, silent form, dost tease us out of thought
As doth eternity: Cold Pastoral!   45
  When old age shall this generation waste,
    Thou shalt remain, in midst of other woe
  Than ours, a friend to man, to whom thou say'st,
"Beauty is truth, truth beauty,"—that is all
    Ye know on earth, and all ye need to know.   50

John Keats, 1795–1821

ODE TO A WATCH AT NIGHT

At night, in your hand
my watch shone
like a firefly.
I heard
its ticking: 5
like a dry rustling
coming
from your invisible hand.
Then your hand
went back to my dark breast   10
to gather my sleep and its beat.

The watch
went on cutting time
with its little saw.
As in a forest   15
fragments
of wood fell,
little drops, pieces
of branches or nests
without the silence changing,   20
without the cool darkness ending,
so
the watch went on cutting
from its invisible hand
time, time,   25
and minutes

fell like leaves,
fibres of broken time,
little black feathers.

As in the forest   30
we smelled roots,
the water somewhere released
a fat plopping
as of wet grapes.
A little mill   35
milled night,
the shadow whispered
falling from your hand
and filled the earth.
Dust,   40
earth, distance,
my watch in the night
ground and ground
from your hand.

I placed   45
my arm
under your invisible neck,
under its warm weight,
and in my hand
time fell,   50
the night,
little noises
of wood and of forest,
of divided night,
of fragments of shadow,   55
of water that falls and falls:
then
sleep fell
from the watch and from
both your sleeping hands,   60
it fell like a dark water
from the forests,
from the watch
to your body,
out of you it made the nations,   65
dark water,
time that falls
and runs
inside us.

And that was the way it was that night,   70
shadow and space, earth
and time,
something that runs and falls
and passes.

And that is the way all the nights   75
go over the earth,
leaving nothing but a vague
black odour, a leaf falls,
a drop
on the earth,   80
its sound stops,
the forest sleeps, the waters,
the meadows,
the fields,
the eyes.   85

I hear you and breathe,
my love,
we sleep.

Pablo Neruda, 1904–1973
(Translated by W. S. Merwin)

A PIANO

If the speed is open, if the color is careless, if the selection of a strong scent is not awkward, if the button holder is held by all the waving color and there is no color, not any color. If there is no dirt in the pin and there can be none scarcely, if there is not then the place is the same as up standing.

This is no dark custom and it even is not acted in any such a way that a restraint is not spread. That is spread, it shuts and it lifts and awkwardly the centre is in standing.

Gertrude Stein, 1874–1946

1. The famous ending of "Ode on a Grecian Urn" often is reprinted as:

    > "Beauty is truth, truth beauty,—that is all
    >   Ye know on earth, and all ye need to know."

    Scholars are not sure whether Keats only intended for the urn to say "Beauty is truth, truth beauty," or if he wanted the urn to say both last lines. How does the shift in punctuation change the meaning?

Georges Braque, *Musical Forms*, 1918.

2. The "mad pursuit" and "wild ecstasy" of the figures are actually fixed forever on the urn. Though the lover chasing the girl will never catch her, he always will be in love and she always will be beautiful. The urn, then, gives them an immortality which they actually cannot have. Compare this idea to the "immortal" song in "Ode to a Nightingale" (page 415).

3. Write a poem that simply presents an object in its context, such as a glass bottle on a windowsill or a motorcycle in the snow or a bowl of peaches on a table. Then try a Stein-like view of the same object.

4. Compare the use of line in "Ode to a Watch at Night" and "The Red Wheelbarrow."

5. The approach to objects in this group of poems varies enormously. Hopkins said, "If you look hard enough at an object, it begins to look back at you." Which object among the poems begins to "look back"—that is, starts to cause reflections and speculations in you? Why?

6. See "Study of Two Pears" by Wallace Stevens (page 93) and "The Great Figure" by William Carlos Williams (page 311). The former has the quality of a still life and the latter has a strong sense of movement. How did each poet accomplish those impressions.?

7. Compare Braque's painting "Musical Forms" to "Piano" by Gertrude Stein.

Poems for Discussion

ALBA

As cool as the pale wet leaves of lily-of-the-valley
She lay beside me in the dawn.

Ezra Pound, 1885–1972

LOVE CALLS US TO THE THINGS OF THIS WORLD

The eyes open to a cry of pulleys,
And spirited from sleep, the astounded soul
Hangs for a moment bodiless and simple
As false dawn.
              Outside the open window   5
The morning air is all awash with angels.

Some are in bed-sheets, some are in blouses,
Some are in smocks: but truly there they are.
Now they are rising together in calm swells
Of halcyon feeling, filling whatever they wear   10
With the deep joy of their impersonal breathing;

Now they are flying in place, conveying
The terrible speed of their omnipresence, moving
And staying like white water; and now of a sudden
They swoon down into so rapt a quiet   15
That nobody seems to be there.
                   The soul shrinks

From all that it is about to remember,
From the punctual rape of every blessèd day,
And cries,   20
         "Oh, let there be nothing on earth but laundry,
Nothing but rosy hands in the rising steam
And clear dances done in the sight of heaven."

Yet, as the sun acknowledges
With a warm look the world's hunks and colors,   25
The soul descends once more in bitter love
To accept the waking body, saying now
In a changed voice as the man yawns and rises,

"Bring them down from their ruddy gallows.
Let there be clean linen for the backs of thieves;   30
Let lovers go fresh and sweet to be undone,
And the heaviest nuns walking in a pure floating
Of dark habits,
            keeping their difficult balance."

Richard Wilbur, 1921–

MADRIGAL

My Love in her attire doth show her wit,
   It doth so well become her;
For every season she hath dressings fit,
   For Winter, Spring, and summer.
     No beauty she doth miss   5
       When all her robes are on:
     But Beauty's self she is
       When all her robes are gone.

Anonymous, 1602

ROSALIND'S MADRIGAL

Love in my bosom like a bee
   Doth suck his sweet;
Now with his wings he plays with me,
   Now with his feet.
Within mine eyes he makes his nest,   5
His bed amidst my tender breast;
My kisses are his daily feast,
And yet he robs me of my rest.
   Ah, wanton, will ye?

And if I sleep, then percheth he   10
   With pretty flight,
And makes his pillow of my knee
   The livelong night.
Strike I my lute, he tunes the string;
He music plays if so I sing;   15
He lends me every lovely thing;
Yet cruel he my heart doth sting.
   Whist,[1] wanton, still ye!

Else I with roses every day
   Will whip you hence,   20
And bind you, when you long to play,
   For your offense.
I'll shut mine eyes to keep you in,
I'll make you fast it for your sin,
I'll count your power not worth a pin.   25

[1] *whist:* be silent.

Alas! what hereby shall I win
   If he gainsay me?

What if I beat the wanton boy
   With many a rod?
He will repay me with annoy,   30
   Because a god.
Then sit thou safely on my knee,
And let thy bower my bosom be;
Lurk in mine eyes, I like of thee.
O Cupid, so thou pity me,
   Spare not, but play thee!   35

Thomas Lodge, 1558–1625

EPITHALAMION

You left me gasping on the shore,
A fabulous fish, all gill
And gilded scales. Such sighs we swore!
As our mirror selves
Slipped back to sea, unsundering, bumped gently there,   5
The room a bay, and we,
Afloat on lapping, gazes laving,
Glistered in its spume.

And all cerulean
With small, speeding clouds: the ceiling,   10
Lights beyond eyelids. So you reeled in me,
Reeling.

Our touch was puffed and cloudy now,
As if the most impaled and passionate thought
Was tentative in flesh.   15
This frail
Smile seemed, in our bodies' wash,
Like a rock-light at sea, glimmering
With all the strength of singleness in space.

Still, you will not turn aside,   20
Your face fallow, eyes touching.
So I cling to your tendrils of hair,
Our two tides turning

Together: towards and away
With the moon, motionless and sailing.   25

O my only unleaving lover,
Even in expiring, you reach again.
Thus we may rest, safe in this sealing
As beached, we lie
Our hulks whitening, sun scaling,   30

While the small sea-foam dries,
And the sea recedes and the beach accedes,
Our bodies piled like casual timber
Sanded, on this pure, solar lift of hour,
Wreathed in our breathing.   35

We will exceed ourselves again:
Put out in storms, and pitch our wave on waves.
My soul, you will anticipate my shouting as you rise
Above me to the lunar turn of us,
As skies crack stars upon our symmetries,   40
Extinguished as they touch this smoky night,
As we exhale again our fume of bliss.

This is my shallow rocking to Orion:
Curling to touch the seaweed at your side.
Wrap my mermaid hair about your wrists   45
And seal my face upon your resinous eyes.

Foundered on finny wastes, we rest
Till dawn, a gilded layer, lies
Across the pallid sky.
The world's a tinted shell borne up where waves embrace.   50
Its thin, convolving valve will close and clasp
This love, so blessed:
Our sea-life, swooning as it swims, to reach
Tentacular and cleaving arms that touch
A milky flank, a drowned, reviving face.   55

Carolyn Kizer, 1925–

THE DAY LADY[1] DIED

It is 12:20 in New York a Friday
three days after Bastille day, yes
it is 1959 and I go get a shoeshine
because I will get off the 4:19 in Easthampton
at 7:15 and then go straight to dinner   5
and I don't know the people who will feed me

I walk up the muggy street beginning to sun
and have a hamburger and a malted and buy
an ugly NEW WORLD WRITING to see what the poets
in Ghana are doing these days   10
                        I go on to the bank
and Miss Stillwagon (first name Linda I once heard)
doesn't even look up my balance for once in her life
and in the GOLDEN GRIFFIN I get a little Verlaine
for Patsy with drawings by Bonnard although I do   15
think of Hesiod, trans. Richmond Lattimore or
Brendan Behan's new play or *Le Balcon* or *Les Nègres*
of Genet, but I don't, I stick with Verlaine
after practically going to sleep with quandariness

and for Mike I just stroll into the PARK LANE   20
Liquor Store and ask for a bottle of Strega and
then I go back where I came from to 6th Avenue
and the tobacconist in the Ziegfeld Theatre and
casually ask for a carton of Gauloises and a carton
of Picayunes, and a NEW YORK POST with her face on it   25

and I am sweating a lot by now and thinking of
leaning on the john door at the 5 SPOT
while she whispered a song along the keyboard
to Mal Waldron and everyone and I stopped breathing

Frank O'Hara, 1926–1966

[1] *Lady:* Singer Billie Holiday, known as "Lady Day."

TICHBORNE'S ELEGY

Written with His Own Hand in the Tower Before His Execution

My prime of youth is but a frost of cares,
My feast of joy is but a dish of pain,
My crop of corn is but a field of tares,[1]
And all my good is but vain hope of gain;
The day is past, and yet I saw no sun,   5
And now I live, and now my life is done.

My tale was heard and yet it was not told,
My fruit is fallen and yet my leaves are green,
My youth is spent and yet I am not old,
I saw the world and yet I was not seen;   10
My thread is cut and yet it is not spun,
And now I live, and now my life is done.

I sought my death and found it in my womb,
I looked for life and saw it was a shade,
I trod the earth and knew it was my tomb,   15
And now I die, and now I was but made;
My glass is full, and now my glass is run,
And now I live, and now my life is done.

Chidiock Tichborne, ?–1586

[1] *tares:* seeds.

ELEGY WRITTEN IN A COUNTRY CHURCHYARD

The curfew tolls the knell of parting day,
    The lowing herd winds slowly o'er the lea,
The ploughman homeward plods his weary way,
    And leaves the world to darkness and to me.

Now fades the glimmering landscape on the sight,   5
    And all the air a solemn stillness holds,
Save where the beetle wheels his droning flight,
    And drowsy tinklings lull the distant folds;

Save that from yonder ivy-mantled tower
    The moping owl does to the moon complain   10
Of such, as wandering near her secret bower,
    Molest her ancient solitary reign.

Beneath those rugged elms, that yew-tree's shade,
  Where heaves the turf in many a moldering heap,
Each in his narrow cell forever laid,   15
  The rude forefathers of the hamlet sleep.

The breezy call of incense-breathing morn,
  The swallow twittering from the straw-built shed,
The cock's shrill clarion, or the echoing horn,
  No more shall rouse them from their lowly bed.   20

For them no more the blazing hearth shall burn,
  Or busy housewife ply her evening care:
No children run to lisp their sire's return,
  Or climb his knees the envied kiss to share.

Oft did the harvest to their sickle yield,   25
  Their furrow oft the stubborn glebe[1] has broke;
How jocund did they drive their team afield!
  How bowed the woods beneath their sturdy stroke!

Let not Ambition mock their useful toil,
  Their homely joys, and destiny obscure;   30
Nor Grandeur hear with a disdainful smile,
  The short and simple annals of the poor.

The boast of heraldry, the pomp of power,
  And all that beauty, all that wealth e'er gave,
Awaits alike th' inevitable hour.   35
  The paths of glory lead but to the grave.

Nor you, ye proud, impute to these the fault,
  If Memory o'er their tomb no trophies[2] raise,
Where through the long-drawn aisle and fretted vault
  The pealing anthem swells the note of praise.   40

Can storied urn[3] or animated bust
  Back to its mansion call the fleeting breath?
Can Honor's voice provoke the silent dust,
  Or Flattery soothe the dull cold ear of Death?

Perhaps in this neglected spot is laid   45
  Some heart once pregnant with celestial fire;

[1] *glebe:* soil.
[2] *trophies:* memorials.
[3] *urn:* funeral urn.

Hands that the rod of empire might have swayed,
Or waked to ecstasy the living lyre.

But Knowledge to their eyes her ample page
Rich with the spoils of time did ne'er unroll;   50
Chill Penury repressed their noble rage,
And froze the genial current of the soul.

Full many a gem of purest ray serene,[4]
The dark unfathomed caves of ocean bear:
Full many a flower is born to blush unseen,   55
And waste its sweetness on the desert air.

Some village Hampden,[5] that, with dauntless breast
The little tyrant of his fields withstood;
Some mute inglorious Milton here may rest,
Some Cromwell guiltless of his country's blood.   60

Th' applause of listening senates to command,
The threats of pain and ruin to despise,
To scatter plenty o'er a smiling land,
And read their history in a nation's eyes,

Their lot forbade: nor circumscribed alone   65
Their growing virtues, but their crimes confined;
Forbade to wade through slaughter to a throne,
And shut the gates of mercy on mankind,

The struggling pangs of conscious truth to hide,
To quench the blushes of ingenuous shame,   70
Or heap the shrine of Luxury and Pride
With incense kindled at the Muse's flame.

Far from the madding crowd's ignoble strife,
Their sober wishes never learned to stray;
Along the cool sequestered vale of life   75
They kept the noiseless tenor of their way.

Yet even these bones from insult to protect,
Some frail memorial still erected nigh,
With uncouth rhymes and shapeless sculpture decked,
Implores the passing tribute of a sigh.   80

[4] *serene:* bright.
[5] *Hampden:* John Hampden, statesman who opposed Charles I; killed in battle during the English Civil War.

Their names, their years, spelt by th' unlettered Muse,
  The place of fame and elegy supply:
And many a holy text around she strews,
  That teach the rustic moralist to die.

For who, to dumb forgetfulness a prey,   85
  This pleasing anxious being e'er resigned,
Left the warm precincts of the cheerful day,
  Nor cast one longing lingering look behind?

On some fond breast the parting soul relies,
  Some pious drops[6] the closing eye requires;   90
Even from the tomb the voice of Nature cries,
  Even in our ashes live their wonted fires.

For thee, who mindful of this unhonored dead
  Dost in these lines their artless tale relate,
If chance, by lonely contemplation led,   95
  Some kindred spirit shall inquire thy fate.

Haply some hoary-headed swain may say,
  "Oft have we seen him at the peep of dawn
Brushing with hasty steps the dews away
  To meet the sun upon the upland lawn.   100

"There at the foot of yonder nodding beech
  That wreathes its old fantastic roots so high,
His listless length at noontide would he stretch,
  And pore upon the brook that babbles by.

"Hard by yon wood, now smiling as in scorn,   105
  Muttering his wayward fancies he would rove;
Now drooping, woeful-wan, like one forlorn,
  Or crazed with care, or crossed in hopeless love.

"One morn I missed him on the customed hill,
  Along the heath, and near his favorite tree;   110
Another came; nor yet beside the rill,
  Nor up the lawn, nor at the wood was he;

"The next with dirges due in sad array
  Slow through the church-way path we saw him borne,—
Approach and read (for thou canst read) the lay   115
  Graved on the stone beneath yon agèd thorn."

[6] *drops:* tears.

The Epitaph

Here rests his head upon the lap of earth
  A youth to fortune and to fame unknown;
Fair Science frowned not on his humble birth,
  And Melancholy marked him for her own.   120

Large was his bounty, and his soul sincere;
  Heaven did a recompense as largely send:
He gave to Misery (all he had) a tear,
  He gained from Heaven ('twas all he wished) a friend.

No farther seek his merits to disclose,   125
  Or draw his frailties from their dread abode
(There they alike in trembling hope repose,)—
  The bosom of his Father and his God.

Thomas Gray, 1716–1771

WHEN LILACS LAST IN THE DOORYARD BLOOM'D[1]

1

When lilacs last in the dooryard bloom'd,
And the great star early droop'd in the western sky in the night,
I mourn'd, and yet shall mourn with ever-returning spring.

Every-returning spring, trinity sure to me you bring,
Lilac blooming perennial and drooping star in the west,   5
And thought of him I love.

2

O powerful western fallen star!
O shades of night—O moody, tearful night!
O great star disappear'd—O the black murk that hides the star!
O cruel hands that hold me powerless—-O helpless soul of me!   10
O harsh surrounding cloud that will not free my soul.

[1] *When Lilacs . . . Bloom'd:* This poem was written as an elegy for Abraham Lincoln.

3

In the dooryard fronting an old farm-house near the
    whitewash'd palings,
Stands the lilac-bush tall-growing with heart-shaped leaves
    of rich green,
With many a pointed blossom rising delicate, with the perfume
    strong I love,
With every leaf a miracle—and from this bush in the
    dooryard,   15
With delicate-color'd blossoms and heart-shaped leaves
    of rich green,
A sprig with its flower I break.

4

In the swamp in secluded recesses,
A shy and hidden bird is warbling a song.

Solitary the thrush,   20
The hermit withdrawn to himself, avoiding the settlements,
Sings by himself a song.

Song of the bleeding throat,
Death's outlet song of life, (for well dear brother I know,
If thou wast not granted to sing thou would'st surely die.)   25

5

Over the breast of the spring, the land, amid cities,
Amid lanes and through old woods, where lately the violets
    peep'd from the ground, spotting the gray debris,
Amid the grass in the fields each side of the lanes, passing
    the endless grass,
Passing the yellow-spear'd wheat, every grain from its shroud
    in the dark-brown fields uprisen,
Passing the apple-tree blows of white and pink in the orchards,   30
Carrying a corpse to where it shall rest in the grave,
Night and day journeys a coffin.[2]

---

[2] *Night . . . coffin:* Lincoln's funeral procession travelled from Washington, D.C., to his
home in Springfield, Illinois, stopping along the way so that citizens could pay respects
to the assassinated president.

6

Coffin that passes through lanes and streets,
Through day and night with the great cloud darkening the land,
With the pomp of the inloop'd flags with the cities draped
  in black,   35
With the show of the States themselves as of crape-veil'd
  women standing,
With processions long and winding and the flambeaus of
  the night,
With the countless torches lit, with the silent sea of faces and
  the unbared heads,
With the waiting depot, the arriving coffin, and the sombre
  faces,
With dirges through the night, with the thousand voices rising
  strong and solemn,   40
With all the mournful voices of the dirges pour'd around the
  coffin,
The dim-lit churches and the shuddering organs—where amid
  these you journey,
With the tolling tolling bells' perpetual clang,
Here, coffin that slowly passes,
I give you my sprig of lilac.   45

7

(Nor for you, for one alone,
Blossoms and branches green to coffins all I bring,
For fresh as the morning, thus would I chant a song for you O
  sane and sacred death.

All over bouquets of roses,
O death, I cover you over with roses and early lilies,   50
But mostly and now the lilac that blooms the first,
Copious I break, I break the sprigs from the bushes,
With loaded arms I come, pouring for you,
For you and the coffins all of you O death.)

8

O western orb sailing the heaven,   55
Now I know what you must have meant as a month since I
  walk'd,
As I walk'd in silence the transparent shadowy night,

As I saw you had something to tell as you bent to me night
    after night,
As you droop'd from the sky low down as if to my side,
    (while the other stars all look'd on,)
As we wander'd together the solemn night, (for something I
    know not what kept me from sleep,)   60
As the night advanced, and I saw on the rim of the west how
    full you were of woe,
As I stood on the rising ground in the breeze in the cool
    transparent night,
As I watch'd where you pass'd and was lost in the netherward
    black of the night,
As my soul in its trouble dissatisfied sank, as where you
    sad orb,
Concluded, dropt in the night, and was gone.   65

9

Sing on there in the swamp,
O singer bashful and tender, I hear your notes, I hear your call,
I hear, I come presently, I understand you,
But a moment I linger, for the lustrous star has detain'd me,
The star my departing comrade holds and detains me.   70

10

O how shall I warble myself for the dead one there I loved?
And how shall I deck my song for the large sweet soul that has
    gone?
And what shall my perfume be for the grave of him I love?

Sea-winds blown from east and west,
Blown from the Eastern sea and blown from the Western sea,
    till there on the prairies meeting,   75
These and with these and the breath of my chant,
I'll perfume the grave of him I love.

11

O what shall I hang on the chamber walls?
And what shall the pictures be that I hang on the walls,
To adorn the burial-house of him I love?   80

Pictures of growing spring and farms and homes,
With the Fourth-month eve at sundown, and the gray smoke
    lucid and bright,
With floods of the yellow gold of the gorgeous, indolent,
    sinking sun, burning, expanding the air,
With the fresh sweet herbage under foot, and the pale green
    leaves of the trees prolific,
In the distance the flowing glaze, the breast of the river,
    with a wind-dapple here and there,   85
With ranging hills on the banks, with many a line against the
    sky, and shadows,
And the city at hand with dwellings so dense, and stacks
    of chimneys,
And all the scenes of life and the workshops, and the
    workmen homeward returning.

12

Lo, body and soul—this land,
My own Manhattan with spires, and the sparkling and hurrying
    tides, and the ships,   90
The varied and ample land, the South and the North in the
    light, Ohio's shores and flashing Missouri,
And ever the far-spreading prairies cover'd with grass and corn.

Lo, the most excellent sun so calm and haughty,
The violet and purple morn with just-felt breezes,
The gentle soft-born measureless light,   95
The miracle spreading bathing all, the fulfill'd noon,
The coming eve delicious, the welcome night and the stars,
Over my cities shining all, enveloping man and land.

13

Sing on, sing on you gray-brown bird,
Sing from the swamps, the recesses, pour your chant from
    the bushes,   100
Limitless out of the dusk, out of the cedars and pines.

Sing on dearest brother, warble your reedy song,
Loud human song, with voice of uttermost woe.

O liquid and free and tender!
O wild and loose to my soul—O wondrous singer!   105
You only I hear—yet the star holds me, (but will soon depart,)
Yet the lilac with mastering odor holds me.

14

Now while I sat in the day and look'd forth,
In the close of the day with ·its light and the fields of spring,
　　and the farmers preparing their crops,
In the large unconscious scenery of my land with its
　　lakes and forests,　　　　　　　　　　　　　　　　　　110
In the heavenly aerial beauty, (after the perturb'd winds and
　　the storms,)
Under the arching heavens of the afternoon swift passing, and
　　the voices of children and women,
The many-moving sea-tides, and I saw the ships how they
　　sail'd,
And the summer approaching with richness, and the fields all
　　busy with labor,
And the infinite separate houses, how they all went on,
　　each with its meals and minutia of daily usages,　　　　115
And the streets how their throbbings throbb'd, and the
　　cities pent—lo, then and there,
Falling upon them all and among them all, enveloping me
　　with the rest,
Appear'd the cloud, appear'd the long black trail,
And I knew death, its thought, and the sacred knowledge
　　of death.

Then with the knowledge of death as walking one side of me,　　120
And the thought of death close-walking the other side of me,
And I in the middle as with companions, and as holding the
　　hands of companions,
I fled forth to the hiding receiving night that talks not,
Down to the shores of the water, the path by the swamp in
　　the dimness,
To the solemn shadowy cedars and ghostly pines so still.　　125

And the singer so shy to the rest receiv'd me,
The gray-brown bird I know receiv'd us comrades three,
And he sang the carol of death, and a verse for him I love.

From deep secluded recesses,
From the fragrant cedars and the ghostly pines so still,　　130
Came the carol of the bird.

And the charm of the carol rapt me,
As I held as if by their hands my comrades in the night,
And the voice of my spirit tallied the song of the bird.

Come lovely and soothing death, 135
Undulate round the world, serenely arriving, arriving,
In the day, in the night, to all, to each,
Sooner or later delicate death.

Prais'd be the fathomless universe
For life and joy, and for objects and knowledge curious, 140
And for love, sweet love—but praise! praise! praise!
For the sure-enwinding arms of cool-enfolding death.

Dark mother always gliding near with soft feet,
Have none chanted for thee a chant of fullest welcome?
Then I chant it for thee, I glorify thee above all, 145
I bring thee a song that when thou must indeed come, come
  unfalteringly.

Approach strong deliveress,
When it is so, when thou hast taken them I joyously sing the
  dead,
Lost in the loving floating ocean of thee,
Laved in the flood of thy bliss O death. 150
From me to thee glad serenades,
Dances for thee I propose saluting thee, adornments and
  feastings for thee,
And the sights of the open landscape and the high-spread
  sky are fitting,
And life and the fields, and the huge and thoughtful night.

The night in silence under many a star, 155
The ocean shore and the husky whispering wave whose voice I
  know,
And the soul turning to thee O vast and well-veil'd death,
And the body gratefully nestling close to thee.

Over the tree-tops I float thee a song,
Over the rising and sinking waves, over the myriad fields
  and the prairies wide, 160
Over the dense-pack'd cities all and the teeming wharves and
  ways,
I float this carol with joy, with joy to thee O Death.

15

To the tally of my soul,
Loud and strong kept up the gray-brown bird,
With pure deliberate notes spreading filling the night. 165

Loud in the pines and cedars dim,
Clear in the freshness moist and the swamp-perfume,
And I with my comrades there in the night.

While my sight that was bound in my eyes unclosed,
As to long panoramas of visions.   170

And I saw askant the armies,
I saw as in noiseless dreams hundreds of battle-flags,
Borne through the smoke of the battles and pierc'd with
    missiles I saw them,
And carried hither and yon through the smoke, and torn
    and bloody,
And at last but a few shreds left on the staffs, (and all in
    silence,)   175
And the staffs all splinter'd and broken.

I saw battle-corpses, myriads of them,
And the white skeletons of young men, I saw them,
I saw the debris and debris of all the slain soldiers of the war,
But I saw they were not as was thought,   180
They themselves were fully at rest, they suffer'd not,
The living remain'd and suffer'd, the mother suffer'd,
And the wife and the child and the musing comrade suffer'd,
And the armies that remain'd suffer'd.

16

Passing the visions, passing the night,   185
Passing, unloosing the hold of my comrades' hands,
Passing the song of the hermit bird and the tallying song of my
    soul,
Victorious song, death's outlet song, yet varying ever-altering
    song,
As low and wailing, yet clear the notes, rising and falling,
    flooding the night,
Sadly sinking and fainting, as warning and warning, and yet
    again bursting with joy,   190
Covering the earth and filling the spread of the heaven,
As that powerful psalm in the night I heard from recesses,
Passing, I leave thee lilac with heart-shaped leaves,
I leave thee there in the door-yard, blooming, returning with
    spring.

I cease from my song for thee,   195
From my gaze on thee in the west, fronting the west,
    communing with thee,
O comrade lustrous with silver face in the night.

Yet each to keep and all, retrievements out of the night,
The song, the wondrous chant of the gray-brown bird,
And the tallying chant, the echo arous'd in my soul,   200
With the lustrous and drooping star with the countenance
    full of woe,
With the holders holding my hand nearing the call of the bird,
Comrades mine and I in the midst, and their memory ever to
    keep, for the dead I loved so well,
For the sweetest, wisest soul of all my days and lands—and
    this for his dear sake,
Lilac and star and bird twined with the chant of my soul,   205
There in the fragrant pines and the cedars dusk and dim.

Walt Whitman, 1819–1892

FROM PENT-UP ACHING RIVERS

From pent-up aching rivers,
From that of myself without which I were nothing,
From what I am determin'd to make illustrious, even if I
    stand sole among men,
From my own voice resonant, singing the phallus,
Singing the song of procreation,
Singing the need of superb children and therein superb
    grown people,   5
Singing the muscular urge and the blending,
Singing the bedfellow's song, (O resistless yearning!
O for any and each the body correlative attracting!
O for you whoever you are your correlative body! O it,
    more than all else, you delighting!)
From the hungry gnaw that eats me night and day,   10
From native moments, from bashful pains, singing them,
Seeking something yet unfound though I have diligently
    sought it many a long year,
Singing the true song of the soul fitful at random,
Renascent with grossest Nature or among animals,
Of that, of them and what goes with them my poems
    informing,   15
Of the smell of apples and lemons, of the pairing of birds,
Of the wet of woods, of the lapping of waves,
Of the mad pushes of waves upon the land, I them
    chanting,
The overture lightly sounding, the strain anticipating,   20
The welcome nearness, the sight of the perfect body,
The swimmer swimming naked in the bath, or motionless
    on his back lying and floating,

The female form approaching, I pensive, love-flesh
    tremulous aching,
The divine list for myself or you or for any one making,
The face, the limbs, the index from head to foot, and what
    it arouses,   25
The mystic deliria, the madness amorous, the utter
    abandonment,
(Hark close and still what I now whisper to you,
I love you, O you entirely possess me,
O that you and I escape from the rest and go utterly off,
    free and lawless,
Two hawks in the air, two fishes swimming in the sea not
    more lawless than we;)
The furious storm through me careering, I passionately
    trembling,   30
The oath of the inseparableness of two together, of the
    woman that loves me and whom I love more than my
life, that oath swearing,
(O I willingly stake all for you,
O let me be lost if it must be so!
O you and I! what is it to us what the rest do or think?
What is all else to us? only that we enjoy each other and
    exhaust each other if it must be so;)   35
From the master, the pilot I yield the vessel to,
The general commanding me, commanding all, from him
    permission taking,
From time the programme hastening, (I have loiter'd too
    long as it is,)
From sex, from the warp and from the woof,   40
From privacy, from frequent repinings alone,
From plenty of persons near and yet the right person not
    near,
From the soft sliding of hands over me and thrusting of
    fingers through my hair and beard,
From the long sustain'd kiss upon the mouth or bosom,
From the close pressure that makes me or any man drunk,
    fainting with excess,   45
From what the divine husband knows, from the work of
    fatherhood,
From exultation, victory and relief, from the bedfellow's
    embrace in the night,
From the act-poems of eyes, hands, hips and bosoms,
From the cling of the trembling arm,
From the bending curve and the clinch,   50
From side by side the pliant coverlet off-throwing,
From the one so unwilling to have me leave, and me just
    as unwilling to leave,
(Yet a moment O tender waiter, and I return,)

From the hour of shining stars and dropping dews,
From the night a moment I emerging flitting out,   55
Celebrate you act divine and you children prepared for,
And you stalwart loins.

Walt Whitman, 1819–1892

DARK SUMMER

Under the thunder-dark, the cicadas resound.
The storm in the sky mounts, but is not yet heard.
The shaft and the flash wait, but are not yet found.
The apples that hang and swell for the late comer,
The simple spell, the rite not for our word,   5
The kisses not for our mouths,—light the dark summer.

Louise Bogan, 1897–1970

THE ALCHEMIST

I burned my life that I might find
A passion wholly of the mind,
Thought divorced from eye and bone,
Ecstasy come to breath alone.
I broke my life to seek relief   5
From the flawed light of love and grief.

With mounting beat the utter fire
Charred existence and desire.
It died low, ceased its sudden thresh.
I had found unmysterious flesh—   10
Not the mind's avid substance—still
Passionate beyond the will.

Louise Bogan, 1897–1970

EXHORTATION

Give over seeking bastard joy
Nor cast for fortune's side-long look.
Indifference can be your toy;
The bitter heart can be your book.
(Its lesson torment never shook.)   5

In the cold heart, as on a page,
Spell out the gentle syllable
That puts short limit to your rage
And curdles the straight fire of hell,
Compassing all, so all is well.   10

Read how, though passion sets in storm
And grief's a comfort, and the young
Touch at the flint when it is warm,
It is the dead we live among,
The dead given motion, and a tongue.   15

The dead, long trained to cruel sport
And the crude gossip of the grave;
The dead, who pass in motley sort,
Whom sun nor sufferance can save.
Face them. They sneer. Do not be brave.   20

Know once for all: their snare is set
Even now; be sure their trap is laid;
And you will see your lifetime yet
Come to their terms, your plans unmade,—
And be belied, and be betrayed.   25

Louise Bogan, 1897–1970

I CARE NOT FOR THESE LADIES

I care not for these ladies,
That must be wooed and prayed:
Give me kind Amaryllis,
The wanton country maid.
Nature art disdaineth,   5
Her beauty is her own.
   Her when we court and kiss,
   She cries, "Forsooth, let go!"
   But when we come where comfort is,
   She never will say no.   10

If I love Amaryllis,
She gives me fruit and flowers:
But if we love these ladies,
We must give golden showers.
Give them gold, that sell love,   15
Give me the nut-brown lass,

Who, when we court and kiss,
She cries, ''Forsooth, let go!''
But when we come where comfort is,
She never will say no.   20

These ladies must have pillows,
And beds by strangers wrought;
Give me a bower of willows,
Of moss and leaves unbought,
And fresh Amaryllis,   25
With milk and honey fed;
　　Who, when we court and kiss,
　　She cries, ''Forsooth, let go!''
　　But when we come where comfort is,
　　She never will say no.   30

Thomas Campion, 1567–1620

FOLLOW THY FAIR SUN

Follow thy fair sun, unhappy shadow;
Though thou be black as night,
And she made all of light,
Yet follow thy fair sun, unhappy shadow.

Follow her whose light thy light depriveth;   5
Though here thou liv'st disgraced,
And she in heaven is placed,
Yet follow her whose light the world reviveth!

Follow those pure beams whose beauty burneth,
That so have scorched thee,   10
As though still black must be,
Till her kind beams thy black to brightness turneth.

Follow her while yet her glory shineth;
There comes a luckless night,
That will dim all her light;   15
And this the black unhappy shade divineth.

Follow still since so thy fates ordained;
The sun must have his shade,
Till both at once do fade;
The sun still proved,[1] the shadow still disdained.   20

Thomas Campion, 1567–1620

[1] *proved:* approved.

FOLLOW YOUR SAINT, FOLLOW WITH ACCENTS SWEET

Follow your saint, follow with accents sweet,
Haste you, sad notes, fall at her flying feet.
There, wrapped in cloud of sorrow, pity move,
And tell the ravisher of my soul I perish for her love:
But, if she scorns my never-ceasing pain,   5
Then burst with sighing in her sight and ne'er return again.

All that I sung still to her praise did tend,
Still she was first, still she my songs did end;
Yet she my love and music both doth fly,
The music that her echo is and beauty's sympathy.   10
Then let my notes pursue her scornful flight:
It shall suffice that they were breathed and died for her delight.

Thomas Campion, 1567–1620

MY SWEETEST LESBIA

My sweetest Lesbia, let us live and love,
And though the sager sort our deeds reprove,
Let us not weigh them. Heaven's great lamps do dive
Into their west, and straight again revive,
But soon as once set is our little light,   5
Then must we sleep one ever-during night.

If all would lead their lives in love like me,
Then bloody swords and armor should not be;
No drum nor trumpet peaceful sleeps should move,
Unless alarm came from the camp of love.   10
But fools do live, and waste their little light,
And seek with pain their ever-during night.

When timely death my life and fortune ends,
Let not my hearse be vexed with mourning friends,
But let all lovers, rich in triumph, come   15
And with sweet pastimes grace my happy tomb;
And Lesbia, close up thou my little light,
And crown with love my ever-during night.

Thomas Campion, 1567–1620

THE CLOD AND THE PEBBLE

"Love seeketh not Itself to please,
Nor for itself hath any care,
But for another gives its ease,
And builds a Heaven in Hell's despair."

So sung a little Clod of Clay,   5
Trodden with the cattle's feet,
But a Pebble of the brook
Warbled out these metres meet:

"Love seeketh only Self to please,
To bind another to Its delight,   10
Joys in another's loss of ease,
And builds a Hell in Heaven's despite."

William Blake, 1757–1828

AH! SUN-FLOWER

Ah, Sun-flower! weary of time,
Who countest the steps of the Sun,
Seeking after that sweet golden clime
Where the traveller's journey is done:

Where the Youth pined away with desire,   5
And the pale Virgin shrouded in snow
Arise from their graves, and aspire
Where my Sun-flower wishes to go.

William Blake, 1757–1828

A POISON TREE

I was angry with my friend.
I told my wrath, my wrath did end.
I was angry with my foe:
I told it not, my wrath did grow.

And I water'd it in fears,   5
Night & morning with my tears;
And I sunned it with smiles,
And with soft deceitful wiles.

And it grew both day and night,
Till it bore an apple bright;   10
And my foe beheld it shine,
And he knew that it was mine,

And into my garden stole
When the night had veil'd the pole:
In the morning glad I see   15
My foe outstretch'd beneath the tree.

William Blake, 1757–1828

THE EXPIRATION

So, so, breake off this last lamenting kisse,
   which sucks two soules, and vapors Both away,
Turn thou ghost that way, and let me turn this,
   And let our selves benight our happiest day.
We ask'd none leave to Love, not will we owe   5
   Any, so cheap a death, as saying, Go;

Go; and if that word have not quite kill'd thee,
   Ease me with death, by bidding me go too.
Oh, if it have, let my word work on me,
   And a just office on a murderer do.   10
Except it be too late, to kill me so,
   Being double dead, going, and bidding, go.

John Donne, 1572–1631

A VALEDICTION: FORBIDDING MOURNING

As virtuous men passe mildly away,
   And whisper to their soules, to goe,
Whilst some of their sad friends doe say,
   The breath goes now, and some say, no:

So let us melt, and make no noise,   5
   No teare-floods, nor sigh-tempests move,
T'were prophanation of our joyes
   To tell the layetie our love.

Moving of th'earth brings harmes and feares,
   Men reckon what it did and meant,   10
But trepidation of the spheares,
   Though greater farre, is innocent.

Dull sublunary lovers love
   (Whose soule is sense) cannot admit
Absence, because it doth remove   15
   Those things which elemented it.

But we by a love, so much refin'd,
   That our selves know not what it is,
Inter-assured of the mind,
   Care lesse, eyes, lips, and hands to misse.   20

Our two soules therefore, which are one,
   Though I must goe, endure not yet
A breach, but an expansion,
   Like gold to ayery thinnesse beate.

If they be two, they are two so   25
   As stiffe twin compasses are two,
Thy soule the fixt foot, makes no show
   To move, but doth, if th'other doe.

And though it in the center sit,
   Yet when the other far doth rome,   30
It leanes, and hearkens after it,
   And growes erect, as that comes home.

Such wilt thou be to mee, who must
   Like th'other foot, obliquely runne;
Thy firmnes drawes my circle just,   35
   And makes me end, where I begunne.

John Donne, 1572–1631

THE RELIQUE

When my grave is broke up again
Some second guest to entertain,
(For graves have learn'd that woman-head
To be to more than one a Bed)
   And he that digs it, spies   5

A bracelet of bright hair about the bone,
  Will he not let us alone,
And think that there a happy couple lies,
Who thought that this device might be some way
To make their souls, at the last busy day,   10
Meet at this grave, and make a little stay?

  If this fall in a time, or land
  Where mis-devotion doth command,
  then, he that digs us up, will bring
  Us, to the Bishop, and the King,   15
    To make us Reliques; then
Thou shalt be a Mary Magdalen, and I
  A something else thereby:
All women shall adore us, and some men;
And since at such time, miracles are sought,   20
I would have that age by this paper taught
What miracles we harmless lovers wrought.

  First, we lov'd well and faithfully,
  Yet knew not what we loved, nor why;
  Difference of sex no more we knew,   25
  Than our Guardian Angels do;
    Coming and going, we
Perchance might kiss, but not between those meals;
    Our hands ne'er toucht the seals
Which nature, injur'd by late law, sets free: 30
The miracles we did; but now alas,
All measure, and all language, I should pass,
Should I tell what a miracle she was.

John Donne, 1572–1631

ON DONNE'S POETRY

With Donne, whose muse on dromedary trots,
Wreathe iron pokers into true-love knots;
Rhyme's sturdy cripple, fancy's maze and clue,
Wit's forge and fire-blast, meaning's press and screw.

Samuel Taylor Coleridge, 1772–1834

NIGHT FEEDING

Deeper than sleep but not so deep as death
I lay there dreaming and my magic head
remembered and forgot. On first cry I
remembered and forgot and did believe.

I knew love and I knew evil: 5
woke to the burning song and the tree burning blind,
despair of our days and the calm milk-giver who
knows sleep, knows growth, the sex of fire and grass,
renewal of all waters and the time of the stars
and the black snake with gold bones.   10

Black sleeps, gold burns; on second cry I woke
fully and gave to feed and fed on feeding.
Gold seed, green pain, my wizards in the earth
walked through the house, black in the morning dark.
Shadows grew in my veins, my bright belief,   15
my head of dreams deeper than night and sleep.
Voices of all black animals crying to drink,
cries of all birth arise, simple as we,
found in the leaves, in clouds and dark, in dream,
deep as this hour, ready again to sleep.   20

Muriel Rukeyser, 1913–1980

THE MOTHER

Abortions will not let you forget.
You remember the children you got that you did not get,
The damp small pulps with a little or with no hair,
The singers and workers that never handled the air.
You will never neglect or beat   5
Them, or silence or buy with a sweet.
You will never wind up the sucking-thumb
Or scuttle off ghosts that come.
You will never leave them, controlling your luscious sigh,
Return for a snack of them, with gobbling mother-eye.   10

I have heard in the voices of the wind the voices of my dim
killed children.
I have contracted. I have eased
My dim dears at the breasts they could never suck.

I have said, Sweets, if I sinned, if I seized
Your luck   15
And your lives from your unfinished reach,
If I stole your births and your names,
Your straight baby tears and your games,
Your stilted or lovely loves, your tumults, your marriages,
    aches, and your deaths,
If I poisoned the beginnings of your breaths,   20
Believe that even in my deliberateness I was not deliberate.
Though why should I whine,
Whine that the crime was other than mine?—
Since anyhow you are dead.
Or rather, or instead,   25
You were never made.
But that too, I am afraid,
Is faulty: oh, what shall I say, how is the truth to be said?
You were born, you had body, you died.
It is just that you never giggled or planned or cried.   30

Believe me, I loved you all.
Believe me, I knew you, though faintly, and I loved, I loved you
All.

Gwendolyn Brooks, 1917–

WHEN THE CEILING CRIES

A mother tosses her infant so that it hits the ceiling.
    Father says, why are you doing that to the ceiling?
    Do you want my baby to fly away to heaven? the ceiling is
        there so that the baby will come back to me, says
        mother.
    Father says, you are hurting the ceiling, can't you hear it
        crying?
    So mother and father climb a ladder and kiss the ceiling.

Russell Edson, 1935–

GIACOMETTI'S DOG

She moves so gracefully on her bronze legs
that they form the letter *M* beneath her.
There is nothing more beautiful than the effort
in her outstretched neck, the simplicity of the head;

Alberto Giacometti, *Dog*, 1951.

but she will never curl again in the comfortable basket,   5
she will never be duped by the fireplace and the fire.

Though she has sniffed out cocaine in the Newark Airport,
we can never trust her good nose again.
She'll kill a chicken in her master's yard,
she'll corner a lamb in the back pasture.   10
She's resigning her post with the Seeing Eye.

Giacometti's *Dog* will not ask for water
though she's been tied to a rope in Naples
for three days under the hot sun.
Giacometti's *Dog* will not see a vet   15
though someone kicks her and her liver fills with blood.
Though she's fed meat laced with strychnine.
Though her mouth fills with porcupine quills.

Giacometti's *Dog* is coming back
as a jackal, snapping at the wheels   20
of your bicycle, following behind in her
you-can't-touch-me-now suit.
Giacometti's *Dog* has already forgotten
when she lost the use of her back legs

and cried at the top of the stairs   25
and you took pity on her.

She's taking a modern-day attitude.
She knows it's a shoot-or-get-shot situation.
She's not your doggie-in-the-window.
She's not racing into a burning house or taking your shirt   30
between her teeth and swimming to the beach.
She's looking out for Number One,
she's doing the dog paddle and making it
to shore in this dog-eat-dog world.

Robin Becker, 1951–

BLACK POET, WHITE CRITIC

A critic advises
not to write on controversial subjects
like freedom or murder,
but to treat universal themes
and timeless symbols
like the white unicorn.

A white unicorn?

Dudley Randall, 1914–

Interpretation: The Wide Response

Try to be one of the people on whom nothing is lost.

Henry James

Folk wisdom has it that spiders hatch their eggs by staring at them. Reading poems requires the same concentration. An African tribe dries reeds for flutes. When the instruments are carved, a musician ceremoniously breathes into each one, imparting a soul. This kind of life-giving is also needed each time you read a poem.

A poem may be analyzed in terms of rhythm, language, metaphor, or any aspect and still remain inert unless the elements fuse. Coleridge coined a word for the ability to fuse the parts of a poem into a whole: *esemplastic*, "to shape into one." The poem's total effect *is* the unity of perception. The best reader puts imagination to work with analysis and listens for the widest possibilities of the words. This requires both staring and giving.

A Close Reading

Think about the craft and meaning(s) of this poem:

LYING IN A HAMMOCK AT WILLIAM DUFFY'S FARM IN PINE ISLAND, MINNESOTA

Over my head, I see the bronze butterfly,
Asleep on the black trunk,
Blowing like a leaf in green shadow.
Down the ravine behind the empty house,
The cowbells follow one another   5
Into the distances of the afternoon.

To my right,
In a field of sunlight between two pines,
The droppings of last year's horses
Blaze up into golden stones.   10
I lean back, as the evening darkens and comes on.
A chicken hawk floats over, looking for home.
I have wasted my life.

James Wright, 1927–1980

First, you might be moved by the poem and surprised by the ending.
The most important immediate response is how the poem affects you.
What emotions does it arouse, what memories does it evoke, where
does it take your imagination, what does it remind you of? Then, *why*?
How do you respond to the images and line use? How does looking at
the craft add to your first impression? What won't "hatch"?
Here are one young writer's notes on Wright's poem:

Wright was the first poet I felt a connection
with. And the first contemporary poet I understood.
When I read the poem ''Lying in a Hammock . . .'' one
afternoon about my junior year in college, I must
have been a bit weary of things in general. Maybe
that's why the title so appealed to me. I had never
seen a poem that had a title so long, or a title that
was so particular. It wasn't simply ''In a Hammock''
or ''Sitting Back and Watching the Time Go By.'' This
actual hammock was tied between two trees or posts on
someone's farm——Oh! to be on a farm at that moment, I
thought, there things are easier, there one can rest,
relax, breathe in that clean country air. Nature! I
thought, that would cure the emptiness, loneliness I
was feeling at the moment. Both my parents grew up on
farms, and I spent many summers there, many, many
weekends.

What line do you think I was struck by? I thought
I might not have read it correctly, so I read it
again. And again. After a number of times, I set the
book down for the day. Several days later I came back
to it, hoping that a little time away would help. I
read it again and again, to the point where I had

memorized it, I had taken it far within me. I still
didn't ''understand'' everything, I felt. I had a
strong feeling but I didn't know what to do with it.
One day I was taking a walk. It was fall, all the
trees were beautiful in their hardwood colors—this
was Minnesota. Fall always brought a certain
sadness, a sadness that came out of the wonderful
beauty of that season, the smells, the colors, the
light, the air. If this isn't a glimpse of beauty,
what is? What is beauty? While I was on this walk,
Wright's poem came into my mind—perhaps it was there
all along—and I started saying it to myself. Being
outside, it was almost as if I were lying in a
hammock, observing the world around me. I remember
looking in the gutter of the street which was filling
up with fallen leaves; mixed in were cigarette butts,
plastic bottles, a can perhaps. The usual litter, but
somehow it all looked transfigured, like Bishop's
looking at the old worn-out fish she caught one day
and proclaiming that everything was ''rainbow,
rainbow, rainbow.'' [See "The Fish," page 67.] I felt
then that I understood the Wright poem—not just
theoretically, but on the level of the senses.

 After this, reading other poems became much
easier. I had made a breakthrough in understanding:
Poems are written by men and women. We all share
common experiences. Everyone has sat in a chair on
the back porch, sat in the sand, in the garden, in a
car stranded in the back country, under a tree,
everyone has looked out on a scene. Poets are
different from others in that they feel their
experience is remarkable—that is, something to make
remarks on. Poets don't simply ignore this kind of
scene. They go one step further.

 I still like the poem. My reasons for liking it
change. Look at the senses Wright touches: Sight: ''I
see'' butterfly, black trunk. He shifts to hearing:
cowbells. Back to sight: field, year-old horse
droppings. Sight: chicken hawk overhead. Not only

these particular ones; he seems to be surrounded with those things that touch his senses. I like his yoking of words that call up a particular emotion: black trunk and empty house. The connotations are surely not happiness of any sort, but more of a kind of despair. The empty house hooks up with the second-to-last line, ''looking for home.'' This kind of emptiness he feels is really populated by some quite amazing sights, feelings. The butterfly is bronze, like a work of art: unreal, very unordinary. It's ''asleep''—though how he knows this, who knows! It just shows that he has been looking at it for a long time, admiring it, the bronze against the black. The color and shape remind him of a leaf, something more ordinary on a tree. And this bronze butterfly is in ''green'' shadow. How a shadow can be green!

The second sentence gives us only sound: he's true to his point of view. He couldn't see the cows; he can only hear the bells—that kind of melancholy sound. Finally, I noticed how the o sounds in the line make the bell notes follow each other across the page. This pleased and surprised me. He thought of that! A poem tries for surprise, tries to get the reader to see something other than what he or she is accustomed to seeing. How pedestrian to have said ''into the distances of the field'' or ''into the late afternoon.''

The third sentence: He sees to the right of him piles of droppings. He thinks they're about a year old. They ''blaze up into golden stones.'' Here we have to say, ''Enough!'' We allowed you to go on about the butterfly turning into a leaf, and there just being cowbells instead of cows, but manure into gold bricks! If we believe this, we'll believe anything!

The last image he gives is less an image than a straight statement. The hawk overhead doesn't seem quite as charged as the other images. What it's doing, though, and what the poet thinks it's doing

might be two different things. What I mean is that
Wright anthropomorphizes the hawk. The hawk is
perhaps looking for its next meal, a rat or a gopher
or a snake: don't hawks hunt at night, or at dusk?
Wright says the hawk is ''looking for home,'' meaning
that it has a home to look for, that it will probably
find one. However, it's Wright (or ''the speaker'')
who is troubled by ''home.'' This kind of projection
seems a shade corny.

What's Wright doing through this poem? On the one
hand, he's simply the observer; that's all he can do.
In a hammock—resting, suspended between earth and
sky. Also, the hammock is on someone else's
place—Wright seems to make a point of that in the
title—he denotes a very specific place. It's as if
he's giving you clues—<u>when</u>, Evening: <u>where</u>, a Farm:
and so on—and wants you to solve some problem he has.

It seems he's giving you clues because of that
last line he throws out, almost like a cry. How to
explain, or respond to, this last line? (My brother,
the literal, anti-imaginative one, says, ''Of course
he's wasting his life, just sitting there feeling
sorry for himself, for whatever reason. He should get
up, get a job, stop writing poetry.'') I take Wright
seriously, but have to ask why he feels this way.
Does the last line follow from the images before it?
It's a very drastic statement to make: what happens
after you say that to yourself? We don't know in the
case of Wright—he doesn't tell us any more; he leaves
us with that statement ringing in our ears. Is his
realization that he has never seen, really seen, this
kind of scene before, or quite in this way, one
strong image after another? Interesting that he ends
the poem with ''my life.'' Key words, I think. He
opens the poem up to some broader considerations.
He's openly saying what many of us at one time or
another will have to confront ourselves with: What
has been the worth of our lives; have we ''wasted''
them; how do you ''waste'' a life? Are there things

you can do to ensure that you do not waste it? This
seems one of the fundamental things that poetry deals
with, questions poetry raises.

This writer fully reacted to and explored the poem. Anything one
does wholly requires a kind of rapt attention that lets the most happen.
Understanding poems sometimes demands living with the poem for a
while, as this writer did.

Wright was familiar with "Archaic Torso of Apollo," by the German poet Rainer Maria Rilke:

ARCHAIC TORSO OF APOLLO

We have no idea what his fantastic head
was like, where the eyeballs were slowly swelling. But
his body now is glowing like a gas lamp,
whose inner eyes, only turned down a little,

hold their flame, shine. If there weren't light, the curve   5
of the breast wouldn't blind you, and in the swerve
of the thighs a smile wouldn't keep on going
toward the place where the seeds are.

If there weren't light, this stone would look cut off
where it drops clearly from the shoulders,   10
its skin wouldn't gleam like the fur of a wild animal,

and the body wouldn't send out light from every edge
as a star does . . . for there is no place at all
that isn't looking at you. You must change your life.

Rainer Maria Rilke, 1875–1926
(Translated by Robert Bly)

Clearly, there's a relationship between the two poems. A further insight
may strike if you read Wright's "A Blessing" and "Autumn Comes to
Martins Ferry, Ohio" again. All four poems hinge on an illumination
at the end. Each leads to a transforming revelation about ordinary
experience. Other poems by an author often illuminate the poem at
hand.

After all this, what about that startling last line in "Lying in a Hammock . . ."? Obviously, it's an electrical charge that arcs back to touch each line with significance. It resists a simple analysis. To some extent, each reader must be the African musician who gives soul to a dried reed by breathing into it. The line says what it says clearly: "I have wasted my life." But exactly *how* that means is richly open to discussion.

What Is Meaning?

Often we hear "What does the poem mean?" That's an odd question, a reductive question which sounds as if the poem is sitting there on the page while "meaning" hovers above it like a little white cloud; as if we must read the cloud formations to find the real poem. Instead, think of **meaning** as *everything* you perceive about the poem. Many poems *suggest* multiple meanings. These are not always paraphrasable. Wright's poem begins with mundane experience (easy enough to talk about), but it ends with a startling perception that bears thinking about at length.

Rather than being *about* experience, think of a poem *as* an experience—sometimes with memorable insights, sometimes not. Every good poem establishes its own parameters. Sometimes sound takes precedence over meaning, sometimes verbal juxtapositions make *a* meaning irrelevant, except as each person interprets the poem. Gertrude Stein's work is an example of this. To read "A Piano" (page 444) and say that it "doesn't make sense" is to miss the point. (After one of Stein's perfectly logical lectures on poetry, a reporter asked her why she didn't write the way she spoke. She replied, "Why don't you read the way I write?") We have to learn to read on the poem's terms. We can't always know what the poet intended, but by carefully reading all the information in the poem we can establish the writer's approach to the subject. Textual analysis, a close reading of the actual text, is the best approach. Poems do not mean what they do not say or suggest. For example, the brother who complained that Wright should get up and get a job was dead wrong as a reader; there is nothing in the poem to suggest that the speaker has not slaved away his whole life at some job. We must trust the text; then we understand by remaining open to the poem's widest possibilities.

The more you bring with you, the more you get back. Reading Rilke's poem and Wright's other work deepens your response to Wright's poem. In his essay "The Prerequisites," Robert Frost wrote:

> A poem is best read in the light of all other poems ever written. We read A the better to read B (we have to start somewhere; we may get very little out of A). We read B the better to read C, C the better to read D, D the better to go back and get something more out of A. Progress is not the aim, but circulation. The thing is to get among the poems where they hold each other apart in their places as the stars do.

Excellent advice: Get *among* the poems and circulate.

Gaps and Holes

Craft. Analysis of the text. Our own interpretations. And still there is something else at work in the poem. Dylan Thomas was aware of significant "holes and gaps" in this passage from "Poetic Manifesto":

> You can tear a poem apart to see what makes it technically tick, and say to yourself, when the works are laid out before you, the vowels, the consonants, the rhymes or rhythms, "Yes, this is *it*. This is why the poem moves me so. It is because of the craftsmanship." But you're back again where you began!
> You're back with the mystery of having been moved by words. The best craftsmanship always leaves holes and gaps in the works of the poem so that something that is *not* the poem can creep, crawl, flash, or thunder in.

In the fragments of Anakreon, a Greek poet of the sixth century B.C., the "gaps and holes" are obvious because parts of the poems are lost. We're drawn toward what is not said, or to what is understated—the poem between the lines. We must participate, supplying our own imaginative complement to what's there. In the fragments below, imagination goes to work on the enticing brackets, which mark lost portions of the ancient worm-eaten papyrus these translations were made from. What's not said but suggested is definitely a part of our experience.

TRANSLATIONS OF ANAKREON[1]

3.

```
[                           ]
[        ] all[nig]ht long [           ]
[                         ]
Both delight and [          [
[                           ]        5
But loving [                ]
Offerings at hand [         ]
Of the Pierides [           ]
[                           ]
And Graces [                ]       10
And then the [              ]
[                           ]
[                           ]
[        ] beaut[iful] [     ]
[                           ]       15
Flitter we all the night [  ]
Fishing with bait [         ]
Golden-helmeted Pallas [    ]
[        ] from afar [      ]
Flowering [                 ]       20
[                           ]
```

20.

Can myrrh rubbed on a chest
Sweeten the great round heart inside?

32.

[   ]
Whose heart is green and young again   25
And dances to a lissome tune on the flute.

39.

[   ] loved pitiful war.

---

[1] *Anakreon:* Anakreon lived in Teos, now Sighalik in Turkey, and later in Athens in the sixth century B.C. His work is often confused with that of an Alexandrian imitation, or homage, to him, written by a group of poets and later misunderstood to be the real work of Anakreon. These fragments are by the real, historical Anakreon.

40.

The servant girl poured
Honied wine from the jug
On her shoulder.   30

85.

[   ] bedroom
In which he, unmarrying,
Was married [   ].

91.

You carry on over it
Far too much.   35

92.

He sleeps soundly
With his bedroom door
Always unbolted.

105.

[   ]
Glowing with desire,   40
Gleaming with spiced oil
[   ].

112.

Walking along with a haughty neck.

113.

Chattering swallow.

114.

Wine-server.   45

123.

Pretty.

124.

Stalks of slim white celery
In a wicker basket.

158.

[   ]

161.

```
[                                ]                          50
Again [                 ] island
[           ] we two in love,
We pray O ears that hear prayers,
Our very solemn [                 ]
[                 ] Lady in the stars                        55
[                 ] Eros stalking
On the balls of his feet [           ]
The happy [                    ] who
Of those I love [                         ]
Until my dream [                          ]               60
Hail! Kyllanas [                          ]
[             ] the sea [                 ]
We kneel at Aphrodite's altar
[                                         ]
Sacred mother [                          ]               65
Of Kypris [                              ]
[                                        ]
Excite [                                 ]
[                                        ]
Glossy [                                 ]               70
[                                        ]
Sweet [                                  ]
Hail [                                   ]
Sight [                                  ]
I hug your knees [                       ]               75
Young [                                  ]
You, boy [                               ]
Come to me! [                            ]
Look [                                   ]
[                                        ]               80
```

Anakreon, sixth century B.C.
(Translated by Guy Davenport)

The jolting phrases of Emily Dickinson invite our participation in a way similar to the fragments of Anakreon:

425

Good Morning—Midnight—
I'm coming Home—
Day—got tired of Me—
How could I—of Him?

Sunshine was a sweet place—   5
I liked to stay—
But Morn—didn't want me—now—
So—Goodnight—Day!

I can look—can't I—
When the East is Red?   10
The Hills—have a way—then—
That puts the Heart—abroad—

You—are not so fair—Midnight—
I chose—Day—
But—please take a little Girl—   15
He turned away!

Emily Dickinson, 1830–1886

Rather than proceeding smoothly, the sense or meaning jerks and jumps. Phrases abut each other like wires that get close enough to spark. The halts (dashes) are, of course, part of the meaning. They connect and separate at once. Here's where the reader's imagination must come into play. We follow the poet's thought process as it occurs, close to the act of perception.

When a poem is extraordinarily difficult to understand fully on first or tenth reading, as much of Dickinson is, we become fascinated, like a mother who prefers the difficult child. We respond strongly without knowing why. The mystery of such a poem is that someday—after we, not the poem, have changed—we may be able to read it. Thomas's "There Was a Saviour," a poem crowded with symbols and private religious associations, seems deliberately cryptic.

THERE WAS A SAVIOUR

There was a saviour
Rarer that radium,
Commoner than water, crueller than truth;
Children kept from the sun
Assembled at his tongue   5
To hear the golden note turn in a groove,
Prisoners of wishes locked their eyes
In the jails and studies of his keyless smiles.

The voice of children says
From a lost wilderness   10
There was calm to be done in his safe unrest,
When hindering man hurt
Man, animal, or bird
We hid our fears in that murdering breath,
Silence, silence to do, when earth grew loud,   15
In lairs and asylums of the tremendous shout.

There was glory to hear
In the churches of his tears,
Under his downy arm you sighed as he struck,
O you who could not cry   20
On to the ground when a man died
Put a tear for joy in the unearthly flood
And laid your cheek against a cloud-formed shell:
Now in the dark there is only yourself and myself.

Two proud, blacked brothers cry,   25
Winter-locked side by side,
To this inhospitable hollow year,
O we who could not stir
One lean sigh when we heard
Greed on man beating near and fire neighbour   30
But wailed and nested in the sky-blue wall
Now break a giant tear for the little known fall,

For the drooping of homes
That did not nurse our bones,
Brave deaths of only ones but never found,   35
Now see, alone in us,
Our own true strangers' dust
Ride through the doors of our unentered house.
Exiled in us we arouse the soft,
Unclenched, armless, silk and rough love that breaks all rocks.   40

Dylan Thomas, 1914–1953

Did Thomas know everything about his poem? Possibly he could join a class discussion and learn something himself. Generally the poet knows his business; otherwise the poems falter or skid. Occasionally a poet writes a luminous, mysterious poem which puzzles him more than the reader. Reader or writer, you do not always understand everything.

The ancient fragments and the obscure Thomas poem require us to sharpen our oyster knives and to pry into them. The active reader always brings an *imaginative complement* to a poem, a readiness to participate fully in the experience. Nothing is as necessary to the poem as a flexible reader.

Power Sources

In his book *On Surgery*, Richard Seltzer says that between the dermis and the epidermis there exists a layer of "pure energy." Dylan Thomas wrote about "the force that through the green fuse drives the flower." Forces and energies also impel or organize the poem.

Most good poems are alive with strong emotion or experience. Thomas's "gaps and holes," though not as apparently as rhythm, meter, and imagery, also fuel the poem. And there are many other discernable forces. Each of the following poems brings to your attention something particular about a poem's infrastructure. A way of proceeding, an idea, a moment of sudden revelation: each is that "layer of pure energy" operating with meaning and craft.

Idea

The primary power comes from an idea that engages our minds. We tend to solve a poem like "The Tortoise" by sorting through our own reactions for agreement. What emotions are behind the idea in this poem?

THE TORTOISE

Always to want to
go back, to correct
an error, ease a

guilt, see how a friend
is doing. And yet   5
one doesn't, except

in memory, in
dreams. The land remains
desolate. Always

the feeling is of   10
terrible slowness
overtaking haste.

Cid Corman, 1924–

Association

A string of associations propels the poem—and the reader's imagination. The mind is naturally associative: one thing reminds you of another, without logical connection. The smell of rain on hot streets may catapult you to a feeling you had for someone, which in turn reminds you of a red motorcycle and pots of hyacinths on a windowsill. No logic, just sensory links buried in the psyche. Poems using this approach depend on the reader's willingness to make imaginative leaps with the author.

In André Breton's "Free Union," each association has to do with a subject, the speaker's wife. The poem is **surreal** (meaning "beyond realism"), a free way of associating by allowing subconscious or dream-like imagery to surface and guide the poem.

Surreal poems often have a dream logic. The poet dips into the psyche, leaps from image to image. The surreal poet values the spontaneity of subconscious associations. **Surrealism** was originally a French movement in poetry spearheaded by Breton, who wrote in 1924:

> Everything leads one to believe that there exists a certain point in the mind from which life and death, the real and the imaginary, the past and the future, what is communicable and what is incommunicable, the high and the low, cease to be perceived as contradictory.

This mysterious "point" was the pole star that inspired and guided the surrealists' fantastic experiments in painting and poetry.

from FREE UNION

My wife with the woodfire hair.
With the heat lightning thoughts
And the hourglass waist
My wife with the waist of an otter in the tiger's jaws
My wife with the mouth of cockade and clustering maximal stars   5
With teeth like the spoor of white mice on white earth
With a tongue of rubbed amber and glass
With a tongue like a daggered host
The tongue of a doll whose eyes open and close
A tongue of unbelievable stone   10
My wife with eyelashes like the strokes of childish writing
With eyebrows like the rim of a swallow's nest
My wife with the temples of slate on a glasshouse roof
And steam on windows
My wife with the champagne shoulders   15
Like a dolphin-headed fountain under ice
My wife with the matchstick wrists
My wife with the fingers of chance and the ace of hearts
With the fingers of new-mown hay
My wife with the armpits of marten and beechnut   20
And Midsummer Night
Of privet and wentletrap nests
With the arms of sea-surf and mill-dam foam
And of wheat and mill mixed
My wife with the spindle legs   25
Moving like clockwork and despair
My wife with the calves of elder pith
My wife with the feet of initials
With the feet of key-bunches with the feet of drinking caulkers
My wife whose neck is pearl barley   30
Whose throat is a golden dale
With rendez-vous in the very bed of the torrent
With the breasts of night
My wife with the breasts of marine molehills
My wife with the ruby crucible breasts   35
With breasts like the ghost of a rose under dew
My wife with a belly like the unfolding fan of the days
A belly like a giant claw
My wife with back like a bird in vertical flight
With back of quicksilver   40
Back of light
With a nape of rolled stone and moist chalk
And the fall of a glass just drained
My wife with the skiff hips

Hips of chandelier and arrow feathers   45
Hips of the ribs of white peacock plumes
And imperceptibly swinging scales
My wife with the buttocks of sandstone and mountain flax
My wife with the swan's back buttocks
My wife with the springtime buttocks   50
And gladiolus sex
My wife with the placer and water-mole sex
My wife with sex of seaweed and stale sweets
My wife with mirror sex
My wife with eyes full of tears   55
With eyes of violet panoply and magnetic needle
My wife with savannah eyes
My wife with eyes of water to drink in prison
My wife with eyes of wood always under the axe
With eyes of water level air level the level of earth and fire   60

André Breton, 1896–1966
(Translated by Kenneth White)

Tension

A major force of the poem is sometimes tension. The use of opposites, words or concepts, gives a push-pull tautness. The poem proceeds by juxtaposition of opposites or by the use of **paradox,** a statement that seems to contradict itself. For example, Shakespeare wrote, "When my love swears that she is made of truth / I do believe her, though I know she lies." Tension operates also in ironic poems. The voice of the duke in Browning's "My Last Duchess" (page 161) says one thing while the reader quickly picks up the unspoken story; we hear the speaker ironically. See also the end of Andrew Marvell's "To His Coy Mistress" (page 262).

BITTER-SWEET

Ah, my dear angry Lord,
Since thou dost love, yet strike;
Cast down, yet help afford;
Sure I will do the like.

I will complain, yet praise;   5
I will bewail, approve;
And all my sour-sweet days
I will lament and love.

George Herbert, 1593–1633

Alogical Structure

An alogical structure proceeds other than by sequential logic. Like surreal poems, these poems refuse to be pinned down to *meaning*. They remain wide open to interpretation, or sometimes just to listening. The first example below is a **sound poem,** written for the ear. The second presents a view of an experience and scene; the words "paint" an impression. When an alogical poem seems composed by chance, it is called an **aleatory** poem.

Both the examples which follow are highly structured and conscious. They don't, however, organize along a one-two-three logical track.

A CHORALE* OF CHEROKEE NIGHT MUSIC AS HEARD THROUGH AN OPEN WINDOW IN SUMMER LONG AGO

uhu wahuhu wahuhu wahuhu wahuhu wahuhu wahuhu wahuhu wahuhu w
guku uguku uguku uguku uguku uguku uguku uguku uguku uguku uguku
huhu huhu huhu huhu huhu huhu huhu huhu huhu huhu huhu huhu huh
u lalu lalu lalu lalu lalu lalu lalu lalu lalu lalu lalu lalu lalu lalu lal
atu talatu talatu talatu talatu talatu talatu talatu talatu talatu talatu t   5
li tsikilili tsikilili tsikilili tsikilili tsikilili tsikilili tsikilili tsikilili
ikiki tsikiki tsikiki tsikiki tsikiki tsikiki tsikiki tsikiki tsikiki tsikik
u kagu kagu kagu kagu kagu kagu kagu kagu kagu kagu kagu kagu kag
ya waya waya waya waya waya waya waya waya waya waya waya waya way
eah yeah yeah yeah yeah yeah yeah yeah yeah yeah yeah yeah yeah y   10
a guna guna guna guna guna guna guna guna guna guna guna guna gun
sasa sasa sasa sasa sasa sasa sasa sasa sasa sasa sasa sasa sasa
unu kununu kununu kununu kununu kununu kununu kununu kununu kun
tu dustu dustu dustu dustu dustu dustu dustu dustu dustu dustu dustu

Jonathan Williams, 1929–

* screech owl, hoot owl, yellow-breasted chat, jar-fly, carolina chickadee, katydid, crow, wolf, Beatles, turkey, goose, bullfrog, spring frog.

THEY DID NOT MAKE CONVERSATION.

A lake as big, the early evening wind at the bather's neck. Something pulling (or was it rising up) green from the bottom. You could lie flat and let go of the white creases. You could indulge your fear of drowning in the arms of shallow wet miles. You did not open your mouth, yet water poured into openings, making you part. Bone in the

throat. That dark blue fading, thinning at the edges. On deck chairs
with bits of flowered cloth across their genitals, the guests called out
in three languages and sometimes pointed, commenting on the simple
beauty of bought connection. The swan-like whiteness of the day.
That neck of waves. There was always a tray with small red bottles.
And pinpointed attentions, at each slung ease.

Kathleen Fraser, 1934–

Epiphany

A moment of epiphany is a sudden revelation or a flash of recognition
when the essence or full meaning of a time, event, memory, or person
is apprehended. Such realizations may also involve a *transformation*,
like the change that occurs after Elizabeth's moment of recognition in
"In the Waiting Room."

DEAR OLD STOCKHOLM

Of course it is snowing
but two city girls,
one blonde the other black-
haired, are preparing for bed
in a warm apartment they share.   5
One is washing her hair in the bathroom sink
while the other does hatha yoga exercises.
They have been dancing with some young men
who spoke nothing but north american english,
one of them from Pittsburgh   10
(from Crawford's Grill up on the Hill)
& the other
a fingerpopper from Leamington, Ontario.

Suddenly, recalling the evening,
the rushing from taxis up inside music clubs,   15
all of them pleased that it should be so,
the bathroom blonde
who,
like a great many scandinavians,
played some instrument in secondary school   20
whistles John Coltrane's whole solo
from the Miles Davis *Dear Old Stockholm*
which had been an old swedish folk song.
In fluorescent abandon
& in time   25

she massages her foamy scalp
with delight.
The young black-haired woman,
hearing all this
—tensed in a shoulderstand,   30
head full of new blood,
filling with new breath—
is overcome with unexpected happiness.

Each girl smiles in private
at the joyfullness of the evening   35
& at the music & the men, wishing
it would never end

                                        Al Young, 1939–

IN THE WAITING ROOM

In Worcester, Massachusetts,
I went with Aunt Consuelo
to keep her dentist's appointment
and sat and waited for her
in the dentist's waiting room.   5
It was winter. It got dark
early. The waiting room
was full of grown-up people,
arctics and overcoats,
lamps and magazines.   10
My aunt was inside
what seemed like a long time
and while I waited I read
the *National Geographic*
(I could read) and carefully   15
studied the photographs:
the inside of a volcano,
black, and full of ashes;
then it was spilling over
in rivulets of fire.   20

Osa and Martin Johnson
dressed in riding breeches,
laced boots, and pith helmets.
A dead man slung on a pole
—"Long Pig," the caption said.   25
Babies with pointed heads

wound round and round with string;
black, naked women with necks
wound round and round with wire
like the necks of light bulbs.   30
Their breasts were horrifying.
I read it right straight through.
I was too shy to stop.
And then I looked at the cover:
the yellow margins, the date.   35

Suddenly, from inside,
came an *oh!* of pain
—Aunt Consuelo's voice—
not very loud or long.
I wasn't at all surprised;   40
even then I knew she was
a foolish, timid woman.
I might have been embarrassed,
but wasn't. What took me
completely by surprise   45
was that it was *me*:
my voice, in my mouth.
Without thinking at all
I was my foolish aunt,
I—we—were falling, falling,   50
our eyes glued to the cover
of the *National Geographic*,
February, 1918.

I said to myself: three days
and you'll be seven years old.   55
I was saying it to stop
the sensation of falling off
the round, turning world
into cold, blue-black space.
But I felt: you are an *I*,   60
you are an *Elizabeth*,
you are one of *them*.
Why should you be one, too?
I scarcely dared to look
to see what it was I was.   65
I gave a sidelong glance
—I couldn't look any higher—
at shadowy gray knees,
trousers and skirts and boots
and different pairs of hands   70

lying under the lamps.
I knew that nothing stranger
had ever happened, that nothing
stranger could ever happen.
Why should I be my aunt,   75
or me, or anyone?
What similarities—
boots, hands, the family voice
I felt in my throat, or even
the *National Geographic*   80
and those awful hanging breasts—
held us all together
or made us all just one?
How—I didn't know any
word for it—how "unlikely" . . .   85
How had I come to be here,
like them, and overhear
a cry of pain that could have
got loud and worse but hadn't?

The waiting room was bright   90
and too hot. It was sliding
beneath a big black wave,
another, and another.

Then I was back in it.
The War was on. Outside,   95
in Worcester, Massachusetts,
were night and slush and cold,
and it was still the fifth
of February, 1918.

Elizabeth Bishop, 1911–1979

Catalogue

Many poems are simply someone's list of ideas, emotions, events,
objects, or whatever. Lists—even someone else's grocery list you find
in the basket of your shopping cart—are intriguing and appealing. We
respond to the possibility of order. Once we list something, we name
it, and naming is one of the writer's passions. As poet Richard Wilbur
says "the itch to call the roll of things" almost always expresses "a
longing to possess the whole world, and to praise it, or at least to feel
it." "Free Union" (page 494) is a catalogue poem, as are "Saying

Things" by Marilyn Krysl (page 38), "Lucky Life" and "If You Saw
Me Walking" by Gerald Stern (page 245 and page 224). You will come
across this mode when you read the Bible's genealogical lists, Milton's
list of fallen angles in *Paradise Lost*, and Vergil's hero lists in *The
Aeneid*. Dip anywhere into Whitman's poetry to experience the cumulative effect of this approach to building a poem.

MANNAHATTA

I was asking for something specific and perfect for my city, and behold!
    here is the aboriginal name!
Now I see what there is in a name, a word, liquid, sane, unruly,
    musical, self-sufficient,
I see that the word of my city, is that word up there,
Because I see that word nested in nests of water-bays, superb, with tall
    and wonderful spires,
Rich, hemmed thick all around with sailships and steamships—an island
    sixteen miles long, solid-founded,
Numberless crowded streets—high growths of iron, slender, strong,
    light, splendidly uprising toward clear skies;
Tides swift and ample, well-loved by me, toward sundown,
The flowing sea-currents, the little islands, the larger adjoining islands,
    the heights, the villas,
The countless masts, the white shore-steamers, the lighters, the ferry-
    boats, the black sea-steamers, well-model'd;
The down-town streets, the jobbers' houses of business—the houses of
    business of the ship-merchants, and money-brokers—the river-streets,
Immigrants arriving, fifteen or twenty thousand in a week,
The carts hauling goods—the manly race of drivers of horses—the
    brown-faced sailors,
The summer-air, the bright sun shining, and the sailing clouds aloft,
The winter snows, the sleigh-bells—the broken ice in the river, passing
    along, up or down, with the flood-tide or ebb-tide;
The mechanics of the city, the masters, well-formed, beautiful-faced,
    looking you straight in the eyes;
Trottoirs[1] thronged—vehicles—Broadway—the women—the shops and
    shows,
The parades, processions, bugles playing, flags flying, drums beating;
A million people—manners free and superb—open voices—
    hospitality—the most courageous and friendly young men;
The free city! no slaves! no owners of slaves!

---

[1] *Trottoir:* a paved footway.

The beautiful city! the city of hurried and sparkling waters! the city of
   spires and masts!
The city nested in bays! my city!
The city of such women, I am mad to be with them! I will return after
   death to be with them!
The city of such young men, I swear I cannot live happy, without I
   often go talk, walk, eat, drink, sleep, with them!

Walt Whitman, 1819–1892

Exaggeration

Exaggeration by overstatement, **understatement,** or comparison fuels
poems with humor and/or surprise. Exaggeration by overstatement is
called **hyperbole.** Hyperbolic figures of speech are common: I slept for
a month, I could eat a horse, he's old as the hills, it's going to snow
forever. In Sonnet CXXX, Shakespeare makes fun of the conventional
exaggerated comparisons made in love poems.

SONNET CXXX

My mistress' eyes are nothing like the sun;
Coral is far more red than her lips' red;
If snow be white, why then her breasts are dun;
If hairs be wires, black wires grow on her head.
I have seen roses damasked,[1] red and white,   5
But no such roses see I in her cheeks;
And in some perfumes is there more delight
Than in the breath that from my mistress reeks.
I love to hear her speak, yet well I know
That music hath a far more pleasing sound;   10
I grant I never saw a goddess go;
My mistress, when she walks, treads on the ground.
And yet, by heaven, I think my love as rare
As any she belied with false compare.

William Shakespeare, 1564–1616

[1] *damasked:* variegated.

Special Knowledge

To understand some poems, the reader needs special knowledge. The
poet may use many foreign phrases or a web of allusions not commonly

recognized. Some poems are written in reply to another poem, perhaps from another era, and the full effect of the one at hand is lessened without knowledge of its "ancestor." Readers gain access to these poems through research.

For the next poem to make full sense, it's necessary to know that William Blake regarded philosophers Voltaire and Rousseau as mockers of faith. Democritus, a Greek philosopher, first taught that all things are made up of atoms. Blake sees Democritus and Newton, who said light was made of particles, as materialists. Blake considers all four of these men irreligious deniers of the transcendental meaning of experience. The final image refers to the children of Israel camping along the Red Sea shore when the Egyptians were pursuing them.

MOCK ON, MOCK ON, VOLTAIRE, ROUSSEAU

> Mock on, mock on, Voltaire, Rousseau:
> Mock on, mock on: 'tis all in vain!
> You throw the sand against the wind,
> And the wind blows it back again.
>
> And every sand becomes a Gem   5
> Reflected in the beams divine;
> Blown back they blind the mocking Eye,
> But still in Israel's paths they shine.
>
> The Atoms of Democritus
> And Newton's particles of light   10
> Are sands upon the Red Sea shore,
> Where Israel's tents do shine so bright.

William Blake, 1757–1828

Synthesis of the poem involves putting together everything that bears on your reading. The examples above, from Thomas's gaps to Blake's complex allusions, will raise your antennae for receiving the full range of each poem. The creative reader responds to what is outward and what is inward, what is stated and what is intuited. "What sets this poem in motion?" is one of the best questions you can ask. Exciting poetry is never just programmatic; the poet constantly surprises our expectations or pours in a secret ingredient. We read carefully and openly if we read to see what makes each poem *that* poem and no other. Similarly, poetry can't be defined or conform to rules. A poem can be a metaphysical argument, an experience of buying aspirin, a word game, or all of these. An exception pops up as soon as you've memorized a beautiful definition.

EXERCISES

1. Karl Shapiro once said of Randall Jarrell, "He was a great, you might say a dangerous, listener." What did Shapiro mean?

2. What would you say in reply to Irving Layton, quoted here from an interview in *Conjunctions #6*, 1984: "I shudder when anyone uses the phrase 'Concrete Poetry.' It has *nothing* to do with poetry. It is a word game. It's like crossword puzzles. Poetry is the passionate articulation of human experience."

3. Try writing a cataloguing poem. It might be a list of qualities you like or dislike in someone, a list of reasons for not dancing or flying. You might start with "It's not too late to. . . ." or "If you loved me you'd. . . ." or "At home, we. . . ."

4. Boustrophedon is the ancient mode of writing in which lines move from left to right then right to left. The root of the word comes from the Greek word meaning the turning of an ox while plowing a field back and forth. Trace the associations of the title through the poem. How many of the "power sources" do you pick up in "Boustrophedon?"

BOUSTROPHEDON

Whereas some poems are baskets catching falling
Things, some line up for the diving board
To add twenty-five laps to their scorecards.
This is such a poem. This is the turn this poem
Has taken. If the title is misleading, it is not
Meandering. Its point, like the needle's,
Only indicates direction to the doubled
Thread it is pulling. It might close up random
Pieces of cloth. Stitching can be satisfying
In itself. Take the anklebone broken from

Stepping in a pothole—it is mending and deserves
A crutch. When the bone ages a million years
It will be a prize for those looking. I have
Zigzagged up hills. I have read it is recommended.
Which is zig and which zag I am confused about:
How long can I zig—or zag—before zig loses
Its meaning and becomes, simply, straight line?
I would like to think I could zag all day, zag
To the mailbox, zag to the flowershop, zag home.
I have worn a furrow to the window and have three
Furrows in my forehead when I am surprised at what
I see. I do not know what the ox in the field
Is thinking, plowing on Sunday, twenty-five turns
It has memorized—better to be here than at the hecatomb[1]!
These U-turns, returns, pull the line, turn, turn the world.

Edward Kleinschmidt, 1951–

[1] *hecatomb:* in ancient Greece, a place where offerings were made to the gods. Often the sacrifice was one hundred oxen.

5.   Write a sound poem—a baby crying in traffic, the noises you hear from your window at night, the washer going through its cycles, or party music and conversation happening simultaneously.

6.   Study the three important poems that follow. Analyze craft, subject, style, voice. What other special powers (such as tension, association, or epiphany) does each have? What meanings does each have? Are there common concerns in the three?

LEDA AND THE SWAN[1]

A sudden blow: the great wings beating still
Above the staggering girl, her thighs caressed
By the dark webs, her nape caught in his bill,
He holds her helpless breast upon his breast.

[1] *Leda and the Swan:* The Greek god Zeus took the form of a swan and sexually assaulted Leda. The result was the birth of Helen of Troy from an egg. Since Helen's beauty was one of the causes of the Trojan War, her conception caused "the burning roof and tower / And Agamemnon dead." Agamemnon, Helen's brother-in-law and commander of the Greek army at Troy, was murdered after the war by Helen's sister, Clytemnestra.

How can those terrified vague fingers push   5
The feathered glory from her loosening thighs?
And how can body, laid in that white rush,
But feel the strange heart beating where it lies?

A shudder in the loins engenders there
The broken wall, the burning roof and tower   10
And Agamemnon dead.
                    Being so caught up,
So mastered by the brute blood of the air,
Did she put on his knowledge with his power
Before the indifferent beak could let her drop?   15

William Butler Yeats, 1865–1939

THE SECOND COMING

Turning and turning in the widening gyre
The falcon cannot hear the falconer;
Things fall apart; the center cannot hold;
Mere anarchy is loosed upon the world,
The blood-dimmed tide is loosed, and everywhere   5
The ceremony of innocence is drowned;
The best lack all conviction, while the worst
Are full of passionate intensity.

Surely some revelation is at hand;
Surely the Second Coming is at hand;   10
The Second Coming! Hardly are those words out
When a vast image out of *Spiritus Mundi*[1]
Troubles my sight: somewhere in sands of the desert
A shape with lion body and the head of a man,
A gaze blank and pitiless as the sun,   15
Is moving its slow thighs, while all about it
Reel shadows of the indignant desert birds.
The darkness drops again; but now I know
That twenty centuries of stony sleep
Were vexed to nightmare by a rocking cradle,   20
And what rough beast, its hour come round at last,
Slouches towards Bethlehem to be born?

William Butler Yeats, 1865–1939

---

[1] *Spiritus Mundi*: Latin for "The Spirit of the World."

AMONG SCHOOL CHILDREN

I

I walk through the long schoolroom questioning;
A kind old nun in a white hood replies;
The children learn to cipher and to sing,
To study reading-books and history,
To cut and sew, be neat in everything   5
In the best modern way—the children's eyes
In momentary wonder stare upon
A sixty-year-old smiling public man.

II

I dream of a Ledaean body,[1] bent
Above a sinking fire, a tale that she   10
Told of a harsh reproof, or trivial event
That changed some childish day to tragedy—
Told, and it seemed that our two natures blent
Into a sphere from youthful sympathy,
Or else, to alter Plato's parable,   15
Into the yolk and white of the one shell.[2]

III

And thinking of that fit of grief or rage
I look upon one child or t'other there
And wonder if she[3] stood so at that age—
For even daughters of the swan can share   20
Something of every paddler's heritage—
And had that colour upon cheek or hair,
And thereupon my heart is driven wild:
She stands before me as a living child.

---

[1] *Ledaean body:* a body like Leda's. See "Leda and the Swan." Yeats is thinking of a woman he loved who told him stories of her school days.
[2] *Plato's . . . shell:* In the parable, man and woman were once inseparable and travelled about as a large egg with four legs and arms. The gods were jealous and split them. Ever since, each man and woman has searched for his or her other half.
[3] *she:* refers to the woman he loved.

IV

Her present image floats into the mind—   25
Did Quattrocento[4] finger fashion it
Hollow of cheek as though it drank the wind
And took a mess of shadows for its meat?
And I though never of Ledaean kind
Had pretty plumage once—enough of that,   30
Better to smile on all that smile, and show
There is a comfortable kind of old scarecrow.

V

What youthful mother, a shape upon her lap
Honey of generation had betrayed,
And that must sleep, shriek, struggle to escape   35
As recollection or the drug decide,
Would think her son, did she but see that shape
With sixty or more winters on its head,
A compensation for the pang of his birth,
Or the uncertainty of his setting forth?   40

VI

Plato thought nature but a spume that plays
Upon a ghostly paradigm of things;
Solider Aristotle played the taws[5]
Upon the bottom of a king of kings;[6]
World-famous golden-thighed Pythagoras[7]   45
Fingered upon a fiddle-stick or strings
What a star sang and careless Muses heard:
Old clothes upon old sticks to scare a bird.

VII

Both nuns and mothers worship images,
But those the candles light are not as those   50
That animate a mother's reveries,

---

[4] *Quattrocento:* the 1400s, an era of great art in Italy.
[5] *taws:* straps.
[6] *Aristotle . . . kings:* Aristotle was the tutor of Alexander the Great.
[7] *Pythagoras:* sixth-century mathematician, musician, thinker. He was reputed to have a golden bone in his thigh.

But keep a marble or a bronze repose.
And yet they too break hearts—O Presences
That passion, piety or affection knows,
And that all heavenly glory symbolise—   55
O self-born mockers of man's enterprise;

VIII

Labour is blossoming or dancing where
The body is not bruised to pleasure soul,
Nor beauty born out of its own despair,
Nor blear-eyed wisdom out of midnight oil.   60
O chestnut-tree, great-rooted blossomer,
Are you the leaf, the blossom or the bole?
O body swayed to music, O brightening glance,
How can we know the dancer from the dance?

William Butler Yeats, 1865–1939

Critical Discriminations

To Coleridge's ideal for poetry—"The best words in the best order"—let's add "with the best mind and imagination writing them." Good poems are greater than the sum of their parts. New readings continue to pay off.

A good poem has the right craft elements working along with an energy, that mysterious X, which makes the poem a world. What works stands out immediately. We've sharpened our discrimination as readers by recognizing all that makes a poem good. It is also valuable to look at how poems fall short, become static and boring, or just grate our nerves by being sentimental or predictable.

Anyone who has read thus far probably doesn't need to hear about the inadequacy of a poem beginning, "It takes a heap o' living in a house t' make it home." Such an opening forbodes a list of clichés and homilies. If a poem verges toward greeting-card sentiment or is riddled with flaws such as love/dove-moon/June-true/blue rhymes, the one question "Is this new?" settles its worth. You may hear that "good poetry is memorable," but being memorable guarantees nothing about quality. "O retard not my motion / For I'm going to the ocean" sticks in the mind and also in the craw.

George Orwell wrote:

> A good bad poem is a graceful monument to the obvious. It records in memorable form—for verse is a mnemonic device, among other things—some emotion which nearly every human being can share. The merit of a poem like "When all the World is Young, Lad" is that, however sentimental it may be, its sentiment is "true" sentiment in the sense that you are bound to find yourself thinking the thought it expresses sooner or later. . . . Such poems are a kind of rhyming proverb.

The good bad poems Orwell described lack intensity or originality. The poet was too easily content. An experimental writer such as Gertrude Stein might proclaim, "If it can be done, why do it?" As readers we might say, "If it *has* been done over and over, why indeed?"

I won't waste space by reprinting much obviously terrible poetry. You can spot inappropriate forms, lame language, clichés, galloping or sing-song rhythms, weak imagery, and worn metaphors. More valuable to study are **"second-intensity"** poems—that is, poetry which could have been better.

What qualities make a poem just miss? In Ernest Dowson's "Cynara" (page 428), we almost can hear mournful violins tuning up. The lover maintains over and over that he has been true in his fashion to Cynara. His "fashion" was to be wildly unfaithful in reality but to hold onto the illusion of Cynara. (Another reality/illusion romantic, Margaret Mitchell, took her famous title *Gone With the Wind* from Dowson's poem.)

Something is out of balance in Dowson's poem. Something keeps the reader from responding fully. Perhaps the poet seems to be tearing his shirt, gesturing. Drama moves just slightly over the edge into melodrama. Our red flags go up. Just a few stanzas in, we start to say to ourselves, "Now, Ernest, you're bragging." So why do we respond strongly anyway? The force of his passion does come through. Perhaps the reader had a similar experience and wants to overlook the melodrama. The poem is not "a graceful monument to the obvious." Dowson had originality, verve. Writing at the tag-end of the reign of Victorian sensibility, he shocked readers somewhat. Readers now cannot experience that shock.

Melodrama: a tempest in a teapot. It's a dangerous quality for a poem. (Emerson said his idea of heaven was a place with no melodrama.) We don't like to be over-convinced. In Dowson's poem we have little imaginative room to act.

The blood relative of melodrama is **sentimentality**. Because poems often deal with emotions, they constantly risk becoming sentimental. Where is the balance between good poetry and simply getting something off one's chest? Sentimentality is a kneejerk emotion. The passion goes purple. You can see that the poet may indeed feel such emotion, but *you* certainly have no reason to. James Joyce defined sentimentality as "unearned emotion." The writer assumes you agree and does not trouble to present the individual case. The sure sign of sentimentality is oversimplification. Watery nostalgia or pure corniness result. "Somebody's Darling," popular during the Civil War, batters out its one message over and over. The author manages to top melodrama with sentimentality.

SOMEBODY'S DARLING

Into a ward of the whitewashed halls,
   Where the dead and dying lay,
Wounded by bayonets, shells, and balls,
   Somebody's darling was borne one day—
Somebody's darling, so young and so brave,   5
   Wearing yet on his pale, sweet face,
Soon to be hid by the dust of the grave,
   The lingering light of his boyhood's grace.

Matted and damp are the curls of gold
   Kissing the snow of his fair, young brow;   10
Pale are the lips of delicate mold,
   Somebody's darling is dying now.
Back from his beautiful blue-veined brow,
   Brush all the wandering waves of gold,
Cross his hands on his bosom now—   15
   Somebody's darling is stiff and cold.

Kiss him once for somebody's sake,
   Murmur a prayer soft and low;
One bright curl from its fair mates take—
   They were somebody's pride, you know.   20
Somebody's hand has rested there:
   Was it mother's soft and white?
Or had the lips of a sister fair
   Been baptized in their waves of light?

God knows best! He has somebody's love,   25
    Somebody's heart enshrined him there,
Somebody wafted his name above,
    Night and morn, on the wings of prayer.
Somebody wept when he marched away,
    Looking so handsome, brave and grand!   30
Somebody's kiss on his forehead lay,
    Somebody clung to his parting hand.

Somebody's watching and waiting for him,
    Yearning to hold him again to her heart;
And there he lies with his blue eyes dim,   35
    And his smiling, child-like lips apart.
Tenderly bury the fair young dead,
    Pausing to drop on his grave a tear;
Carve on the wooden slab at his head,
    "Somebody's darling slumbers here!"   40

Marie LaCoste, 1840?–1936

EXERCISE

The craft and emotion in the next two poems are more complex and developed. Discuss the conclusions of both. Are they earned by the poem or do we seem expected to agree? What qualities make these "second intensity" poems? Are you still moved by either? Why?

THE SECOND WIFE

She knows, being woman, that for him she holds
The space kept for the second blossoming,
Unmixed with dreams, held tightly in the folds
Of the accepted and long-proper thing—
She, duly loved; and he, proud of her looks   5
Shy of her wit. And of that other she knows
She had a slim throat, a nice taste in books,
And grew petunias in squat garden rows.
Thus knowing all, she feels both safe and strange;
Safe in his life, of which she has a share;   10
Safe in her undisturbed, cool, equal place,
In the sweet commonness that will not change;
And strange, when, at the door, in the spring air,
She hears him sigh, old Aprils in his face.

Lizette Reese, 1856–1935

PIANO

Softly, in the dusk, a woman is singing to me;
Taking me back down the vista of years, till I see
A child sitting under the piano, in the boom of the tingling strings
And pressing the small, poised feet of a mother who smiles as she sings.

In spite of myself, the insidious mastery of song   5
Betrays me back, till the heart of me weeps to belong
To the old Sunday evenings at home, with winter outside
And hymns in the cosy parlour, the tinkling piano our guide.

So now it is vain for the singer to burst into clamour
With the great black piano appassionato. The glamour   10
Of childish days is upon me, my manhood is cast
Down in the flood of remembrance, I weep like a child for the past.

D. H. Lawrence, 1885–1930

Six Danger Signals

Sentimentality and melodrama are two of the worst offenders in a poem. Watch for these more subtle problems also.

1. Redundant **syntax** *can* make a poem static and monotonous. If too many sentences begin the same way—"I saw . . ." "I told . . ." "I felt . . ." "I went . . ."—the poem can begin to plod. Just as in prose, the syntax of a poem generally needs to be varied. The form of sentences has a psychological effect. If that form repeats, it should be a conscious repetition for a desired effect. For instance, choosing all declarative sentences imparts an authoritative tone. Using many modifying phrases and prepositions imparts a softness, perhaps qualifying the subject. If the writer unthinkingly uses thirteen compound sentences in a short poem about speed, the syntax is at war with the subject.

2. Not enough "muscle" in the language. Too much use of nonspecific designators (*these*, *this*, *it*) blurs effect, as do too many passive verbs or strings of adjectives and adverbs. The misuse of the preposition *of* is especially "flabby." Some writers get into the habit of letting *of* name a metaphor without really *showing* the image to the reader: sea of life, mattress of the soul, river of death, crops of grief, raven of anguish, tiger of desire, moon of loss, rose of forget-

fulness, or (perhaps the worst) briefcase of sorrow. A single concrete noun can't carry an abstract word over into an image. This is a weak construction which, if overused, can fade the language of a poem into white noise.

3. Lack of movement from beginning to end. We feel the poem running in place. Not enough happens. The poet writes more than the subject warranted. Our interest ends before the poem does.

4. **Overwriting** puts words out of balance with their content. Hopkins constantly *risks* this. His results dazzle us while others' runaway experiments merely daze us. To over-describe gives a poem a topheavy feeling: "The stark green pines against the swirling gray clouds on a late fall day." A series of double modifiers bogs down the sound as well as the sense. Note the following detrimental overuse of imagery. Too much imagery becomes absurd. The subject gets hidden.

THE QUARREL

Rolling down the lane like waves in an angry sea
we outdistance our words in tosses of hair and chin.
Stirring the rust of misunderstanding
with large sticks of silence, we each
are prisoners in the other's eyes.   5
Our mouths squeezing out words like lemon pips,
lips sour with the juice of the unspoken.
Our steps
            are distant echoes.
We pace, we stare up at the blue illusion and   10
only our eyes reflect sparks of expectation.

5. Decorum can go awry. **Decorum** is the writer's instinct for appropriate form, subject, and language. Louise Bogan wrote to another poet reprimanding her for using the word *kitty* in a poem. Bogan insisted that one should say "cat." "Kitty" violated her sense of decorum. In his poem on Lord Hasting's death from smallpox, Dryden loses all sense of decorum:

Was there no milder way but the Small Pox,
The very Filth'ness of *Pandora's Box*?
So many Spots, like *naeves*,[1] our Venus soil?
One Jewel set off with so many a Foil?
Blisters with pride swell'd; which th'row's flesh did sprout   5
Like Rose-buds, stuck i' th' Lily-skin about.
Each little Pimple had a Tear on it,
To wail the fault its rising did commit:
Who, Rebel-like, with their own Lord at strife,
Thus made an insurrection 'gainst his Life.   10
Or were these Gems sent to adorn his Skin,
The Cab'net of a richer Soul within?

[1] *naeves:* blemishes.

6.   *Moralism* can run around a well-intentioned poem. Tidy moral
     summations tacked on the end mar the reader's sense of participa-
     tion. We feel force-fed if a poem seems to say, "And the moral of
     this story is. . . ." Some writers mount a soapbox. The "Take this,
     it's good for you" attitude produces sermons, not poetry. When
     the poet has a political or **didactic** purpose—that is, when the poem
     teaches—the best strategy is to show the situation rather than
     instruct from on high. In Randall Jarrell's "Protocols" (page 185),
     for instance, the subject is the gassing of children in concentration
     camps. By letting the two children speak for themselves, Jarrell
     allows the reader to "overhear" them. His choice of first-person
     speakers gives immediacy to the situation. Probably he made this
     choice in order to avoid *describing* the children of the Holocaust.
     He might have wanted to make a moral point but knew that he had
     nothing new to comment on. Poets don't want to repeat. Through
     Jarrell's choice of speakers, we hear something new in this poem:
     that possibly the children regarded the journey to the camps as an
     adventure. Their perspective increases our awareness of their
     tragic deaths. We do not have Jarrell looking at the children but
     the children speaking for themselves. The poet knew that their
     voices would speak more clearly than his.

EXERCISES

1. Read "Soldiers Bathing" by F. T. Prince (page 386) and "Dover Beach" by Matthew Arnold (page 338), two successful poems dealing with moral issues. Analyze and compare the strategies of these poems.

2. Compare Gogarty's version of the Leda myth with Yeats's "Leda and the Swan" (page 505). What language in Gogarty's poem would you not find in Yeats's? Where is there humor in Gogarty's version? Compare the questions asked in each poem. Does Gogarty's poem fall into any of the dangers discussed above?

LEDA AND THE SWAN

Though her Mother told her
　　Not to go a-bathing,
Leda loved the river
　　And she could not keep away:
Wading in its freshets　　　　　　　　　　　　5
　　When the noon was heavy;
Walking by the water
　　At the close of day.

Where between its waterfalls,
　　Underneath the beeches,　　　　　　　　　10
Gently flows a broader
　　Hardly moving stream,
And the balanced trout lie
　　In the quiet reaches;
Taking all her clothes off,　　　　　　　　　15
　　Leda went to swim.

There was not a flag-leaf
　　By the river's margin
That might be a shelter
　　From a passer-by;　　　　　　　　　　　20
And a sudden whiteness
　　In the quiet darkness,
Let alone the splashing,
　　Was enough to catch an eye.

But the place was lonely,   25
    And her clothes were hidden;
Even cattle walking
    In the ford had gone away;
Every single farm-hand
    Sleeping after dinner,—   30
What's the use of talking?
    There was no one in the way.

In, without a stitch on,
    Peaty water yielded,
Till her head was lifted   35
    With its ropes of hair;
It was more surprising
    Than a lily gilded,
Just to see how golden
    Was her body there: 40

Lolling in the water,
    Lazily uplifting
Limbs that on the surface
    Whitened into snow;
Leaning on the water,   45
    Indolently drifting,
Hardly any faster
    Than the foamy bubbles go.

You would say to see her
    Swimming in the lonely   50
Pool, or after, dryer,
    Putting on her clothes:
"O but she is lovely,
    Not a soul to see her,
And how lovely only   55
    Leda's Mother knows!"

Under moving branches
    Leisurely she dresses,
And the leafy sunlight
    Made you wonder were   60
All its woven shadows
    But her golden tresses,
Or a smock of sunlight
    For her body bare.

When on earth great beauty   65
    Goes exempt from danger,
It will be endangered
    From a source on high:
When unearthly stillness
    Falls on leaves, the ranger,   70
In his wood-lore anxious,
    Gazes at the sky.

While her hair was drying,
    Came a gentle languor,
Whether from the bathing   75
    Or the breeze she didn't know.
Anyway she lay there,
    And her Mother's anger
(Worse if she had wet hair)
    Could not make her dress and go.   80

Whitest of all earthly
    Things, the white that's rarest,
Is the snow on mountains
    Standing in the sun;
Next to the clouds above them,   85
    Then the down is fairest
On the breast and pinions
    Of a proudly sailing swan.

And she saw him sailing
    On the pool where lately   90
She had stretched unnoticed,
    As she thought, and swum;
And she never wondered
    Why, erect and stately,
Where no river weed was   95
    Such a bird had come.

What was it she called him:
    Goosey-goosey gander?
For she knew no better
    Way to call a swan;   100
And the bird responding
    Seemed to understand her,
For he left his sailing
    For the bank to waddle on.

Apple blossoms under 105
    Hills of Lacedaemon,
With the snow beyond them
    In the still blue air,
To the swan who hid them
    With his wings asunder, 110
Than the breasts of Leda,
    Were not lovelier!

Of the tales that daughters
    Tell their poor old mothers,
Which by all accounts are 115
    Often very odd;
Leda's was a story
    Stranger than all others.
What was there to say but:
    Glory be to God? 120

And she half-believed her,
    For she knew her daughter;
And she saw the swan-down
    Tangled in her hair.
Though she knew how deeply 125
    Runs the stillest water,
How could she protect her
    From the wingèd air?

Why is it effects are
    Greater than their causes? 130
Why should causes often
    Differ from effects?
Why should what is lovely
    Fill the world with harness?
And the most deceived be 135
    She who least suspects?

When the hyacinthine
    Eggs were in the basket,
Blue as at the whiteness
    Where a cloud begins; 140
Who would dream there lay there
    All that Trojan brightness;
Agamemnon murdered;
    And the mighty Twins?

       Oliver St. John Gogarty, 1878–1957

3. What advice does Niedecker offer? How might you apply this to reading poetry?

from NORTH CENTRAL

consider at the outset:
to be thin for thought
or thick cream blossomy

Many things are better
flavored with bacon

Sweet Life, My love:
didn't you ever try
this delicacy—the marrow
in the bone?

And don't be afraid
to pour wine over cabbage

Lorine Niedecker, 1903–1970

Poems for Discussion

WHAT IS POETRY

The medieval town, with frieze
Of boy scouts from Nagoya? The snow

That came when we wanted it to snow?
Beautiful images? Trying to avoid

Ideas, as in this poem? But we
Go back to them as to a wife, leaving

The mistress we desire? Now they
Will have to believe it

As we believe it. In school
All the thought got combed out:

What was left was like a field.
Shut your eyes, and you can feel it for miles around.

Now open them on a thin vertical path.
It might give us—what?—some flowers soon?

John Ashbery, 1927–

CHORUS SACERDOTUM[1]

Oh, wearisome condition of humanity,
Born under one law, to another bound;
Vainly begot, and yet forbidden vanity,
Created sick, commanded to be sound.
What meaneth nature by these diverse laws?   5
Passion and reason self-division cause.
It is the mark or majesty of power
To make offenses that it may forgive.
Nature herself doth her own self deflower,
To hate those errors she herself doth give.   10
For how should man think that he may not do,
If nature did not fail and punish too?
Tyrant to others, to herself unjust,
Only commands things difficult and hard,
Forbids us all things which it knows is lust,   15
Makes easy pains, unpossible reward.
If nature did not take delight in blood,
She would have made more easy ways to good.
We that are bound by vows and by promotion,
With pomp of holy sacrifice and rites,   20
To teach belief in God and still devotion,
To preach of heaven's wonders and delights—
Yet when each of us in his own heart looks
He finds the God there far unlike his books.

Fulke Greville, Lord Brooke, 1554–1628

[1] *Chorus Sacerdotum:* priest's chorus.

ETHICS

In ethics class so many years ago
our teacher asked this question every fall:
if there were a fire in a museum
which would you save, a Rembrandt painting
or an old woman who hadn't many   5
years left anyhow? Restless on hard chairs
caring little for pictures or old age
we'd opt one year for life, the next for art
and always half-heartedly. Sometimes
the woman borrowed my grandmother's face   10
leaving her usual kitchen to wander
some drafty, half imagined museum.
One year, feeling clever, I replied
why not let the woman decide herself?
Linda, the teacher would report, eschews   15
the burdens of responsibility.
This fall in a real museum I stand
before a real Rembrandt, old woman,
or nearly so, myself. The colors
within this frame are darker than autumn,   20
darker even than winter—the browns of earth,
though earth's most radiant elements burn
through the canvas. I know now that woman
and painting and season are almost one
and all beyond saving by children.   25

Linda Pastan, 1932–

THE FLOATING CANDLES

For my brother Mahlon (1944–1980)

You lit a firebrand:
old pine was best.
It lasted, the black
pitch fume cast odors
that, kindling a campfire   5
or such, today
can bring tears. You held
the torch to one dwarf
candle stub then another
and others till each   10
greased cup filled up

and the stiff wicks stood.
Ten minutes a candle,
but we were young
and minutes seemed long   15
as the whole vacation.
We chafed and quarreled.
The colors bled
like hues in jewels.
At last we carried   20
a tub of the things
down the path to the Swamp
Creek pond through seed-
heavy meadows where katydids
whined like wires   25
in mid-August air's
dense atmosphere.
An hour before bedtime.
Reluctant grownups
would trail behind,   30
bearing downhill
the same dull patter
and cups brimful
of rye, which they balanced
with the same rapt care   35
that balanced our load.
The bullfrogs twanged
till you touched a wick
with the stick, still flaming,
then quieted. We heard them   40
plop in the shallows,
deferring to fire,
and heard in the muck
turtles coasting in flight.
The night brought on   45
a small breeze to clear
the day that all day
had oppressed us, to dry
the sweat that our purposeful
hour had made,   50
to spread the glims
like dreamboats of glory
in invisible current.
That slow tug drew
the glowing flotilla   55
south to the dam.
The bank brush—hung
with gemmy bugs—shone
and made great shadows

as the candles slipped by,   60
erasing the banal
fat stars from the surface.
This was, you could say,
an early glimpse
of a later aesthetic.   65
Nonsense. We know
it was cruder than that
and profounder, far.
It showed us the way
the splendid can flare   70
despite the flow
of the common. Now,
despite the persistence
of heat and quarrel,
the thickness of wives   75
and children and time,
such shinings on water
are fact. Or sublime.

Sydney Lea, 1942–

TWO YEARS LATER

The hollow eyes of shock remain
Electric sockets burnt out in the skull.

The beauty of men never disappears
But drives a blue car through the
                                    stars.   5

John Wieners, 1934–

THE WORLD SO WIDE

The worlde so wide, th'air so remuable,°	*changeable*
The sely° man so litel of stature,	*helpless*
The grove and ground of clothing so mutable,[1]	
The fire so hot and subtil of nature,	
5 The water never in oon°—what creature,	*the same*
That made is of these foure thus flitting,	
May stedfast be as here in his living?	

---

[1] *grove . . . mutable:* trees and earth so variable in their clothing.

The more I go the ferther I am behinde,
  The ferther behind the neer° my wayes ende;   *nearer*
10 The more I seche° the worse can I finde,   *seek*
  The lighter leve the lother for to wende;[2]
  The bet° I serve the more al out of mende.°   *better, mind*
Is this fortune—n'ot I°—or infortune?   *I know not*
Though I go loose, tied am I with a lune.°   *leash*

Anonymous, fifteenth century

[2] *The lighter . . . wende:* The easier the leaving the more loathe to go.

NOT WAVING BUT DROWNING

Nobody heard him, the dead man,
But still he lay moaning:
I was much further out than you thought
And not waving but drowning.

Poor chap, he always loved larking   5
And now he's dead
It must have been too cold for him his heart gave way,
They said.

Oh, no no no, it was too cold always
(Still the dead one lay moaning)   10
I was much too far out all my life
And not waving but drowning.

Stevie Smith, 1902–1971

HOT SUN, COOL FIRE

Hot sun, cool fire, tempered with sweet air,
Black shade, fair nurse, shadow my white hair.
Shine, sun; burn, fire; breathe, air, and ease me;
Black shade, fair nurse, shroud me and please me.
Shadow, my sweet nurse, keep me from burning;   5
Make not my glad cause cause of mourning.
    Let not my beauty's fire
    Inflame unstaid desire,
    Nor pierce any bright eye
    That wandereth lightly.   10

George Peele, 1557–1596

BOY RIDING FORWARD BACKWARD

Presto, pronto! Two boys, two horses.
But the boy on backward riding forward
Is the boy to watch.

He rides the forward horse and laughs
In the face of the forward boy on the backward   5
Horse, and *he* laughs

Back and the horses laugh. They gallop.
The trick is the cool barefaced pretense
There is no trick.

They might be flying, face to face,   10
On a fast train. They might be whitecaps
Hot-cool-headed,

One curling backward, one curving forward,
Racing a rivalry of waves.
They might, they might—   15

Across a blue lake, through trees,
And half a mile away I caught them:
Two boys, two horses.

Through trees and through binoculars
Sweeping for birds. Oh, they were birds   20
All right, all right.

Swallows that weave and wave and sweep
And skim and swoop and skitter until
The last trees take them.

Robert Francis, 1901–1987

ADAM'S CURSE

We sat together at one summer's end,
That beautiful mild woman, your close friend,
And you and I, and talked of poetry.
I said, "A line will take us hours maybe;
Yet if it does not seem a moment's thought,   5

Our stitching and unstitching has been naught.
Better go down upon your marrow-bones
And scrub a kitchen pavement, or break stones

Like an old pauper, in all kinds of weather;
For to articulate sweet sounds together   10
Is to work harder than all these, and yet
Be thought an idler by the noisy set
Of bankers, schoolmasters, and clergymen
The martyrs call the world."

                  And thereupon   15
That beautiful mild woman for whose sake
There's many a one shall find out all heartache
On finding that her voice is sweet and low
Replied, "To be born woman is to know—
Although they do not talk of it at school—   20
That we must labor to be beautiful."

I said, "It's certain there is no fine thing
Since Adam's fall but needs much laboring.
There have been lovers who thought love should be
So much compounded of high courtesy   25
That they would sigh and quote with learned looks
Precedents out of beautiful old books;
Yet now it seems an idle trade enough."

We sat grown quiet at the name of love;
We saw the last embers of daylight die,   30
And in the trembling blue-green of the sky
A moon, worn as if it had been a shell
Washed by time's waters as they rose and fell
About the stars and broke in days and years.

I had a thought for no one's but your ears: 35
That you were beautiful, and that I strove
To love you in the old high way of love;
That it had all seemed happy, and yet we'd grown
As weary-hearted as that hollow moon.

William Butler Yeats, 1865–1939

HARLEM SWEETIES

Have you dug the spill
Of Sugar Hill?[1]
Cast your gims
On this sepia thrill:
Brown sugar lassie,   5
Caramel treat,
Honey-gold baby
Sweet enough to eat.
Peach-skinned girlie,
Coffee and cream,   10
Chocolate darling
Out of a dream.
Walnut tinted
Or cocoa brown,
Pomegranate-lipped   15
Pride of the town.
Rich cream-colored
To plum-tinted black,
Feminine sweetness
In Harlem's no lack.   20
Glow of the quince
To blush of the rose.
Persimmon bronze
To cinnamon toes.
Blackberry cordial,   25
Virginia Dare wine—
All those sweet colors
Flavor Harlem of mine!
Walnut or cocoa,
Let me repeat: 30
Caramel, brown sugar,
A chocolate treat.
Molasses taffy,
Coffee and cream,
Licorice, clove, cinnamon   35
To a honey-brown dream.
Ginger, wine-gold,
Persimmon, blackberry,
All through the spectrum
Harlem girls vary—   40

---

[1] *Sugar Hill:* a section of Harlem.

So if you want to know beauty's
Rainbow-sweet thrill,
Stroll down luscious,
Delicious, *fine* Sugar Hill.

Langston Hughes, 1902–1967

SILENT POEM

backroad	leafmold	stonewall	chipmunk	
underbrush	grapevine	woodchuck	shadblow	

woodsmoke   cowbarn   honeysuckle   woodpile
sawhorse   bucksaw   outhouse   wellsweep

backdoor   flagstone   bulkhead   buttermilk   5
candlestick   ragrug   firedog   brownbread

hilltop   outcrop   cowbell   buttercup
whetstone   thunderstorm   pitchfork   steeplebush

gristmill   millstone   cornmeal   waterwheel
watercress   buckwheat   firefly   jewelweed   10

gravestone   groundpine   windbread   bedrock
weathercock   snowfall   starlight   cockrow

Robert Francis, 1901–1987

IMAGE

Old houses were scaffolding once
          and workmen whistling.

T. E. Hulme, 1883–1917

WESTERN WIND

Western wind, when will thou blow,
   The small rain down can rain?
Christ, if my love were in my arms
   And I in my bed again!

            Anonymous, fifteenth century

THE SCRUTINY

Why should you swear I am forsworn,
   Since thine I vowed to be?
Lady, it is already morn,
   And 'twas last night I swore to thee
That fond impossibility.   5

Have I not loved thee much and long,
   A tedious twelve hours' space?
I must all other beauties wrong,
   And rob thee of a new embrace,
Could I still dote upon thy face.   10

Not but all joy in thy brown hair
   By others may be found;
But I must search the black and fair,
   Like skillful mineralists that sound
For treasure in unplowed-up ground.   15

Then, if when I have loved my round,
   Thou prov'st the pleasant she,
With spoils of meaner beauties crowned
   I laden will return to thee,
Ev'n sated with variety.   20

            Richard Lovelace, 1618–1657

THE NYMPH'S REPLY TO THE SHEPHERD[1]

If all the world and love were young,
And truth in every shepherd's tongue,
These pretty pleasures might me move
To live with thee and be thy love.

Time drives the flocks from field to fold   5
When rivers rage and rocks grow cold,
And Philomel[2] becometh dumb;
The rest complains of cares to come.

The flowers do fade, and wanton fields
To wayward winter reckoning yields;   10
A honey tongue, a heart of gall,
Is fancy's spring, but sorrow's fall.

Thy gowns, thy shoes, thy beds of roses,
Thy cap, thy kirtle,[3] and thy posies
Soon break, soon wither, soon forgotten—   15
In folly ripe, in reason rotten.

Thy belt of straw and ivy buds,
Thy coral clasps and amber studs,
All these in me no means can move
To come to thee and be thy love.   20

But could youth last and love still breed,
Had joys no date[4] nor age no need,
Then these delights my mind might move
To live with thee and be thy love.

Sir Walter Raleigh, 1552–1618

---

[1] *The Nymph's Reply to the Shepherd:* see "The Passionate Shepherd To his Love" by
Christopher Marlowe (page 157).
[2] *Philomel:* nightingale.
[3] *kirtle:* a long undergarment.
[4] *date:* ending.

KUBLA KHAN

In Xanadu did Kubla Khan
A stately pleasure-dome decree:
Where Alph, the sacred river, ran
Through caverns measureless to man
　　Down to a sunless sea.   5
So twice five miles of fertile ground
With walls and towers were girdled round:
And there were gardens bright with sinuous rills,
Where blossomed many an incense-bearing tree;
And here were forests ancient as the hills,   10
Enfolding sunny spots of greenery.
But oh! that deep romantic chasm which slanted
Down the green hill athwart a cedarn cover!
A savage place! as holy and enchanted
As e'er beneath a waning moon was haunted   15
By woman wailing for her demon-lover!
And from this chasm, with ceaseless turmoil seething,
As if this earth in fast thick pants were breathing,
A mighty fountain momently was forced:
Amid whose swift half-intermitted burst   20
Huge fragments vaulted like rebounding hail,
Or chaffy grain beneath the thresher's flail:
And 'mid these dancing rocks at once and ever
It flung up momently the sacred river
Five miles meandering with a mazy motion   25
Through wood and dale the sacred river ran,
Then reached the caverns measureless to man,
And sank in tumult to a lifeless ocean:
And 'mid this tumult Kubla heard from far
Ancestral voices prophesying war!   30
　　The shadow of the dome of pleasure
　　Floated midway on the waves;
　　Where was heard the mingled measure
　　From the fountain and the caves.
It was a miracle of rare device,   35
A sunny pleasure-dome with caves of ice!

　　A damsel with a dulcimer
　　In a vision once I saw:
　　It was an Abyssinian maid,
　　And on her dulcimer she played,   40
　　Singing of Mount Abora.
　　Could I revive within me
　　Her symphony and song,
　　To such a deep delight 'twould win me,

That with music loud and long,   45
I would build that dome in air,

That sunny dome! those caves of ice!
And all who heard should see them there,
And all should cry, Beware! Beware!
His flashing eyes, his floating hair!   50
Weave a circle round him thrice;
And close your eyes with holy dread,
For he on honey-dew hath fed,
And drunk the milk of Paradise.

Samuel Taylor Coleridge, 1772–1834

Note: After taking a little opium for illness, Coleridge fell asleep while reading a travel and history book. He dreamed a long, complex poem. When he woke and began to transcribe it, he was interrupted by a man from Porlock who had a message for him. After the interruption, Coleridge was unable to reconstruct the rest of the poem. "Kubla Khan" is the portion he remembered.

THOUGHTS ABOUT THE PERSON FROM PORLOCK

Coleridge received the Person from Porlock
And ever after called him a curse,
Then why did he hurry to let him in?
He could have hid in the house.

It was not right of Coleridge in fact it was wrong   5
(But often we all do wrong)
As the truth is I think he was already stuck
With Kubla Khan.

He was weeping and wailing: I am finished, finished,
I shall never write another word of it,   10
When along comes the Person from Porlock
And takes the blame for it.

It was not right, it was wrong,
But often we all do wrong.

May we enquire the name of the Person from Porlock?   15
Why, Porson, didn't you know?
He lived at the bottom of Porlock Hill
So had a long way to go,

He wasn't much in the social sense
Though his grandmother was a Warlock,   20
One of the Rutlandshire ones I fancy
And nothing to do with Porlock,

And he lived at the bottom of the hill as I said
And had a cat named Flo,
And had a cat named Flo.   25

I long for the Person from Porlock
To bring my thoughts to an end,
I am becoming impatient to see him
I think of him as a friend,

Often I look out the window   30
Often I run to the gate
I think, He will come this evening,
I think it is rather late.

I am hungry to be interrupted
For ever and ever amen   35
O Person from Porlock come quickly
And bring my thoughts to an end.

I felicitate the people who have a Person from Porlock
To break up everything and throw it away
Because then there will be nothing to keep them   40
And they need not stay.

Why do they grumble so much?
He comes like a benison
They should be glad he has not forgotten them
They might have had to go on.   45

These thoughts are depressing I know. They are depressing,
I wish I was more cheerful, it is more pleasant,
Also it is a duty, we should smile as well as submitting
To the purpose of One Above who is experimenting
With various mixtures of human character which goes best,   50
All is interesting for him it is exciting, but not for us.
There I go again. Smile, smile, and get some work to do
Then you will be practically unconscious without positively having to go.

Stevie Smith, 1902–1971

THE DEFINITION OF LOVE

My love is of a birth as rare
As 'tis for object strange and high:
It was begotten by Despair
Upon Impossibility.

Magnanimous Despair alone   5
Could show me so divine a thing,
Where feeble Hope could ne'er have flown
But vainly flapped its tinsel wing.

And yet I quickly might arrive
Where my extended soul is fixed,   10
But Fate does iron wedges drive,
And always crowds itself betwixt.

For Fate with jealous eye does see
Two perfect loves, nor lets them close:
Their union would her ruin be,   15
And her tyrannic power depose.

And therefore her decrees of steel
Us as the distant poles have placed,
(Though love's whole world on us doth wheel)
Not by themselves to be embraced,   20

Unless the giddy heaven fall,
And earth some new convulsion tear,
And, us to join, the world should all
Be cramped into a planisphere.[1]

As lines, so loves oblique may well   25
Themselves in every angle greet;
But ours, so truly parallel,
Though infinite, can never meet.

Therefore the love which us doth bind,
But fate so enviously debars,   30
Is the conjunction of the mind,
And opposition of the stars.

Andrew Marvell, 1621–1678

[1] *planisphere:* a map of a sphere on a plane.

POEMS WE CAN UNDERSTAND

If a monkey drives a car
down a colonnade facing the sea
and the palm trees to the left are tin
we don't understand it.

We want poems we can understand.   5
We want a god to lead us,
renaming the flowers and trees,
color-coding the scene,

doing bird calls for guests.
We want poems we can understand,   10
no sullen drunks making passes
next to an armadillo, no complex nothingness

amounting to a song,
no running in and out of walls
on the dry tongue of a mouse,   15
no bludgeoness, no girl, no sea that moves

with all deliberate speed, beside itself
and blue as water, inside itself and still,
no lizards on the table becoming absolute hands.
We want poetry we can understand,   20

the fingerprints on mother's dress,
pain of martyrs, scientists.
Please, no rabbit taking a rabbit
out of a yellow hat, no tattooed back

facing miles of desert, no wind.   25
We don't understand it.

Paul Hoover, 1946–

A THEOLOGICAL DEFINITION

A small room, the varnished floor
Making an L around the bed,

What is or is true as
Happiness

Windows opening on the sea,   5
The green painted railings of the balcony
Against the rock, the bushes and the sea running

George Oppen, 1908–1984

OVERLAND TO THE ISLANDS

Let's go—much as the dog goes,
intently haphazard. The
Mexican light on a day that
"smells like autumn in Connecticut"
makes iris ripples on his   5
black gleaming fur—and that too
is as one would desire—a radiance
consorting with the dance.

                         Under his feet
rocks and mud, his imagination, sniffing,   10
engaged in perceptions—dancing
edgeways, there's nothing
the dog disdains on his way,
nevertheless he
keeps moving, changing   15
pace and approach but
not direction—"every step an arrival."

Denise Levertov, 1923–

SONNET 61

Since there's no help, come let us kiss and part;
Nay, I have done, you get no more of me,
And I am glad, yea glad with all my heart
That thus so cleanly I myself can free;

Shake hands forever, cancel all our vows,   5
And when we meet at any time again,
Be it not seen in either of our brows
That we one jot of former love retain.
Now at the last gasp of love's latest breath,
When, his pulse failing, passion speechless lies,   10
When faith is kneeling by his bed of death,
And innocence is closing up his eyes,
    Now if thou wouldst, when all have given him over,
    From death to life thou mightest him yet recover.

Michael Drayton, 1563–1631

PRAY TO WHAT EARTH DOES THIS SWEET COLD BELONG

Pray to what earth does this sweet cold belong,
Which asks no duties and no conscience?
The moon goes up by leaps her cheerful path
In some far summer stratum of the sky,
While stars with their cold shine bedot her way.   5
The fields gleam mildly back upon the sky,
And far and near upon the leafless shrubs
The snow dust still emits a silver light.
Under the hedge, where drift banks are their screen,
The titmice now pursue their downy dreams,   10
As often in the sweltering summer nights
The bee doth drop asleep in the flower cup,
When evening overtakes him with his load.
By the brooksides, in the still genial night,
The more adventurous wanderer may hear   15
The crystals shoot and form, and winter slow
Increase his rule by gentlest summer means.

Henry David Thoreau, 1817–1862

A LETTER FROM THE CARIBBEAN

Breezeways in the tropics winnow the air,
Are ajar to its least breath
But hold back, in a feint of architecture,
The boisterous sun
Pouring down upon   5

The island like a cloudburst. They
slant to loft air, they curve, they screen
The wind's wild gaiety
Which tosses palm
Branches about like a marshal's plumes.   10

Within the filtered, latticed
World, where spools of shadow
Form, life and change,
The triumph of incoming air
Is that it is there,   15

Cooling and salving us. Louvers,
Trellises, vine—music also—
Shape the arboreal wind, make skeins
Of it, and a maze
To catch shade. The days   20

Are all variety, blowing;
Aswirl in a perpetual current
Of wind, shadow, sun,
I marvel at the capacity
Of memory   25

Which, in some deep pocket
Of my mind, preserves you whole—
As wind is wind, as the lion-taking
Sun is sun, you are, you stay:
Nothing is lost, nothing has blown away.   30

Barbara Howes, 1914–

THE LATE LATE SHOW

It must be judgment day
the dead
are playing tonight
flickering through the clammy hours
while the world sleeps
just me and long gone Laurel and Hardy
watching
the piano fall
down the sad decades.

Hazel Lane, 1929–

RETURN

I ask for nothing more than the old house,
those same sails of fragrant pine,
the windows tied to the green afternoon
and its whole night pounding in my pillow.

Nothing more than the calm morning,   5
the clatter of a horse with rubber shoes,
the clothes fluttering on suspended wires,
all those essences tumbling in white wine.

My children playing with the wheel of fortune,
the roses courting the adobe, doubtful,   10
the cat reading things into himself,
our grandparents resting in the shadows.

Everything still, the family sitting down,
the dead ones navigating tenderly,
you with the branch of basil reborn,   15
your silence filled with love and nostalgia.

It will always be too early for the shy elm,
the cherries will open their fragile parasol,
the street will keep track of the rains winter left
and new young couples will wander into oblivion.   20

The piano moored to its worn-out rugs,
we'll all be tangled in smiles,
I'll look in your eyes for the ring we gave away,
It will be like stroking the morning open.

The bits of glass falling out of the trees,   25
the letters we never read,
a fear of having said nothing
when a word was enough to light up the family.

We'll carry a little fire in our hands,
we'll set a sun in our chests   30
and it will be singing time.
We'll close the blinds.

Fernando Alegría, 1918–
(Translated by Stephen Kessler)

SPECIAL HANDLING

The light is four o'clock light
though it's only three   & Mediterranean
    Soon   shadows of someone's back steps
have solidified   and take on depth
        like a door you might   5
            want to enter   or
how a black dog's shadow rubs
                        the side
                            of the
                                house and   10
goes down into that same light with little hammer sounds
    On a simulated roof
            footsteps   drag against green diagonals
                        & beige
                asbestos siding (fire-proof)   15
                    because everyone worries about fire
                        sometimes
            how flame lights up the body   licks holes

Inside the house   she takes baths
        to make the fire go away   20
    The water holds   has its own   open arms
        a wet bridge under her
            carrying her forward   away from mud
    She tries for similar effects in blue pools
            though bodies do bump up   25
                against her
in the reverie of a smoothly executed
            lap in which no
                error appears in the stroke
    But in a tub   above pacific waters   you just float   30
        going nowhere
                    a boat moored inside a hill
                        with the moon stuck
            alee   & spilt wherever
                            hair's free   35
        Entering
the underground water   it will be warm
            with minerals that tattoo   their shadows beneath
        the silver rings on your fingers

But don't worry   go in   40
by the back road   and know any mud
    is just darkness getting thick

The risk is
    in stillness   to rub up against   45
that special handling light gives us

Kathleen Fraser, 1937–

NOTHING TO DECLARE

When I lived here
the zinnias were brilliant,
spring passed in walks.
One winter I wasn't so young.
I rented a house with Ann Grey   5
where she wrote a book and I could not.
Cold as we were on the mountain
we wouldn't be moved to the plain.
Afternoons with no sun
a blanket is left on the line.   10
Hearts go bad
like something open on a shelf.
If you came to hear about roosters,
iron beds, cabinets of ruby glass—
those things are long gone;   15
deepscreen porches and Sunday's buffet.
This was the school
where they taught us
the Russians send their old
to be melted down for candles.   20
If I had a daughter I'd tell her
Go far, travel lightly.
If I had a son he'd go to war
over my hard body.
Don't tell me it isn't worth the trouble   25
carrying on campaigns
for the good and the dead.
The ones I would vote for
never run. I want each and every one
to rejoice in the clotheslines   30
of the colored peoples of the earth.
Try living where you don't have to see
the sun go down.

If the hunter turns his dogs loose
on your dreams   35
start early, tell no one
get rid of the scent.

                                        C. D. Wright, 1949–

NIGHT JOURNAL

—I think of Issa,[1] a man of few words:
The world of dew
Is the world of dew.
And yet . . .
And yet . . .
                                                                      5
—Three words contain
                      all that we know for sure of the next life
Or the last one: close your eyes.
Everything else is gossip,
                      false mirrors, trick windows   10
Flashing like Dutch glass
In the undiminishable sun.

—I write it down in visible ink,
Black words that disappear when held up to the light—
I write it down   15
                      not to remember but to forget,
Words like thousands of pieces of shot film
                                 exposed to the sun.
I never see anything but the ground.

—Everyone wants to tell his story.   20
The Chinese say we live in the world of the 10,000 things,
Each of the 10,000 things
                      crying out to us
Precisely nothing,
A silence whose tune we've come to understand,   25
Words like birthmarks,
                      embolic sunsets drying behind the
                                 tongue.
If we were as eloquent,
If what we say could spread the good news the way that dogwood does,

---

[1] *Issa:* Japanese haiku poet.

Its votive candles   30
                  phosphorous and articulate in the green haze
Of spring, surely something would hear us.

—Even a chip of beauty
                  is beauty intractable in the mind,
Words the color of wind   35
Moving across the fields there
                  wind-addled and wind-sprung,
Abstracted as water glints,
The fields lion-colored and rope-colored,
As in a picture of Paradise,   40
                  the bodies languishing over the sky
Trailing their dark identities
That drift off and sieve away to the nothingness
Behind them
                  moving across the fields there   45
As words move, slowly, trailing their dark identities.

—Our words, like blown kisses, are swallowed by ghosts
Along the way,
                  their destinations bereft
In a rub of brightness unending: 50
How distant everything always is,
                            and yet how close,
Music starting to rise like smoke from under the trees.

—Birds sing an atonal row
                  unsyncopated   55
From tree to tree,
                  dew chants
Whose songs have no words
                  from tree to tree
When night puts her dark lens in,   60
One on this limb, two others back there.

—Words, like all things, are caught in their finitude.
They start here, they finish here
No matter how high they rise—
                            my judgment is that I know this   65
And never love anything hard enough
That would stamp me
                  and sink me suddenly into bliss.

Charles Wright, 1935–

DEGREES OF GRAY IN PHILIPSBURG

You might come here Sunday on a whim.
Say your life broke down. The last good kiss
you had was years ago. You walk these streets
laid out by the insane, past hotels
that didn't last, bars that did, the tortured try   5
of local drivers to accelerate their lives.
Only churches are kept up. The jail
turned 70 this year. The only prisoner
is always in, not knowing what he's done.

The principal supporting business now   10
is rage. Hatred of the various grays
the mountain sends, hatred of the mill,
The Silver Bell repeal, the best liked girls
who leave each year for Butte. One good
restaurant and bars can't wipe the boredom out.   15

The 1907 boom, eight going silver mines,
a dance floor built on springs—
all memory resolves itself in gaze,
in panoramic green you know the cattle eat
or two stacks high above the town,   20
two dead kilns, the huge mill in collapse
for fifty years that won't fall finally down.

Isn't this your life? That ancient kiss
still burning out your eyes? Isn't this defeat
so accurate, the church bell simply seems   25
a pure announcement: ring and no one comes?
Don't empty houses ring? Are magnesium
and scorn sufficient to support a town,
not just Philipsburg, but towns
of towering blondes, good jazz and booze   30
the world will never let you have
until the town you came from dies inside?

Say no to yourself. The old man, twenty
when the jail was built, still laughs
although his lips collapse. Someday soon,   35
he says, I'll go to sleep and not wake up.
You tell him no. You're talking to yourself.
The car that brought you here still runs.

The money you buy lunch with,
no matter where it's mined, is silver   40
and the girl who serves you food
is slender and her red hair lights the wall.

Richard Hugo, 1923–1982

THE HOUSE WAS QUIET AND THE WORLD WAS CALM

The house was quiet and the world was calm.
The reader became the book; and summer night

Was like the conscious being of the book.
The house was quiet and the world was calm.

The words were spoken as if there was no book,   5
Except that the reader leaned above the page,

Wanted to lean, wanted much most to be
The scholar to whom his book is true, to whom

The summer night is like a perfection of thought.
The house was quiet because it had to be.   10

The quiet was part of the meaning, part of the mind:
The access of perfection to the page.

And the world was calm. The truth in a calm world,
In which there is no other meaning, itself

Is calm, itself is summer and night, itself   15
Is the reader leaning late and reading there.

Wallace Stevens, 1879–1955

11

Writing about Poetry

To say it quite simply, the critic has one pre-eminent task—the task of easing or widening or deepening our response to poetry. There are, of course, many ways of performing this task. But no critical method will satisfactorily perform it if there is not respect both for the poem and for the reader.

C. Day Lewis, from *The Poetic Image*

A good critical paper is lively exploration of the significance and craft of a poem. When Scott Fitzgerald remarked that he wrote to find out what he thought, he uncovered a truth common to most of us. The attention writing requires almost always results in a deeper relationship to the work. Reactions become more organized, more objective. Good criticism is not only good writing, with well-organized paragraphs, a coherent point of view, and proper organization of priorities; it is also a creative act. The poem is more than what is said, of course, and with your own concentration and imaginative attention you discover the span of the poem.

Every critical paper needs a specific focus. You might explicate (interpret) a whole poem; or you can choose to shine a spotlight on one aspect of a work, such as the color imagery in "The Eve of St. Agnes" or the use of contradictions in John Donne's "Song." A teacher may give you a broad assignment—write a ten-page paper on the craft and meanings of "Sunday Morning"—or ask you to compare two poems. You may have the leeway to write a critique in connection with an idea or a quote such as Dickinson's "I write to drive the awe away yet awe impels the work." Some essays require library research and extensive reading of the author. Quick responses to a poem in class, fifteen- to thirty-minute essays, are a familiar and useful part of most poetry classes.

In many ways, writing essays about poems is no different than writing you're used to. Probably you've had assignments to write an essay explaining how something functioned, describing a character or place, or telling an important personal experience. Probably you've had to compare or define or discuss cause and effect. All these approaches fall under the four "shuns": narration, description, exposition, and persuasion. These (often overlapping) categories exercise different writing skills. Critical papers in poetry fall into the four "shuns": one will be the major tack you'll take in your paper. Once a direction is established, the destination must be kept in sight. The purpose of criticism is enlightenment. Ideally, the writer and reader of a critical paper both widen their perceptions.

Steps in the Development of a Critical Paper

1. Find your subject. If you may choose your own topic, gear your subject to the length required. A three-page paper needs a narrowed approach: the relationship of speaker and listener in Browning's "My Last Duchess," Hopkins's use of hyphenated words in three poems, or sound images in Keats's "Ode to a Nightingale." A long term paper encompasses more: a comparison of Louise Bogan's twentieth-century lyrics to Thomas Campion's seventeenth-century ones, the use of metaphor in ten Plath poems, or the subject of death in Keats's odes. Choose what most interests you. Do you like the work? Why? Study and read aloud what you've selected. Look up words and allusions (references to people, events, history) you don't know. Write down three or more ideas, emotions, and/or responses. If you find you have less than three strong responses, your paper will probably be too thin, and you'll find yourself reiterating the same point in different ways.

2. Paraphrase each line. This is not interpretation. Don't say that "leafy green" symbolizes money or cabbage; just write, in your own words, what the lines actually say. This technique is useful as you get started. You make sure that you understand the basic level of the poem. Paraphrasing is a limited response. It is to the poem as the idea of chocolate cake is to a real chocolate cake. The real thing is a luscious *combination* of ingredients, measured and balanced and baked. What the poem literally says is a beginning step to take.

3. Reread each line. Beyond what it specifically says, what does the line *suggest?* Meaning includes everything you experience from the poem. Think of *how* the poem's meanings come across to you. Note connotations of words and images. What triggers your imagination? Where, beyond the literal level, does the poem take you?

4. Analyze the poet's craft. As your knowledge of craft builds with each chapter of the text, put your new information to use. After the chapter on Images, for instance, start to notice precisely what *kinds* of imagery the poem uses. The papers you'll write at first will be different from the later ones. Consult the Craft Checklist which follows these pointers. *How* the poem works is a major focus of your analysis. Your expanding critical vocabulary will give you new ways to talk about poems.

5. You're ready to begin. Will you compare, focus on an aspect, use library research? This text has encouraged you to think for yourself, to ground yourself solidly in a knowledge of craft so that your emotional and intellectual reactions can be articulated. Many of your assignments probably will reflect this orientation; however, you may sometimes be asked for papers involving published criticism. At the outset, set your limits—what you will and will not consider. Which of your responses is most important? Identify your most important idea, even if you have many. What should you stress? Establishing a priority of emphasis will help you organize your material. List supporting evidence or reasons for your response. Be sure you're not ignoring alternative positions. If you think Yeats affirms the value of art in "Sailing to Byzantium," you should analyze any evidence to the contrary.

6. Write a first draft, getting down in any manner all your important connections and perceptions. You can write spontaneously and then see whether you have established an order that follows your priorities. Or you can make an outline first and write from that. As new thoughts not in the outline occur, note them separately. Then, when you've finished the draft, see if the new ideas fit in. You may need to expand your original outline. Are you forcing ideas? Are you writing from plethora or dearth of response? (Obviously, a selection from *more* is better.) Is your draft logical? You might take the scissors to your draft, cut out the paragraphs, and try different arrangements for a more dynamic or logical order. Are

your points clearly made? Take risks with your criticism: Argue
with a critic or an idea in the text if you disagree. Don't be afraid
to give a reaction contrary to the "accepted" view of a poem.
Thomas Campion's famous

> There is a garden in her face
> Where roses and white lilies grow
> A heavenly paradise is that place
> Wherein all pleasant fruits do flow

might strike you as grotesque rather than lovely. Say so, but say
why. *A face covered with lilies and fruit?*

7. If you get stuck, consult critics, teachers, friends. Brainstorming
    with others helps—especially after you've established your own
    ideas about the work. When writing a research paper, the reference
    librarian is your ally. She or he can guide you to these and other
    useful books: *Contemporary Authors* (see index volume first), *Cur-
    rent Biography*, *The Oxford Companion to American Literature*,
    The Oxford Companion to English Literature, *The Penguin Com-
    panion to English Literature*, and *The Penguin Companion to
    American Literature.* The current *MLA International Bibliography
    of Books and Articles on the Modern Languages and Literatures*
    will lead to you criticism published on writers. Try looking at the
    poem from others' perspectives. You may need to look deeper or
    in a different direction. Reorganization may be necessary.

8. Write your next draft. Bring into your writing the good example of
    poems: precision of language. Vary your sentence structure; use
    repetition effectively; use concrete images rather than abstractions
    or generalizations; find a form that works best; notice each word.
    Check your diction: no jargon, slang, or messy colloquialisms. No
    overblown critical rhetoric. Your own clear voice is the best style.
    Your style is the voice *only* you could write. Avoid an "equitone"
    voice. Let your own strong reactions show. Ask yourself what you
    would get out of reading the paper for the first time. Make each
    paragraph move the paper along. Without summing up methodi-
    cally, find the right closure so the reader realizes fully what you've
    said.

9. Check your mechanics. Proofread for spelling mistakes and typo-
    graphical errors. A spelling check on a word-processing program
    isn't adequate, since it won't recognize that you meant *youth* but

typed *your.* Check your grammar. Are the parallel sentences in agreement? Are pronoun references clear, with no stray *it* or *this* referring to nothing the reader can find? In addition to regular grammatical considerations, writing about poetry requires knowledge of certain particular mechanics:

Quotation marks are used around titles of poems. Book titles, periodicals, and titles of long poems are underlined, indicating italics (if you're using a computer, type these in italics).

When quoting three or more lines from a poem (or four or more lines of prose), separate the quote from your text by three spaces. Follow the poet's line breaks exactly and double-space the quote:

And then went down to the ship.

Set keel to breakers, forth on the godly sea, and

We set up mast and sail on that swart ship,

Bore sheep aboard her, and our bodies also

Ezra Pound, from *Canto I*

If you had already been writing about Pound's *Canto I* and had identified it as a subject previously, you would not need to note the name of the poem and author after the quote. When quoting a shorter passage, incorporate it within your text: ". . . down to the ship. / Set keel to breakers. . . ." Use a slash line with a space on either side of it to indicate a line break. Use elipses (. . .) to indicate words omitted. Two slashes (//) indicate a stanza break.

Any facts or ideas not your own must be attributed to their sources. Note an outside source briefly within the paper:

. . . this breakthrough in style occurred in the summer of 1902 when she revised the third section of her epic "Momentary Days" (Carter 16–22).

and cite the full source information on a separate "Works Cited" page at the end. The reader refers to this and finds:

Carter, Megan. *The Modern Epic.* London: Spanscript Editions, 1926.

For more examples of documentation, see the student research paper "Sailing to Byzantium," which follows in this chapter. Your instructor might not require a "Works Cited" list for short papers with limited use of outside sources. You may, in this case, include your source and page within the text:

As Carmen Sadler says in *Images of the Tropics in the Work of Anthony Cox* (Hartford: Michaelmas Press, 1986), palm trees and fireflies appear in twenty-two poems (38).

If you quote Sadler later, simply note the page number of the information:

Sadler insists, though I think she is wrong, that Cox "became too dependent on esoteric naming, a practice which reached an extreme in *Gloxinia, Cinnabar, and Frangipani*" (109).

In recent years, the format for footnotes and bibliography has been simplified. For special cases of documentation of outside sources which may be necessary, you will need a reference such as a current edition of the *Harbrace College Handbook* or the *MLA Handbook for Writers of Research Papers*.

Craft Checklist

For your analysis of a poem, consider these aspects of craft.

Words

What is the quality of the words in the poem? Are any overused? Are they fresh? Concrete? Vague? Abstract? If you would run your hand over the surface of the sounds, would they be smooth, rough, jagged, soft? Is this texture fitting to the subject?

Voice

Is the poem anchored in a particular speaker's voice? Whose? What is the tone of voice? Does the tone change? Who is the listener?

Images

How many senses are evoked in the poem? What are they? Is the imagery effective? Is the poem immediate or distant? In what end of the telescope does the poem take place—that is, does it seem to take place right here and now, or far away? Does the same image reappear? What is the effect of this?

Movement

What is the activity of the poem like? Look at the verbs: are they generally active or passive? Are the tenses consistent? Does the poem keep on moving? Does each stanza do different work from the previous stanza? Does the poem stay on the track? Or does the train take a side trip into other subjects?

Line

Is the line taut like the lively tension in the string of a helium balloon? Are the end words the ones you linger on? Usually poetry is written in lines, prose in sentences. Although the lines of poetry usually add up to sentences, the construction is line to line. Cover the left half of the poem. Does the right side consistently trail off from an energetic beginning? A sure sign of this is many lines ending with prepositional phrases. Cover the right side. Are both sides of the line equally strong? Do most lines end-stop or enjamb (run over to next line)? Does the poem start immediately or does the poet need a one-minute wind-up to get to the subject? How does the poem end? A bang? A whimper? Is the end overstated, telling the reader what the conclusion is in case it wasn't clear? Generally, a slow start and a drawn-out end "frame" the poem too much, giving a blocked-in feeling.

Form

What does the poem's shape say about the subject? Does each line start with a capital letter? Why? Are the lines irregularly placed? Why? Are the rhymes forced, or do they work for the poem? Does repetition emphasize or detract? Is there a metrical pattern?

The checklist also helps you judge the craft of poems you write.

Student Essays

Analyze these responses to "In the Waiting Room" by Elizabeth Bishop (see page 498). Near the beginning of an introductory poetry course, students were asked to explicate the poem or to describe their personal reactions to it.

Essay 1

Insights Into a Poem

''You are one of <u>them</u>. / <u>Why</u> should you be one, too?'' Life is full of complexities. Perhaps one of the most difficult to understand is the fact that although every person has unique traits, in our most basic form we are all similar. But what determined that we would be human in the first place? Elizabeth Bishop's poem ''In the Waiting Room'' captures the horror that she experiences as a young child, when she realized the ''unlikeliness'' of this occurrence.

There are three main parts to this rather long poem. The first section takes the reader through a description of the setting. At first glance, there doesn't seem to be anything of importance here. Elizabeth has gone with her Aunt Consuelo to the dentist's office. She sits in the waiting room while her aunt is inside with the dentist. This waiting room is just like any other that we have all experienced. There are lamps, other people waiting, and, of course, magazines. We soon realize that this room is actually a microcosm. The confining boundaries of the room permit Elizabeth to view a subset of life. Inside this small room Elizabeth is with the variety of people existing in the larger, real world. It is possible to see an even smaller unit of life by extrapolating upon this view, and a magazine becomes the vehicle towards this end. While waiting, Elizabeth picks up an issue of <u>National Geographic</u> and begins to read. More importantly, however, she looks at the pictures, which expose her to a world of strange new people with unique customs and traditions. She sees

Babies with pointed heads

wound round and round with string;

black, naked women with necks

wound round and round with wire

like the necks of light bulbs.

For the child, the realization that these people in
all their strangeness are still the same as she is a
terrifying one. How did she come to be Elizabeth and
not someone else such as a black baby living in an
African tribe?

Here the poem alters dramatically. From the
relative tranquility of the setting, the reader is
suddenly tossed into the upheaval of a mind reeling
with confusion:

I said to myself: three days

and you'll be seven years old.

I was saying it to stop

the sensation of falling off

the round, turning world

into cold, blue–black space.

Aunt Consuelo has cried out in pain. The sound sends
Elizabeth into a crisis of mistaken identity.
Elizabeth can find no reason for that sound to have
come from her Aunt instead of from her or anyone else

in the room for that matter. ''Why should I be my
Aunt, / or me, or anyone?'' thinks the child.

As Elizabeth's mind jerks spasmodically, so does
the form of the poem. The reader is faced with
sentences that no longer flow from one to the other
as they did in the first stanza. The confusion taking
place in the girl's mind is shadowed by a confusion
in the written lines. This is because we, the
readers, are taken from the mental thoughts of a
girl's mind as she endures a crisis into a comparison
of the hard reality that she can see existing in the
room. She can see similarities between herself and
the others in their

boots, hands, the family voice

I felt in my throat, or even

the <u>National Geographic</u>

and those awful hanging breasts

but coming to grips with ''what made us all just
one?'' is something that her mind can barely handle.
This is not particularly surprising. After all, this
question is not easily dealt with by grown, educated
minds.

Finally, Elizabeth manages to put her fears
behind her. She hasn't come to any conclusions, but
as the poem begins its last section we realize that
she has come back to reality. In this very short
conclusion, cold hard reality has replaced the
topsy-turvy confusion. ''The War was on'' is stated
with certainty. There is nothing to indicate the
crisis that went before. The reader has been given a
calm beginning and calmer end, with a middle that
confirms the feeling that ''. . . nothing stranger /
could ever happen.''

Scott Berrison

Essay 2

Becoming Real

I sat on a balcony church pew one Sunday morning in February. I was surrounded by my two brothers, my sister, and my parents, all towering above me, diminishing me. The priest's voice droned on and on about Christ rising. Suddenly I felt lost—— overwhelmed. Were these people really my family, directly related to me? What did that mean, anyway? How did I get to be part of this world, and how did the world begin? Who <u>am</u> I? Often when I was little, in elementary school, I got surges of these ''lost'' feelings. I realized that I was a very insignificant part of a vast, complex world. Elizabeth Bishop considers this same reaction in her poem, ''In the Waiting Room.''

''Real,'' as defined in <u>The Velveteen Rabbit</u>, is the ''process of becoming a complete person.'' Becoming ''real'' begins at a very early age; the age when a child begins to question and analyze. It is at this time when a child questions everything from ''Why do socks stick?'' to ''How can a radio talk?'' (Often parents can talk with their child for ten minutes or so with the child only saying, ''Why, why, why?'') This ''why'' stage in a child's life is the beginning of his ''becoming real.'' A child learns a lot from the answers to his questions. His many ''realizations'' can often make him confused and boggled, overwhelming him with complexity, but they will also help him to grow and become a more ''complete'' person.

I had a small ''realization'' and became confused in the church, just as six–year–old Elizabeth did in ''In the Waiting Room.'' Possibly for the first time, she really became aware that the world was very complex: a world of strange people and strange phenomena. It was all suddenly brought before her mind with ''vividness and clarity'' by the <u>National</u>

<u>Geographic</u> magazine she read while waiting for her
aunt in the dentist's office.

I often felt lost, empty, and confused during
elementary school. I shuddered while imagining
myself perched precariously on the edge of the
massive earth, spinning dizzily through dark, empty,
infinite space in wobbly circles, wondering how
darkness could possibly go on forever. My head
whirled when Dad patiently tried to explain (when I
was only six), all about the geological process of
Death Valley, with its complex alluvial fans,
peculiar salt build—ups, gigantic faults and
limestone deposits. I was overwhelmed when he tried
to explain anything to me about electricity or
anything ''mysterious'' (a TV, toilets, geysers,
sky—scrapers, stoplights). Once when I was ten I even
stomped away from the dinner table nearly in tears
when I could not understand—even though Dad not—so—
patiently tried to explain with two carrot sticks and
a stalk of celery—how the 1976 Olympic torch became
magically lit. I identify with ''In the Waiting
Room'' because in grade school, I read magazines for
hours, staring at all the unfamiliar people and
wondering who they were and why <u>I</u> got chosen to be
part of <u>my</u> family. Were my parents <u>really</u> my parents
or did I actually belong to the Amish man and lady
shown milking their gigantic, brown, spotted cow in
the March 1974 issue of <u>National Geographic</u>?
Familiar scenes snapped me out of my pensive moods—
watching our German shorthair chase a rock always did
the trick—and made me feel comfortable with my
surroundings once again.

Elizabeth, a secure but naive six year old, also
got bewildered when she read and became exposed to
the wonders of <u>National Geographic</u> in the dentist's
waiting room. Her shielded bubble created by her
family burst as she realized she was such a small
part of the extremely complex world. Elizabeth was
very observant and spunky. She noticed details:

> The waiting room
>
> was full of grown—up people,
>
> arctics and overcoats,
>
> lamps and magazines.

The reader can actually picture her marching along with her aunt into the office, carefully checking over the place where she was to wait. The reader sees her spunk when she makes it clear that she could read: ''I read the <u>National Geographic</u> / (I could read). . . .'' Because of the selection of her observations of particulars, the reader knows that she was young and naive, not understanding many different ways of life other than her own limited, secure environment.

The window to a complicated world previously unrealized by Elizabeth was the <u>National Geographic</u>. It baffled her. She read it with wide eyes, ''. . . straight through. / I was too shy to stop.'' She sees ''the inside of a volcano, / black and full of ashes,'' a couple dressed in riding breeches,'' ''A dead man slung on a pole,'' ''Babies with pointed heads,'' and

> black, naked women with necks
>
> wound round and round with wire. . . .
>
> Their breasts were horrifying.

All this alarming new information made Elizabeth's head reel with confusion. She couldn't imagine that people could ever be so different and peculiar. Her realization stupified her——she desperately stared

at the cover ''the yellow margins, the date'' to try
to keep something in touch with the life she knew, to
steady herself. Her swirling confusion led her to
believe that her aunt, in the dentist's chair, let
out a scream: a scream which probably came from
Elizabeth herself. It was a result of her sudden
feeling of helplessness—she cried out for an
explanation—she was overwhelmed:

> What took me
>
> completely by surprise
>
> was that it was <u>me</u>:
>
> my voice, in my mouth.
>
> Without thinking at all
>
> I was my foolish aunt.

It was too much for Elizabeth to digest. She
became nauseated.

> The waiting room was bright
>
> and too hot. It was sliding
>
> beneath a big black wave,
>
> another, and another.

She tried to steady herself by staring at the cover
once again, and by reassuring herself that she was
herself, and not one of the terrifying tribal women
with the wire-wound necks. ''You are an <u>I</u> / you are an

<u>Elizabeth</u>.'' She also glanced around the room to get
a grip on anything familiar:

> I gave a sidelong glance . . .
>
> at shadowy gray knees,
>
> trousers and skirts and boots
>
> and different pairs of hands
>
> lying under the lamps.

Elizabeth's confusions stimulated two main
questions which she actually asked the reader in the
poem. She asked, ''What similarities'' hold us
''. . . all together / or made us all just one?'' and
''How had I come to be here?'' These questions, even
if left unanswered, begin to expand Elizabeth's
knowledge of her own reality. Thus, by becoming
confused, just as I did while sitting on the church
pew, Elizabeth realized that the world is actually
much more complex and vast than her comfortable,
secure little world in Worcester, Massachusetts. She
became aware that nothing would ever be stranger than
this basic realization of separateness and oneness.
    Both Elizabeth and I popped out of our confused
states of mind almost as quickly as we popped in.
Elizabeth snapped out of it by walking out of the
dentist's office with her aunt. In the night and
slush ''. . . it was still the fifth / of February,
1918.'' I snapped out of it by walking out of the
church with my family; the sun glaring in my eyes,
the birds chirping in the trees, and the wind
whipping through my hair—it was still Sunday
morning, February, 1972.

Gretchen Maurer

Student Research Paper

The next paper responds to an assignment to write a short research paper on a single poem that the student found puzzling. The poem, "Sailing to Byzantium," appears on page 296 of this book. "Puzzling" is an understatement for "Sailing to Byzantium." Without research into Yeats's theories and allusions, this poem yields only a fraction of its potential meanings.

One purpose of the paper was to practice using correct format for noting outside sources of information. You must credit any idea not your own, any quote, or even a way of presenting an idea if you found it first in an outside source. The following paper uses correct notation for simple critical documentation.

''Sailing to Byzantium'' by W. B. Yeats

In form, ''Sailing to Byzantium'' is a four—part poem in stanzas of eight lines each. The lines rhyme abababcc, although many seem to chime (young/song) rather than actually rhyme. The meter is iambic pentameter, with variations. My overall impression of the form is that it is compact, especially considering the profound meanings Yeats covers in only thirty—two lines. The tight, carefully made poem suits the subject matter. A looser structure would not fit the poem at all because of the subject: the release from subjectivity and time that art gives one.

This is a complicated poem. The title, ''Sailing to Byzantium,'' is important. Byzantium became Constantinople, then modern—day Istanbul, and so, of course, it no longer exists. Sailing there, literally, is impossible. Therefore this will be an imaginary journey from the speaker's real home to a place far back in time. The significance of Byzantium for Yeats is clear from his book <u>A Vision</u>, which attempts to interpret history, behavior, and art by Yeats's invented system of wheel and cone symbols and number theories. In it he states, ''I think that in early Byzantium, maybe never before or since in

recorded history, religious, aesthetic and
practical life were one . . .'' (279). The voyage
then is a quest for such wholeness. According to
Yeats's theory, the height of Byzantine art
coincides with a peak in a cycle of civilization.
Every two thousand years a new cycle begins. The
reign of the Emperor Justinian represented a high
point in that cycle (279). The journeyer seeks a
return to that point.

In imagination, the speaker, in stanza 1, is
sailing to Byzantium where the artists are

> Almost impersonal, almost perhaps without
> the consciousness of individual design, absorbed
> in their subject matter and that the vision of a
> whole people . . . the work of many seemed the
> work of one, that made building, picture,
> pattern, metal—work of rail and lamp, seem but a
> single image (280).

In contrast, he thinks back to the country he
left:

> That is no country for old men. The young
>
> In one another's arms, birds in the trees
>
> ——Those dying generations——at their song

There, the old are not part of the ''sensual music.''
The dying generations of birds remind me of Keats's
''Ode to a Nightingale'' (Keats 144) with its idea of
the immortality of song contrasting with the brevity
of human life. In that country, everything revolves
around bodily life. Even the sea is ''mackerel—
crowded.'' Fecundity is everything. There, back on
the speaker's native shores, everyone neglects
''monuments of unaging intellect'': art.

Stanza 2 continues this lament. Again looking
back ''there,'' the soul has to sing louder and
louder for each ''tatter in its mortal dress,'' in
its attempt to overcome age. There is no ''singing
school'' to teach one how to do this. An old man there
is no more than a ''tattered coat upon a stick,'' a
figure reduced to a scarecrow. At the end of the
second stanza, the aging poet has ''sailed the seas''
and sets his imagination down in the ''holy city of
Byzantium.'' Art historian Rene Huyghe describes the
Byzantine belief that ''in this world, the soul
inevitably became defiled and had therefore to
escape from the physical body, 'to traverse the waves
of the sensual world' and aspire towards God
transcendent'' (18). Now that the speaker has
crossed from the sensual, the rest of the poem is
about the aspiration for the transcendental.

Once in ''the holy city of Byzantium,'' he
immediately implores the sages who are

standing in God's holy fire

As in the gold mosaic of a wall,

Come from the holy fire, perne in a gyre,

And be the singing—masters of my soul.

No singing schools existed where he came from, we
remember from stanza 2. The soul is still full of
desire though the body is ''a dying animal.'' He
invites the sages to teach him to sing and to spiral
down through historical time to him. He uses the
movement of a bobbin thread, perne (or pirn), as a
verb to indicate movement within the gyre. The gyre
in Yeats's theory is two interpenetrating cones
representing ''antithetical elements in every

man's, nation's, and era's nature'' (Unterecker 25).
The sages appear as an artwork themselves; Yeats sees
them in intense light, a holy fire like a gold
mosaic. In extreme contrast, the speaker's image of
himself is of a ''dying animal.'' In the Byzantine
philosophy of the time, all matter is darkness, while
the spirit is light. ''Likewise in art, concrete and
visible nature should only figure in so far as it
leads to the spiritual'' (Huyghe 18). The sages are
like muses who can lead him to be an artifice like
themselves, transformed into a oneness with this
unified culture.

At the end of the third stanza, ''the artifice of
eternity'' lets him finally ''out of nature
. . . ,'' out of the ''dying animal.'' In a note on
the poem (Collected Works 453), the author says he
''read somewhere that in the Emperor's palace at
Byzantium was a tree made of gold and silver, and
artificial birds that sang.'' In the fourth stanza he
imagines himself transformed into such an
''artifice,'' a hammered gold bird, one of the
impossible ''unaging'' monuments of the first
stanza. At this point, remember the birds in the
first stanza, endlessly dying and regenerating. Over
the real ''birds in the trees . . . at their song,''
the speaker prefers the beautiful gold bird who will
sing of the past, the present and the future. The
word which continues to puzzle me is drowsy. It seems
close to the neglected monuments of the first stanza.
The poet must mean that at least in Byzantium the
monuments endure, whether the people are engaged by
them or not. The most important moment of the poem is
the last line. One critic says, ''The poet—in—the—
poem thus reaches totality by objectification of the
self . . . but it is a totality in which . . . his
tongue's a stone'' (Requeiro 127). I disagree with
her conclusion. I think Yeats would not have bothered
to write the poem if that was all it came to. The last
words, that the hammered gold bird can sing ''Of what

is past, or passing, or to come'' refer both to the
''Whatever is begotten, born, and dies'' (the
sensual music) in the first stanza and to the ''perne
in a gyre,'' the escape from all the vicissitudes of
time in the third stanza. Byzantium, I conclude, is
in history as art is in human life, a rare
representation of unity in a chaotic world.

Elizabeth Andrews

Works Cited

Keats, John. <u>The Poems of Keats</u>. Boston: Houghton
Mifflin, 1899.

Huyghe, Rene, gen. ed. <u>The Larousse Encyclopedia of
Byzantine and Medieval Art</u>. New York: Prometheus,
1963.

Requeiro, Helen. <u>The Limits of Imagination</u>. Ithaca:
Cornell UP, 1976.

Unterecker, John. <u>A Reader's Guide to William Butler
Yeats</u>. New York: Noonday, 1959.

Yeats, William Butler. <u>A Vision</u>. New York:
Macmillan, 1956.

———. <u>The Collected Poems of William Butler Yeats</u>. New
York: Macmillan, 1968.

A Poet's Handbook

We do what we know before we know what we do.

Charles Olson

Invoking Your Muse

The desire to write feels something like a power surge: If you have it, you know it. Many writers say they write because they *have to*, there's no choice; the rush that runs through them simply demands to be expressed in words. This may be an occasional phenomenon or the sign of a lifelong involvement with the word.

Your own process of writing will be a long discovery. When the power surge strikes, you may or may not pick up your pen. Writers are quirky beings. Some write in the moment of intensity. Others let a thought or experience drift about in the unconscious, then calmly draw on it later. After writing, almost all new writers fear that they will never write again, especially if the work seems wonderful. An experienced writer learns to trust a process and to realize that there may be an unpredictable tide, but that the tide *will* come back in. One of the best poets I know must write in a darkened room. He starts by writing random words only on the left side of the page, meditating and freely associating for an hour. When a word or phrase suddenly takes his attention, he moves it to the right and quickly writes the whole poem. His process makes no sense to others but works for him. Another poet "writes" by speaking into a tape recorder while taking long walks, then transcribes and revises at the computer. You may be a late-night writer or one who must clear off the desk entirely. While driving, showering, bathing, when the mind is occupied but oddly free, you might get your best ideas.

Many writers keep dream journals to get closer to their unconscious lives, or record important thoughts and details in blank books.

You may need blue paper, like Colette, or a cork-lined room, like Proust. Weird though these things might sound to someone else, writers find what works.

I am devoted to art sketch books. In them I keep quotes, images, observations, lists, and hundreds of phrases and single words such as "ocarina," "lithic," "pond slider turtle" and "cut out the light"—sounds I like when I come across them. When I begin a poem, I put down—only on a white legal pad—as much raw material as I can. Then I go to my great thick repository and take what I need for that particular poem. The selections I've included in my sketch book, of course, are not whimsical, even though I don't know at the time why I'm including certain definitions, phrases, quotes, or newspaper articles. Gradually, an unwieldy body of material forms, which I then shape and reshape. Sometimes I realize that the poem still wants something more. If I don't know what that is, I put the poem away until that *something* that seems right lands in my head. For a time I kept a parallel book I called an image bank. I collected old photos, art postcards, ads, and drawings. With colored pencils, I tried first to draw what I wanted to write about. Writing from a visual image intrigued me then. *Elephrasis* (description), a useful word from classical rhetoric, means a literary exercise using words to evoke a visual effect. In addition, poets want a complex of emotional, associative, intellectual and sensual effects. I liked the process of description and sharpened my sense of imagery by practicing accurate reproductions in words of something I looked at. Gradually I stopped that approach; my process shifted.

The discovery of your own best process is helpful because once you identify it, you can recognize and create the climate you respond to. "Act in the little ways that encourage good fortune," as poet William Stafford put it. You also can realize what won't work—you will know if you can't write while job hunting, visiting troublesome relatives, or writing a term paper on Yeats. Forget writing for the moment; you can relax and later on find the natural time and place. There is a large, irrational aspect to writing. It's good to begin with that in mind. In an essay, Wallace Stevens writes about the "transaction between reality and the sensibility of the poet from which poetry springs." The moment you raise the pen is the moment of that transaction. You are suddenly in two worlds. Your process of arriving at that moment is crucial to the words that fall across that large, white expanse, the page.

Beginning with a White Page

The epigraph to this chapter—"We do what we know before we know what we do"—speaks to a mysterious subterranean level of ourselves. If you have a desire to write, even an inner sense that you *will* write, this quote invites you to trust yourself. You do know something important about who you are and what is in you that wants *saying*. Starting out, you may not yet know what works and what doesn't. Later, you will. As a writing teacher, I've been amazed at how many people have talent. Some simply let it go; they take up broadcasting or urban planning or go back to their jobs. The students who abide with their talent, who voraciously read and think about poetry, who attend readings, memorize poems, and who try out anything that will broaden the experience of writing—those are the ones who generally have the peculiar love and discipline that it takes to become a writer. You don't, however, have to sign a dotted line. You can enjoy reading and writing poetry while making your living delivering babies or pizzas.

Einstein said that the theory of relativity came to him as a "feeling." How then did he translate that vague sensation into theory? And how, once you've generated pages of notes from exercises, do you write a poem?

Suggestions for Writing and Revising

Write poems that matter very much to you, whether they are memories of childhood, meditations, or sound experiments. The quality of deep feeling, thought, or intense energy will guarantee that your poem, at least, has life.

You may not know what you're writing about as you hunt and gather in your mind for your material. Be as generous to the white page as you can; give it everything you've got at the moment. Underline all the important sounds, ideas, phrases—and ruthlessly throw away any clichés. A good rule to remember: If you've heard it before, don't use it. Start crafting and revising as soon as you have written down all the raw material you think you need. Some poets go through thirty revisions. Chances are, any poem will need work beyond the first draft, unless you've had a true gift.

Try to push aside the censor, that demon who whispers "Not good" and "Don't dare say that" and "Who cares about your life?"

Poets write about the same basic human subjects over and over. Your inner voice is one that never has been heard in the world before. Though there are thousands of love poems and death poems, your version will be new if you can catch your own sound. Give yourself a lot of leeway with writing exercises. Anne Sexton said she sometimes wanted to write but didn't know what she wanted to say: "I will fool around on the typewriter. It might take me ten pages of nothing, of terrible writing, and then I'll get a line, and I'll think, 'That's what I mean.' What you're doing is hunting for what you mean, what you're trying to say."

Refer to the Craft Checklist (page 552). It's a handy reference for all the craft issues in a poem. Go over all the possibilities for improvement that the list suggests. At the revision stage, the same objective standards you study in each chapter of the text are brought to bear on your own poem.

Try different line lengths and line breaks, searching for a natural rhythm that fits your sense of the subject. Perhaps you will want to try arranging phrases into iambic pentameter or iambic tetrameter, the two most useful meters in English. The text, of course, will help you review the metrical patterns, if you want your poem in a particular measure. If lines don't seem to work, perhaps your form is the prose poem. Does any line bear repeating? A repeating line, when it comes around again, needs to intensify in meaning. Invent your own forms, arranging the words so that they interact with the white space on the page (the silence).

Don't be too cryptic. This is very important. It's the most common flaw in students' writing. You might have so much respect for the distilled language of poetry that you forget to give the reader enough clues. You might boil down your poem too much so that each word is incredibly important to you but not to the reader, who has no idea what you're talking about! Cut, cut, cut is what you may hear over and over in a poetry workshop. You sometimes need to do the opposite and add.

Write the poem, then put it aside and write what you truly wanted to say. Always push yourself to go further. Some poems are simple and some don't want to be. Ask if you have done all that the poem requires of you. Does it want more?

Polish and shine your language. See that your diction supports the tone you want the poem to have. If it's an angry poem, you don't want passive verbs and soft sounds. Fold the poem down its center axis and read all the right half's lines than all the left half's lines. Does the energy trail off on the right side? Do you want this poem to be a strong-lined poem, with energy deployed down the page? If so, work on the lines that let down the momentum. Check to see if you have the habit of ending lines with prepositional phrases or weak words (the, an, of, etc.).

Read aloud as you go. Anything that bothers your ear or trips your tongue should be reexamined. If you can, tape-record the poem and listen to it for clues to improving rhythm.

If you are in a workshop, ask the other members specific questions about your poem when you have them. Does this have any emotional effect? Is this hard to follow? Does this image draw too much attention to itself? Do you believe the poem? Does this word stick out? Anything you suspect is a problem needs to be clarified. Give the other writers the kind of criticism you would like to get: the hard, kind approach. What you all want is for each poem to be the best it can be. You do not want it to sound like the teacher's poetry or anyone's. Beware of criticism that comes from a dogmatic reader who knows all the answers or who wants everyone to sound like him or her. When reacting to someone's poem, remember the old saw "constructive criticism." It gives the writer more of a sense of possibility for revision if you make a definite suggestion for improvement rather than just saying what you don't like. Always think in terms of re-vision—seeing the poem anew and reworking from its original source.

Give yourself a chance to try various writing exercises. Good ones can do anything from warming you up to uncovering your deepest material. Gimmicky ones can be fun, but you don't learn much from them. Mechanistic ones produce lifeless work. My heart sinks when I hear teachers ask students to list the objects in their rooms. The exercises below are divided into several categories, each with a real purpose. You can return to ones that work for you at different stages of your writing. For some, the muse just won't be invoked this way but for many, especially when writing is hard, the objective demands set forth in an exercise prove to be freeing. Why? The odd fact is that when you are challenged from outside, you frequently do unexpected work. The other facet is crucial: play. We may bring a dampening seriousness to writing. The exercise casts it as a kind of play. Nothing rides on it so we are at liberty. We can be wild, funny, dark, meditative all at once.

Try anything—but meanwhile also write what you normally would write on your own. There's a synergy to exercises when used in a class or writing group. When you have twenty minutes to complete an exercise, the pressure squeezes out writing that you didn't know you could do. Hearing others' responses to an exercise makes you more aware of your own voice and your own unique material. Varied responses can make you realize you need to dig toward the core, listen harder to yourself, or take a different perspective on the material.

EXERCISES

Getting Started   These exercises are for warming up, limbering the imagination, letting ideas flow through your pen, unfettering the mind. Turn off the premature editor and try to write copiously. It's better to pare down from abundance than to pad a meager beginning.

1. Take the first line of a poem and write from that line. If you get stuck, take lines from other poems or texts and use them along the way. Write twenty or more lines. Later, you may want to revise the lines you've borrowed. Those lines probably are linked to issues that matter to you and the exercise opens you to those concerns.

2. Cut out fifty or so phrases, words, sentences you like from a magazine. Select some as possible titles. On a large, white page, arrange these cutouts into a collage poem, without forcing the words into a preconceived subject. You may need to change your title when you're through. It's amazing how many fine poems come from this exercise. The mind is shapely even when playing; you're cutting out something of your own. The pleasure here is the discovery of the poem you didn't know you were creating.

3. Freely write for twenty minutes without lifting your pen from the paper. Write anything, without trying to connect logically what you're doing. Then, underline any lines or words you like. Note recurrent ideas, images, themes. The purpose is spontaneity. List anything that strikes you as important in the free writing. Is there a poem for you?

4. Keep a dream journal. Watch for patterns. Do you often dream of houses with secret rooms or attics? Are you under siege in your dreams? Who is after you in each? Read books on dream interpretation. Whatever mysteries and clues you record may be valuable in poems, though dream poems identified by "And then I woke up" are seldom interesting.

5. Generate as many titles for poems as you can think of. Look for titles when reading biology texts, tax manuals, foreign language phrase books. Keep a list of possible titles. Choose one anytime and try to work from it. The mind throws out little gifts all the time. The seemingly random titles may hit an important subject just waiting to be tapped.

6. Write a poem in the style of a poet you admire or despise in this text. This opens up the work further and allows you to experience the poet's modes of crafting and expressing.

7. Take a poem you already have written and start a new poem with the last lines. If you *had* to continue a finished poem, where could you go with it? This pushes you to explore a subject you thought you were through with.

8. Make lists. Write poems with titles like "Reasons for Not Moving," "Places I Would Not Want To Go Without You," "Why I Don't Travel Well," "Some Stars, Some Galaxies," etc. Especially for congenital list makers, this exercise can uncover real motives.

9. Take one word and write everything you can from that one word—all your associations, the dictionary meaning, the etymology, the sound associations. Where does the word lead you? Flesh it out as fully as possible. This plumbs the richness of a single word and gives you a framework for constructing and imagining. The root of "trellis," for instance, connects with "page." The climbing vines can link with the scrawl of words—connections you have no way of making without probing into meanings. Spending time with word roots will make clear that every word is a fossil poem.

10. This is a strange exercise that works famously for some and not at all for others. It is close to free writing in technique but far from it in material it uncovers. Ask someone to select three books

from different fields (an instruction manual, guide book, history book, an art book, or philosophy text) and to read to you for fifteen minutes, switching from book to book at two- or three-minute intervals. You type while listening, typing as fast as you can. Don't edit or try to control. Type your thoughts, phrases you hear, associations from what you hear, anything, just keep typing. Use the material as you would the free-writing material described in number 3; it's guaranteed to produce raw material you could not consciously have written.

11.   Write opening lines to ten poems as quickly as possible. Choose one immediately and finish the poem in twenty minutes. See if time constraints inspire you. Work fast!

12.   Write to music, closing out all other sound. Try to follow the emotions or rhythms of the sounds.

Home Ground   The next exercises work from prime territory: personal experience, the "I" voice, the family matrix, memory, the heart, and the heart of the heart. Many writers have observed that you have enough material for a lifetime if you've survived a childhood. First causes, moments of change, realizations, early loves and passions, places—these are rich sources for poetry. The accepted wisdom is "Write about what you know," but I think it's important to seek what new insights and facts you can unearth about what you know. Or, to enlarge this idea, think about John Logan's statement, "It's not the skeleton in the closet we are afraid of, it's the god."

1.   Write out in prose, in as much detail as possible, your earliest memories. Think about why you remember these events and images and not others. What connections to emotions you now have can you make? Select the most powerful memory and work on a poem, with the object of finding meaning in the memory. Virginia Woolf remembered the pattern of her mother's dress, the Venetian blind cord trailing across the windowsill in the wind. Each memory opened her writing to her first connections with her mother and to a childhood place she loved.

2.   Write about a symbolic object from childhood: a ruby your aunt wore in the hollow of her throat, a pistol in your father's bedside table, your mother's stack of yellowed love letters in the hall closet, a set of trains you loved—any object that has become

larger than itself. Explore the ramifications in your life then and now.

3. List the sayings you heard over and over while growing up. Did this wisdom stick or did you rebel? Try a poem using the repetition of a single expression.

4. Begin with the phrase, "My mother (brother, father) always . . ." or "My sister never . . . ," and list as many things as you can think of. Try writing a portrait of that relative.

5. Family photos are fertile ground. Write a full response to the image: all the details you see and remember, including color, smell, touch. Imagine before and after incidents of the image, stories that may or may not be true. Photos of grandparents you never knew, your parents before the divorce, your mother at sixteen, you as an infant pulling over the Christmas tree or screaming—all these are wide open to your imagination and reinterpretation.

6. List the absolutes you live by. What would you always do? Never? How did you arrive at one of these standards?

7. Write about the rituals, conscious or unconscious, that you practiced as a child. Did you have to have the bed turned down just so, did you torture ants, or did you get ready for school in an unalterable regime? What family rituals were you a part of when growing up? What rituals do you practice today? What is the significance of ritual to you?

8. Try to remember what it was like to be inside your six-year-old body, then your sixteen-year-old body. Think of specific moments—ice skating at night, driving too fast, the first day of school—during those two ages and write active poems using the size, muscles, point of view of yourself then. "I sing the body electric," Whitman wrote.

9. List the major changes in your life and see if you can identify a moment when you realized that you were changing or that nothing would be the same after that. The changes will be vastly different—a move to a new town, the drowning of a friend, a moment of triumph or defeat. Write from within that moment.

10. In your mind, walk through a significant house or apartment from your childhood. Record your memories, all the sensory details of

each room, how you feel as you revisit. Why does this house still occupy you?

11. Write a self-portrait.

12. Write about a love relationship that changed your idea of love.

13. When were you first aware of being *girl* or *boy*? With what emotional resonances?

14. Revisit a family meal, an ordinary evening in the family circle, the smells, the atmosphere, the conversations. Or a meal at a time of celebration.

15. What are the mysteries in your past? Focus on someone you never figured out or an occurrence that should have worked out otherwise.

16. What lie did you tell? Why do you still remember it? Did you steal something? What attraction did the object have and how did you feel?

17. In prose, write out fully a description of the landscape you can't help but call home. The red clay hills of Georgia, the broken doorways of the lower East side, the misty islands of Washington: wherever your pulse tells you *this is unmistakably home*. Describe your feelings on returning to this place after an absence.

18. Is there a subject you've forbidden yourself to write about? Are you ready to look at it?

19. Weddings, wakes, births, birthdays, divorces, trips, all the big occasions of life provoke powerful memories. Character and conflict tend to come to the fore in these times.

20. What did you say that you would like to unsay?

21. Use other poets' titles to suggest subjects, for example, "Why My Mother Made Me," "Breaking Points," "The Close of Summer," "Random Panic in the U.S.A."

22. Write out a specific memory of a childhood friend. What would you say to that friend now?

23. What events in your life changed your own perception of who you are?

24. Write a poem in letter form to an important person you've lost touch with.

25. Do you have a fear or phobia? My own was explored in "Sestina for the Owl," (page 350). What do you think is the origin of your fear? What does the spider, snake, or bird remind you of?

26. Record your pleasures.

The Expanded Sphere   This set of exercises focuses on encountering objective experience. Of course, your own experience often enters into poems that are not specifically about you. The work suggested below puts you in touch with an otherness, a place to perceive something about yourself, another, or the world.

1. Choose a person from history or a person you are curious about and in that person's voice ("I") recount an event or an emotion. You may want to do some research. Speaking as John Kennedy en route to the hospital, Hitler in the bunker, a baker at 3 A.M., a mortician going to work, or as Marilyn Monroe looking in the mirror, puts you in a new voice.

2. Spend some time reading mythology. Select a myth that intrigues you and rewrite it in contemporary terms, with contemporary characters. The practice will reveal the inner archetype of the myth and its relevance to your life today.

3. Observe an animal, either an exotic one at the zoo or a domestic one in your neighborhood. Spend an hour describing every detail of its appearance, personality, and actions. What is your connection with this animal? Try to recreate in words something essential of your perceptions.

4. Find an article in today's newspaper. Using the factual details expand the article, obituary, or review, imagining causes and consequences. Write a dramatic poem, emphasizing a narrative progression.

5. Select a painting and describe its colors and images minutely, including sensory impressions that you imagine, such as the iron smell of blood or the satiny flank of the horse. Write all your reactions to the painting: its story, impact, what it reminds you of, what you imagine the painter thought and felt. If there are people in the painting, where are they, what is going on in their minds? Finally, explore why you chose this particular painting.

6. Take on a social or political issue you feel strongly about. If it's the homeless, for instance, you might focus on a particular man

who sleeps under the bridge in your neighborhood. Close attention, rather than general reactions will keep the poem in your voice.

7. Write "portraits" of someone (corner grocery clerk, dental hygienist, a neighborhood character) you encounter but don't know well, imagining his or her real and secret life. As a link to the next set of exercises, practice here the craft of the speaker. Let your subject speak as "I," then rewrite your portrait using "you" or the third-person pronoun.

Craft Exercises   The focus is on imagery, language, line use, and association. A study of these can improve your writing quickly. Throughout the text are other craft-oriented exercises. By trying out all the meters and forms, you will absorb a tremendous amount of "feel" for rhythm and for the psychological effects a form has on writer and reader. The challenge of a fixed form usually brings out something unforeseen. When writing a sonnet, don't try to sound like Shakespeare or Keats—use your own language. The life of forms depends on their rediscovery for our time, not reuse from a past time. To hone your skills, try each of these:

1. Rewrite a poem you've already finished, changing *all* the nouns, verbs, and adjectives. Read the old and new versions aloud then see if you want to revise your original poem with some of the new words. This helps you go beyond a word choice that might have been too easy and to wake up your language.

2. Write a one-page poem using only one sentence. How far can you go with a stretched out sound that pulls the reader along without any stops? After this, write the same poem using extremely short sentences. How do the two approaches change the meaning of what you've written?

3. Select three unrelated objects—a broken doll, a wine bottle, a hat—and place them in front of your writing table. Describe, using the most exact and literal words you can. Notice everything. Do you then see relationships among the three objects? Is there a story involving all three? Can you, as Hopkins advised, look hard enough at any object that it begins to look back at you?

4. Select a color and list ten images for that color, taking care to present the image in a context, so that a reader can experience it.

For example, white: a frozen white sheet on the line, cracking in the wind. Yellow: the last tooth in an old man's mouth. Red: arterial blood spurting on a white tile floor. Putting the image in *action* or in *place* creates the reader's full sensory response. This is the first writing exercise I ever tried. My freshman teacher said a white feather from a goose's breast was not enough. I've always remembered the teacher saying, "Activate! Activate!" I made the feather slowly zigzag to the ground. Try this exercise over and over to heighten your awareness of how to form an image. The variations listed below are challenging. This writing exercise is one of the most valuable you can try.

5. Try the above exercise with emotions such as fear, elation, peace, wonder, guilt, regret, joy, grief. Make these abstract words concrete through imagery.

6. Try the above with softness, hardness, coldness, humidity, speed, fading, roughness, rain, snow, abrasiveness. For example, hailstones in one result of this exercise appeared in a poem as "blank eyeballs of an angel looking to heaven," "the jar of gallstones," "a soft turtle egg," "all the faraway moons of Jupiter hitting the roof," and "mothballs melting in the folded seams." One's first response is often not good enough. Hailstones falling like golf balls surprises no one, especially not the poet! Let the hailstones strike the roof of the Subaru like gunshots—something that imparts energy and meaning.

7. This may seem difficult, but it's actually fun. The purpose is to let yourself make sound associations. Take a poem in a language you don't know at all and "translate" it simply by making up a version from the way the poem sounds to you. Stick to the stanza form as it is in the original. Listen carefully to each word; what does it "say" to you? For example, *sangre de pato*: sand grates the patio, song of the parrot, some day in the ghetto, the angry potato; *kindheit*: kind heart, kind heights, Clondike.

8. Working on associating might seem like a contradiction in terms but this exercise does give you access to a way of thinking that may be blocked to you by an overly literal mind. Have someone call out a list of words to you. Evocative words or phrases work best: boxcar, 1982, stairway, pocket watch, map of England, hairbrush, plum, Do Not Enter, noon, falling. With each one, try to

call up an *image* of that word, something that shows the word's meaning to you. Poet Paul Hoover's image for shy: "When I go to a party I hold a picture of you, Mother, over my face." Coleman Barks's image for midnight is, "A miner buries his hands in a woman's hair." For bruises, he wrote, "paint samples." This is hard at first and the harder it is, the more valuable the exercise will be to you. Be sure to study the image chapter.

9. Start with two opposing ideas in your first two lines. This opens the poem to dramatic tension.

10. Keep a nature notebook. Write daily observations of weather, trees, crops, urban flower boxes, rain, snow, humidity. Write not factually but descriptively and fully. This is objective practice in noticing details and learning to convey them. Or, keep a bus notebook, describing people and events on your daily route. Your job, a person, a particular interest—all these can be part of your practice as a poet.

11. Write a dramatic monologue (see page 160), one that you can imagine as a performance piece, perhaps with props, a setting, actions. Gear your monologue to an experiment with diction, trying to capture actual speech rhythms and the natural diction of your speaker.

12. Revise a poem you've written so that all lines are enjambed. Then revise it so that all lines are end stopped. Compare the two versions with your original.

Review these Writing Suggestions within the Text:

Words: Texture and Sound:

Page 42	Exercise 1
Page 42	Exercise 2
Page 57	Exercise 3

Images: The Perceptual Field:

Page 87	Exercise 2
Page 91	Exercise 3
Page 91	Exercise 4
Page 113	Exercise 1
Page 114	Exercise 3
Page 114	Exercise 5
Page 120	Exercise 1

Rhyme and Repetition:

Page 201	Exercise 1
Page 225	Exercise 1

Meter: The Measured Flow:

Page 281	Exercise 2

Free Verse:

Page 321	Exercise 3
Page 322	Exercise 4
Page 322	Exercise 5

Traditional and Open Forms:

Page 365	Exercise 4
Page 365	Exercise
Page 368	Exercise 3

Subject and Style:

Page 419	Exercise
Page 421	Exercise 3
Page 421	Exercise 4
Page 425	Exercise 7
Page 431	Exercise 4
Page 446	Exercise 3

Interpretation: The Wide Response:

Page 504	Exercise 3
Page 505	Exercise 5

Your Poems Out the Door

If you are interested in publishing, nothing could be simpler than the submission process. Spend some hours in the library or a good bookstore reading current literary magazines. If they are not available, ask the reference librarian for a *Literary Market Place*, or order *The International Directory of Literary Magazines and Small Presses* (Dustbooks) or the *Directory of Literary Magazines* (Moyer Bell) from a bookstore. If you are in an isolated area, check out books of poems and look at the acknowledgements pages to see where the poet previously published the poems. Then write to each magazine that interests you and request a copy. See which magazines appeal to you and publish poetry you respond to. It's a waste of time to send blindly to publications you are not familiar with.

Send three to five poems, impeccably typed, to the editor. If a poem is longer than a page, indicate whether or not there is a stanza break at the bottom of every page. Your name and address should appear on each sheet you submit. Don't send a résumé or write an involved letter, but it is nice to say something about yourself: that you work as a reading tutor or taxi driver, that you study film in Arkansas or work on the school literary magazine. If you admire the magazine, no one minds hearing what you especially like. If that seems awkward, just enclose the poems, list them by name, and thank the editors for reading and considering them. Always enclose a stamped, self-addressed envelope (called SASE) for return. Everyone gets rejected. It always hurts. Send the poem out again right away. If you have received an encouraging note with your poems, you might try the same magazine again soon. Usually, editors write brief responses, if any, because they are frantically busy. Some respected magazines receive a staggering 100,000 poems a year. If months go by, with no reply at all to your poems, write and inquire about their status.

To avoid many hard rejections, show your work to trusted friends or teachers. Ask if they think you're ready to publish. Of course, they may be wrong, but in general, you are operating in the dark if you just have your own opinion. We all love our own writing. Sending out work too soon often means crushing discouragement, when it would have been better to concentrate on clarifying the style and intensifying the experience of writing.

New writers often ask about copyrighting their work before they send it out. It's not necessary and actually the circled C on a poem looks amateurish. Most poets are far too enamored of their own words to take anyone else's. Books, of course, are copyrighted, and poems that are accepted for publication are copyrighted by the magazine, usually with all rights belonging to the author, who simply acknowledges the magazine when a poem is reprinted elsewhere.

As you write more and more, you may have an urge toward more than one genre, non-fiction, fiction, or plays. If you have the opportunity, it's helpful to take introductory classes in all of these, in order to explore the structures and possibilities of each. All the genres join at some deep taproot. More and more, writers feel the connection of all the genres, and many are reluctant now to tie themselves forever to only one. For any writing, poetry offers the most precise and, at the same time, the most imaginative training. Leafing through the chapters in this book, you'll notice how many of the topics covered carry over to the concerns of other genres. Image making or using repetition patterns or selecting a certain diction have everything to do with short stories, novels, and plays. This chapter's exercises help you search your most important material, plus aspects of the craft of poetry. The art can't go far without the craft. Read and reread the text, with *writing* in mind. What you need to know as a writer of poetry is also what you need to know as a reader, and then some.

Backboards: Quotes on the Art of Poetry

> The poet's eye in a fine frenzy rolling,
> Doth glance from heaven to earth, from earth to heaven;
> And as imagination bodies forth
> The forms of things unknown, the poet's pen
> Turns them to shapes, and gives to airy nothing
> A local habitation and a name.

William Shakespeare, from *A Midsummer Night's Dream*

All plain styles, except the very greatest, raise a troublesome question for the critic. Are they the result of art or of accident?

C. S. Lewis, from *The Allegory of Love*

> The spider's touch, how exquisitely fine!
> feels at each thread, and lives along the line.

Alexander Pope, from *An Essay on Man*

90 percent of American poets do not exist. They are androids, manufactured from Randall Jarrell by the lost-wax process.

Kenneth Rexroth, quoted by Jonathan Williams in *The Magpie's Bagpipe*

A work of art is good if it has grown out of necessity. In this manner of its origin lies its true estimate: there is no other.

Rainer Maria Rilke, from *Letters to a Young Poet*

A work of art is an expressive form created for our perception through sense or imagination, and what it expresses is human feeling. The word "feeling" must be taken here in its broadest sense, meaning *everything that can be felt*, from physical sensation, pain and comfort, excitement and repose, to the most complex emotions, intellectual tensions, or the steady feeling-tones of a conscious human life.

Suzanne K. Langer, from *Problems of Art*

An artist, then, expresses feeling, but not in the way a politician blows off steam or a baby laughs and cries. He formulates that elusive aspect of reality that is commonly taken to be amorphous and chaotic; that is, he objectifies the subjective realm. What he expresses is, therefore, not his own actual feelings, but what he knows about human feeling. Once he is in possession of a rich symbolism, that knowledge may actually exceed his entire personal experience. A work of art expresses a conception of life, emotion, inward reality. But it is neither a confessional nor a frozen tantrum; it is a developed metaphor, a non-discursive symbol that articulates what is verbally ineffable—the logic of consciousness itself.

Suzanne K. Langer, from *Problems of Art*

The great poet has less mark'd style, and is more the channel of thoughts and things without increase or diminution, and is the free channel of himself. He swears to his art, I will not be meddlesome, I will not have in my writings any elegance, or effect, or originality, to hang in the way between me and the rest like curtains. I will have nothing hang in the way, not the richest curtains. What I tell I tell for precisely what it is. Let who may exalt or startle or fascinate or soothe, I will have purposes as health or heat or snow has, and be as regardless of observation. What I experience or portray shall go from my composition without a shred of my composition. You shall stand by my side and look in the mirror with me.

Walt Whitman, from *Preface to Leaves of Grass*

To find my home in one sentence, concise, as if hammered in metal. Not to enchant anybody. Not to gain a lasting name in posterity. An unnamed need for order, for rhythm, for form, which three words we oppose to chaos and nothingness.

Czeslaw Milosz, from "Notes and Inscripts"

I write poems to preserve things I have seen/thought/felt (if I may so indicate a composite and complex experience) both for myself and for others, though I feel that my prime responsibility is to the experience itself, which I am trying to keep from oblivion for its own sake. Why I should do this I have no idea, but I think the impulse to preserve lies at the bottom of all art. Generally my poems are related, therefore, to my own personal life, but by no means always, since I can imagine horses I have never seen or the emotions of a bride without ever having been a woman or married.

As a guiding principle I believe that every poem must be its own sole freshly created universe, and therefore have no belief in "tradition" or a common myth-kitty or casual allusions in poems to other poems or poets.

Philip Larkin, from "Statement"

No tear in the writer, no tears in the reader. No surprise for the writer, no surprise for the reader. For me the initial delight is in the surprise of remembering something I didn't know I knew. I am in a place, in a situation, as if I had materialized from cloud or risen out of the ground. There is a glad recognition of the long lost and the rest follows. Step by step the wonder of unexpected supply keeps growing. The impressions most useful to my purpose seem always those I was unaware of and so made no note of at the time when taken, and the conclusion is come to that like giants we are always hurling experience ahead of us to pave the future with against the day when we may want to strike a line of purpose across it for somewhere. The line will have the more charm for not being mechanically straight. We enjoy the straight crookedness of a good walking stick.

Robert Frost, from "The Figure a Poem Makes"

Re-vision—the act of looking back, of seeing with fresh eyes, of entering an old text from a new critical direction—is for women more than a chapter in cultural history: it is an act of survival. Until we can understand the assumptions in which we are drenched we cannot know ourselves. And this drive to self-knowledge, for women, is more than a search for identity: it is part of our refusal of the self-destructiveness of male-dominated society. A radical critique of literature, feminist in its impulse, would take the work first of all as a clue to how we live, how we have been living, how we have been led to imagine ourselves, how our language has trapped as well as liberated us, how the very act of naming has been till now a male prerogative, and how we can begin to see and name—and therefore live—afresh. A change in the concept of sexual identity is essential if we are not going to see the old political order reassert itself in every new revolution. We need to know the writing of the past, and know it differently than we have ever known it; not to pass on a tradition but to break its hold over us.

Adrienne Rich, from ''When We Dead Awaken''

A poem is not reason enough for us to unleash our imagination in reckless wanderings. Rather, what I want to say is this: that poets, if their poetry is good, draw on a deep-rooted experience of life, which all of us, young and old, have within ourselves; how much we feel this, I don't know. These are the roots through which they communicate with us. What forms, what vestments this common experience, this common feeling of life, will take in a historical moment no one can tell. It depends, I think, not only upon the idiosyncrasy of the individual who expresses himself but also upon many intellectual, social, and political mores of the time.

George Seferis, from *A Poet's Journal*

A simple test: if you open the book and say hmm, isn't that true! then you know you've read it all before. Put the book back on the shelf and try to find one that irritates you to a state of wakefulness—the grand alerting that poetry is best at.

Robert Kelley, from an interview, *The Mississippi Review*

Why write? To read what I've written. *Why read what you've written?* Because, for all its possible flaws and omissions, no one else could have written it.

Joyce Carol Oates, Journal, 1989

Form is never more than a *revelation* of content.

Denise Levertov, from *The Poet in the World*

The poet's task is to hold in trust the knowledge that language, as Robert Duncan has declared, is not a set of counters to be manipulated, but a Power. And only in this knowledge does he arrive at music, at that quality of song within speech which is not the result of manipulations of euphonious parts but of an attention, at once to the organic relationships of experienced phenomena and to the latent harmony and counterpoint of language itself as it is identified with those phenomena.

Writing poetry is a process of discovery, revealing *inherent* music, the music of correspondences, the music of inscape. It parallels what, in a person's life, is called individuation: the evolution of consciousness toward wholeness, not an isolation of intellectual awareness but an awareness involving the whole self, a *knowing* (as man and woman "know" one another), a touching, a "being in touch."

Denise Levertov, from *The Poet in the World*

Prosody is the articulation of the total sound of a poem.

Ezra Pound

I think poetry should surprise by a fine excess, but not by singularity; it should strike the reader as a wording of his own highest thoughts, and appear almost as a remembrance.

John Keats

Poetry is mostly hunches.

John Ashbery

Like a piece of ice on a hot stove the poem must ride on its own melting. A poem may be worked over once it is in being, but may not be worried into being. Its most precious quality will remain its having run itself and carried away the poet with it.

Robert Frost, from "The Figure a Poem Makes"

A mannered style, that of Gongora or Henry James, for example, is like eccentric clothing: very few writers can carry it off, but one is enchanted by the rare exception who can.

W. H. Auden, from "Writing"

Since writing is not only an art but a trade embodying principles attested by experience, we would do well not to forget that it is an expedient for making one's self understood and that what is said should at least have the air of having meant something to the person who wrote it—as is the case with Gertrude Stein and James Joyce. Stewart Sherman one time devised a piece of jargon which he offered as indistinguishable from work by Gertrude Stein, which gave itself away at once as lacking any private air of interest. If I may venture to say again what I have already said when obscurity was deplored, one should be clear as one's natural reticence allows one to be.

Marianne Moore, from "Idiosyncrasy and Technique"

The poet, described in ideal perfection, brings the whole soul of man into activity, with the subordination of its faculties to each other according to their relative worth and dignity. He diffuses a tone and spirit of unity, that blends and (as it were) *fuses*, each into each, by that synthetic and magical power, to which I would exclusively appropriate the name of Imagination.

Samuel Taylor Coleridge, from *Biographia Literaria*

Accuracy of observation is the equivalent of thinking.

All poetry is experimental poetry.

There is no wing like meaning.

One reads poetry with one's nerves.

Poetry is a pheasant disappearing in the brush.

Wallace Stevens, from *Adagia*

I believe that the proper and perfect symbol is the natural object, that if a man use "symbol" he must so use them that their symbolic function does not obtrude; so that *a* sense, and the poetic quality of the passage, is not lost to those who do not understand the symbol as such, to whom, for instance, a hawk is a hawk.

Ezra Pound, from "Credo"

I have said that poetry is the spontaneous overflow of powerful feeling: it takes its origin from emotion recollected in tranquillity: the emotion is contemplated till, by a species of reaction, the tranquillity gradually disappears, and an emotion, kindred to that which was before the subject of contemplation, is gradually produced, and does itself actually exist in the mind. In this mood successful composition generally begins, and in a mood similar to this it is carried on; but the emotion, of whatever kind, and in whatever degree, from various causes, is qualified by various pleasures, so that in describing any passions whatsoever, which are voluntarily described, the mind will, upon the whole, be in a state of enjoyment. If Nature be thus cautious to preserve in a state of enjoyment a being so employed, the Poet ought to profit by the lesson held forth to him, and ought especially to take care, that, whatever passions he communicates to his Reader, those passions, if his Reader's mind be sound and vigorous, should always be accompanied with an overbalance of pleasure.

William Wordsworth, from Preface to *Lyrical Ballads*

Poetry indeed seems to me more physical than intellectual. A year or two ago, in common with others, I received f.om America a request that I would define poetry. I replied that I could no more define poetry than a terrier can define a rat, but that I thought we both recognized the object by the symptoms which it provoked in us. One of these symptoms was described in connection with another object by Eliphaz the Temanite: "A spirit passed before my face: the hair of my flesh stood up." Experience has taught me, when I am shaving of a morning, to keep watch over my thoughts, because, if a line of poetry strays into my memory, my skin bristles so that the razor ceases to act. This particular symptom is accompanied by a shiver down the spine; there is another which consists in a constriction of the throat and a precipitation of water to the eyes; and there is a third which I can only describe by borrowing a phrase from one of Keats's last letters, where he says, speaking of Fanny Brawne, "everything that reminds me of her goes through me like a spear." The seat of this sensation is the pit of the stomach.

A. E. Housman, from *The Name and Nature of Poetry*

Real mysteries cannot be solved but they can be turned into better mysteries.

Griel Marcus, from *Lipstick Traces*

We are happy when for everything inside us there is a corresponding something outside us.

W. B. Yeats, from a letter to Dorothy Wellesley

Copyrights and Acknowledgments

HOUGHTON MIFFLIN COMPANY Ai, "The Anniversary" from *Cruelty* by Ai. Copyright © 1970, 1973 by Ai. Galway Kinnell, "The Bear" from *Body Rags* by Galway Kinnell. Copyright © 1965, 1966, 1967 by Galway Kinnell. The preceding reprinted by permission of Houghton Mifflin Company. All rights reserved.

BARBARA HOWES "A Letter from the Caribbean" by Barbara Howes from *A Private Signal* published by Wesleyan University Press (1977). Copyright © 1977 by Barbara Howes. Reprinted by permission of Barbara Howes.

INDIANA UNIVERSITY PRESS Josephine Miles, "Ride" from *Poems 1930–60* by Josephine Miles. Reprinted by permission of Indiana University Press.

INTERNATIONAL CREATIVE MANAGEMENT, INC. Muriel Rukeyser, "Effort at Speech Between Two People" and "Night Feeding" from *The Collected Poems of Muriel Rukeyser,* McGraw Hill Books, Inc. Reprinted by permission of International Creative Management.

MARK JOHNSTON "War Movie in Reverse" by Mark Johnston. This poem first appeared in *The New England Review/Bread Loaf Quarterly,* vol. 5, no. 43. Reprinted by permission of Mark Johnston.

KELSEY ST. PRESS Frances Phillips, "Salt" from *Celebrated Running Horse Messenger.* Reprinted by permission of Kelsey St. Press.

ASHLEY KING "Untitled" by Ashley King. Reprinted by permission of Ashley King.

CAROLYN KIZER "Epithalamion" from *The Nearness of You,* Copper Canyon Press. Reprinted by permission of Carolyn Kizer.

EDWARD KLEINSCHMIDT "Boustrophedon" from *First Language* published by University of Massachusetts Press, 1990. "University of Iowa Hospital, 1976" from *Magnetism,* published by The Heyeck Press, 1987. The poem first appeared in *Poetry.* Copyright 1986 by Modern Poetry Association. The preceding reprinted by permission of Edward Kleinschmidt.

YUSEF KOMUNYAKAA "Facing It" from *Dien Cai Dau.* Reprinted by permission of Yusef Komunyakaa.

MARILYN KRYSL "Saying Things" and "Sestina: Vanishing Point" from *More Palomino, Please, More Fuchsia,* Cleveland State University Press. Reprinted by permission of Marilyn Krysl.

HAZEL LANE "Late Late Show" by Hazel Lane. Copyright © Hazel Lane. Reprinted by permission of Hazel Lane.

JOSEPH LANGLAND "Hunters in the Snow: Brueghl" from *The Wheel of Summer,* Dial, 1963. Copyright © Joseph Langland. Reprinted by permission of Joseph Langland.

LATIN AMERICAN LITERARY REVIEW PRESS Fernando Alegría, "Return" from *Changing Centuries: Selected Poems.* Reprinted by permission of Latin American Literary Review Press.

LEVIN, GANN, & HANKIN Gertrude Stein, "A Very Valentine" excerpted from "A Valentine to Sherwood Anderson." Reprinted by permission of Levin, Gann & Hankin.

LITTLE, BROWN AND COMPANY Emily Dickinson, "My Life Had Stood—a Loaded Gun" from *The Complete Poems of Emily Dickinson* edited by Thomas H. Johnson. Copyright 1929, 1935 by Martha Dickinson Bianchi; Copyright © renewed 1957, 1963 by Mary L. Hampson. "Good Morning—Midnight" from *The Complete Poems of Emily Dickinson* edited by Thomas H. Johnson. Copyright 1929 by Martha Dickinson Bianchi; copyright © renewed 1957 by Mary L. Hampson. Stanley Kunitz, "The Knot" from *The Poems of Stanley Kunitz 1928–1978* by Stanley Kunitz. Copyright © 1979 by Stanley Kunitz. The preceding reprinted by permission of Little, Brown and Company.

LIVERIGHT PUBLISHING CORPORATION e. e. cummings, "Buffalo Bill's" and "in Just-" are reprinted from *Tulips & Chimneys* by e. e. cummings by permission of Liveright Publishing Corporation. Copyright 1923, 1925 and renewed 1951, 1953 e. e. cummings. Copyright © 1973, 1976 by George James Firmage. (This poem is an excerpt from "Portraits.") "somewhere i have never travelled" is reprinted from *ViVa* by e. e. cummings by permission of Liveright Publishing Corporation. Copyright 1931, 1959 by e. e. cummings. Copyright © 1979, 1973 by The Trustees for the e. e. cummings Trust. Copyright © 1979, 1973 by George James Firmage. Robert Hayden, "Those Winter Sundays" is reprinted from *Angle of Ascent, New and Selected Poems* by Robert Hayden, by permission of Liveright Publishing Corporation. Copyright © 1975, 1972, 1970, 1966 by Robert Hayden.

LOUISIANA STATE UNIVERSITY PRESS Lisel Mueller, "What the Dog Perhaps Hears" and "The Concert" are reprinted by permission of Louisiana State University Press from *The Private Life* by Lisel Mueller, Copyright © 1976. "Night Song" is reprinted by permission of Louisiana State University Press from *The Need to Hold Still* by Lisel Mueller, Copyright © 1980. This poem originally appeared in *The Ohio Review*. Marilyn Nelson Waniek, "Century Quilt" is reprinted by permission of Louisiana State University Press from *Mama's Promises* by Marilyn Nelson Waniek. Copyright © 1985 by Marilyn Nelson Waniek.

SUSAN MACDONALD "A Smart* Dithyramb" from *A Smart Dithyramb,* The Heyeck Press, 1979. Reprinted by permission of Susan MacDonald.

MACMILLAN LONDON LTD. Wilfred Gibson, "Breakfast" and "Troopship: Mid-Atlantic" from *Collected Poems 1905–1925* by Wilfred Gibson. Reprinted by permission of Macmillan London Ltd.

MACMILLAN PUBLISHING CO., INC. Thomas Hardy, "Snow in the Suburbs" reprinted with permission of Macmillan Publishing Company from *The Complete Poems* by Thomas Hardy, edited by James Gibson. Copyright 1925 by Macmillan Publishing Company, renewed 1953 by Lloyds Bank Ltd. Hugh MacDiarmid, "Crystals Like Blood" reprinted with permission of Macmillan Publishing Company from *Collected Poems of Hugh MacDiarmid.* © Christopher Murray Grieve, 1948, 1962. Marianne Moore, "To a Steam Roller" reprinted with permission of Macmillan Publishing Company from *Collected Poems of Marianne Moore.* Copyright 1935 by Marianne Moore, renewed 1963 by Marianne Moore and T. S. Eliot. "By Disposition of Angels" reprinted with permission of Macmillan Publishing Company from *Collected Poems of Marianne Moore.* Copyright 1951 by Marianne Moore, renewed

Index of First Lines

Index of Titles

Index of Authors and Titles

Index of Terms and Topics